Estranging Dawn

THE LIFE
AND WORKS OF
WILLIAM VAUGHN MOODY

By MAURICE F. BROWN

Southern Illinois University Press   Carbondale and Edwardsville

Feffer & Simons, Inc.   London and Amsterdam

LIBRARY OF CONGRESS CATALOGING IN PUBLICATION DATA

BROWN, MAURICE F   1928–
  ESTRANGING DAWN.

  BIBLIOGRAPHY: P.
  I. MOODY, WILLIAM VAUGHN, 1869–1910.
I. TITLE.
PS2428.B7   818'.5'209 [B]   73–252
ISBN 0–8093–0618–2

CONTENTS

ILLUSTRATIONS (between pages 154–155)

PREFACE

IN THIS first biography of William Vaughn Moody, my major concern has necessarily been to present accurately and to define clearly the life and development of an American writer. Moody was a talented and intelligent poet and dramatist, caught between the gestures of a dying nineteenth-century tradition and the emerging demands of twentieth-century experience. His commitments as man and writer were to his tradition, but he was aware of the issues of his time and increasingly flexible in his responses. A central problem in presentation is that Moody's personality and work have seemed alien to modern sensibility. Only recently, in the context of a resurgence of youthful idealism—with its ranging moods of deep despair and extravagant hope, its involvement in a quest for ritual regeneration, and its attraction to mystical modes of knowing—are Moody's commitments and conflicts open once more to some degree of sympathetic understanding. Of contexts appropriate to such understanding, those of Moody's life and of his immediate cultural situation are most valuable and least available to us. I have sought to present Moody's life as a writer in these contexts.

In one sense every poet is a kind of archetypal hero of his period: he acts out his version of its own particular *agon*. In a very central way Moody became such a hero for his times by virtue of the scope of his cultural concern and of the contemporary recognition his work received. In the first decade of this century, he was seen as the most successful serious poet and dramatist of his generation. World War I brought revolutionary changes in the stance of the American writer to his experience, his medium, and his audience. As a result, Moody and his work have been relatively ignored by several generations of readers, scholars, and critics. But only relatively ignored. Somehow Moody's work has survived in a critical climate not only inhospitable but hostile to his stylistic concerns. Gay Wilson Allen, Walter B. Rideout, and James K. Robinson include a generous selection of Moody's work in *American Poetry* (New York, 1965), the most distinguished anthology in the field since F. O. Matthiessen's *Oxford Book of American Verse* in 1950. Critics as diverse as Matthiessen, Lewis E. Gates, Ludwig Lewisohn, Arthur Hobson Quinn, R. P. Blackmur, Howard Mumford Jones, and Robert Bly have identified Moody as a modern or pre-modern writer of interest and significance. Yet Moody has been a controversial and somewhat enigmatic figure, and estimates of the ultimate value of his work have varied as widely as critical approaches to it.

Moody's life is particularly attractive because of the range and in-tensity of his commitments and activity. That range is reflected in the scope and stylistic variety of his writing. He was a literary scholar and critic, a brilliant and vigorous writer of personal letters, an imaginative dramatist, and a poet of great versatility. His work embodies and re-cords his passionate search for a medium adequate to his experience in the bewildering dawn of the twentieth century. The search led to the drama. The skirmish of Moody, his friends, and their associates in the theatre against an entrenched theatrical tradition was a prelude to that later series of anti-establishment rebellions which have reinvigorated American theatre throughout the century. Yet American poetry of the first decade affords a sharp and revealing contrast which perhaps best defines Moody's stance as a writer and the nature of his achievement. Until 1912 American poetry *was* William Vaughn Moody and Edwin Arlington Robinson, although Robinson's work had not yet been widely acclaimed. Robinson was more sensitive than Moody to psycho-logical complexity and to irony in human experience. He used the English language with a mastery which Moody did not approach. Yet Moody's work embodies more fully than his friend's the concerns and spirit of the Progressive period, just as it is caught more completely in the period's limitations. Moody probes the temper of his times in its own terms: the myriad natural, social, and spiritual formulations of Darwinian theory; the rediscovery of myth and ritual by the cultural anthropologists and the scholars of Greek, Hebrew, and Sanskrit litera-tures; the promise in nonrational modes of human inquiry and means to power, stimulated by Nietzsche and others; currents of nineteenth-century utopian thought, manifested in increasing concern for social and political injustice and corruption; and a wide-ranging eclecticism, which sought within Western culture and beyond it for materials of contemporary relevance. Moody's particular genius, unlike Robinson's, was for the larger structures of literature, structures developed in thematic complexity, in dramatic contrast, and in intricate interlocking systems of symbol and patterns of myth. He found his most appropriate medium in the drama, and it is here he treats the issues of his times in greatest depth. I have accordingly been most interested in the complex structure of *The Fire-Bringer* and in Moody's development of its implications in his later poems and plays.

It is in the concerns and structures of these later works of the writer that Moody is most relevant to our times. Moody the poet is treated in this book as heir to the nineteenth-century poetic tradition, less in its American than its British and continental forms. In terms of poetic texture, rhythmic variety, and symbolist technique, he extends its achievements to their limits and sometimes beyond. Particular forebears—among them Emerson, Browning, Whitman, Wagner, and Milton—have been suggested. And I have singled out those contemporaries beyond his immediate circle with whom Moody has most in common: Francis Thompson, Gabriele D'Annunzio, and Frank Norris, among others. Moody's relationship to more recent writers has interested me as well. If the gestures of his poetic language are not often those of a modern style, his treatments of personal and social regeneration in the context of deepening malaise and sharpening disillusionment represent early formulations of the issue central to twentieth-century poets as diverse as Ezra Pound, T. S. Eliot, Wallace Stevens, and William Carlos Williams. Moreover, his formulations seek breadth and intensity of life in mystical, mythic, and sexual dimensions of human experience. This thrust of Moody's work suggests its relevance to that of D. H. Lawrence, Hart Crane, Eugene O'Neill, Thomas Wolfe, and the nonacademic, neo-Whitmanic poets of the 1960s. But to explore these affinities in any detail would be to turn from the task at hand.

Most of the documents on which this—a first biography of Moody —rests are the letters, journals, reminiscences, and books written by Moody and his friends. They were among the most lively and penetrating writers of their generation, and they speak for themselves and live on their own terms in this work. I have consulted Moody's uncollected poems and articles, his manuscript drafts of published and unpublished work. A full bibliography and accurate chronology have been established as aids to a clearer view of the writer's development. Most of Moody's major critics and editors were his personal friends. Their work has been generally competent and they have supplied invaluable biographical detail. Yet a number of errors, due to incompleteness of information, to personal involvement, or to obscured recollection, have marred their accounts. I have corrected them on the basis of fuller documentation or accounts of greater validity. Though my

sources are often identified in the narrative, students of Moody and of
the period will wish to consult the notes appended to this book.

For their interest and generous permission to quote from and reproduce previously unpublished materials, I am indebted to the following: to Frederick J. Fawcett, 2nd, for permission to use William
Vaughn Moody materials; to Joanne C. Hamlin and Priscilla C. Ball
for use of and citation from the unpublished memoirs of Julia Moody
Schmaltz; to Alison P. Marks for citations from Josephine Preston Peabody Marks; to William B. Mason for quotations from Daniel Gregory
Mason; to David S. Nivison for citations from Edwin Arlington Robinson; to Jean Torrence Bales for Ridgely Torrence materials; and to
Wallace L. Anderson for use and citation of his unpublished Uni-
versity of Chicago doctoral dissertation on Moody's reception. For
generous aid and permission to reproduce materials in their collections,
I wish to thank librarians of the Harvard College Library, the Princeton
University Library, the Library of the University of Chicago, the New
York Public Library, and the Huntington Library, San Marino, California. For their assistance in tracking down materials I am indebted
to librarians of the New Albany (Indiana) Public Library, the Indiana
Historical Society, the Columbia University Library, and the Kresge
Library of Oakland University. For permission to quote from published
materials I am grateful to copyright owners listed at the end of this
preface. And my notes at the end of the volume indicate the extent of
my indebtedness to a host of others. I wish to thank the *Colby Library
Quarterly,* the *New England Quarterly,* and the *Bulletin of Bibliography* for permission to republish materials which first appeared in their
pages, sometimes in a different form.

The collection of materials for this biography began some ten
years ago, and segments of my work have been conducted under a
series of small grants from faculty research funds of Colby College and
Oakland University. Writing of my final draft was essentially completed under a grant of sabbatical leave from the latter institution. I
am grateful for this support. For special interest and assistance I am
indebted to Alexander P. Clark, Curator of Manuscripts at Princeton,
and to Margaret McFadden, Assistant Curator for Manuscripts and
Archives at Chicago. I am grateful to Robert Hoopes and to Merton M.
Sealts for aid and encouragement, and to Lyman L. Leathers, Richard
M. Ludwig, and Gertrude M. White, who have read the manuscript of
this book in first draft and offered useful suggestions for its final form.
I thank Wallace L. Anderson for his careful reading of the manuscript
and for valuable assistance with Moody-Robinson materials. I am
grateful to Marian Wilson for her knowledgeable editorial assistance
and her patient and painstaking typing of the manuscript. I owe a

special debt of thanks to Howard Mumford Jones, who read portions of the manuscript in various stages of revision and who drew my attention to Moody in the first place.

The author is indebted to the publishers and authors' representatives for permission to quote from the following sources: Edwin Arlington Robinson's letters to William Vaughn Moody in E. S. Fussell, "Robinson to Moody: Ten Unpublished Letters," *American Literature* 23 (May 1951), copyright © 1951 by the Duke University Press. Maurice F. Brown's William Vaughn Moody bibliography (reproduced in expanded form in this book), published in the *Bulletin of Bibliography* 28 (October–December 1971). *Diary and Letters of Josephine Preston Peabody,* edited by C. H. Baker (Boston: Houghton Mifflin Company, 1925). The Estate of Daniel Gregory Mason for passages from Daniel Gregory Mason, *Music in My Time, and Other Reminiscences* (New York: The Macmillan Company, 1938). Seán Haldane and The Ladysmith Press for permission to reprint from Seán Haldane, *The Fright of Time: Joseph Trumbull Stickney, 1874–1904* (Ladysmith, Québec: The Ladysmith Press, 1970).

Rochester, Michigan   Maurice F. Brown
October 1972

CHAPTER I THE SWEET
AND HEAVY YEARS

A SIXTH CHILD and third son was born to Francis Burdette and
Henrietta Stoy Moody in Spencer, Indiana, July 8, 1869. His mother
named him William Vaughn Stoy Moody after a favorite younger
brother. On his father's side the child was descended from a line of
New England Moodys, beginning with one William, who migrated to
Ipswich, Massachusetts, in 1634 and then settled in Newbury. His
son Joshua, a graduate of Harvard College, had been an active preacher
in Portsmouth, New Hampshire, participating in the Andros rebellion
and the resistance to the witchcraft proceedings of the 1690s. A
penchant for richness of language was already a family trait; for
Joshua's sermons, in their elaboration of diction and metaphor, ex-
ceeded the limits generally observed in the Puritan plain style.

Early in the nineteenth century, Will Moody's grandfather,
Stephen, left New England to settle in the rich farming country of
western New York state. He acquired land, married a well-to-do widow
with three daughters, and prospered. Burdette Moody, born in 1826,
was the first of three sons.[1] After their father's death in the late 1840s,
Burdette and his brothers headed west. With little idea where to go,
they gathered in the family schoolroom of their Cortland farmhouse.
Each was blindfolded, spun around, and headed for a map of the
western territory with a pointer in his hand. Gideon Moody touched
down in the Dakotas, Norman in central Illinois, and Burdette in
southern Indiana.[2] Burdette Moody took the dare seriously; he arrived
in New Albany, Indiana, in March 1849.[3]

Because of its position at the head of navigation on the lower
Ohio River, New Albany was a thriving, rough, commercial center of
eight thousand people. It was the largest city in Indiana, challenging

Louisville, Kentucky, across the river for supremacy and hoping to
emulate Cincinnati and Pittsburgh as its future unfolded.⁴ Trained as
an accountant, Burdette quickly found a job with the newly formed
New Albany and Salem Railroad, financed by local merchants. In
September 1852 he married Henrietta Stoy, of a large New Albany
business family.⁵ Henrietta's deceased father, Peter Stoy, had been successful in commerce and owned a New Albany shipyard which his
widow ran in the fifties with the help of her sons.⁶ A year after Burdette's marriage, the romance of the river captured him, as it captured
Sam Clemens of Hannibal. He became captain and part owner of two
Pittsburgh-New Orleans packets—first, the *Jesse K. Bell*, and later, the
Louisville.⁷ Life on the Mississippi gave form to the personality of Will
Moody's father, tempering his New England heritage. Henrietta accompanied him on an occasional trip to New Orleans, Memphis, or
Pittsburgh, and with him gained access to a range of social and cultural
experience that New Albany alone could not have provided.

The Civil War brought a sudden end to Burdette Moody's enterprise. The *Louisville* was on the lower Mississippi when war broke out,
and the boat and its cargo were seized by the Confederates at Memphis.
In 1862 Moody moved his family north to Spencer, Indiana, in an
attempt to make good his losses by business activity and land speculation along proposed railroad lines. He tried marketing maple sugar,
flour milling, and dry goods, but after eight years Burdette was able
to list for tax purposes only $2000 in real estate and a personal estate of
$1500. His work provided a modest competence, but it fell far short
of the success he had desired and was but a fraction of the estate listed
by the neighbor in whose dry goods business Burdette Moody worked.⁸
In the fall of 1870 he moved his family back to New Albany to live in
his mother-in-law's house and work for his brothers-in-law as secretary
of the Ohio Falls Iron Works. Burdette was to spend the remainder of
his life in this frustrating, perhaps humiliating, position. His son, William Vaughn Moody—then fifteen months old—was to spend his youth
and adolescence in New Albany.

The father Will Moody knew was a tall and impressive man in
his forties. A maverick in the rich Stoy pasturelands, he was an accountant only north-northwest. At heart, he was an adventurous romantic. In his life on the river he had found the identity which best
suited him, and in New Albany Burdette was always known as "Captain Moody." ⁹ He accepted the pattern his life had taken with resignation, but he told his children tales of his young manhood, of his Moody
forebears, and of shadowy, exciting origins of the Moody family in
European nobility. He sometimes read to them in the evenings from
Shakespeare or Dickens, his favorite writers. Will grew up with a

sense of the nobility and excitement of the past and of travel in quest of adventure and fulfillment not offered by day-to-day life in New Albany. But if Burdette Moody communicated to his young son his early dreams and his restiveness in the restricted world of Stoy values, he provided more directly a model for the acceptance of duty. Will Moody, later writing about his father, drew attention only to Burdette's stoicism and his "Antique nobleness." [10]

The Moodys lived with Grandmother Mary Stoy, who dominated the household Will knew as a child. Mary Stoy had spent her girlhood, womanhood, and widowhood in New Albany. Daughter of one of the settlers of the city, she was a hard-headed businesswoman and a sturdy Methodist, known to her acquaintances as "the iron woman." [11] Mary Stoy frowned on waste and frivolity and remembered the Sabbath by devoting it to religious activity and allowing no cooking on that day. She was self-appointed hostess to the stream of itinerant preachers who appeared at revival meetings of New Albany's Wesley Chapel and at camp meetings held in and around the city. Her grandson was to draw on his memories of the household she ruled for his play, *The Faith Healer*.

Will Moody respected his father and his grandmother, but he was closest to his mother. The effect was to direct his energy and ambition more toward his mother's cultural goals than those of his father, toward the romance of refinement and culture to be found in art, music, and literature. Henrietta Moody was delicate and dark-eyed. A graduate of the Anderson Seminary, she played the piano and enjoyed drawing.[12] Her family was proud of the prize she had won as a schoolgirl for her crayon work, and several of her landscapes had been framed and hung in the house. While Henrietta shared her mother's practical moral sense, her Methodism was one of sentiment and sensibility. Henrietta liked to keep the blinds low in the front parlor so that the room would have a religious glow.[13] She believed fervently in personal divine guidance and was to tell her children of a miraculous salvation. Sensing danger one evening at dinner, she had gone directly to the room that Will, still a baby, shared with a sister. An overturned candle had started a fire, which was quickly extinguished. The source of her warning was divine, Henrietta declared.[14] During Will's childhood, Henrietta Moody suffered periods of intermittent invalidism. A back ailment and nervous disorder confined her at times to her bed or chair. During Will's youth the periods of invalidism gradually lengthened and Henrietta was able to join her family only in the late afternoon or early evening. Early in the 1880s, when she had been unable to walk for more than a year and specialists in Louisville seemed unable to help, Burdette took his wife to doctors in the East. They were unable to arrive at a clear diagnosis or to determine the causes of Mrs. Moody's illness.

Throughout Will's childhood his mother's affection for him was marked, and her older children accepted the fact that their brother was favored. She fondly called him "My Sweetheart," and young Will brought his mother his problems, his secrets, and his aspirations. He ran her errands, helped care for her plants, learned to draw under her guidance, and brought her his schoolboy exercises.[15] The image of his mother that was to remain with Will Moody appears in a poem he wrote at thirty-one, "The Daguerreotype." In a daguerreotype of his mother at seventeen, the poet finds none of the haunting sense of weary disappointment and baffled grief he remembered as characteristic of the woman he knew. Yet what he emphasizes in Henrietta as invalid mother is the sweetness of the mystical aura surrounding her. He calls up

> the sweet and heavy years
> When by her bed and chair
> We children gathered jealously to share
> The sunlit aura breathing myrrh and thyme,
> Where the sore-stricken body made a clime
> Gentler than May and pleasanter than rhyme,
> Holier and more mystical than prayer.

A major theme of the poem is the pride and hope his mother centered in him. Henrietta Moody nourished her son's first movements toward painting and writing, and shared with him her tendency to mystical and aesthetic apprehension of experience. His relationship with his mother was to dominate Moody's relations with women and provide the immediate source for the most persistent theme in his work.

Conflicts in the personalities and values of his grandmother, father, and mother provided the strong and vaguely turbulent undercurrents of Will Moody's childhood. But the major implications of the pattern of personality they helped create were to be apparent only later. The surfaces of Will's life were relatively calm. The New Albany home provides an index to that life. Located in the middle-class residential section of town just west of the central business district, the house was separated from newer sections of housing for workers which edged the city on the north and east. Wooden porches ran the height and width of the two-story brick house. The yard was large, with fruit trees and a huge chestnut tree in the rear. The front parlor, lit by candles in wall brackets and a green-globed lamp, contained a reproduction of the Charlotte Corday portrait by J. R. Story and a marble-topped table with wax flowers under a glass bell. The family Bible was on a ledge under the table. The back parlor housed Mrs. Moody's piano, her plants and vines, and a secretary where the household accounts and a few books were kept.[16]

The house had been almost empty when Burdette Moody and his family returned to it in 1870. Only Henrietta's youngest brother, William Vaughn Stoy, was living with his mother.[17] Of the five Moody children, the eldest, Mary, was sixteen and had been attending a school for young ladies in New Albany. A son, Francis, was thirteen, and there were Charlotte, seven, Julia, three, and Will.[18] A last child, named Henrietta for her mother, was born in 1871. The immediate household thinned during Will's childhood. In 1873 Mary Moody married. William Vaughn Stoy left to set up a dry goods and decorating business in Lafayette, and Francis Moody joined him there later in the decade. Yet young Will was aware of his membership in a larger family group, which gathered at church and on special occasions. Not only did Mary visit, bringing her children, but the Moodys maintained close associations with the families of four of Henrietta's brothers, all established in and around New Albany.

Will Moody's Stoy heritage became important to his adult personality, the source of a part of himself he fought and rejected. Some sense of the nature of that heritage can be inferred from the positions Moody's four uncles had established in New Albany. Besides the young William Vaughn Stoy, whom his mother and older brothers had set up in the dry goods business, there were Henry, Peter, Jr., and Raymond. Henry Stoy worked on a newspaper in Louisville; he and his wife lived on a farm near New Albany. Peter Stoy, Jr., the head of the family and the most successful of the brothers, had gone from local hardware and dry goods businesses into manufacturing. In the 1870s and 1880s, the major Stoy investment was in the Ohio Falls Iron Works, part of Washington C. De Pauw's financial empire and one of the city's largest enterprises. Peter Stoy was vice-president and superintendent. Raymond Stoy, Will's fourth uncle, was treasurer, and Burdette Moody had joined the firm as secretary.[19]

In addition to several other financial ventures, Peter Stoy was a founder and director of the First National Bank of New Albany. In the year Will graduated from high school, his uncle and W. C. De Pauw served as bondsmen for the school district, each posting bond in the amount of $90,000. Both Peter and Raymond served as city councilmen, and the Stoys were active in their church. They had turned from their Presbyterian religious origins to become mainstays of the city's Wesley Chapel Methodist. For most of the nineteenth century they served as its trustees and superintended the Sunday school.

Old Peter Stoy had been a trustee of the chapel and taught a Sunday school class from 1821 until his death thirty years later. His sons carried on the tradition, heading the church building committee when a new structure was erected in the fifties. They served the church as trustees, and Burdette Moody was to join them on the board in the 1870s. Peter, Jr., and Raymond Stoy alternated as superintendents of the Sunday school through a forty-year period until their deaths in the 1890s. In addition, young Will's Great Uncle William Wicks was a Methodist minister; he often visited and delivered an occasional guest sermon in Wesley Chapel during Will's boyhood.[20]

As a child, Will entered eagerly into the casual play of his sisters and his cousins. He was petted, not only by his mother, but by Grandmother Stoy and his older sisters, who eased their potential jealousy by excessive attentiveness. When their brother was ill with "malarial fever," caught on a trip to Uncle Henry's river-bottom farm, Charlotte and Julia took turns nursing him back to health. Charlotte, six years his senior, was especially devoted, and it was to her Will went for the pieces of bread covered with butter and sugar that he loved as a child. Major passions of Will's boyhood were solitary: reading and hiking. The Moody children were raised on Bible stories, fairy tales, the Greek myths, the plays of Shakespeare, and the novels of Dickens and Louisa May Alcott. Will's own early preferences were for historical romance—Dickens, Dumas, and Scott. In his adolescence he read the then-popular New England authors, admiring particularly Emerson and Whittier. In high school he discovered Browning. He carried a copy of the poems in his pocket, declaiming his favorites to anyone who would listen. With a succession of dogs, which he habitually rescued and adopted, the boy explored the countryside, hiking out to Henry Stoy's farm or back into the wooded Silver Hills, the "Knobs," which rose to the north and west of the plateau on which New Albany was built. He explored the banks of the river itself. In high school Moody and a friend constructed a skiff and explored the debris left by the great Ohio flood of 1884.[21]

Eager for the admiration of those around him, Will was determined to excel. Much in his environment quickened his ambition: the Stoy middle-class Protestant tradition, parents bitterly disappointed in their own hopes who found new hope in him, and older sisters to urge him on. As a schoolboy Will Moody was well coordinated and active, though chunky and smaller than most of his classmates. He was quick to try to emulate older or larger boys, however, and worked to become something of a local expert on the horizontal bar, if not in more active group sports.[22] Alert and well mannered, Will pleased his teachers. He began to enjoy playing with words and is today remembered chiefly in

New Albany as the nine-year-old grammar school student who won a contest by finding two hundred and thirty-two separate words in the letters of the word *Constantinople*.[23] A second public display of Will's verbal abilities came at the height of the temperance movement in New Albany. The issue aroused the Methodists to a torchlight parade in which illuminated signs were carried. Will not only marched but gave a speech on temperance to the group which gathered afterwards in the Wesley Chapel.

In high school Will joined with two classmates to edit and distribute a newspaper which they called the *Minute-Man*. They solicited advertisements and subscriptions. Their motto was "Eternal Vigilance Is the Price of Liberty," and they declared in their prospectus that they meant to strike "through custom and prejudice and demigogism [sic]" and attack the "evil institutions and abuses" of their society. Fourteen-year-old Will Moody began his attack with an article on "Ingersollism" in the newspaper's first issue. He described followers of Robert Ingersoll in these words:

They cast aside all the faith and promises that have sustained our fathers in the dark hours, and substitute in their place a miserable makeshift of "Reason" and "Common-sense." They are *progressive,* and the religion of our fathers must needs be swept away in the whirling tide of Nineteenth Century cynicism, and all the hopes of a Christian give way to the hollow teachings of a bar-room loafer. . . . They get behind their petty bulwark of science, and claim that there is no God; that the mighty machinery of the universe is run by chance, or by some vague force which they call nature.[24]

Moody was treating issues which were to become major to his poetry, but his youthful approach is a sign of the extent to which he was immersed in the ethos of his home and community.

Moody's early interests in art were developing as well. While a student in high school, Will enrolled in a summer course in crayon drawing at the Pritchett School of Design across the river in Louisville. He worked on a grand scale, doing a life-sized Venus de Milo and large portraits of his father and mother, which were exhibited at the Louisville Exposition. His family encouraged him, hanging the portraits and giving him a little room behind the back parlor to use as a studio. Moody continued his work during the school year, taking lessons in oils from a New Albany artist with Paris in his background. Will painted still lifes, family portraits, and his dogs. He took his oils with him on tramps into the hills and painted from nature.

Moody's education was guided by a gifted teacher-principal of

New Albany High School, Professor R. A. Ogg, who later became a member of the faculty at DePauw University. Ogg helped channel Will's diffuse ambition, encouraging him to write and to continue his education at a college in the East. In his junior year Will read one of his classroom essays in a Lincoln's birthday oratorical contest. He won the prize. In his essay, "The Evolution of History," Western civilization is treated in terms of progressive development. The Middle Ages presented problems—Will was not yet a lover of medievalism. It is suggested that in some yet undiscovered way the period "worked out its destined part in the task." [25] The essay became the high school valedictory address in June 1885 when Moody graduated first in a class of twenty.

Moody's family and relatives, the environments of church and school, provided the contexts of his youth. As an adolescent he became increasingly familiar with the larger life of the city. In the 1880s, New Albany was an established business and manufacturing center of over twenty thousand inhabitants. Perhaps most important to Moody's tendency to express conflicts of values in geographical terms, the city was a crossroads. New Albany had always been a Northern city, but sympathies arising out of its economic and cultural ties with the South remained strong even in Moody's boyhood. If the city's primary orientation was to the North and the East in the seventies and eighties, the West cast its spell on the young and enterprising. The city had pretensions of which Will became increasingly aware. Its merchants liked to boast of a street railroad, an opera house seating twenty-five hundred, twenty flourishing churches, and diversified industry. But a Chicago visitor of the period characterized the place as "a big country village with city clothes on." [26] The Moodys sampled fare at the New Albany Opera House and in Louisville, having the choice of such offerings as Victoria Woodhull's lectures, a German opera troupe, local choruses and bands, James Whitcomb Riley, the Yale Glee Club, *East Lynne*, the Parisian Cyclorama, Robert G. Ingersoll, General Lew Wallace, and Gilbert and Sullivan operettas.

On the periphery of Will's middle-class life were the wealthy and the laborers, many of whom were skilled European immigrants who worked in W. C. De Pauw's glass factory. Indeed, 20 percent of New Albany's population was made up of first generation immigrants. Neither the conditions of New Albany's laborers nor Will Moody's acquaintance with factory life from his father's point of view were inclined to arouse his interest or concern. W. C. De Pauw was cut from the pattern of America's nineteenth-century "captains of industry." His organization was strongly paternalistic, but since much of the labor in New Albany's industry was highly skilled, wages were high.

His early perspectives were to color Moody's later attitudes toward problems of industry and labor. Will was equally aware of the life led by New Albany society, headed by De Pauw and his friends. He knew of the schools their children attended, their large homes with rich furnishings, and their frequent trips abroad. Uncle Peter moved in their circles, and Will and his sisters sometimes looked longingly toward a more luxurious life and opportunities beyond those offered by New Albany. At the other extreme was the life of the New Albany waterfront—the life naturalistic novelists would begin to explore in another ten or fifteen years. Local newspapers featured stories of the brawls, murders, and intemperance of segments of the population less respectable than the Moodys, choosing the sensational or the senti-mental for focus. They editorialized on racial problems, on the influx of harlots from Louisville, the depredations of bums and loafers, cases of bastardy, fistfights, and drunkenness.

If Will had his occasional brushes with this life as an adolescent, it was not his life or his particular concern. The crucial experience of his adolescence was immediate and personal. From Will's earliest childhood a sense of impending doom had hovered over the family because of the state of his mother's health. Family prayers, when led by Great Uncle William Wicks, included the wish that Mrs. Moody be prepared for a death which seemed imminent and for eternal life with God.[27] When Will was not yet ten, the death of Grandmother Stoy left a gap in the family. In November 1883, in Will's fourteenth year, his sister Mary died, still in her early thirties. Only two months later, her family gathered around Henrietta Moody's bed in a final farewell.[28] If the earlier deaths had created anxiety, the effect on Will of his mother's death was traumatic. In the spring he planted a rosebush at the foot of her grave and hurried to the cemetery after school to care for it and to lie on the grave, meditating. Captain Moody began stopping at the graveyard after work to bring his son home for supper.[29]

Moody's anguished sense of betrayal led to an idealization of his adolescent love for his mother and an awareness of life's urgency. Periods of exaltation, deriving from the vague mysticism his mother had stimulated in him, alternated with depression and a sense of guilt and exile. The exaltations involved a sense of spiritual rebirth, the memory of which haunted the poet years later as he tried to recapture what he called "Lost verses from my youth's gold canticle." The re-ligious contemplations Moody engaged in partook of and yet departed significantly from the evangelical Protestantism of his childhood. In the works of the Pre-Raphaelite poets and of Robert Browning he began to find his way to a reinterpretation of his tradition. Similarities between the situation of the Brownings and that of his own parents were compelling. And Will Moody found in Browning what many of his countrymen found: a liberating mutation of the religious faith of the American Protestant middle class. Browning provided a medium through which the values of work, of striving and conquest, of salvation and damnation through passion could be realized in a realm of spirit, beauty, and idealized love.

The memory of a walk taken in the spring after his mother's death—a memory which remained vivid to his sister Julia years later—preserves Will Moody's expanding sense of life. He was full of speculation and felt he was standing on the threshold of life. Most of all he longed for experience. "I don't care how I have to work," he said. "I don't care how I have to suffer. I want to experience *everything*." A second statement seemed significant to his sister: "If it wasn't for Mama—her love and all—I don't believe I could understand Christ." [30] In his youth, Will's mother had been his means of entry into world of spiritual and aesthetic experience. Participation in her love and suffering now became the mode of human reconciliation with God as well. The whole conversation was suffused with a strange sense of liberation, and Will and Julia felt they were treading on stars.

The year after graduation from high school Will attended daily classes at the Pritchett School, worked in the little room he had converted into a studio, and took frequent solitary sketching trips. He read and began to write until late in the night. If his drawing and painting were public knowledge, Will's writing was secretive. He tore up his poems as soon as he finished writing them. Captain Moody fell victim to a kidney ailment in the fall and his condition became serious by winter. In the spring complications set in and he lost interest in life. At the end of May 1886 Captain Moody died. The employees of the iron works—over a hundred men—attended his funeral and sent a resolution of condolence praising Burdette Moody's "probity, manliness, devotion to duty, generous heart, and tender love." [31] Arrangements were quickly made for the survivors. Henrietta, fifteen, joined the Francis Moody family in Lafayette, while Julia, twenty, and Charlotte, twenty-three, were invited to Poughkeepsie, New York, to visit with Charles Rowley, widower husband of one of Burdette's half-sisters. The young ladies intended to prepare for careers in teaching by enrolling at the Oswego Normal School in the fall. The estate would have provided about $2000 for each child, but Will resigned his share in favor of his sisters.[32] He contracted to teach country school in the Corydon Pike school near New Albany, hoping to save enough of his salary to go on to a university in a year or two.

2

The years between the dissolution of Will's family and his matriculation at Harvard College in 1889 were hardly a preparation for "experiencing *everything.*" Last of the Moodys left in New Albany, Will was invited to live with Henry and Elizabeth Stoy on their Ohio River farm near Will's country schoolhouse. Will's desire for solitude had deepened, and the Stoys found him shy and retiring.[33] Developing the self-deprecatory wit characteristic of his maturity, Will called the three of them the Star and Cuttlefish Association. He was the cuttlefish—a squidlike mollusk with a hard internal shell. It ejects a cloud of black fluid when in danger. Will's source for the self-characterization is probably the fourth satire in Horace's first book. There the cuttlefish is associated with a disguised malice, which damns under cover of friendship and praise. Moody's personality was developing its shell through aggressive melancholy, self-protective irony, benign detachment, and poetic projection.

Moody's energies were directed to his teaching in the fall. His rural schoolhouse primarily served children of immigrant German peasants. For the first time, Will came into contact with the poor. His conscience was engaged, and he was torn between a growing sense of responsibility to his charges and his desire for a very different life. Finally, it was the boredom and drudgery of his life which impressed him most strongly. Still devoted to Browning, he sometimes read and discussed the poet with Elizabeth Stoy. He read constantly, either in his room or perched in one of the large elm trees that surrounded the house. He enjoyed rowing to and from his school on the river, and he preferred rowing against a stiff current. Will worked over his poems and began to keep the best of them, but he showed them to no one. In January a sympathetic cousin persuaded him to return to New Albany. Another of Will's uncles had returned to the city to live in the old Stoy homestead, and an invalid daughter, Armon, almost thirty, was interested in literature. Will began joining her in her room after his day of teaching, and they talked.[34] He found a relationship with her which paralleled that with his mother. Toward the end of the year Will showed Armon Stoy his poems and asked for her reactions.

Moody's work flowered that spring in gifts of small handwritten volumes which he sent to Charlotte and Julia in the East. Mottoes for the volumes were taken from Emerson. *To Julia*[35] contains eleven poems written between 1885 and 1887. The poems are imitative of Victorian practice in the lyric and the Petrarchan sonnet. Influences

of the popular poetry of the period and of the Pre-Raphaelite poets
are stronger than that of Browning—an indication that Browning was
more a solace for Moody than a master to be imitated. Most of the
poems are reveries, developed largely in terms of scenic description.
Imagery and allusions are drawn from Moody's reading in English and
American poetry of the nineteenth century, in the schoolboy's classical
mythology, and in the Bible. The poems show a special attraction to
images and scenes of apocalyptic terror and vision. The apocalyptic
landscape in one poem is projected through description of organ music
in the heart of a dim cathedral. In "Wagner," a snake threatens the
glory seat, but it is repelled and falls in "bestial yellings and a shriv-
elled, dead,/ Contorted horror cleaving the abyss—/ One wild eye
glaring." Yet another poem is set in the landscapes of a woman's soul,
in which the speaker "can but grope/ In the great darkness helplessly."
There is a hush "before the smothered boom/ Of some far-off erup-
tion," and the poem ends in a scene of midnight ecstasy. In the rich
symbols of the Pre-Raphaelite poets, with their suggestive sexual overtones, Moody was finding the means to express the turbulence of his
adolescent conflict.

The most interesting of these early poems are two which rise out
of meditations on the death of his mother. The first is a short lyric
which treats the symbolic implications of the rosebush Moody had
planted on his mother's grave. He called it "To a Wild Rose by a
Tomb":

> Out of the broken life,
>   The choking tomb,
> Out of the storm and strife
>   The glare and gloom—
> Soul, it is meant for thee,
> Take thou the prophecy—
> Beauty and bloom!

Moody's second poem takes the curious form of a sonnet octave to
which the refrain, "When sunset dies," is added. It is followed by a
full sonnet and refrain. In the first section, Moody describes himself
at sunset, going "Across a dusky church-yard that I know,/ To one
low mound that loves the mellow glow." This is the concluding full
sonnet:

> When sunset dies the curtains of deceit
> That bar our vision from the shining Why
> We look and long for when the blood-hound's cry

Is in our ears, and sink our bleeding feet
Beneath the noon's mad curse of dust and heat—
Are drawn aside, and in a dumb delight
We feel the revelation of the night
Kiss from our brows the burning Judas-cheat.
Then I can press my lips upon the stone
Calmly as though my life did not lie there
With the wild-rose and ivy over-grown;
Then I can clasp again the conscious air,
Because I feel what was is still mine own—
Knowing what things the yearning stars declare
When sunset dies.

The poem is a confused expression of the youth's bewildering sense of betrayal in the loss of his mother. The bloodhound seems to have been drawn from a lingering impression of the chase in *Uncle Tom's Cabin,* and Moody's expression of faith gropes clumsily through a maze of metaphor toward expression. The reference to Judas identifies Will with Christ and illuminates his statement that his mother enabled him to understand Christ better. Like Christ he has been betrayed by one who had been loved and trusted, betrayed into a life involving separation, suffering, and death. But the declaration of "the yearning stars" permits mystical union with the spirit of Henrietta Moody, a living soul which survives in "the conscious air." The boy makes love to the stone "calmly," as though his "life did not lie there." The theme and motifs of this early poem were to reappear in poems of the writer's maturity—particularly "Good Friday Night" and "The Moon-Moth."

Will Moody's life opened to new possibilities when a letter arrived in the spring from Charles Rowley in Poughkeepsie. Moody was invited to help tutor Charles, Jr., for entrance examinations at Yale. Moody himself could enroll at nearby Riverview Academy to prepare himself for college. Although Rowley's wife had recently died, leaving him with an only son, he maintained a large home which he called Tendring Hall. His offer to Will was more charitable than business-like, for the young man was more suitable as a companion than as a tutor to Charles Rowley, Jr.

Moody arrived at Tendring Hall in the summer of 1887 and was to be at home there for the next two years. In the fall he threw himself into his studies at Riverview Academy with an energy all the more intense after his year of drudgery and boredom. Moody found that he was behind the advanced preparatory classes in Latin and Greek, but he caught up by doing two years' work in his first year. If Will's knowledge was limited, his zest to learn and his power of endurance were strong. He was an excellent model for Charles Rowley, who was amazed at Will's ability to study late into the night, long after Charles had retired in exhaustion.[36]

In his first year at the academy Moody was a day student, living at Tendring Hall. The following year he lived at Riverview, where he helped teach the younger boys. The head of the academy was an effective young master, Harlan P. Amen, later headmaster at Exeter for many years. Dr. Amen was by background and character a lucky find for Moody. He, more than anyone the young man was later to meet, helped develop Moody's intellectual interests and give shape to his goals. Amen had worked his way through Exeter and then Harvard. He enjoyed talking literature with his students and he shared Moody's own taste for tramping through the countryside. Amen's primary interest was Greek literature, and he communicated his sensitivity to it to Moody. Indeed, he found Moody's appreciation for the Greeks remarkable, and their communication was lively.

A host of activities beyond his study and tutoring indicates Moody's dedication to the preparatory school ideals. The academy had moved away from early connections with West Point, but it retained a military atmosphere. The only Riverview memory Will later communicated to Robert Morss Lovett was of marching around the drill field with others who had broken the rule against smoking.[37] Lovett suggests that Will looked back with distaste on the discipline at Riverview, and it is likely that he did. At the time, however, he made a determined effort to perform well, and he may have welcomed the discipline, for he was captain of the best-drilled company in the school in 1888. There was ample opportunity for a broad social life as well. The atmosphere of the Rowley home was warm, and Will formed a close friendship with young Charles Rowley. He joined the family for trips to New York City, to nearby lakes, to the Rowley farm in South Cortland, New York, and to their summer home on Martha's Vineyard. He dated an occasional girl from nearby Vassar College. And his associations with fellow students were stimulating. On one summer hiking trip Moody, John Otis, Fred Morgan, and Amen walked from Burlington, Vermont, into the White Mountains. They climbed Mount Washington and went on to Lake Winnepesaukee. From there they took the train to Boston and Cambridge for sightseeing. Morgan remembered Moody as vocal and sociable on the trip. His religious views were already radical and he loved argumentation.[38]

Relaxation of the tensions of Will's early poetry appears in a Browningesque monologue he wrote in reaction to the portrait of a mournful nun in Charles Rowley's collection.[39] In the monologue Sister Angelica speaks of her frustrated love for the young painter who chose her as model for the Virgin when he painted the nunnery's walls. At the poem's end, Moody recurs to his image of a rose by a tomb. Sister Angelica dreams of plucking the rose. It turns into the young painter and the poem ends with the suggestion of fulfillment of their love. The poem is passionate, but there is a new detachment in the way Moody uses the tension-laden symbol from his New Albany experience.

In spite of evidence of a new sociability, Moody's outward manner changed little. His was already a personality which, as Daniel Gregory Mason was later to observe, "combined intellectual candor and personal reserve in a way that many found bewildering." [40] Charles Rowley, Jr., found him dutiful, gentle, and modest. Will's deepest feelings were communicated to no one, and the manner he presented the world was one of quiet poise. Moody's devotion to the goals set by Riverview was the result of his own high ambition and his rigid sense of duty. Moody won the Riverview medal for highest scholarship at the end of his first year, together with a number of prizes in special subjects. Among his prizes was a set of Matthew Arnold, which was in his undergraduate library. He was graduated in 1889 with the highest record ever attained by a student at the academy. A scholarship of $400 awaited him at Harvard College.

CHAPTER 2 SUBTLE THREADS THAT BIND

WHEN WILL MOODY entered Harvard College in the fall of 1889, it was rapidly developing into the modern university.[1] President Eliot's free elective system, and expansions of the faculty and the course offerings had created a new sense of freedom and challenge.[2] One of the citadels of the American cultured middle class, Harvard was heir to what George Santayana was later to call the "Genteel Tradition." The easy, sometimes urbane, sometimes provincial spirit of a college dedicated to the creation of the gentleman still pervaded student life. It was preserved in the teaching of men like Barrett Wendell, George H. Palmer, and Charles Eliot Norton. But the old tradition was pressed by a multitude of intellectual and social problems. They took the form of antitheses: the American moral sense had found in Hegelian thought congenial methods of analysis and the promise of salvation in synthesis. Antinomies were identified in idealism or realism, religion or science, man or machine, wealth or commonwealth, Europe or America, Hebraism or Hellenism, the world as Will or the world as Idea. Harvard students and faculty sought viable positions in the moral earnestness of a social gospel or a gospel of culture, in aestheticism, pessimism, and neo-primitivism. The environment that produced Moody, the writer, provided the soil for *The Strenuous Life*, *The Will to Believe*, and *The Philosophy of Loyalty*, as well as for *The Sense of Beauty* and *Italian Painters of the Renaissance*. Will Moody found his personal conflicts darkly mirrored in the larger problems of his place and time. At Harvard he moved toward self-definition in terms of his culture.

Moody took a huge battery of examinations, passing those in elementary and advanced Greek and Latin, elementary French and

German, physics, geometry, algebra, English, and ancient history. The advanced standing he gained was to enable him to complete course work in three years. Moody's Riverview training directed him to a classical education with a heavy emphasis on language and literature, and one-third of his college work was to be taken in Latin and Greek. In his first year Moody took courses in these languages, English A, German poets from Kleist through Heine, the history of modern Europe, and chemistry. His one semester of work in chemistry was to be Moody's only excursion outside the humanities.[3]

The dedication to academic duty developed at Riverview remained with Moody, and he took his classes seriously. His dedication was a result of genuine appetite for learning, of high ambition, and of the desire to justify the expense of his education. He had been awarded the Gambrill scholarship, Harvard's largest. While $400 was a princely sum at the time, it was not sufficient to cover all his needs. From the Dakotas, Uncle Gideon Moody sent help in the form of a thousand dollars.[4] Will treated it as a loan and eventually repaid it. Besides his own expense, Will was expected to contribute to the support of his sisters. Some of his earnings as New Albany teacher and as tutor at Riverview had gone into the family coffers, and he continued to make contributions out of his funds during his college years. He did countless odd jobs as a student, but most of his income came from tutoring. Preparation of students for college was a popular means of support for the bright student, and this occupied several of his summers.

Robert Morss Lovett has described Will Moody at twenty as "a well-knit figure, of medium height, a ruddy face under wavy flaxen locks, eyes of cold blue except for frequent gleams of humor, lips sensitive and sensuous." His eyes and his voice—"full, clear, rich in overtones"[5]—were his most distinctive characteristics. More casual acquaintances than Lovett found Moody either poised and self-contained or snobbishly aloof. He gave the impression of someone who had "been around a good bit." Moody entered the casual life of the college undergraduate with relative ease. There were informal poker games and long sessions of earnest talk. Moody played some football, enjoyed rowing, and followed Harvard athletic contests with enthusiasm. Weekend hiking trips were a popular activity and Will went off with groups— once to Plymouth, another time to Concord, and still again to Lexington.

In the preceding summer Will had met Grace Hurd, a relation of the Rowleys. A romance began that was to continue for the next four years. Like Moody, Grace had lost both parents. She lived with her grandparents in Elma, in western New York. In the fall Will began a correspondence with Grace that is highly literary in content and reveals the richly romantic quality of his imaginative life. In one letter the young poet and Grace take the roles of Endymion and Diana; in a Valentine letter they are Hero and Leander. Moody knew much of Shakespeare at twenty, and he found his love mirrored in the gently idealized love scenes in *As You Like It, The Merchant of Venice,* and *The Tempest.* He draws his reading in Browning, Carlyle, and Kleist into the service of his correspondence. Moody's letters are often scenic, and he sometimes weaves elaborate fabrics of fantasy. In one letter Moody describes a picturesque Boston street musician and imagines the man is thinking of his youth in Italy, where he sang to a beautiful woman standing "in a balcony perhaps, with its old carvings flushed into rose and gold by the mellow sunset and its latticed vines weaving a trembling lace of shade on the marble floor." [6] In another letter Will places himself and Grace "next door to Ali Baba or just around the corner from Aladdin." Grace is languishing, "clad in cool Persian silks" in an arbor "smothered in citron flowers and roses that bloom in the month of Ramadahu," when "a cloudy something falls through the orange boughs" and Will in the guise of Hafiz appears on his wishing rug.[7] Will attempts to arouse jealousy with casual reference to possible Christmas festivities involving Cambridge girls. He complains that Grace's letters are "coldblooded," and he casts himself as Pygmalion, praying to ox-eyed Hera in an attempt to wake Grace "from her ivory sleep."

Moody was finding public outlets for his writing at Harvard. In his first year he published five short poems and a short story in the undergraduate literary magazines, the *Advocate* and the *Monthly.* None of the poems was new. Under the stimulus of a lively under-graduate literary renaissance at Harvard,[8] Moody revised his early work and sent it out. The most ambitious of his poems is "A Chorus of Wagner," first written in New Albany three years earlier.[9] It is a good example of the direction Moody's impulses to craftsmanship were taking. After intensive reworking, the poem looked like this:

> From sheer-walled sunless mountain-gorge so deep
> That fierce-tongued torrents steal thence faint and sweet
> As milk-maid's laugh across the spangled wheat,
> Rumbleth some shade-born monster up the steep
> Dragging its folds, a coiled and clammy heap,
> Up, up the slant cliffs to the glory-seat
> Where rings on rings of circling beat
> From the clear air a rainbow's jewelled sweep.
> A rush intense—a sudden storm of rays
> Hurled clanging on the brute's sepulchral head—

> Dim bestial yellings—and a shrivelled, dead,
> Contorted horror cleaving the abyss,
> One wild eye glaring—and a hateful hiss
> Plunging and splintering down the craggy ways.

The sonnet searches almost desperately through a maze of florid diction for the evocative image. While Moody is concerned with a dramatic action, the poem is basically scenic. He strives for energy in a concentrated piling of phrases, in hyphenated nouns and adjectives, in a welter of powerful verbals, in fragmented syntax, and in violent rhythmic breaks through the sestet. The style created is an example of the Victorian sublime pushed to its limits: four verbs sustain the weight of twenty-six adjectives and twenty-five nouns. Moody's search for new poetic energy had begun in an attempt to raise the intensities of the poetic tradition he inherited. Stylistically the poem suggests a major direction in Moody's poetic practice throughout the nineties, and thematically it anticipates his first poetic drama, *The Masque of Judgment.*

Moody's poetry so impressed Norman Hapgood and his board of editors that they invited him to join the board though he was but a first-year student. The *Monthly* was both a literary magazine and an informal writers' club. It became central to most of Moody's friendships. When he entered Harvard, Robert Herrick was editor. In the early nineties the *Monthly* was controlled by Moody and his closest friends—Robert Morss Lovett and the Hapgood brothers, Hutchins and Norman. Moody met Philip Henry Savage, Pierre La Rose, Joseph Trumbull Stickney, and others through his association with the publication. And he met recent ex-editors, who kept in touch with their successors. Among them were George Rice Carpenter, Mark Antony De Wolfe Howe, Bernard Berenson, George Pierce Baker, and George Santayana.

Through much of the century, moral earnestness at Harvard had taken the form of the complacent Unitarianism Emerson had attacked some fifty years earlier. The tradition had finally absorbed Emerson, adjusting comfortably, but by the nineties it was being directed into new channels by *Monthly* editors. They keenly felt their provinciality and wanted to do something about it. Reading in Ruskin, Arnold, and others gave them their tools. Articles on foreign writers and subjects form the bulk of the magazine's material. And the articles were drawn from sources calculated to supplement America's abundant Hebraism with the necessary leaven of Hellenism. When American writers are treated, they are generally attacked. Lowell is too "narrow"; Henry James is a mere realist, good at social chitchat but at little else; and

Howells's work bears the fatal curse of life's universal dryness in New England. Hugh McCulloch's article on Walt Whitman suggests one important attitude, on the basis of which the American tradition was rejected. "Whitman," he writes, "stands for the America which might have been, but which never can be now." Whitman's Americanism is seen as the product of a less corrupt, less complex world than that of Moody and his associates. Whitman's poetic vision had been "founded on data which time has shown to be insufficient." [10]

The redirection of moral earnestness into cultural channels struck familiar chords in Will Moody. The Methodist training of his childhood had already taken on the coloration of his reading in Emerson, Browning, and Arnold. And, while Will felt the conflict of his Indiana background with an Eastern foreground, he was becoming even more sensitive to the contrast between America and Europe. He wrote a theme presenting his dilemma in the form of a thinly masked character sketch of a midwesterner studying engineering in the East. Moody describes his subject as "a curious product of the ignorant, matter-of-fact, able West and the hysterically civilized East," who has come to the conclusion that he is "an impossibility." Moody's engineer "accepts life quietly as a place for building bridges and aquaducts but is predoomed to failure because of a smothered conviction that life is nothing of the sort, but some remote experience, some over-sea place—Art, Love, Italy." [11]

In the quandary of the young man "predoomed to failure," Moody touches on a second of his preoccupations as an undergraduate. He responded to the pessimism which permeated Harvard Yard in the early nineties in much the same way that Existentialism spread across university campuses in the 1950s. The poetry of Matthew Arnold and Arthur Hugh Clough was basic reading for undergraduates. Fitz-Gerald's *Rubáiyát* was at the height of a popularity that was to continue through the nineties. Dobson and Swinburne were the contemporary poets of note, and Harvard literati were delving into Obermann, Leopardi, and Musset. Edgar Saltus's *Philosophy of Disenchantment* and *The Anatomy of Negation*, published in the mid-eighties, helped swell undergraduate interest in Schopenhauer, Leopardi, and Leconte de Lisle.

Harvard pessimism tended to take the form of an aestheticism tinged with the manners of *fin-de-siècle* decadence. The pervasiveness of its appeal is evident in the college fiction of the period.[12] It is best caught in the figure of the aspiring young poet presented in the Harvard stories of Charles M. Flandrau and Waldron K. Post. Flandrau's undergraduate literary man is playfully cynical and coolly aloof, scornful of the Philistinism of the common herd. His "apparent ac-

quaintance with most of the sensations a jaded century has to offer"
led others to suspect that the literary man had at some time lived reck-
lessly. But Flandrau suggests that the cynicism and decadence are no
more than a cultivated pose.[13] George Santayana was high priest of
the Harvard aesthetes and elder statesman to the *Monthly*, which he
had helped found in 1885. He had returned from graduate study in
Europe to join the Harvard philosophy department in Moody's freshman year. Through the early nineties the editors of the *Monthly* often
deserted their unadorned staff quarters to meet in Santayana's rooms
in the Yard, where they could talk in greater comfort over a punch
compounded of lukewarm tea and Tokay. Santayana was writing
quietly poised Petrarchan sonnets in the nineties—poems which seek
detachment from the passionate world of will. He continued to publish poetry and an occasional prose piece in the magazine. He entered
the controversy over Whitman with a dialogue on the poet, and he
urbanely dissected the Philistine in an article which delighted his
undergraduate associates. The article ends with a sophisticated ironic
thrust at the enemy's materialistic orientation to values: "You have the
happiness of knowing that, when nothing I value endures, the earth
may still sometimes, because of you, cast a slightly different shadow
across the craters of the moon." [14]

Caught in the popular mood, Will interpreted his relation to
Grace Hurd in terms of *fin-de-siècle* psychic drama. He wrote her that
she was a saint—his personal salvation. He had followed a vision of
Grace into a Cambridge church, and he observed that he was prepared
to turn Catholic upon her canonization. When Grace viewed the experience as an idle fancy, Moody protested his seriousness and presented his "life-story" in evidence:

> You do not know, nobody can know the awfulness, the terror, the
> ghastliness of those spirit-lands across which, from my very nature, I have
> had to journey; the days when men have seemed like midges dancing above
> miasmas and stagnations unfathomable, when life and all its butterfly-
> flutterings have seemed the hollowest mockery that shamed the sun, when
> I could have crushed the whole blind sick universe into powder and thrown
> myself into the infinite nothingness with a laugh.
>
> One by one I saw the things I loved fade away, the things I trusted
> fail me—and then there came a time of which I do not wish to think,
> for I came out of it not the unselfish gentle-hearted boy I went in, but one
> who had tasted the wine cup of sin and knew its dregs were death.[15]

This is spiritual biography in the form of the Victorian quest poem.
Moody's journey through a distorted landscape of terror culminates in
a gesture of Byronic hyperbole. The second paragraph echoes the motifs

of *fin-de-siècle* poetry, with its images of innocence and the dregs in life's wine cup. On another occasion Moody writes out of the depths of a mood of frustration and desperate nostalgia:

We are so fatally woven about with circumstance! We catch glimpses of fair and happy uplands of life, and look about us if we may somehow struggle up to them, but the valley closes round us again and there is nothing but tangled thicket and swamp and darkness.

So we keep on living our little days out, one after another,—trying to forget those sunny fields of the *Might-be,* trying to forget the void out of which we came and the void into which we are going, trying—but so despairingly—to forget the great hunger of our hearts, which cry out for something real and will not be satisfied with shadows.[16]

In spite of the extravagant posturing, the anguish and despair to which these passages reach are genuine. Moody was searching the models available to him—as all writers must—for a style answerable to his experience.

As Will put his freshman year behind him, he became more free in personality, indulging a love of caprice and breaking through petty restraints. Personal and study habits became more erratic, but his course work continued to engage him. He studied Pliny, Tacitus, and Horace in Latin, and took courses in French and in seventeenth-century European history. Moody's concern for intellectual problems had deepened, and he joined the Philosophy Club and elected a philosophy course. It and his course in Greek were his greatest interests. Philosophy was a three-ring circus, taught by Palmer, James, and Santayana. The influence of William James proved most lasting. He introduced Moody to Taine and convinced him of the serious philosophical objections that should be made to the work of Herbert Spencer. James quickened Moody's interest in psychology as well, and Moody was one of a group of students who attended a series of psychic exhibitions in Boston with James.[17] But Moody was most caught by his teacher's infectious enthusiasm for a variety of experience and his emphasis on the basic fact of experience itself.

The interest in Greek that Moody had developed at Riverview was deepening, and he was excited by his reading in the drama, particularly *Alkestis, Oedipus,* and *The Bacchae.* The Harvard Greek department was avant-garde in the nineties, and Moody's teachers engaged him by emphasis on the poetic and dramatic values of the plays he read and by their interest in the dramatic patterns taken by Greek myth and ritual. Of the two Greek modes Moody and his friends distinguished, he preferred that which was "lawless, glad, and beautiful" to that characterized by "simplicity, repose, and sanity." The preference appears in an early poem, "To the Nike of Paionios," and finds later expression in "The Moon-Moth." Of English poets, it was Keats who Moody began to feel best caught the true poetic spirit of the Greeks. But he did not turn to Hellenism with the total devotion of his friends, Philip Becker Goetz and Joseph Trumbull Stickney. He admired the caryatids of the Erechtheum, observing in a class theme that they "seemed to carry in their calm limbs and firm-poised breasts all the health and frank physical beauty of old Greece." But his first allegiance was to the mystical Christian vision embodied in Tintoretto's depiction of Paradise "with its soaring rings of beatific spirits, brooded over by the mystc dove." He decided that our great loss of the Greek spirit was a greater gain, and he declared himself content to be a modern.

Moody's closest friends, however, were unwilling to find their relief in the aestheticism of the nineties, and he was increasingly drawn to their position. For values appropriate to their times, Lovett, the Hapgood brothers, and finally Moody turned to a neopaganism which emphasized the power of the will, emotional regeneration, and impulsive action. Moody's best friend, Robert Morss Lovett, admired William Morris's rejection of a "ghastly hedonism" and a "mournful epicureanism" for active resistance and protest. Engagement in the world of will was, Lovett felt, the only response to pessimism.[18] True to his theories, he founded the Prospect Progressive Union, a settlement house in Central Square, Cambridge, which enlisted professors and students willing to lecture to audiences of tradesmen and clerks. Santayana was somehow recruited, though he was not attuned to the spirit of the enterprise. He gave a lecture on St. Francis and the virtue of poverty to the assembly of aspiring Philistines.[19]

The Hapgoods were midwesterners. More rebellious in temper and tradition than Moody and Lovett, they had learned to admire Robert Ingersoll at their father's knee. Hutchins Hapgood shared Moody's sympathetic response to pessimism, however. He could oppose "all that is dark and evil" in the universe only with the hope that his "Alma Mater," Harvard, could somehow help him retain into maturity the simple faith and delight of a child.[20] His brother, Norman, dissected the stance of pessimism and decadence for the *Monthly* group in an article titled "The Apologist." "When Ibsen and others kick over the traces of custom, and tell us our sins, they make more noise than need be," he wrote. "So when Mr. Wilde tells us there is a world without the moral, and Mr. Saltus proves the necessity of disenchantment, their tone is a trifle high. . . . Their manner lacks repose." Pessimism itself he considered a form of "literary capital" and an indirect confession of "personal littleness." "The gentleman," Hapgood wrote, "who shouts at us our speedy decay is not a charlatan, he is a weakling."[21]

Hapgood believed in truth, honor, and goodness, he maintained, simply because he had the will to believe. Yet, he wrote, "I cannot help wishing occasionally that my intellect and my senses would join my will and give me the child's whole-souled belief in all it wishes to believe." [22]

Under the new dispensation, Moody's attitudes shifted from the scenic and pictorial to the human and dramatic. For example, his interest in Shakespeare had changed by the end of his sophomore year: he turned from passages of gentle idealism and fancy to sterner stuff. "One must be very human," Moody decided, "very conscious of a fierce heart throbbing in his side, that will not be reasoned with nor gainsaid, very glad that he is a man, born under the terrible white sun to laughter and wrath and tears—in order to like Shakespeare." [23] The shift in attitude made itself increasingly felt in the pages of the *Monthly*. In rebellion against Santayana's leadership, Moody and his friends published three articles on Stevenson, three on Whitman, and three on Browning. Vigor, youthfulness, strength, and intensity of emotion are the qualities admired in these writers. Whitman now emerges as *"a man"* and is praised for being "in our pessimistic age the apostle of joy." Maeterlinck has "too much depth and masculinity" to be decadent, one article asserts. He too is hailed as "a man." William James, a prophet ready at hand to the movement, was asked for an article on the undergraduate program. He wrote to reject "the golden and dreamy and amateurish ideal" of college as inferior to a "more strenuous and professional" one, "not only as a participant in the struggle for existence, but as an agent in the formation of *character*." [24] The editors happily published Dickinson S. Miller's "The Over-Production of Opinion" [25]—a total rejection of reason as a guide to life. Miller argues that intellectual controversy produces only confusion. He observes, "A mind open on too many sides, a sensibility too exposed, will find the springs of action shattered and resolution 'sicklied o'er' with thought." The answer is that "We must give up the hope of living by reason" and turn to "rapid judgment" and "sure instincts." A similar set of values runs through the fiction which Moody and his friends found most attractive. The protagonist of one story,[26] a Harvard man, is interested in a beautiful farm girl from Kansas. He loses her to "a thick-set young man with the countenance of a brakeman." The Harvard man is too refined: he is unable to enter into the elemental struggle for possession that is necessary in these matters. Another tale [27] traces the decline and fall of a young epicure who is unable to act because his assumed dilettantism has fatally weakened his will.

Encouraged by his literary success and stimulated by his associates on the *Monthly*, Moody had turned to new work. Except for one poem, Moody avoided the popular Petrarchan sonnet now—it was a vehicle of the Harvard aesthetes. Neither did he write ballads, another popular *fin-de-siècle* form. His most persistent model is Browning, though there are hints and echoes of richer styles of the Pre-Raphaelites, of Swinburne, and of the minor English poets of the eighties. One poem, "Dance Music," is an attempt to evoke a hypnotic spell in driving trochaic meter, but modern ears respond only to the artificiality of the measure. The scene is a dance of death, in which imagery and suggestion of Greek Bacchanalia mingle with references to medieval dragons and castles. In another poem, "The Sun Virgin," a passionate young Peruvian declares his love for a maiden dedicated to service in the temple of the sun. He is about to steal her away, an action which is assertive but will lead to inevitable *Liebestod*. In "The Picture," an old woman, viewing her portrait as a young beauty, recalls the way she proudly ruined the life of an enamored painter. Mannerisms of William Morris's poetry mix with the Browningesque theme. "A Sick-Room Fancy" is a quiet monologue. Stimulated by the beauty of a bedside rose, a dying man sinks into a reverie and foresees possible reunion with his beloved after death. In a passage like this one the language is compressed and restrained:

> What finger can unwind
> All subtle threads that bind
> Body and soul and mind?
> What thought may stand and say
> "Thus flies the shade away?"
> What knowledges may scan
> The unimagined plan,
> Saying "Cannot" and "Can"?

A more extravagant passage pushes sound and rhythm to Swinburnian limits. The speaker sees himself and his love moving off quietly together, through

> Starlight and sky and sea,
> Wandering, while on while,
> Nearer that argent isle
> Which from the dawn of time,
> Gemmed in seas hyaline,
> Wrapped in a cloudless clime,
> Bird-song, bee-humming,
> Ever through soft sky-shine
> Bided their coming.[28]

2

As a sophomore Will had written to Grace Hurd out of the depths
of a period of self-analysis, complaining, "Life is not leading anywhere."
Self-definition was becoming increasingly necessary, and a struggle
with his identity surfaces in experiments Moody was making with his
name. In signing his work, he had tried various combinations. Sometimes he was merely a set of initials. He finally decided, and by the end
of his sophomore year William Vaughn Stoy Moody—a name he had
tried several times—became William Vaughn Moody. The gesture
suggests rejection of that part of his heritage that was most Philistine.
His choices had included the less assertive possibilities of W. V. S.
Moody and W. V. Moody. The signature, Will Moody, would have
suggested a Whitmanic stance. The young poet's choice confirmed
Moody's sense of a public identity presented in the form most ac-
ceptable to the Genteel Tradition.

Moody's choice of a public name is a sign of new, clear commitments. He decided to become a college teacher and to prepare himself
to enter Harvard's graduate program in English language and literature. Moody's academic work as a junior turned decisively to an
emphasis on English. He sat through three courses with Professor
Child, two in Anglo-Saxon and one in Shakespeare. He took a course
in the seventeenth century with Dean Briggs and one in the nineteenth
century with Professor Hill. There were several courses in the modern
languages: one in Goethe and the Romantics, another in the *Song of
Roland,* and a third in beginning Italian. Moody wandered outside
languages only to elect Norton's Roman and medieval art. For the poet
the effect of this curriculum was more negative than positive. It served
primarily to solidify his strong tendency to a literary academicism.
Moody was to be firmly rooted in the almost overwhelming problems
of the English and American poet working in a cultural and poetic
tradition already caught in a number of dead ends.

Moody had arrived at a new dedication to his writing as well. It
rings most clearly in a remark made to Lovett. They were discussing
their futures, and Lovett was discouraged by the difficulties he foresaw
in achieving any significant success in the world, already crowded with
successes. Moody tended to agree, but he replied—with solemnity,
Lovett recalled: "No man can refuse to run at Olympia." [29] Moody's
poetry had brought him local recognition, but wider success now began to seem possible. In his junior year the number of poems Moody
published in the *Monthly* doubled, and they were ambitious. In ad-

dition he was submitting his best work to the national magazines. In November 1891 *Scribner's* published one of them: "Dolorosa." The publication, however, illuminates a new problem inherent in the ideal of the gentleman scholar and writer on which the Genteel Tradition rested and to which Moody had committed himself. As a sophomore, using *The Ring and the Book* as his touchstone, Moody observed that life was but the "crude ore" of art. The artist's task was to burn away the dross so that "the rude mass becomes a work of art." [30] But for Moody the burning away involved a transmutation so complete that no sense of immediate personal experience remained. Grace Hurd had been one source for "Dolorosa," though even a reader who knew the fact would have difficulty finding personal reference in the poem. Yet Moody regarded its publication as a serious breach of decorum. He wrote Grace a letter which ranges from ill-concealed excitement to abject apology for the poem's appearance in "a professional magazine." [31] Combining disdain for crudities of the business world with a sense of impropriety in public display of one's personal feelings, the attitude of gentleman-poet Moody adopts places severe limits on his range and treatment of subject.

Moody's commitments are clearly operating in a letter of September 1891, in which his rebellious pessimism is expressed in new terms. He wrote Grace,

I . . . am bitterly sick of living a life of judgment and reason, where every action is the result of forethought and calculation, where every liking and every hatred can be dissected, and its motive spring uncovered. I want to just *feel* for a while, to love and hate without knowing the reason why—I want to get drunk with the sweet old life-wine. . . . I refuse to be a brain—I will pitch Plato out of the window and turn woodchopper first.[32]

Moody's mood is permeated with the anti-intellectualism of the *Monthly* literati. But the context for conflict is Moody's immediate environment, and the battle is one between his commitment as a student of literature and that as a writer.

If Harvard was helping Moody to self-definition in terms of his culture, its impact on his social manner was slight. His habit of reticence was as marked as ever. Even his friends found him shy and sometimes eccentric. Lovett has written that Moody's most usual attitude was that of "calm self-possession." [33] Another friend remembered him for his delight in cryptic comment and his general unworldliness.[34] Moody retired into the background in any group, and he seldom referred to himself, his family, or his past. His greatest pleasure was taking a long walk, and he often set off with Lovett, Norman Hapgood, or Philip Goetz for Arlington Heights, Mount Auburn Cemetery, Spy Pond, or Boston. Moody's conversation, one friend remarked, tended to consist of chasing a metaphor through an elaborate set of convolutions.[35] Beneath his calm, detached manner, Moody's friends found the frank, companionable, direct, and practical young man he sometimes was, or they recognized in him the spiritual zest of a "young Euphues." When he was comfortable in a small group, "a guarded joy looked out from his eyes, with gleams of ironical amusement," Lovett found, and sometimes Moody's "whole being would flame up in laughter." [36] His friends liked him best in these moods, and they began referring to Will Moody as "the faun."

Yet Moody was by no means solitary and withdrawn. His writing and membership on the board of the *Monthly* helped precipitate him into a variety of undergraduate activity. He joined Delta Upsilon, a fraternal society which gathered for literary Monday evenings. Members read their work and occasional plays were produced. Moody was elected to the O.K. and the Signet, other literary groups in which the younger faculty participated—Kittredge, Santayana, and Gates particularly. He was president of Signet as a junior, and a member of the Western Club. Moody was not viewed as "an organization man," but he brought to these extracurricular associations the same sense of duty with which he pursued his studies. Lovett observed, "You had only to say, 'You ought to do that,' and with dogged obedience he went about it." [37]

Moody, Lovett, and the Hapgoods mingled with the girls of the Annex, as Radcliffe College was then known, in activities of the Comedy Club, the Browning Club, and a Peripatetic Club which planned hikes and canoeing trips. The groups often met in Cambridge homes or in the rooms of the Harvard members. But, as Hutchins Hapgood later recalled, strict proprieties were observed and "The higher life . . . was always insisted upon." [38] Moody reveals something of the young gentleman's attitude toward women in a class theme. Why, he asks with light irony, are female bicyclists "so shocking to the nerves"? The reason, he decides, is that "to the healthy male mind, woman is not a forked animal. . . . She has a head, two arms, an an undivided trunk cunningly contrived in some mysterious and private manner to the purposes of locomotion." [39] This explains our preference for the Venus of Milo and the Samothracian Nike to the Medicean Venus and Callipygia. The tale of one of Moody's dates became a minor legend for his friends. He took a bright Radcliffe girl to a cultural event in Boston. She was generally admired for her "attractive and baffling personality," and she displayed none of "the soft sentimentality which

the superior young Harvard man disliked." After walking her home in
meditative silence, Moody said, "good night." "If you hadn't said that,"
the girl remarked, "I would have had some respect for you." [40]

The Boston theatre had been an interest for Moody from the first,
but it became a passion for him as a Harvard junior. Hollis Square
Theatre was a familiar haunt, and Moody was able to see the Kendals
or Julia Marlowe play Shakespeare by serving in Portia's jury or by
carrying a spear in *Macbeth*. He began analyzing performances and
rating actors in his themes and letters, writing of Miss Rehan's Viola —
"she misses the delicate seriousness and quiet humor" of the role; of
Mrs. Langtry in decline — "at the core she is unconquerably a peasant";
and of Julia Marlowe, his favorite — "she was more charming than ever
this year." Moody took the role of Monsieur Sangfroid in a Comedy
Club production of his junior year, and he began to develop a technical
interest in the drama as well. In 1892 he published an article in the
Monthly, "On the Introduction of the Chorus into Modern Drama." [41]
In it Moody draws a contrast between Greek choral drama and modern
"illusion" drama. "Schiller . . . goes straight to the crucial point,"
Moody writes, "by declaring that once for all the drama has nothing
to do with illusion. What the poet has to deal with . . . is . . . ideal
truth." Virtues of the dramatic chorus are enumerated: it raises "tone"
of the drama, introduces the lyric element, and provides symmetry
through repetition of phrase and dominant motifs. Most important, the
chorus lends a degree of objectivity to the action, holding the mimic
life "at arm's length," and providing "universality and range." The
Greek drama is healthy drama, Moody maintains. The Greeks lived
rich, full lives and did not need the escape illusion provides. In contrast Moody sketches the condition of modern man, caught in an intellectual maze, in the rigors of a complex struggle for existence, in the
high pressures of a modern environment, and in a frigid, nonanimal
climate. Because modern man, thus trapped, is unhealthy, his drama
is unhealthy; it seeks an illusory dream world. But drama could and
should send the spectator back to the real world, Moody maintains,
"refreshed by the ideal vision" and able to use it to master reality. He
was to base his own dramatic practice on extensions of this early
analysis.

Moody's new seriousness as a writer is manifest in his publication
of a flood of poems in 1891 and 1892. Love is his central theme, treated
in a variety of forms and styles. "The Amber-Witch" and "The Lady
of the Fountain" develop the theme of the *femme fatale,* the first in
terms of a poet's enchantment by a sea witch and the second in
Arthurian narrative. In the first, a lyric, the poet confronts the sea
witch's allurements in a symbolic landscape dominated by a mad sea

and a bewitching moon. Moody was to return to the situation and the motifs of the poem several years later in "Jetsam." In "The Lady of the Fountain," a pure but naïve hero, Owain, is drawn to an unholy, forbidden lust by an enchanted water fay. Variations on the theme appear in "Angelle" and "Dolorosa." The first is an ambitious Browningesque piece in which Moody's narrative moves in four monologues, those of Count Bertram, of Angelle (an uncloistered nun who falls in love with him), of a minstrel, and finally of Angelle's abbess. The love is passionately consummated, but the count soon dies in a tournament. "Dolorosa," which appealed to the editors of *Scribner's*, is a dramatic monologue in which blind Lippo, a medieval cleric, regains his sight in a vision of the Mater Dolorosa. The vision, vibrant with glad life and love, is one in which the Mother of Sorrows, madonna of the lilies, merges with the image of a gypsy girl associated with the poppy and the wild rose. In "Harmonics," a sonnet, the artist is shaken from his complacent sense of mastery of technique by the heaven-scaling, regenerative inspiration of an untutored old man and the memory of his own instinctive youthful ardor.

Moody's most successful early synthesis of narrative and lyric is a new poem, "How the Mead-Slave Was Set Free." It is the monologue of an Italian boy, caught in the service of Germanic "drunken sea-thieves." Themes are developed in terms of a subtle juxtaposition of the values of North and South. The Nordic sea-rovers are about to kill the boy, but their queen recognizes the poet in him and saves him. The North is identified with rude and aggressive materialism, the South with love, freedom, art, and life. Images of the North—the poison weed, the salt sea, spears, the black bull's horns, and the thieving ships (becalmed in one shift of image and staggering at the poem's end)—clash with a cluster of images associated with Italy and love—the red and white of the queen's face, repeated in roses, blood, fog, and light. Metaphor does not impede the narrative, and Moody retains control of his difficult stanza. Beyond the poem's association of business, aggressiveness, and the northern ships, the figure of Captain Moody looms, and the young singer is rescued by a protective female figure embodying both mother and lover. The poem glances ahead toward *The Fire-Bringer* and *The Death of Eve*, works of Moody's maturity.

A second poem is of interest because of its experimental nature. In "Sea Shells" Moody moves toward directness, a new colloquialism, and ellipsis. The poem arises out of the immediate contexts of Moody's life. Norman Hapgood and Louis Dow had become intrigued by the sleight-of-hand of a Boston shell-game artist. After careful study they were convinced they could beat the game. They played and, of course, lost.[42] The experience intrigued Moody and he wrote this poem:

Hold your ear close to this shell;
    Wait while I coax the sea note
    Out of my deep organ's throat.
Hold your ear close, listen well,
Hear the cool sea-music swell.

Nay, I've a note to my hand;
    If I but sound it—Farewell,
    Sea-music's gone from your shell!
Now for the thirsty white land;
All that this note means is sand.

Nothing discordant to hear?
    Even my desert-note breaks
    Into the song the surf makes?
All the parched hills eddy near,
Billow and boom at your ear?

Hold your ear close to this heart;
    Wait while I find the love chord
    On the world's wide organ-board.
There! your eyes tell me in part
How the good harmonies start.

Hold your ear closer awhile:
    One more note—dare you await
    This bitter treble of hate?
God has some shells in the pile!
That's plain enough from your smile.[43]

The poem's early stanzas suggest a dramatic situation involving two antagonistic voices, but both voices belong to the poet, a master of illusion addressing a listener. Interpreter of God to man through nature, the poet has become shell-game artist, revealing his confidence game to the onlooker, whose smile at the poem's close is a recognition of the irony. The promise in the "cool sea-music" swell is juxtaposed to the threat of wasteland. Imagery merges in the third stanza and sea becomes desert: "All the parched hills eddy near,/ Billow and boom at your ear?" The poem's unusual tone captures the effect of Moody's gently mocking smile on his friends. It is developed skillfully through a rhetoric which balances informal command, brief and extended exclamation, and ironic leading questioning. Moody's experimentation extends even to the uncharacteristic punning financial reference in "note to my hand." As it stands, the poem may be too confusing to be fully successful: reference to the central dramatic situation is too oblique and the poem breaks through toward a new poetic medium almost completely foreign to Moody's contemporaries. It was a direction he could not take if he expected anyone to read his poetry in his own time.

3

In the spring of 1892, having essentially completed requirements for graduation, Moody secured a position as tutor to Ingersoll Bowditch, who was to spend a year in Europe before entering college. In July Moody sailed with the Bowditch family, having confirmed plans to join Lovett, Norman Hapgood, and Louis Dow in a European hiking trip. His education had developed in Moody the perspectives of the young sophisticate, and he viewed his shipmates from those perspectives. The people, Moody felt, were "of very slight interest compared to the sea," and he spent hours observing the "swift changes of its moods" and the "shifting harmony of its colors." [44]

The Bowditch party began Europe with the Rhine. At Coblenz Moody and young Bowditch split off to join Moody's friends for a month of boating, hiking, and climbing. They continued up the Rhine, heading for Switzerland. The group was filled with an energetic dedication to absorb culture and setting. Moody responded to the visual, the scenic, and the atmospheric. When he caught Norman Hapgood lying on his back looking at the sky instead of the Rhineland scenery, Will reprimanded him. "I can see more this way than I can understand," Hapgood objected. But Moody did not approve of daydreaming and told Hapgood he could do that with his eyes shut. [45] Moody had planned a schedule of reading and writing, but he was not following it. He explained in a letter to Charlotte Moody, "There is so much to see over here that I begrudge every minute which is not spent in getting acquainted with the wonderful and beautiful things which I may never again be lucky enough to behold." [46]

The high point of the tour for Moody was a climb over the crest of the Cima di Jazzi and down into the bright Italian sunlight and green foothills of Domodossola. [47] Will wrote Grace that he had "somehow stumbled into Paradise." In Italy's "magical atmosphere of purple and gold," he felt "at home almost for the first time" in his life. The hikers parted at Lake Como. The undergraduates moved down into Italy, and Moody and Bowditch joined the boy's family in Geneva. Much of August and September were spent in Scotland, the

English Lake Country, and London. There was cycling in Warwick-
shire and sightseeing in Stratford and London. Moody wrote Lovett,
"These midland counties are excellently beautiful, to use Mr. Howells's
solemn phrase, and beautiful in a fresh wide awake way which will
appeal to you doubly after the sultry splendor of Italy." [48] He bought
Grace a set of Browning in London as a birthday gift.

Traveling with the Bowditches introduced Moody to the leisurely
and often elegant life of nineteenth-century Americans in Europe. He
was enchanted. In the mornings he fulfilled his tutoring duties. Afternoons and evenings were spent in the usual tourist activities and in
attending the theatre. The comparison with life in America was not
favorable. From England Will wrote:

This rich and courteous life, made fine by twenty generations of culture,
has left me heartsick—it is so painfully in contrast with our vulgar, bare
and hurried way of living in America. Of course I do not forget that with
all her crudeness America is still the best—the fortunate land—and that
her faults are only the faults of youth—but for all that I cannot help longing for the gifts of art, of old association, and of delicate and courtly living
which Europe has to give.

If anything, considering the appeal of European culture to undergraduates in Harvard literary circles, the extent of Moody's dedication
to America rather than his response to Europe is surprising.

The fall was spent in Paris, and the life was heady. Will and
young Bowditch spent hours in the Louvre and the Luxembourg gal-
leries. He reveled in the elegance of the "vrai-monde" in Sunday
afternoon drives, was elbowed by the "demi-monde" at the races, and
went to masked balls and to the theatre. The opera *Manon* became a
favorite. Generally, Moody would take coffee and rolls in bed on
awakening at eight. Then he spent some time with a morning paper—
the *Figaro* or the *Matin*. After a chapter of Zola or Bourget and several
hours of study with his charge, they would saunter forth for the Tuile-
ries gardens or an hour at the Louvre before a Guido Reni or a Botti-
celli. At twelve Will preferred to breakfast at the Café Anglais "with a
lot of jolly fellows who are spending their fathers' money and pretend-
ing to study art at the Ecole des Beaux-Arts," he observed. The afternoon brought more sightseeing. Moody dined with the family and
spent his evenings at the Théâtre Français or the Opéra Comique.
Theatre was followed by supper, served with ample quantities of wine.
After seven weeks of this life, Moody came to know Paris "tolerably
well," he thought. Having spent several evenings exploring Parisian
night life under the guidance of a French officer he had met, he felt
the city was best described as a "dainty Sodom," observing to Lovett

that "never in the history of man was the scarlet robe so delicately
woven or of so gossamer a texture." [49]

The approach of winter drew the Bowditches to Italy, and Moody
became more meditative. He had some preparation for Florence. Among
the reviews he had done for the *Monthly* was one of Charles Eliot
Norton's translation of *The Divine Comedy*. It was Moody's introduction to the poet who was to assume importance in his later work; here
was a man whom the inspiration of ideal womanhood had awakened
to the highest kind of poetic vision. In Florence, Moody turned to a
study project of his own: the reading of Dante in Italian. He visited
the museums and the churches, walked the hills rising above Florence
on both sides of the Arno. He was roused to melancholy joy as he
contemplated the city from Bellosquardo. A hazy sunset faded from
gold to purple as he thought, "poor Florence, sadly changed since
Dante saw Beatrice in the orchard of apples and loved her so that now
all men love both her and him—yes, but happy Florence too, since so
much is left to her of the grace and loveliness of her great time." The
group was in Rome for the carnival days and then set off for Naples,
Sorrento, and Capri. Pompeii and Paestum filled Will with a sense
of the decline of empire and the pettiness of human desire. Contemplating the "unsatisfied hearts of men, their long endeavor, their
paltry gains," he decided that "There is nothing in life but love, it is
all of life."

In March the Bowditch party set out for three weeks in Greece
with Edward Lowell and his family. Moody steeped himself in famous
sites and monuments as they toured Eleusis, Phylae, Aegina, and
Marathon, moving on to Nauplia in the Peloponnesus. From there
side trips were taken to Epidaurus, Argos, and Mycenae. By the time
Moody returned to Athens, the rich emotion Italy had inspired was
exchanged for a Greek sense of clarity and calm beauty. In a visit to
the Acropolis in "the long-dreamed-of, the pilgrim city," his imagination possessed him and for "one strange minute" Moody felt himself "a
Greek in a Greek world." But he decided his own overseas world was
better—"full of hope and love and splendid struggle." Moody and the
Bowditches went on to Constantinople, dined with the sultan, and
then returned to Italy. In April Moody and Ingersoll Bowditch went
north together to live with a family in Dresden in the hope of im-
proving the boy's knowledge of German. They soaked in German music
of the opera and the church. Will heard the whole of Wagner's Ring
cycle with awe and joy. He attended Easter services in the cathedral,
writing Grace of his response to the music. He found in "the bright
foam of human voices floating on the surge and sweep of the billowy
violins, the Beyond of hope; the troubled and multitudinous voice of

the organ, the Beyond of struggle; and the exultant shout of the silver trumpets the Beyond of victory." There was enough time before sailing in late May to go to Venice, "the dream-city," where Will spent a day on the canals "in delicious indolence watching the magical color of the crumbling walls and smooth water." Moody had been introduced to a new world in which the lures of culture, wealth, and courtesy were all strong, and his imagination supplied deficiencies it found in the reality. The taste of Europe was to prove addictive— Moody had discovered his promised land.

In Europe Moody's sense of himself and of his relationship to Grace Hurd changed. The continent had afforded opportunity for sexual and romantic adventure: there had been excursions into the night life of Paris and a brief love affair with a girl in Dresden. But the new, broad horizons opened by travel were themselves compelling. Will began addressing Grace as "Dearest Gretchen," feeling the Faustian challenge in his exploding world. Grace had written him expressing doubts about their relationship, and Will replied:

I feel that you have misunderstood me all along—inevitably misunderstood me, not through your fault or perhaps even through my own, but because of the curious labyrinthine nature which heaven has seen fit to give me—and which I do not understand myself.

But for all the mystery of his own personality, one thing had been clear, he continued: "My mind kept crying out to my heart that it must be free—absolutely free to sound the heights and depths of human life and human thought." Misunderstandings multiplied because of Moody's cavalier tone, because letters were miscarrying, and because Grace's voice from Elma, New York, seemed thin beside the voices of Europe.

By March Moody was ready to admit his love was dead. He suggested, "If it were not for duty, how more than best it would be to break the cup after the first long delicious draught, for fear of the dust and the insects that may defile." He wondered, "Is there really love which renews itself against the years?" From Venice, however, Moody reiterated his love with a qualification. He returned to the Faustian stance of earlier in the year: "I do love, you," he wrote, "only it is a misfortune of my nature that with this human happiness in my hands —I cannot rest quite quiet always; something drives me out into space to seek, to seek, I do not know for what—." Moody needed love and stability, but he desired it primarily as a basis for a larger freedom. His conflict embodies both the egocentricity of youth and the commitment to breadth of human experience expressed years earlier in New Albany.

In June Will was back in Cambridge for his graduation. He was second in his class and had been honored by election as class poet. His sisters were on hand for the festivities—crew races, a baseball game with Yale, a traditional junior-senior battle, and a round of parties. Bishop William Lawrence addressed the class at Commencement. Grace Hurd was unable to attend but sent a pen and a paper knife.

CHAPTER 3 LASSITUDES
OF FIN DE SIÈCLE

MOODY SPENT his next two years in Cambridge, the first working toward a Master of Arts degree, and the second as Instructor in English at Harvard. His movement to a career in which he might combine creative work with college teaching was not unusual. A number of young Harvard writers had chosen the path marked by Longfellow and Lowell earlier in the century. Of the group associated with the *Monthly*, George Rice Carpenter had begun teaching at Columbia; George Santayana, Hugh McCulloch, and George Pierce Baker had joined the faculty at Harvard; and Robert Herrick was teaching at the Massachusetts Institute of Technology. Lovett had completed his work at Harvard in the spring of 1893 and he and Herrick were preparing to leave for positions at the new University of Chicago.

Moody spent much of his summer in the Harvard Library. He worked with Lovett on a revision of Bulfinch, for which the young men received a fee of $100. The project suggests that Moody's knowledge of and interest in classical mythology was already unusually extensive. In August Moody went to Chicago with a group of friends to see the World's Columbian Exposition. The trip was an introduction to the ambitious city which loomed in the immediate future of his friends, Lovett, Herrick, and Hapgood. And Moody's impressions were not entirely unfavorable, since he was to join them two years later. The impact of the Exposition on Moody is implied in a casual reference to it as "the World's Fake." [1]

Moody's graduate program provided a steady diet of medieval literature and philology. His work habits resembled those of earlier years. On at least one occasion his irregularity brought on a minor illness—he had dissipated for three nights and studied for the next three days and nights to right the balance. By midyear he was tired and unhappy, writing Lovett, "Philology and Minerva are destined to part with mutual scorn and vituperation." [2] Shakespeare's line, "Bare ruin'd choirs, where late the sweet birds sang," kept running through his mind, but Moody had already decided to take honor examinations in June and he had begun an ambitious thesis on the sources of Sidney's *Arcadia*.

Moody's "dissipations" were, if anything, of a greater variety than those of his undergraduate years. He had established a local reputation as a promising scholar and poet, and he moved freely in society. While the undergraduate literary circles remained open to him, he was increasingly invited to faculty gatherings of an artistic and literary nature. Two of the poet's frequent hostesses were Mrs. Crawford H. Toy and Louise Chandler Moulton. Mrs. Toy had been a warm friend to Moody in his undergraduate years, and he spent Christmas in the Toy home. She entertained frequently and always included students. Moody liked the good talk, and there was often music as well. An accomplished pianist, Mrs. Toy played selections from the romantic composers she admired—Chopin, Rubinstein, and Wagner. Mrs. Moulton was a poet of some reputation. On one occasion Moody boasted that he had "bearded a whole den of lions at Mrs. Moulton's —From old Dr. Holmes to Robert Grant." And he had happily exchanged words with "an Oxford prof who has dined with Dodo at the Master of Baliol's." [3]

Moody began attending the meetings of a newly organized Folk Lore Society in preference to those of the Browning Club. The interest of Harvard scholars in myth and legend was penetrating the academic community, and Moody's own concerns were changing. The change was to lead him from work in the dramatic monologue and lyric toward the drama. But the society, like the Browning Club, was coeducational, and it was the social interest that Moody emphasized to the absent Lovett. He characterized the society as "an organization much affected by voluptuous young ladies yearning to walk in the cold clear light of science." The girls, he continues, "are all saturated with sun-myths, and ghosts, trolls and witches are their daily walk and conversation." [4] The theatre continued to attract Moody and he regularly deserted Middle English dialects for evenings with Irving and Miss Terry, Coquelin and Jane Harding, and the operas of Wagner.

Grace Hurd briefly resumed her position in Moody's imagination as spiritual inspiration and incarnation of the beauty he found in literature. In a letter of the fall, Will outlined the heavy responsibilities he placed on her, observing, "I do not meet a woman anywhere in Poet-land without making you stand beside her, while I judge you by her and her by you." After listing among her competitors Helga in the hall at Borgfjorth, Miranda on Prospero's enchanted island, Manon "as she lies dead in the desert," Beatrice in paradise, and Pompilia in the "curse of the sunset," he charged Grace, "You are and must be all these women to me, and at the same time remain yourself and only you." [5] Moody had visited with Grace during the summer. Renewed association quickened their love, but it raised practical issues that had been blurred during Moody's year of absence. By late fall the correspondence began to wither away. Moody did not accept Grace's invitation to spend Christmas in Elma, and during the winter their relationship turned into friendship at a distance. Neither Moody's financial situation nor the nature of his idealized love for Grace Hurd had boded well for the future. Moody's growing sense of reality, his involvement in his work, and the increasing gap between their situations all worked toward a gradual loosening of ties.

In spite of a depressing outlook for poetry on the national scene, Moody's associations involved him in a new sense of literary enterprise. As established models for the serious young American poet there were only the genteel poets of the second generation—Edmund Clarence Stedman, Richard Henry Stoddard, and Thomas Bailey Aldrich. The literary periodicals of the early nineties echoed and re-echoed *fin-de-siècle* complaints against the age. The role envisioned for poetry was defensive and peripheral. Charles Leonard Moore, writing on "The Future of Poetry" in *Forum* [6] in 1893, is representative. He contemplates Matthew Arnold's assertion that poetry's future is "immense" without enthusiasm, tabulating killing foes of the poetic spirit: the hypothesis of evolution, the rationalistic method of inquiry, and the comforts and contentments of wealth. Poetry's appropriate materials are identified as "the happiest and loftiest images and impressions." It should provide contentment, inspiration, charm, and consolation, permitting the reader to put off problems of mortality, actuality, and utility. Critics like Oscar L. Triggs and W. J. Rolfe affirmed this analysis in the pages of *Poet-Lore*.[7] Triggs, for example, concludes: "Art is, then, an exponent of the evolution of ideality."

Though they did not disagree with this general position, Moody's Cambridge friends tended to ignore it. There was an air of promise and portent in the loose group of young writers clustered in and around Cambridge. Most of them used the *Monthly* as an outlet for their work even after graduation from Harvard. Robert Herrick, who had published Carpenter's translation of Ibsen's new *The Lady from the Sea* while editor of the magazine, continued to submit short pieces. William A. Leahy, from his position as literary and art critic for the Boston *Traveler*, contributed energetic lyrics and quasi-philosophical dramatic pieces. George Santayana and Hugh McCulloch were represented by a poem or an essay every few issues, and George Pierce Baker and Lewis Gates sometimes contributed an essay or a review.

Most of these writers were, like Moody and Herrick, already looking beyond their immediate literary environment. *Scribner's* had published two of Moody's best poems, and national magazines were beginning to open their doors to the stories Herrick was sending out. Poets were preparing volumes for the press. Leahy had been the first in print with *The Siege of Syracuse* in 1889, and another volume was in preparation. Herbert Bates, who had left the East for an instructorship in English at the University of Nebraska, was working on poems for his *Songs of Exile*, which appeared in 1896; and Mark Anthony De Wolfe Howe privately published a first volume, *Rari Nantes*, in 1893. A second volume, *Shadows*, was to appear in 1897. Copeland and Day were to publish Philip Henry Savage's *First Poems and Fragments* in 1894 and a second volume four years later. Bliss Carman, who had taken some work at Harvard in the eighties, had given up his job in New York journalism and was frequenting the literary circles of Boston and Cambridge. The *Monthly* printed six of his poems between 1893 and 1895. Carman's *Guendolen and Marjorie* had appeared in 1889, and when *Low Tide on Grand Pré* appeared in 1893, George Pierce Baker reviewed it for the magazine. Small and Maynard published Carman and Hovey's energetic, irreverent *Songs from Vagabondia* in 1894 and the book was in its third edition by the end of 1895.

The hospitality of Boston publishers Copeland and Day and of Small, Maynard and Company to first volumes by these poets was a stimulus of major proportions. And the formation early in 1894 of a "young Harvard" publishing house provided a third outlet. The wave of Harvard literary interest had stimulated two seniors—Herbert S. Stone and Ingalls Kimball—to venture into avant-garde publishing. They set up office in the Caxton Building in Chicago where Stone's father, a banker and general manager of Associated Press, offered his support. As early as February 1894 Moody suggested that Herrick try Stone and Kimball as likely publishers for a first volume of stories:

They are known to smile on Harvard men and would I am sure be glad to publish it at their own risk. They are getting out volumes of verse for Mac and Santy, and have even approached *me* with harp and psaltery, though so far I have had grace from God to resist their blandishments.[8]

Stone and Kimball published McCulloch's *The Quest of Heracles and Other Poems* and Santayana's first volume, *Sonnets and Other Verses*, in 1894. Their list was soon to range from an imposing edition of the works of Edgar Allan Poe to Richard Hovey's pioneering translation of four of the plays of the young Maurice Maeterlinck.

In May the house founded the *Chap-Book,* which looked to England's popular *Yellow Book* for a model. The magazine had a brief but lively four-year career. Bliss Carman was enrolled as associate editor, and the magazine was open to young American writers and to discussion of contemporary currents in European art and taste. While the *Chap-Book* was national in scope, printing work by established writers like Hamlin Garland and drawings by John Sloan, it drew heavily on the talents of the greater Cambridge circle. Early issues included work of Carman, Hovey, McCulloch, Louise Imogen Guiney, Louise Chandler Moulton, Lewis E. Gates, and P. B. Goetz. Moody yielded to blandishments, submitting a poem which appeared in June 1894 and is included in his *Poems* (1901) as "The Ride Back." But he was furious with Stone for giving a second poem to Carman for judgment,[9] and their quarrel ended his relations with the firm.

Moody's closest friend in this group of Cambridge and Boston poets was Philip Henry Savage. Like Moody, Savage had entered Harvard in 1889, and the two poets met frequently in the undergraduate literary clubs and in *Monthly* gatherings. Beyond a mutual distaste for effete aestheticism, it is unlikely that Moody shared any of Savage's specific poetic aims. The poetry of Savage has much in common with that of the English poet William Watson, and the influence of Wordsworth is strong. Yet his work displays a quiet integrity which Moody admired. Of Moody's associations with undergraduates, the most significant were a continuing friendship with the poet Trumbull Stickney and the inauguration of a lifelong friendship with Daniel Gregory Mason. Stickney entered Harvard in 1891. At seventeen he was already more cosmopolitan and self-sufficient than most of the students. His father, Austin Stickney, had left a professorship in Latin and Greek at Trinity College in the sixties to embark upon the life of the Europeanized American that Henry James studied in such detail. Trumbull Stickney was born in Geneva, Switzerland, and except for two terms spent in an American preparatory school he was educated by his father, developing the social grace, refinement, and sophistication appropriate to such a childhood. Moody and Lovett welcomed Stickney to the inner circle of *Monthly* editors at the end of his first year. He began publishing thoughtful literary essays as well as lyrics and sonnets which moved toward the subtle control of tone he was to achieve in his mature work. In spite of vast differences in background, personality, and taste, a friendship which would later flower in Europe flourished between Moody and the young cosmopolitan.

In the spring of 1894 Pierre La Rose introduced Moody to his

roommate, Dan Mason. Mason was son of a founder of the Mason and
Hamlin Company. He shared Moody's interest in music and literature
— his great enthusiams of the nineties were Brahms and Thoreau. The
three men met by chance in one of the small restaurants off Harvard
Square. Mason has left a record of the meeting.[10] As they talked, Moody
tended to his habitual detachment. He "smoked a pipe ponderingly,
pressing it with thoughtful fore-finger, and from time to time dropped
brief comments, often hardly more than resonant ejaculations," which
Mason felt were liberating. He was accustomed to conversation salted
with the mannered epigrams fashionable among sophisticates in the
age of Oscar Wilde. Startled by Moody's florid and careless manner of
dress and observing a "barbaric taste for magnificence in waistcoats and
neckties," Mason decided Moody's manner "breathed the freshness,
almost uncouth, of the West." However, the poet's unconventionality
soon seemed "delightfully friendly and intimate," and Mason began to
prefer Moody's "rich silences" to the attempts at cleverness to which
he was accustomed.

Moody's manner at twenty-five expresses his disaffection for the
customary modes of fin-de-siècle sophistication. For Mason the effect
was that of the freedom and freshness of a Walt Whitman in Harvard
Square. Indeed, Whitman was to become an increasingly important
influence on Moody, and Whitman's stance has been modified in many
ways by American writers wishing to declare their independence and
their poetic vocation. Moody's sense of alienation from his Harvard
environment deepened during his two postgraduate years in Cambridge. Harvard had been a citadel from which to attack the Philistinism of America. But Moody was increasingly turning his sights on the
college itself—on the sterilities of his graduate work and of fin-de-siècle
tastes. He preserved the values of the poet with surfaces of indifference
which masked the quiet depths at which he sought to live. The manner
was, in effect, an act of judgment, as Mason suggests. Moody gained a
reputation as a snob with those whom he so judged.

The affirmations revealed in Moody's "resonant ejaculations" and
his "barbaric taste for magnificence" were supported by what Mason
called the "inverted snobbishness of the radical." [11] It too was a symp-
tom of growing rebellion; as Josephine Peabody was later to observe,
Will Moody was "tolerant of everybody except Episcopalians." As yet,
his tolerance was condescending and more theoretical than actual,
corollary to Moody's growing interest in the raw materials of life. He
had begun to express admiration for Whitman's "humane inclusiveness" and to desire more vivid human contacts than his year of study
was providing. Moody was avoiding the usual Boston and Cambridge
student haunts and searching out mixed environments. Toward the

end of the year Mason began accompanying Moody on his explorations. He records an important "find"—Pritchard, a Cambridgeport
workingman whom they decided represented "divinity in the average
man." [12]

Moody's growing malaise was in large part a reaction to the
poetic stalemate into which his work had been moving. In his last year
as an undergraduate he had published a group of poems which brought
his early style to its maturity. Two poems, "Faded Pictures" and "Song
of the Elder Brothers," are competent works in the stanza of "In
Memoriam." The first, published in *Scribner's* while Moody was
abroad, is a quiet meditation on a girl's portrait. Moody read "Song of
the Elder Brothers" at his Commencement. The "elder brothers" are
graduates—among them Longfellow, Emerson, and Wendell Phillips—
who helped create a noble tradition. "By the Evening Sea," a poem in
two sonnets, was published in the *Monthly* early in 1893 and was later
collected under the title of "The Departure." The sonnets present an
allegorical vision in the manner of Rossetti. The first develops a scene
in which the listless poet, the strings of his lyre "Crushed in the rank
wet grasses heedlessly," contemplates a boat with saffron sails spread,
ready to depart into evening. Fair women embark with spring blossoms
in their hair. The octave of the second sonnet presents a tableau which
the sestet dissolves. The tableau depicts four women:

> One gazed steadfast into the dying west,
> With lips apart for joy of one faint star;
> And one, with eyes that caught the strife and jar
> Of the sea's heart, followed the sunward breast
> Of a lone gull; from a great harp one drew
> Blind music like a laugh or like a wail,
> And in the purple shadow of the sail
> One wove a crown of berries and of yew.
> Yet even as I said with dull desire,
> "Once all were mine, and one was mine indeed,"
> The smoky music burst into a fire;
> And I was left alone in my great need,
> My foot upon the thin horn of my lyre,
> And all its strings crushed in the dripping weed. [13]

Moody develops his theme with taste and technical skill; balanced
tensions in the poem's "smoky music" of dissolving promise are delicately maintained. The tableau quietly evokes a sense of possible fulfillment through involvement in passion and desire, but emotion is
suspended in frozen gesture and blind or uncertain movement. Moody

introduces sophisticated rhythmic variation to maintain movement, but tonal balance is not disturbed.

The longer poems of Moody's first graduate year, however, can be approached with little more than dismay: he falls back into some of the more deplorable excesses of his early work. "The Hawthorne Bush" and "The Picture and the Bird" are medieval in theme and setting and lack the precision and control of the shorter lyrics. The first is a dramatic lyric in skipping couplets, the second a perfunctory longer narrative after Browning. Two other poems of 1894 are skillful enough but are quest poems in Moody's well-worn medieval contexts. The major interest of "The Briar Rose" is in its hint of themes to be developed in later poems. Moody's questing minstrel is sympathetic to ordinary human suffering, and he mourns the unfulfilled promise of his childhood in a stanza of evocative images:

> His childhood's trust seemed as a bough
> Uncomforted of bud or leaf,
> His boyhood's pride a poor hedge row
> Of ragged thorn, and manhood's grief
> A stony field without a sheaf.[14]

In Moody's *Chap-Book* poem, "The Ride Back," a wounded knight rides through a threatening landscape to reach his beloved. He does reach her but dies kissing her lips. When Moody republished the poem in 1901 he prefaced it with a passage in italics, setting the central quest in the frame of a young man's dream:

> *Before the coming of the dark, he dreamed*
> *An old-world faded story: of a knight,*
> *Much like in need to him, who was no knight!*
> *And of a road, much like the road his soul*
> *Groped over, desperate to meet Her soul.*
> *Beside the bed Death waited. And he dreamed.*

The poem's speaker has become a dying Miniver Cheevy, finding relevance in the old motif only as dream. The frame is a gesture through which the maturer writer attempted to make viable a poem which in 1894 he saw as his best work.[15]

These poems—both the successes and the failures—give evidence of the poetic dead end into which Moody had worked himself. His achievement in the sonnet and the short stanza of the Pre-Raphaelite tradition represents an outer limit of mastery. He could do what Rossetti had done in both—no small matter in itself. The longer poems of 1893 and 1894 are attempts to do something more, something bigger, and—in "The Picture and the Bird" and "The Ride Back"—to reach toward the more positive statement of faith he desired to make. Yet they represent no new successes. Moody reworks old materials and reiterates familiar themes. In the expansions of these poems he falls back upon excesses of the Victorian sublime. There is not only a full return to archaisms of diction and syntax but a general flabbiness. Moody seeks vitality in the unusual adjective—"labyrinthine," "amaranthine," "skyey"—and is drawn to imitation of Francis Thompson's yoking of nouns through verbal transformations. Hopes are "vistaed," fears are "chasmed" and hours are "pillaring." The tighter stanza of "Faded Pictures" had limited Moody to "heapy hair," but the Commencement song had risen to the inflated rhetorical grandeurs of "The opalescent seas of thought" and "Song's amaranthine buds of fire."

The longer poems Moody wrote in 1893 and 1894 may have been attempts to pad out a first volume of poetry in response to the Cambridge publishing atmosphere. But Moody had written enough poetry for a volume by summer 1894. The poetic taste demonstrated in his choice of the submissions to *Scribner's* and in his refusal to submit a volume to Stone and Kimball indicates that his aims were high and that he was aware how far short most of his work had fallen. While fading inspiration, unfulfilled promise, and betrayed quest were familiar themes in the poetry of the period, Moody's statement of them reached to deeply felt personal problems in his life and writing. The wisdom of hindsight comes all too easily: any college freshman today could point out new possibilities in the use of colloquial diction and rhythms, in materials and themes drawn from immediate experience, in realistic prose drama or the naturalistic novel. But few serious poets of Britain and America were less trapped than Moody in 1894. In America there was only the young Robinson, beginning to publish some of the poems he would collect in his first volume, *The Torrent and the Night Before*, in 1896. None of the poets of Moody's circle were of any help. The lively but trivial "vagabondia" of Carman and Hovey was irrelevant to Moody's involvements and aims. The silky mysticism and pale medievalism of McCulloch and of Carman, the minor perfections of Santayana, the youthful struggles of Stickney to develop a viable post-Symbolist style—all led to foreseen closures of the circle. And Moody was already the technical master of these poets, competent through a broader range of style and effects.

In late spring Moody finished his work on the sources of Sidney's *Arcadia*. Its only value today lies in the evidence it gives of the knowledge and taste of the poet. Sidney's combination of gallantry and

literary imagination appealed strongly to Moody. He relishes retelling
Sidney's tales, sharing "the pleasure which Sidney found in reviving
these faded tales, and decking them out in all those gay robes of rhetoric
and fancy which keep them fresh and pretty even to this day." [16]
Moody liked the "wild charm," "romantic color," and "generous chivalry" of the work, objecting to an occasional touch of "insipid sentimentality." Moody's growing interest in Greek myth illuminates his
final section. He argues that in certain descriptions of knightly splendor
Sidney was drawing on the "beautiful passages in which Heliodorus
brings before us the majesty of the Delphic cult and the fictitious
splendors of Ethiopian sun-worship." [17]

Moody's work on Sidney's revision of the old *Arcadia* helped
shape the commitments basic to the poetic dramas he was to write.
He sympathized with Sidney's developing interest in dignity of style,
epical form, and complex structural unity. Sidney seemed to offer a
relevant synthesis of romantic and classical values, and his cultural
cosmopolitanism reinforced the position Moody and his friends held
with regard to America. Sidney's position is firmly advanced: "He
believed that the literature of his country could be regenerated only
from without, either directly from Greece and Rome, or from that
country where the great classic traditions had been preserved—Italy." [18]
The view was to influence Moody through much of his life. Yet Sidney's efforts, Moody points out, bore no fruit in practical, commercial
England "stung into life by new-won religious freedom and newly
roused national pride." [19] Sidney's *Arcadia* could only be seen as a
"link between a past which might have been revived and a future
which might have been realized." [20] The tone of this passage repeats
the familiar wistful paralysis of Moody's poems, but it carries no hint
of recognition of common limitations, no suggestions of personal irony.

2

Will Moody spent the summer of 1894 with his sister Charlotte
in a cottage at Endion Camp, Long Lake, New York. Will had been
closer to Charlotte than to his other sisters from early boyhood, and
the fact that she alone remained unmarried strengthened their bond.
Suffering from an affliction of the lungs, Charlotte had been advised
to seek treatment at Saranac, and Will was the only member of the
family free to accompany her. [21] The easy pace of the health resort
was welcome, and Moody let himself sink into the uneventful life.
"I have melted into a spiritual jelly fish," he wrote Mason, but the
summer crowd roused him to the energies of disdain. He found them

"dull spawn, only human by virtue of being made in the likeness of an outraged God." [22] Friendship with Mason, who was fascinated by the ideas of Josiah Royce, stimulated contemplation. And so did Moody's friendship with Mrs. Toy, to whom he wrote in August:

As you lie on your back under these gigantic pines and listen to the inarticulate multitudinous life of the thing, you find yourself reversing the Fichtean telescope, and coming reluctantly to believe that perhaps God could manage to think his thoughts without pouring himself through just your highly ingenious brain. [23]

But Moody's response is not systematic or even basically philosophical. He imaginatively explores ideas as feeling for their potential quality and their existential implications.

At the summer's end Will returned to spend what was to be his last year in Cambridge. He proctored in Grays Hall and assisted in Lewis E. Gates's writing course, annotating papers with the conscientious care that was to characterize his teaching. Frequent exploration of city and countryside had become habitual. Brattle Street and Fresh Pond were favorite haunts. There were walks into the surrounding countryside (on one that spring, Moody spent the night in a field, sleeping in the new-mown hay). There was canoeing or boating on the Charles. There were excursions into Boston. Sometimes Moody was alone, but Mason, who had become an adoptive younger brother, was a frequent companion. Mason remembered long winter talks over hot rum toddy beside the open coal fire in his room, walks in the gray sunsets of winter into Boston to dine at Marliave's (where they could capture the feeling of being in Italy), evenings at the symphony (the *Pathétique* and Dvořák's *New World* were fresh and exciting), and discussions afterwards "over beer and welsh rarebits at the Old Elm." Interlacing the talk were Moody's "imagination-releasing figures of speech, his fertile silences, his irresponsible humor, comical slang and shouting gusto of laughter, his deep contagious sense of the infinite mystery and richness of life." [24]

While Mason's appreciative companionship was gratifying, it had little immediate impact on Moody's writing. Of greater significance was Lewis Gates, who helped provide critical perspective and pointed a way out of *fin de siècle*. Gates taught courses in poetry and nineteenth-century literature. Steeped in the Victorians, he followed with interest the work of new poets of Britain and the Continent. He shared Moody's interest in music and responded to values of sound and rhythm in poetry. He was a sensitive critic with a touch of genius, an important guide to a number of American writers. [25] Herrick respected him and

Stickney took his writing course as an undergraduate. In 1894, when
Moody was assisting him, both Josephine Preston Peabody and Frank
Norris were writing under his guidance. Gates read Norris's *McTeague*
in manuscript that year. Looking for a synthesis of romantic achievement and the newer urges to realism, Gates demanded literature with
an immediate and direct relation to life. As early as the fall of 1892
he had condemned Tennyson's tendency to desert life for a dream world
and his "morbid love" of nature.[26] He admired moral earnestness and
emotional fervor and was intolerant of the posing in so much of the
writing of the nineties. Among contemporary poets, Francis Thompson
was Gates's favorite. The poetic virtues to which he was dedicated
gather in his description of the essential quality of Thompson's work.
In it he found a beauty which, unlike that of Swinburne's poetry,
"emancipates and strengthens"; "beauty spiritual as well as sensuous;
beauty quintessential, primordial, regenerative; beauty that stings the
spirit into keener activity and more passionate aspiration." [27] Evangelical
fervor rings in the mission Gates set for literature—the redemption of
life through a vision of its spiritual beauty. Gates's interest in contemporary French poetry and his continual testing of literature against
genuine experience bolstered half-formed impulses in Will Moody
and faced him toward the new century.

Moody and the brilliant young teacher became close companions,
but the relationship was not an easy one. Gates was sensitive and
withdrawn, alternately open and suspicious, gentle and bitterly aggressive. He was already suffering from the periods of nervous exhaustion that would lead to his early resignation in 1902.[28] Yet the
friendship matured. Through the winter and spring Gates and Moody
often attended Cambridge literary gatherings together. In April they
called on a twenty-year-old girl in Gates's class who had the audacity
to submit some poems to the *Monthly*—Josephine Preston Peabody.
She was to be the third close friend Moody found in his graduate years.
Indeed, the astonishing Josephine was a force which drew and held
together a group of young writers. Early her "Fellowship" included
Moody, Mason, and Gates. As Gates moved to the fringes, Savage and
then Robinson entered Josephine's circle. In the first decade of the
twentieth century Ridgely Torrence and Percy MacKaye were gathered in.

Josephine was a charming and talented young woman. A tendency
to fragility did not dim her creative energy nor her passion for freedom.
Her family was an old and distinguished one in New England. Since
the age of ten when her father, Charles K. Peabody, died, Josephine
had lived in the greater Boston area with her mother and grandmother
in genteel frugality. At fourteen she published her first poem; more

followed, to be printed in the *Woman's Journal* and *Wide Awake*. As she put her teens behind, she felt more and more cut off from the associations necessary to a writer. A sense of loneliness alleviated only by her native good spirits pervades her early journals. In the spring of 1894 Josephine had longed for closer contact with life, writing:

> One must, then, think thoughts that have more common vital interest.
> And how is it that one thinks them? One must come into closer relationship with people and things.
> So it all resolves itself into the old drawback of loneliness—not merely that—but literal solitude. . . . It has not, I think truly, been my fault—this loneliness of the past—and present. But if it is going to make my voice a far-away sound, if it is going to throw me upon my far-off dream resources, so that I shall seem an incomprehensible thing—I will dig, break stone—sweep streets, before I give myself up to it for life.[29]

The situation is not unlike Emily Dickinson's, but Josephine's sense of isolation is militant, and she refuses to fall back on "far-off dream resources" for life and poetry. Josephine was to break out of the charmed circle through strenuous effort, but it left its mark on her personality and her poetry.

Josephine's rebellion led her to enroll as a special student at the Harvard Annex, and she took courses with Gates and George Pierce Baker. Her poems were now appearing in the *Atlantic Monthly*, *Scribner's*, and the *Chap-Book*. She was reading widely and developing an enthusiasm for Leopardi, Christina Rossetti, Alfred de Musset, Plutarch, Aeschylus, and Sophocles. Horace Scudder, the genial editorial consultant to Houghton Mifflin, had taken Josephine under his wing, introducing her into the larger society of writers in Boston and Cambridge and escorting her to literary gatherings—among them meetings of the Folk Lore Society. Will and Josephine were formally introduced at a gathering of the English Club in March 1895. They went into the library and talked poetry in the bay window. Moody called on her in Dorchester the following Sunday and she agreed to accompany him to a performance of *Die Meistersinger*. Upon her submission of poems to the *Monthly*, Moody and Gates called, and eventually her poem, "Dreams," appeared in the hitherto masculine publication. The spring was filled with activity—walks, literary and social gatherings, a dancing party, trips to Boston museums and musical events. Sometimes Moody took her, sometimes Gates, sometimes both, sometimes Moody and Mason. At social events Josephine generally encountered both Moody and Gates, but she and Moody began to tire of Gates's presence. In June Moody evaded a group picnic with a lame excuse and took Josephine canoeing instead. In one of a number of spring walks, Moody suggested they roll down a hill—a hint of incipient bacchanalia—but Josephine refused.

Josephine noted the quality of their companionship in her journal, writing in April:

One thing about Mr. Moody is absolutely new to me. He has a way of saying "Tell me about it" whenever I mention anything that interests me or has held depths for me, or even when I don't mention those depths, and this unexpected *Tell me about it* is a thing that strikes great wonder through me and almost puts two tears in my eyes before I know it.[30]

After attending a symphony concert with Will, she wrote, "Fellowship is very astonishing." She grew to suspect that he "has been or is, in love: not with *me* at *all*," but she thought he might have liked to talk about it. They joined in attacking the insincerities of "Philistia," and Moody's frustrations erupted in a note of May: "My God . . . what is to make life endurable—but the privilege now and then of being sincere,—of being real?"[31] But Moody's intensity and his tendency to confessional sometimes grated on Josephine, who observed to herself on May 20 that "William Vaughn Moody seems to think that anything less than rehearsing the articles of thy belief isn't *talking*."[32]

When talk turned to articles of belief, Josephine's enthusiasm for participation in life became a frequent topic. She had gathered her desires and her faith together in a quest for what she called "It." While Moody's identification with Josephine's youthful idealism was limited, "It" evoked the major tenets of his own faith. He was amused but involved, and began to sign an occasional note, "Yours in the Service of It." On one occasion, by way of parenthetical apostrophe to "It," he wrote, "Ah! The vague sweet-shrouding mute arch vocable!"[33] Mason, however, became a serious devotee, defining "It" this way: "'It' is everything, taken together, that may be the object of a youthful idealist's devotion; it is the sum total of all that is beautiful and worthy of loyalty in the world; it is what it is happiness to remember, wretchedness to forget."[34] In other contexts, less Roycean in emphasis, "It" is seen as the source of creative energy and identified with the "Atman" or fount of Godhead that is evoked in the *Bhagavad-Gita*. But the choice of the Hindu formulation is less an indication of serious study of the scriptures than of casual acceptance of a convenient term to indicate a mystical reality orientation. Bernard Berenson had been caught up in the quest for "It" at Harvard in the late eighties. His formulation of the concept emphasized rebellion against outmoded forms, intensity as a sign of ultimate value, and exaltation of immediate experience as ultimate.[35] Devotion to "It" involved the "graduation" from myth and dogmas which was common to the thought of Santayana and Moody and central to contemporary interest in comparative mythology. Josephine herself, identifying "It" with the will of God, best defined it as *"Radiance, Radiance,* Truth true enough to be beautiful."[36] The genuine seeker of "It" attempts to be "so full of love and truth as to become a part of the very fabric of divinity," she declared.

If Moody participated in the quest for "It" with protective detachment, Josephine's personality and conversation marked a turning point in his creative life. He was not slow to realize it, and his own analysis of the impact in a letter of the following fall is perceptive. He wrote that his first desire had been for a "free open-air converse" and a "quiet putting aside of the social dulnesses" that had become more and more oppressive to him in the Cambridge environment. He was searching for "a girl-mind—a naïve peanut-eating attitude, and unhorizoned truancy." But in Josephine he found the sensitive intelligence he needed. "Your mind was the first I had known at once strong enough and fresh enough to help me," he wrote, "and I pounced upon you with rapacious egotism."[37] The "pounce" involved more than the socializing and the talk: Moody was reading and discussing his poems with Josephine. The result was a general displeasure with his work. On a canoeing outing on which he brought along some of his poems, he abruptly tore up a poem as he was about to read it and threw the scraps in the river.

Either because he was writing little that year or because he destroyed much of what he did, little evidence of his activity survives. One more quest poem, later called "The Golden Journey," appeared in the *Monthly* that spring, however. It takes the pattern of earlier work. In theme and manner it resembles "The Briar Rose," but it demonstrates the same shift of interest found in Moody's early story, "The Joyless Asphodel": the context for the fatal quest is now the world of pagan Greece.

On one of his outings with Josephine, Moody read a new poem, "Ethics in a Gondola." She liked the poem and he sent her a copy.[38] It is not particularly successful and was never published, yet it is of thematic interest. The poem is a dramatic monologue in which a gondolier sets his Venetian ethic against a Christian-Hebraic ethic he associates with northern Europeans. His immediate subject is a sculpture of Venice's Gentucca entwined with a serpent. Gentucca, who merges with a Lilith figure, is contrasted with Eve. In the contrast, an ancient Eastern wisdom of sensuous immersion in experience is

celebrated in preference to Puritan rationalism. Had Eve had her wits
about her, the loquacious gondolier maintains, she would not have
bruised the serpent's head:

> But taking thought of Lilith's snowy limbs
> Hugged by the gilt green of the amorous snake,
> She would have stroked the red-veined sinuous throat,
> Looked reptile love into the jacinth eyes,
> Mingled a sleep-song with the drowsy noon,
> And when the green balls glittered kindliest
> Whispered, "Sweet serpent, hiss me in the ear
> The secret of the darling dangerous tree!"
> And sat and hearkened 'neath Jehovah's smile,
> And been forevermore as are the Gods.

At the end of the poem Moody's gondolier extends his contrast to
include that between the heaven-scaling passion of Venetian heroes
and the methodical common sense of English foot soldiers. The gondolier's symbolism is daring in its frank sexuality, and the monologue
explores a non-Protestant ethic to which Moody had been attracted
in various earlier forms. Woman is here the agent of human reconciliation with God, but she no longer takes the shape of the static Pre-
Raphaelite ideal: she is passionate lover of the serpent. Gentucca was
to be developed as Pandora in Moody's Promethean play; and in his
much later work on Eve she merges with Eve in a single rebellious
figure.

Moody's association with Josephine quickened his revolt against
the defensive patterns his art and life had taken. His responses to
experience were prestructured by the attitudes and gestures appropriate
to *fin-de-siècle* literary experience. Much of common human experience
was excluded as irrelevant to a quest for beauty and truth, and a high
degree of detachment from immediate experience was fostered. It is
important to recognize the fact that Moody was not merely an apprentice writer, experimenting with styles which he saw as avant-garde.
Moody's affinity for English post-Symbolist styles is remarkable, and
they provide extremely congenial means for objectification of the deep
structure of his personality. As his poems float relatively free from
stimuli in immediate experience, so do the gestures of his Cambridge
life. A strong sense of unreality is pervasive. Seldom is there a sense of
genuine and compelling experience which demanded and found its
own necessary and unique form of response. Like the protective
shields he erected against close human relationships, Moody's poems
represented a form of detachment from life that was grounded in

adolescent trauma resulting in fear of involvements that might lead to loss. To be sure, he was increasingly dissatisfied with a life he was beginning to see as a melodrama in which he was the only actor. Yet if he cried out for genuine experience, for "the privilege . . . of being real," he had only begun to come to grips with an issue basic to his life and art.

In April the possibility of a change of scene in the fall appeared.[39] Robert Herrick, at the University of Chicago, was planning to spend the coming year abroad. He and Lovett approached Moody with the offer of an instructorship. Will's inclination was to remain at Harvard, and he was also eyeing the possibility of a traveling fellowship after another year of teaching. But the pressures for leaving Cambridge were strong. Both Herrick and Lovett were convinced that continued life in the cloistered Cambridge environment would not contribute to Moody's growth. Although he was hardly prepared to recognize Chicago as the appropriate spot for his salvation, Moody tended to agree. He accepted a position as instructor in English and rhetoric,[40] planning to save a portion of his salary for a long sojourn in Europe. Once the decision was made Moody welcomed it, and his dissatisfactions with Cambridge intensified. He wrote Herrick,

Now that under the stress of circumstances the die has been cast, I am heartily glad of it and look forward to beginning work out there with zeal. I shall of course have to endure a pang or two at leaving Harvard but at bottom I shall feel a certain sense of liberation. Harvard is a nourishing mother, but she keeps her children in leading strings till they reach an unseemly age.[41]

Lewis Gates was planning a summer in Europe and Dan Mason was urging Moody to join him on a summer's walking trip. Having committed his soul to Mammon for the fall and the unforeseeable future, Moody could justify a summer in Europe. Mason, Moody, and Gates made plans accordingly for a tour of Belgium and northern France. The impending change compounded Moody's conflict and plunged him into gloom on the eve of his departure for Europe. He poured out his heart to Josephine, leaving her pondering, "He is strange,—strange." When Will was in the abyss, she observed to herself, he didn't stop halfway. She noted his habit of silence, his way of "raising his eyelids suddenly" and "the strangely repressed feeling in his voice" as he explained the sources of his despair. "I see the most beautiful light, ardency,—love—purity," he complained, ". . . and the next moment it is nothing but cheap electric light." [42] Josephine was not particularly sympathetic, and a day or two later Moody asked if he might make a final call before leaving, promising not to bring with him "the Stygian gloom of that vaguely confessional night." He was afraid he had appeared to be melodramatic and promised to try to eradicate the impression "by the display of a fine spring line of high-priced optimism." "By virtue of your trade," he suggested, "you ought to have a feeling for all peddlers and mountebanks—even when they peddle nothing prettier than opinion, and fool nobody with their penny miracles but themselves." [43] Moody's gloom had been a reversion to a familiar pattern of melodramatic self-pity, but Josephine's sensible confusion disgusted him with the stereotyped patterns his despair took.

On July 3 Moody and Mason sailed on the *Rhynland*. In Antwerp the young men were joined by Gates, who had been spending some time in London. [44] The hikers moved down across Belgium into France and west toward Normandy. A sense of quest set the dominant mood. Moody was drinking in impressions, but he did not follow Mason's lead and keep a journal. Instead, he returned to his sketching, as if to reach truer reactions by a change of medium. Stimulated by Gates's discussion and by his setting, Moody was reading in French poetry and in Maeterlinck. Maeterlinck merged with his own mood and he found the writer's importance in his "human querulousness." [45]

Moody was putting his most striking impressions into poetic draft, taking careful, tentative steps toward something new. In Caen came the sketch of a "moon theme" that would be worked into a poem in the fall. Stirred by regimental bugles at Tessy-sur-Vire, Moody began work on a fragment that finally found its way into *The Masque of Judgment*. In the bare reaches of Normandy he and Mason passed an old man singing a haunting song with the reiterative lyric content, "Pourquoi?" The experience seemed archetypal to the two questing young men, and some years later Moody returned to the incident to make a poem of it. In shaping these fragments Moody was seeking for affirmations more genuine than "penny miracles" by virtue of their sources in human conflict.

Both Moody and Mason had promised to write Josephine from Europe, but neither did. Moody, taking a position appropriate to the highest mores of the time, maintained it was too unconventional. Perhaps it was. The plot of Howells's *The Landlord of Lion's Head*, published two years later, turns on the assumption that to associate closely with a marriageable girl without intending to marry her is the distinguishing mark of a cad. But Moody himself, in a frank letter of the fall to Josephine, suggests a deeper motive for his actions—"rapacious egotism," perhaps "jealousy." [46]

By September, Josephine was perplexed and disturbed. When Moody called on his way through Cambridge, Josephine confronted him with what seemed to be the disintegration of her fellowship. She recorded the scene in her diary:

Who should come, yesterday evening, but William Vaughn Moody. He arrived in New York Saturday night after a most turbulent voyage. He said that the summer had been pleasant,—and dolorous in some respects; not "splendid." We talked such commonplaces for a while and then fell into catechism. He had not written a line he said; he had not even kept a journal; he had sketched much but refused to show me any of his work. . . . At length, said I: "I wish that you would tell me please, why you never sent me the poem that I asked you for. Was it that you forgot, merely?"

W. V. M. meditated calmly and said that he had not forgotten it at all.

"And the local color that you were both to send me?—Did you forget that?"

"No, we did not forget it."

"Won't you tell me then why you did not send them?"

W. V. M. studied the frieze critically and then meted out reasons with some economy. "I had several good reasons," he said coolly. "In the first place, I did not wish to send you the verses; I should have preferred to have you see much better ones. Secondly, I did not write any better ones. —I did not write anything at all, as I say. In the third place, I did not believe that you really wanted them."

After further probing, during which Moody continued to study the frieze, Josephine observed, "There are more reasons." At this, Moody made a "most withering speech," speaking slowly and quietly in a manner that left his companion "inly [sic] enraged and astonished." He said, "There are occult and inscrutable reasons for every human performance. I have mine. Nevertheless, the reasons which I have given you are all true; and all plausible. And I have told you . . . as much as I wish to tell." Josephine concluded her entry with anger and resolution:

It is wholly W. V. M.'s fault that Mr. Mason and he and I are not that dream of my existence,—the artistic fellowship,—wonder of the ages and model for youths and maidens. It shall be: it must be. I will not be stamped by the machine of the age into the everlasting pattern of Isolated-Girl-Worshipper-of-Art.[47]

Two days later she decided to make her doctrine clear to Moody and Mason, and she found her chance when Mason called on her, bringing roses. Fixing Mason with a straight and unfaltering gaze, she said, "Look here, here are the bylaws anyway: we are all young: we respect each other's work: we are worshippers of It: and so my being a girl doesn't count! At any rate that's the only way the world can be saved!" [48] Harmony was restored. Mason accepted Josephine's bylaws and wrote a limerick, commemorating "Fellowship" but indicating some restiveness under Josephine's stricture against recognition of difference between the sexes:

> In a Fellowship truly harmonic
> Impersonalism is chronic:
>   *We* run *ours* by steam,
>   And the whole blessed scheme
> Is impossibly hyperplatonic. [49]

Will Moody, already in Chicago, received letters from his two reconciled comrades and responded immediately, entertaining the mood that had been established. "The twentieth century dates from yesterday," he wrote, "and we are its chosen; if not as signs set in the heavens of its glory, at least as morning birds that carolled to it, mindless of the seductive and quiet palpable worm—." [50] But hardly mindless of the seductive worm, Moody characteristically undercut his extravagance, breaking off the letter with a determined gesture to reality: "More later—brutally busy—." Though hardly the carol of a morning bird, the gesture points toward the twentieth century.

CHAPTER 4 CHICAGO'S ALCHEMICAL POWER

MOODY ARRIVED in Chicago in late September 1895. The city's sprawling, violent contrasts were to wean him from Cambridge and thrust him into contact with the forces molding twentieth-century America.[1] He mulled over his first impressions in a letter to Josephine. "Cambridge—mellow and autumnal—," he wrote, "begins already to take on really mythic colors—to loom symbolic, under the stress of this relentless prairie light and vast featureless horizon." He fell immediately under the power of the city, sensing an "alchemical power to change and transmute"; explaining, "It is appallingly ugly for one thing—so ugly that the double curtain of night and sleep does not screen the aching sense. For another thing it is absorbing—crude juice of life—intellectual and social protoplasm." Moody's old stances to experience suddenly seemed irrelevant, and he recognized the pretentious artificiality of the patterns of his life. "I begin to believe that your charge against me of theatricality was just," he wrote, "that all my life there in the East was a sort of tragi-farce, more or less consciously composed, so rudely awake and in earnest is everything here." [2]

Moody became immediately and fully involved in his work. As a new instructor, his assignment was two composition courses, one of forty students and another of twenty. Uneasy about class procedures and afraid of his competence to lecture four times a week, Moody spent the fall writing out lectures and working through piles of student compositions. He and Mason, who was working in New York, exchanged comment about the loss of ideals in the workaday world, and Moody foresaw little chance to do his own writing. His students, many fresh from the small towns of the Middle West, awakened a sense of his own past, deadened by the Cambridge years. He felt he could help them and that some of them were distinctly worth helping.[3]

Robert Lovett had married in June and taken Herrick's large house on East End Avenue. The Lovetts rented a room to Moody and one to Ferdinand Schevill. Kenneth Rand and William Hapgood boarded with the group and expenses were shared. Moody's weekly costs came to $8.38. Life *en ménage* proved to be congenial; horizons were broad and spirits were usually high.[4] Moody occasionally contributed to the sociability by singing to the accompaniment of his guitar or by reading aloud from his current poetic enthusiasms. Shelley and Francis Thompson—significant models for the poet seeking expression of spiritual energy—were frequent selections, and there were memorable readings of the latter's "The Hound of Heaven," "Dream Tryst," "The Poppy," and "To Monica." At times they dined out. On one of their "gaudy" evenings in a private room at the Bismarck Restaurant, the fare was steak and continental beer. In the course of the evening's entertainment Will danced in tails an interpretation of "Twinkle, Twinkle, Little Star."[5] There were explorations of the city. Moody and his friends either walked or traveled by the cable car which ran the length of old Cottage Grove Avenue into town. Chicago's major lure for Moody was music. In a sense of desperation at the thought of cultural vacuum he shored up defenses by purchasing tickets for the full season of twenty-two symphonies and twelve chamber concerts.[6]

The shock of change, if exhilarating and liberating, was thrusting Moody back upon himself, arousing deep nostalgia. In one of his rare references to his origins in New Albany, Indiana,[7] he wrote Josephine in October,

I cannot help feeling out here, a few hundred miles from the place were [*sic*] I was born and brought up, a vast regret—no, let me say it, an unspeakable remorse, for the things that have not come to fruition. I have gone back in these weeks through ten years of crowded living—so crowded that I have not once before had time to feel my way back through the underwood tangle—and the light of promise that lies over those early landscapes wrings my heart.[8]

Moody continued, rejecting the intervening ten years as "a private sickness of the vision," a mockery of his early boyish dedication to poetry and to beauty.

In November Moody's conflict erupted into poetry. He began working over his "moon theme"—the fragment he had written in France during the summer. By Thanksgiving he had fought his way through to a new draft, expanding the fragment into a long poem. He called it "Jetsam" and sent it off to Josephine with a long letter of explanation.[9] A night walk taken near Chartres was the poem's base.

Moody and Mason had set off after supper and walked the narrow
lanes and footpaths through the fields until, lost in thought and talk,
they had no idea where they were. They followed the path of the
moon across the fields back toward the tower of the great cathedral,
caught up in the mystical sense of peace and union with spiritual
reality which is central to the finished poem. Deep in Dante and rereading the *Vita Nuova*, Josephine had written reviving discussion of
"It." Moody wrote of his own awareness of the agonizing difficulties of
full spiritual communication with Christ "through hours and days
when the brain is burnt out and the heart sluggish." But even so, he
continued, "Here, with all that star-dust between me and such quenchless radiance of welcome, I have nevertheless heard the passing knock
and snatched the door open in an agony of expectation." The context
is central to "Jetsam." The desire for complete union with the source
of spiritual beauty, together with remorse for halfhearted response to
the "quenchless radiance of welcome" is the poem's impetus. Discussion of Dante suggests an important dimension of the haunting
moon figure—muse, saint, and *femme fatale*—in which the poet's devotion centers. In the second controlling image of the poem—that of
the poet as a boy—the memory of Moody's own early faith is summoned up.

"Jetsam" is set in Chicago, symbolically evoked, and the moon
theme is charged with the conflict of the antithetical context. The
resulting poem is Moody's first major achievement. It is a quest poem,
and Shelley and Thompson in particular have contributed to the
materials and method of the poem.[10] But there is a new assurance and
independence in Moody's development: the context of the quest is
contemporary, the poem's central figure is developed in unexpected
psychological complexity, and the poem rises from compelling sources
in his experience, displaced much less than earlier. "Jetsam"[11] is a
dramatic monologue which begins as a young man walks at sunset
through a limbo of broken, betrayed human beings. He is tormented
by two visions: the face of his lost youth and that of a virgin, identified with the moon, who sings "Rich verses" from the poet's "gold
canticle." He follows the streets of a satanic city to the river, "Coiled
in its factory filth and few lean trees." He goes along the river to a sea
of light, "a new world, undreamed of, undesired,/ Beyond imagining
of man's daedal heart." A second section recircles this simple narrative
movement, clarifying theme and issues in a poetry of achieved power:

> My heart is man's heart, strong to bear this night's
> Unspeakable affliction of mute love
> That crazes lesser things: the rocks and clods

Dissemble, feign a busy intercourse;
The bushes deal in shadowy subterfuge,
Lurk dull, dart spiteful out, make heartless signs,
Utter awe-stricken purpose of no sense;
But I walk quiet, crush aside the hands
Stretched furtively to drag me madmen's ways.
I know the thing they suffer, and the tricks
They must be at to help themselves endure.
I would not be too boastful: I am weak,
Too weak to put aside the utter ache
Of this lone light just long enough to see
Whether the moon is still her white strange self
Or something whiter, stranger—even she
That by the changed face of my ghostly youth
Sang, globed in fire, the golden canticle.
I dare not look again; another gaze
Would drive me to the wavering coppice there
Where bat-winged madness brushed me, the wild laugh
Of naked nature crashed across my blood.
So rank it was with earthy presences
I could have hugged the warm slow-breathing earth,
Barked, whinnied, hissed, danced fawn-foot rings,
Bitten and rolled in bestial rage of fight,
But that within me, smiting through my lids
Lowered to shut in the thick whirl of sense,
The dumb love ached and rummaged; and without,
The soaring splendor summoned me aloud
To leave the low dank thickets of the flesh. . . .
I came out in the moon light cleansed and strong, . . .
And looked up at the lyric face to see
All sweetness tasted of in earthen cups
E'er it be dashed and spilled, all radiance flung
Beyond experience, every benison dream,
Treasured and mystically crescent there.[12]

The psychology of the conflict is carefully drawn in Moody's sophisticated handling of a familiar *fin-de-siècle* theme. Spiritual love is the affliction and the world of nature is a surrealistic dance of madness, feigning the love it seeks and can only parody, just as human faces of the poem's first section had been the dull mockery of love caught in sensuality. The speaker dares not refresh his sense of the goal for fear it will drive him to its antithesis in "naked nature." But the ordeal is essential to fulfillment of the vision, and the speaker comes out into the moonlight "cleansed and strong."

The third section of the poem is a displaced recollection of Moody's youth, which invokes his early love of imaginative beauty symbolized in the figure of the moon virgin. The lush manner in which Moody's imagination wove his experience is evident in this passage describing the moon's rise:

> Of all the sights that starred the dreamy year
> To young eyes opened on my southern hills,
> For me one sight stood peerless and apart:
> Wild bell-towers tacit; strong hills prone and dumb;
> Vineyards that hushed their tiniest voice to hear;
> Skies for the unutterable advent robed
> In purple like the folded iris-buds,
> And by some lone expectant pool, one tree
> Whose grey boughs shivered with excess of awe,
> As with preluding gush of amber light,
> And horns of herald silver surgent through,
> Across the palpitant horizon marge
> Crocus-filletted came the singing moon.[13]

In later revision of this passage Moody excised line two with its personal, if generalized, reference to the hills of New Albany; he also removed the detail which places the scene in Italy, Moody's spiritual homeland. "Wild bell-towers" became "Bright rivers"; "strong hills" became "low hills"; and "Vineyards" turned into "Forests." For Moody in 1895, however, the heavy rococo elaboration was necessary to make experience in New Albany palatable as poetry.

Of the moonlight the poet wove himself "A place to dwell in sweet and spiritual." His early poems, which once seemed "futile adorations," have become a "mystic garment" the moon virgin wears for her bridal: they are the "burden" of the song she breathes between her "passion-parted lips." The song calls him out "along the flowering road/ That summers through the dimness of the sea," and the poet enters the sea to unite with the moon maiden. The motif is familiar enough— that of *Liebestod*—here involving mystical union with the alluring source of spiritual beauty in the moon. The young man goes to physical death in the faith that full dedication to the vision is life's only value. But the moon figure embodies characteristics of the *femme fatale* of romantic poetry as well. The final effect depends on a deliberate ambiguity.

Writing of his new poem to Mason, Moody presented a casual surface, observing, "Having a few hours last week for ecstatic contemplation of my navel, I emitted a more or less piercing yawp thereconcerning, in the form of a new treatment of the moon theme."[14]

But beneath the surface was tension and concern. The poem marked a crisis for Moody—a test of his ability to find a new direction as a poet. After he completed the poem, he confessed to Josephine, a deep revulsion immediately set in. He lost faith in it, in himself, and in the future. He reread his lines to find them "graceless, repulsive, without the dignity or pathos of death." [15] But Josephine had been immediately struck with the new direction and with the poem's quality. She wrote with enthusiasm for "the amazing poetry," so "splendid in color and vividness and passion." [16] Moody's spirits revived and he sat down to rewrite the poem.

Moody had developed sensitivity to the flaws in his style. Of his experience while writing "Jetsam," he observed,

It is an odd baffling thing, this of expression, isn't it? For as soon as you say a thing with emphasis, you straightway perceive that you have either said something false, or have been bellowing insignificance into the preoccupied ear of Space.[17]

Moody's revisions indicate the working of a keen and detached critical sense. The poem was improved in clarity and coherence, and the significance of the ordeal further developed in depth. In four places the poet achieved greater exactness or concreteness of adjective; in three, he strengthened structure. The section of the poem quoted above, describing the conflict with nature, had been revised and expanded from its earlier version. Moody reworked his lines treating nature's enticements, and he introduced the seven lines beginning, "I am weak . . . ," increasing the psychological complexity of the speaker's mood and reinforcing his moon figure. Moody's two major expansions of the poem come between the body of the poem and its last eleven lines, lines in which the poet moves into the sea. The intention of both was to clarify and define the final dramatic act. In revision Moody added a fifty-two-line section, defining the act as an acceptance of the spiritual call and describing three denials of that call before its final acceptance. The addition strengthens understanding of the speaker's motivation. In a final revision several years later, Moody added another section as long, which functions as a "letter to the world." In it the speaker justifies his action, though he takes a glance at other ways of union with beauty—fruitful ways of mature life as opposed to his own carelessly impulsive Liebestod. As a judgment of an older Moody, this final addition need not concern us here.

In the fall Moody took up a second project as well—one which marks an even more startling departure from the work of his Cambridge years than "Jetsam." He began losing sleep over an idea for a play that was much later to become *The Faith Healer*. The news-papers were carrying stories concerning Francis Schlatter, who mys-teriously disappeared in mid-November from the home in Denver where he had been performing feats of faith healing. Schlatter had begun his career in Albuquerque and was known as the "New Mexico Messiah." His followers noted a striking resemblance to Christ and some felt he was Christ returned to earth. Schlatter was a simple man. He dressed as a worker, and he refused to take money when his power aided someone. His following was tremendous: his mail totaled 42,000 letters in the month before his disappearance, and a crowd of over a thousand persons was waiting when he disappeared. He left a simple message: "My mission is finished. The Father takes me away. F. Schlatter." People continued to report seeing the missing healer for the next few weeks, and an appearance in Chicago had been expected at the end of November. But he was nowhere to be found. At the end of the year a group of seekers reported seeing him in Mexico, headed south.[18] Moody was interested in reconstructing the web of conflict and motive leading to the apparent rejection of role by a man with a sense of spiritual mission. The incident provided both a character and a situation which he found "intensely significant and eloquent." [19]

Moody spent the holidays in the East. The Fellowship gathered joyously; there were three or four days of intense talk, moonlight walks, and house partying at the home of Mrs. Mary Mason, Dan's sister-in-law in Milton. Somehow, typically, the visit ended in mis-understanding and recrimination. Upon his return to Chicago, Moody sent Josephine a long letter of explanation of his actions. He seems to have been totally unnerved by seeing Josephine again. "As a Voice, a Psyche-in-the-Niche," she had been "an element of wonderful good" in his life, but by a deep instinct, he observed, he was "impelled to abstract" her "from the empirically real in the world." A totally spiritual relationship was the only possibility for them, and he explained why:

I came to acquaintanceship with you out of an experience which, while leav-ing the outward conversation of my days almost unruffled, had left my in-stinctive inner life crippled near to death, and I brought from it a nervous, almost insane, dread of those intimate relations of friendship where impulse is the guide. I have sufficient self-knowledge to know that when I am face to face with a person, and especially a woman, who interests me, I am the absolute creature of impulse.[20]

In meeting Josephine again, Moody had felt "something subtle and fine" wither away in their relationship, and he found himself "left dangling rather aghast." The neurotic dread of intimacy, avoided by attenuated spiritualization of the relationship, is the distinguishing

mark of Moody's relations with women and characteristic of his treatment of all experience in his early poetry. Josephine tried to unwind
the threads of the holiday confusion in her journal, complaining about
complication of honest, artistic friendship with other matters.[21]

Moody was slowly working toward a more immediate relation to
experience, though theory preceded action. To Josephine's sister, who
was nursing her through an illness, he wrote, "I feel now that Cambridge, gracious as it is, comely as are its words and its ways, is dangerous to whatever in life or in art is crescent, burgeoning, determinedly
contemporary." [22] Health, he maintained, was to be found in hearty
embrace of the commonplace. He prescribed for Josephine "a vigorous
taking possession of what comes handy, an easy humorous ratification
and assimilation of it." Yet Moody's quarrel with Cambridge did not
preclude continuing castigation of varieties of "the commonplace"
offered by Chicago. He raged at his "gigantic ink-blot of a town," in
which he declared there was "no city life to gaze at, nothing to relieve
the gaseous tedium of a mushroom intellectuality, no straining wicked-
ness or valiant wrestling with hunger to break the spectacle of Gospel-
peddling comfort." [23] The drudgery of work in Chicago's "Godless
vineyard" was Moody's greatest burden, and the frustrations of teaching
cry through his letters: "A hundred passionate powers and live hungers
tingle through me and I want to use them. By way of doing so I de-
liver reptilian lectures on the structure of the paragraph. Bah!" [24]

Will Moody's Protestant moral stamina combined with his faith
in the value of the "alchemical power" of his situation. His best admonitions to himself were to keep alert and alive, and he advocated
service to human and mythic dimensions of life rather than to multipli-
cation of intellectual subtleties. "Demeter," he maintained, "is as good
to pray to as the Ding an Sich." To Mason, who was having trouble
with his wrist and had been forbidden the piano, Moody wrote on
February 16: "If you can only throttle your Daemon, or make him
forego his leonine admonition 'Accomplish,' and roar you as any sucking dove the sweet vocable 'Be,'—you ought to live." By way of illustration, Moody observed that he picked up "shreds of comfort out of this
or that one of God's ash barrels." [25] One such shred came when skating
with a slim Irish girl of fifteen. They caught hands and skated alone
and silently for an hour "while the rag of sunset rotted to pieces."
Moody was mystically shaken and elated by the sensation of "the
warmth of her hand through the ragged glove, and the pathetic curve
of the half-formed breast" where the back of his wrist touched her body.

Moody demanded for himself a life that was itself poetic, a life
nourished by an environment which stimulated transcendent imaginative experiences. He identified such an environment with Europe. If

Chicago had furnished materials for life and art in "Jetsam," it was only by virtue of the relation between beauty and its polar opposite. As yet the "shreds of comfort" Moody found in Chicago were highly limited in their nature by his temperamental and theoretical bias. But his responses made the pale dreams of *fin-de-siècle* aestheticism more and more inappropriate. If the cultural shock created an inner life of turbulence, Moody instinctively dramatized it and vented his spleen on all available targets. And the passionate turmoil of *Sturm und Drang* had its satisfactions and values for the passionate poet. Josephine and Mason talked it over in the middle of March. Mason was deeply concerned for his friend, but Josephine's sympathy had limits. Although she was only partially right, there was a bright shrewdness in her guess that Will Moody was probably "very cheerful and entertained" in Chicago.[26]

2

Moody entered into his spring-term teaching with a new ease, soaking himself in the Keats and Shelley he was presenting to his classes and spending evenings reading Spenser and Hardy. The Chicago April lured him to long walks in which he drank in the silvers and blues of the early morning sunrise over the lake. "I walk about," he wrote, "in an amber clot of sensuousness, and feel the sap mount, like a tree." [27] With the warmer weather he lingered in his wanderings about the city, stopping occasionally on street corners to talk with whomever he might meet. He had written no poetry since "Jetsam," but he was "living a great deal." "I compel incident, as per formula," he wrote Josephine, "and the world breaks into lambencies and corruscations at the least jostle. It's a wizard's jar." [28]

The shreds "from God's ash barrels" Moody was picking up were beginning to flower into poems. In May Moody completed a poem dealing with his subtle, spiritual love for a girl he had sat near at the symphony concerts but had never spoken to. The poem weaves Moody's sense of the fragile relationship under the presiding genius of the music. It was later published with major deletions and changes as "Heart's Wild Flower." Though not strikingly successful, the poem is important for its source in a real event and its indication of the single-minded Dantesque experience in which the poet found the highest manifestation of love. He sent the poem to Mason, observing that it was almost the first thing he had done that represented "a direct impulse from 'real' life." [29] In his original version Moody celebrated the fact that the relationship, totally spiritual in nature, would endure forever, a "bubble of dream sky." Identifying his anonymous love as a "fadeless flower" placed on the girl's forehead, he rejoices that it is:

> Not such a sign as women wear
> Who bow beneath the shame
> Of marriage insolence, and bear
> A house-wife's faded name;
> Nor such as passion eateth bare
> With its carcanet of flame.

Instead, his love bore a power "Of strange beatitude"—the "dearest of God's dowers" to man.

A series of letters [30] survives which records both the criticism Moody was getting from Mason and Gates and his responses to it. Mason objected to the poem's "obscurities, overloadings, and verbal disingenuousnesses," vagueness of the syntax, and turgidity in Moody's heaping up of adjectives and in his "catachrestical and grotesque" phraseology. Moody accepted most of his friend's strictures, agreeing on issues of syntax, turgidity, and certain phrases which now seemed "rococo as hell" to him. In more general defense against Mason's demand for simplicity, however, he wrote,

I think you are not tolerant enough of the instinct for conquest in language, the attempt to push out its boundaries, to win for it continually some new swiftness, some rare compression, to distill from it a more opaline drop. Isn't it possible, too, to be pedantic in the demand for simplicity? It's a cry which, if I notice aright, nature has a jaunty way of disregarding. Command a rosebush in the stress of June to purge itself; coerce a convolvulus out of the paths of catachresis. Amen!

Gates's critique arrived at the end of the month with an even more slashing attack on Moody's diction. But Gates's major thrust was for the tenuousness of the central experience. He found Moody decadent in his exaltation of a purely imaginary love. Ironically, Gates had missed what Moody considered a new concern for the "direct impulse from 'real' life."

The barrage of criticism coincided closely enough with Moody's own changing taste that he was not dismayed. In revising the poem in early June he ruthlessly cut five of the thirteen stanzas away and made a number of changes in those that remained.[31] Still undecided about it, he set the poem aside, writing Mason: "At worst it is only one more failure, success only looms a little haughtier, a little more disdainful of conquest. Esperance and set on!" [32]

In June Moody set off with Ferd Schevill for a trip in Wisconsin. He traveled on a new English bicycle for which he had paid sixty-five dollars. They headed for the northern lake country, which charmed Moody and reminded him of the country around Dresden.[33] All his life he would continue to approach unfamiliar American landscapes through European analogies, yet another instance of his tendency to impose idealized forms on his experience. The cyclists, who averaged a healthy fifty miles a day on their trip, were back in Chicago for the opening of the summer term in early July. Moody's teaching was a repetition of the rhetoric and composition of the preceding three terms.[34] But he had passed beyond the elaborate rebellions of the winter and was enjoying the city itself, wandering the streets in search of "compelling incident." Moody became, he declared, "a prowler in slums, a rapt visitor at Salvation Army gatherings, a hanger about stage doors, a talk-provoker at quick-lunch counters (locally known as *snatcheries*), a Lovelace of the public parks, a patient scavenger of the odds and ends of street adventure." [35]

Under the new spiritual dispensation of the summer, Moody broke through to a stream-of-consciousness technique in this passage of a letter to Josephine:

Mr. Ruskin would not be happy in Chicago. God is a very considerable personage—So is Mr. Rockefeller—So am I, but for a different reason—Towers of Babel are out of fashion—Ride a Rambler—Fourfifths of William Blake would not be accepted for publication by the Harvard Advocate—Life at a penny plain is d——d dear—Eat H.O.—The poet in a golden clime was born, but moved away early—A man may yearn over his little brothers and sisters and still be a good Laodicean—Art is not long, but it takes a good while to make it short—There will be no opera or steel engraving in the twentieth century—An angle-worm makes no better bait because it has fed on Caesar—Wood fires are dangerous. So is life at a penny plain, but for a different reason. Towers of Babel, though out of fashion, are well received in Chicago—There were no birds in the Tower of Babel—God is a very considerable personage. So is Olga Nethersole—So are you, but for a different reason—I am owner of the spheres, and grow land-poor—Literature is a fake and Nordau is its prophet—God bless McKinley—Love is not Time's fool: he was turned off for lack of wit—Eve was born before Ann Radcliffe, so the world goes darkling—Tom's acold—I am old—rose, quoth 'a. God's pittykins 'ield ye, gany, for thy apple-greenness! T'would gi'e the Ding-an-Sich a colic to set eyes on 'e—Natheless Monet was a good painter, *and* color-blind— [36]

Moody was to retain his nineteenth-century sense of generic decorums. He would have been amazed had he been told that the passage is twentieth century in sensibility and provides the basis of a modern

poetic style in its fragmentation, its alogical intuitive leaps, its semi-
obsessive repetitions, its wide-ranging mixture of diction, and its juxtaposition of "images" drawn from Western tradition against those of
contemporary popular culture.

In his expansive, Whitmanic mood, Moody celebrated the commonplace and sought an "open-air freedom," assailing a letter from
Gates which, he wrote Josephine, "breathed Culture like a pestilence"
and almost drove him back to the wilderness. After reading the letter,
he observed, he "had to eat a whole onion, raw, to make peace with
fact." [37] A sign of Moody's growing desire to "make peace with fact"
was the new interest aroused in him by the color and excitement of
the Democratic convention in Chicago in July. William Jennings Bryan
gave his Cross of Gold speech, took the convention by storm, and
began the long circuit of stump speeches which carried the issue to the
country. Moody became concerned for the desperate condition of western farmers and felt the Free Silver movement might offer relief. But
his immature social and political thinking is made apparent in a comment to Mason [38] that he was thinking of stumping, though he was
still not sure on which side! And he identified his concern as "the utmost abyss and downward of my recreancy." The recreancy was of
course to the aesthetic and spiritual idealism of the Fellowship.

For literary discussion Moody had found a friend in Paul Shorey,
a classicist interested in contemporary literature. Shorey approached
the problems of literature in the nineties with a fresh conservatism in
an article he published in the August issue of the *Atlantic Monthly*.[39]
He gave short shrift to the flabby laments for the age that filled such
influential literaries as *Dial* and *Poet-Lore*. Not a tear is shed over the
materialism of the Philistines, "the decay of spirituality," or the icono-
clasm of science. Nor does Shorey take the familiar sentimental view of
art as "a pleasureable beguilement" through which man may escape the
burden of reality through the "joy of elevated thoughts." [40] During
1895, *Poet-Lore* had encouraged writers to explore the possibilities in
evolutionary and democratic thought for new poetic forms and ideas.
Though his friend attacked the suggestion as nothing new, Moody was
to find it useful to the development of breadth and contemporary relevance in his work. Shorey's faith in the potential of the drama for a
more realistic treatment of life coincided, however, with Moody's own
interest in his materials on the New Mexico "messiah." Shorey's was
yet another voice to swell the ranks of friends urging him toward
something new.

But Moody was having little success. During the summer he
wrote only one poem. It drew on an experience described in a letter of
late June to Mason.

I have had an enormous little adventure since I wrote last. Another Girl, of course. This time a Westerner par excellence—a Californian, dating mentally from the age of Rousseau and Chateaubriand, with geysers and cloudbursts of romanticism, not to say sentimentality; dating spiritually from the Age of Gold, or some remoter purity, some Promethean dawn, some first foam-birth in hyperborean seas. She likes Gibson's drawings, adores Munsey's, and sings "Don't Be Cross, Dear" with awful unction.[41]

Moody's approaches to the girl were repelled, and he worked the incident into a poem, "Dawn Parley," [42] which attempts to maintain a serious tone. But the poet's lively sense of the situation turns his elevated treatment into unconscious parody. The failure is a dramatic illustration of the enfeebling effect of Moody's myopic view of poetry as necessarily lofty and ennobling.

During the summer Moody completed work on an edition of Bunyan's *Pilgrim's Progress* for Scott, Foresman's Lake English Classics. It was the first of a number of textbooks he was to edit for the series. He found in Bunyan what he felt was the true poetic temperament—one very like his own. He praised Bunyan's "uncontrollable waves of feeling which plunged him into maniacal despair, and without warning lifted him to heights of mystical ecstasy." [43] He liked Bunyan's realistic detail, observing of the book, "It sprang racy of the soil; it had its root in daily fact, and drew its sap from the immediately human." [44] But Bunyan's major achievement was in his transmutation of these materials, in his "glowing pictures concrete as . . . field-flowers, yet bathed inexplicably in the delicate effulgence of dream." [45] It was the effect toward which Moody's own most recent poetry had aimed.

But Moody understood how those poems had failed, though he turned his self-disgust into an attack on Shelley: "poor chap—he was trying to say something worth while, with all that intolerable mouthing!" [46] In search of a new style, Moody was returning to the roots of Victorian poetry in the work of the great Romantics. The influence of Keats, Blake, and Shelley on Moody's work in the nineties was pervasive and can be suggested in the context of his treatment of their work in *A History of English Literature*, written at the end of the nineties. The character of Keats, like that of Sidney, combined imaginative vigor, personal courage and nobility, and great human warmth in a way Moody found extremely attractive. Both poets became personal models. Keats's view of life "as the Valley of Soul-making," [47] was central to Moody's commitments and to his Fellowship with Josephine and Mason. Like Keats, Moody was unusually responsive to sensuous stimuli. The responsiveness found outlets in his painting and in the rich textures of his poetry. But the rightness of Keats's develop-

ment toward the objectivity and energy of dramatic forms gave Moody
guidance in his own career. Shelley's passionate version of Neoplatonic
idealism was compelling: indeed, Shelley's example was the major influence on Moody's two most recent lyrics. What Moody identified as
Shelley's "myth-making" power was to have its effect on visionary
passages in Moody's poetic drama. But he felt that Shelley's program
was ultimately misguided. As a child of the French Revolution, Shelley
assumed that only external tyrannies stood between man and his realization of the ideal. The true tyrannies Moody knew were internal.[48]
Blake's orientation to experience, his theological position, and the
power and grandeur of his symbolism attracted Moody. Blake's lyrics
were to become the major influence on Moody's own short lyrics. But
in all of these cases, Moody's admiration was qualified. In much of
their work he found a lack of form and restraint which made for
marked unevenness in quality, inhibited power, and ultimately restricted
communication. If Shelley was guilty of "intolerable mouthing," most
of Blake was inaccessible, and Moody was later to attack his work,
writing: "The greater part of his message was so obscure, so wild, so
incoherently delivered, that even now, after much study, his com-
mentators have succeeded in making clear only a portion of what he
wrote." Blake's lyrics are "some of the most powerful short poems in
the language," but Moody concludes, "It must be admitted that he is
at his best very rarely, and then, as it were, by accident." [49] The influence of the English Romantic poets on Moody's work of the later
nineties was to be balanced by his commitment to the essentially classic
criteria of form and clarity in art.

In September Robert Herrick returned from his year abroad, and
the six months to follow were Moody's first period of close association
with the novelist. At twenty-seven, but a few months older than
Moody, Herrick had already published several volumes of fiction; and
he returned from Europe with his draft for *The Gospel of Freedom*,
a novel to be published in 1898. Herrick's puritanism was sterner than
Moody's, and his interests spanned the spectrum of Chicago life. He
prodded the city's business and political activity, the intricacies and
corruptions of speculation in traction stocks, and the mores of the
enterprising newly rich families building imposing homes on Chicago's
south side. Herrick's social conscience was as strong as Lovett's, yet he
was responsive to Moody's vague, romantic longings for a vibrant life,
rich in love and beauty. Both attitudes were crossed by his strong, clear
sense of irony, and Herrick reserved his harshest disapproval for the
detached aesthete of the nineties, the egocentric connoisseur of shades
of sensuous and emotional experience. Herrick was to attack the amoral
drifter in sensibility through the judgment of his hero, Jennings, in
The Gospel of Freedom.

They are all much alike, these sighers after art and beauty. A poor lot, take them as a whole, who decide to eat honey all their lives! I have seen more of them than anything else in Europe,—dilettantes, connoisseurs, little artists, lazy scholars. Chiefly Americans, who, finding America too incomplete, come here and accomplish nothing. . . . The environment they run after atrophies their faculties; the very habits of life which are best for these people hurt *them;* they sink into laziness.[50]

Association with Herrick, a hardheaded sceptic resembling Gates in the sharpness of his tongue, was bracing for Moody, and Herrick's was yet another voice raised to encourage the poet to temper his extravagance.

In addition to his composition course, Moody was teaching an advanced writing course in the fall of 1896. One of his students, who explains that the course was "artistic" in emphasis, has left a description of the course and a record of her class notes that gives some idea of Moody's emphasis as well as his effect on an interested student.[51] In the classroom, the student writes, Moody spoke in a "slight, soft, natural drawl" and frequently read passages from Browning, Stevenson, Carlyle, Pater, or Dante in Italian, merely "to illustrate the beauty of the lines." Daily themes were standard, with an occasional change of pace provided by assignment of a longer piece of writing. Three possible emphases for writing were suggested: the informal journal, the projection of inner experience; the "ordinary journal," leaning to observation and description of outer reality; and the "sketch book," in which the writer "should imagine himself an artist and his blank page, his canvas." Special technical emphasis seems to have been placed on the values of contrast and suggestiveness. The major prescription noted is this: "To have power in writing Poetry, drench every word and line in suggestiveness." As an example of drenched lines, Keats is quoted: "The sedge is withered on the lake/ And no birds sing." The major effect of the course, for one student at least, was that Moody had made clear "the Greek Ideal": "Life and beauty for its own sake." Such a record cannot be approached as a mature statement of Moody's artistic aims. Yet "Jetsam" and later works of the nineties depend on contrast as a major formal principle. And if the emphasis on suggestiveness is stated too baldly, it is basic to Moody's poetic practice in its achievements and its occasional bathetic lapses.

Primarily because of the pressure of work, Moody did not go East for the holidays. Much of his vacation was spent preparing the two new courses for the winter, one on English literature of the first half of the seventeenth century, the other on the history and principles of versification. The literature course gave Moody great pleasure and was the occasion for his first concentrated work on Milton. He found the poets of the period stimulating, declaring to Mason that he was "read-

ing in them all night and writing lectures on them all day." Moody felt
he was making "some rare finds" and was having "good fun." [52] The
statement is one of his few expressions of enjoyment in teaching. The
intricacies of versification also stimulated Moody. His description of
the course states that the "ability to make use of French text-books is
presumed"—an important indication of the significance he attached to
the experiments in versification of the post-Symbolist movement in
France.

Under the pressure of teaching and his inability to define a new
poetic direction, Moody had written little since the summer. By the
end of the winter only two short lyrics were done.[53] "A Bracelet of
Grass" and "On the River" draw upon personal experience and represent more mature and fully achieved performances than the comparable
"Dawn Parley" and "Wilding Flower." The speaker of the first poem,
as a thunder storm gathers, bracelets his love's wrist with a ring of
sedge grass. The storm arouses the poet to thoughts of the transience
of human love; and the last of the poem's three stanzas rises to impassioned outcry:

> We gazed from shelter on the storm,
> And through our hearts swept ghostly pain
> To see the shards of day sweep past,
> Broken, and none might mend again.
> Broken, that none shall ever mend;
> Loosened, that none shall ever tie.
> O the wind and the wind, will it never end?
> O the sweeping past of the ruined sky!

In "On the River" the scene is sketched in swift strokes, transitions are
dropped, and the outcry is abruptly juxtaposed. The poem suggests a
break toward ellipsis in Moody's experimentation with techniques of
symbolism. His central figure is a silent woman of "wild pathetic grace"
sphered by the "watchful blue" of the cosmos. She embodies the poem's
central tension between the call of mundane love and man's desire for
spiritual fulfillment.

In the course of negotiating for a leave, Moody had to alter his
plans for an extended European trip. The work of the department was
heaviest in the fall and winter. "Times are hard," Will wrote Charlotte, "and the funds of the university somewhat involved, and the
President [Harper] unwilling to make an extra appropriation for a
new instructor to fill my place." At the end of March 1897 Moody left
for Europe, having arranged to spend the light spring and summer

quarters abroad, returning in October for the opening of the fall term. Before sailing he sent Charlotte Moody a revealing, analytical letter:

I am keenly conscious of the apparent selfishness of my own position; very few people can understand, perhaps even you do not *fully* understand, how entirely my earning-power, and living power depend upon my keeping awake and elastic, nor how soon I should lose my grip if it were not for these occasional plunges into what must seem to a Puritan mind (and we are all Puritans at heart—I mean, all of our family) mere "sensation baths." As you know I have never been content from the first to play for any but the highest stakes which my spiritual bank account rendered possible to me. If I lose, as I very well may, I shall accept my punishment without whining; but until then, I cannot bring myself to pitch the game lower. . . . If I come out, I shall have you to thank for much of it.[54]

The full strength of Will Moody's heritage moves in the letter. The stern Protestant mores of Moody's youth were basic to his mature personality, and Charlotte's generous support of his artistic aspirations left Moody with a heavy residue of guilt. The poet could indulge his senses only in the name of high spiritual purpose, if his life were to be justified. Moody's fine old metaphors, drawn from a seventeenth-century world of spiritual accounting, suggest the appropriate context for his innermost spiritual drama. The cost of failure would be, inevitably, "punishment." The poet's Puritan forebear, Joshua Moody, would have no difficulty interpreting the struggle. Will Moody, like Dr. Faustus, was gambling with his soul.

3

On March 27, 1897, Moody embarked on the *Kaiser Wilhelm* for Naples. The trip was to be his *Italiënische Reise*. Italy was the glory of his first trip to Europe and had been an imaginative homeland even earlier. Though at twenty-eight Moody would have rejected the view that life was "some remote experience, some over-sea place—Art, Love, Italy," spiritually and emotionally Chicago had not convinced him that he was wrong. Now, however, the trip was a poet's business trip: Moody was headed for the land where experience itself was poetry. His anticipation was not chimerical. The trip was to provide the sources for Moody's work until the turn of the century.

Out of harbor Moody began a journal [55] in which impressions for possible poems were stored. The charm began working in the Azores, where Moody recorded his sense of the landscape, held in tension with comparisons to the Chicago scene. He noted,

To my American mind, used to sprawling masses of architectural make-shift held together only by a commercial urgency, there is something primitive, touching, intimately remembered by the heart, in these little Latin towns, built by the old citizen instinct under the guidance of some provincial Romulus.

Landing in Naples, Moody set out for a week of cycling in the vicinity.[56] The beauty of Sorrento, with its rising terraces of lemon trees in blossom, captivated him, and a Good Friday procession of the crucifix and the Virgin plunged him into an experience of communion with Christ. He began work on the poem that was to be "Good Friday Night." Upon the arrival of Ferdinand Schevill the cyclists left for Rome. Moody conjured up the poetry of place by reading Dante and Gabriele D'Annunzio, devouring the latter's recent popular success, *Trionfo della Morte,* a novel dealing with the passionate turmoil of an imaginative young hero caught in adulterous love for a fascinating woman. She combined the characteristics of a virginal saint and a voluptuous temptress. D'Annunzio focuses on the psychological states and morbid imagination of his hero, who alternately writhes in voluptuous sensuality or contemplates an ideal asceticism modeled after St. Francis. The novel is weighted with Christian and pagan symbolism, culminating in a *Liebestod* as the mad hero, after long contemplation of Wagner's *Tristan and Isolde,* hurls his mistress and himself over a cliff into the sea. The book cast its intoxicating spell across the landscape, contributing to the motifs and tone of "Song-Flower and Poppy," and to the masque Moody would begin in June.[57]

The presence of Schevill was of incalculable importance: his knowledge of Italian history and art was already impressive, and the historian's interest in place and time tempered Moody's tendency to sheer sensuous and emotional response. They toured the museums and churches, and looked at paintings and frescoes, with a special interest in places that figure in Dante's life or in the *Divine Comedy*. Moody collected impressions, jotting down reminders of specific scenic detail— cloud effects, the vividness of a man on a donkey here, of a group of workmen there, the charming effect of farm girls' faces, the sense of color and form as a landscape composed. Moody was contented and relaxed. He describes the mood of an afternoon as he lay upon the side of a hill, resting from cycling:

. . . a sense of unhorizoned freedom, a voluptuous absence of care for the morrow—what I *might* call a cosmic content—which I do not remember since boyhood. Perfect happiness, perfect success, in life, would be to recover this sense as a permanent possession, because out of it comes all poetry, all true contemplation.[58]

For touchstone Moody returns characteristically to boyhood's instinctive sense of union with nature, identifying "cosmic content" as the source of all poetry. But Moody's more active self demurs. True contemplation may come from cosmic content, Moody adds, but "Perhaps not true action? That is the eternal vexing question."

On May 1 the cyclists went to Assisi; Moody's fullest record is of this experience, which finally became the central motif of "Song-Flower and Poppy." He wrote,

Sky clouded in, and served to heighten impression of ascetic strenuousness which began to grow upon us as we climbed the hill toward the gate. Ferd plucked a poppy on the way. The passionate flame of the blossom seemed strangely incongruous and a little devilish there, but the ground was thick with them. He put it in his button hole as a flag of truce to the spirit of the place, he said; it seemed to me rather a flaunting denial of that spirit.

There was further matter for poetry in an evening spent in intoxicated vision and talk. It combined with an early morning trip out of Orvieto to provide the experiences that formed the core for "Road-Hymn for the Start." [59]

Moody and Schevill cycled north to Florence, Bergamo, and Milan, separating in Lugano as Schevill left for passage home to a summer of teaching. Moody went on to Venice where he joined the Lovetts in a villa they had rented for several months.[60] Sightseeing was avidly pursued. On one excursion to a modern art exhibition Moody became engrossed with a triptych of the Last Judgment, and the idea for *The Masque of Judgment* took form. Moody gave up his journal and began working directly with the host of ideas for poems already running in his head. On June 8 he wrote Schevill that he had finished his Good Friday poem, and he diffidently set forth the plan for his masque, which he characterized as "a rather hopelessly fantastic thing." His subject, the day of judgment, he thought to present "from the point of view of the accusing human." Moody's plan was well in mind, for he included a listing of his unusual characters, observing, "I foresee great possibilities,—a kind of Hebrew Götterdämmerung, with a chance for some real speaking-out-in-meeting—hoop-la!—Excuse my barbaric yawp; it is merely meant to express enthusiasm." [61]

In mid-June Moody and the Lovetts were moving north, settling for a few weeks in Cortina d'Ampezzo in the Dolomites. Moody was working mornings on the masque, drawing on the awesome surroundings for his setting. By July the travelers were in the Tyrol, where Moody, his imagination outrunning his pen, often gave up "a night in the starlit grass" for a night "of lamp-oil and muddy ink." [62] Moody was back in Florence by the end of July, considering his return home

and recuperating from overexertion. He wrote Mason, "I have lain on
my gorgeous heap of sensation like Fafnir on the Glittering Hoard,
growling from my *papier-mâché* throat to all importunate duties and
memories 'Lass mich fühlen! Ich lieg und besitze.'" Meditating his
luxurious mood, he observed,

My golden bath, my Semele-shower of sensation, has only strengthened my
conviction that the adventures of the mind are beyond all compare more
enthralling than the adventures of the senses, that no twining of amorous
limbs can bring the intoxication of the airy grappling of the Will to Beauty
with the feminine latency of thought toward being beautifully created
upon.[63]

Moody's playful adaptation of Keats's idea of the "negative capabil-
ity" of the dramatic poet offers suggestive insight into his view of the
poet's role. Thought, feminine and latent, is roused to adventure by
God-showered sensation, the manifestation of the Will to Beauty in
the universe. An adjunct to Moody's temperamental mysticism, the
view was to continue to balance his major impulse to press his poetry
and drama into being by the sheer power of his own will.

In mid-July Moody had written to Horace Scudder, accepting the
commission for an edition of Milton's poetry.[64] And he was preparing
another volume for the Lake English Classics. He left Europe to spend
September working in Boston on these projects. In the course of the
summer, however, Moody had completed "Good Friday Night," "Road-
Hymn for the Start," and had made progress on his masque.[65] In addition, there was probably something in draft for the poems that were
to be "Song-Flower and Poppy" and "A Dialogue in Purgatory."

Moody was striking out in new directions with considerable success. "Good Friday Night" is deceptively simple, presenting Moody's
experience in Sorrento without editorial comment. The poet is casually
watching the Good Friday procession. His "glad spirit" does not respond to the image of the suffering God: "Unspiritual, dead/ Drooped
the ensanguined Head." But as a fellow stranger kneels to the image of
the Virgin, the poet feels ashamed and joins him. Suddenly he sees in
the image "the dear mortal grace" of his own mother's face. Feeling
deep fellowship with the stranger, Moody walks the lemon-scented hill
with him. The risen moon reveals that his companion is Christ. The
implication is that man unites with Christ and all mankind in brotherhood, not by sharing in suffering and death but through mutual recognition of the grace of the mother, source of all life human and divine.
Moody's handling of an English imitation of Horace's alcaics is sophisticated, and his stanza establishes the quiet tone of the poem's early
movement:

> At last the bird that sang so long
> In twilight circles, hushed his song:
> Above the ancient square
> The stars came here and there.

Imagery is similarly muted, and syntax and diction rise from a base in colloquial language when dramatically appropriate. Compared to "Jetsam" with its passionate overstatement, the poem marks a new control and balance in Moody's work.

"Road-Hymn for the Start" provides a statement of the mature poet's dedication to transcendent reality. Moody characterizes the inaugural baptism of pilgrims of the spirit:

> We have felt the ancient swaying
> Of the earth before the sun,
> On the darkened marge of midnight heard sidereal rivers playing;
> Rash it was to bathe our souls there, but we plunged and all was done.
> That is lives and lives behind us—lo, our journey is begun!

In the stanzas that follow, Moody welcomes the pilgrims' lack of a clear sense of identity and of destination. They follow the day star as the failing moon flames up, shrivels white, and falls: they seek in a world of reality which lies through and beyond the world of imagination ruled by the moon. The poem represents Moody's reinterpretation of Whitman's call to the open road. It ends appropriately in rejection of the sweet anguish of a hidden bird's song—an allusion to "Out of the Cradle Endlessly Rocking." The world of Whitman's bird was that of suffering nature and human beings, comprehended in song. Moody's desire is for totally transcendent identity.

In late September Moody returned to his teaching in Chicago. He roomed and boarded with Robert Herrick and his family. Moody's conviction that he should be able to flourish in Chicago if he exerted sufficient will power was waning. He was puzzled over his dilemma. In many ways he was much more in sympathy with the West than with the East. But western "robustness" he found mingled with an overwhelming lack of aesthetic discrimination, even if New England as he knew it had its element of effeteness and smug complacency. Perhaps the real burden was teaching. He had hardly begun work once again when he was "heartily sick of theme work," feeling it was emasculating. "Every week I spend over it makes it more impossible for me to take my day-to-day existence seriously," he wrote Josephine; and he felt more and more "sheepish" in the face of "men who are doing the virile thing in a virile way." [66] He was reading and quoting Whitman for sustenance.

Through the Chicago fall and winter Moody scarcely touched his

"Glittering Hoard" of materials for poetry. He devoted the scraps of
time that became available to his work on the edition of Milton.[67] And,
with his left hand, he quickly worked up his volume for the Lake
English Classics—an edition of "The Rime of the Ancient Mariner"
and "The Vision of Sir Launfal" for high school students. As if this
time-consuming work were not enough, Moody had been reading the
newly collected poems of Edmund C. Stedman and the eight-volume
collected edition of the writings of Thomas Bailey Aldrich for an
Atlantic review. It appeared in January 1898, under the title "Our
Two Most Honored Poets." [68] The article demonstrates Moody's gracious, if somewhat equivocal, stance toward the poetic establishment. It
was a position which made self-definition outside the tradition difficult
and tended to obscure the liberating impulses in Moody's own thought
and art. He begins by observing that both poets "are too justly appre-
ciated to make criticism very pertinent." Aldrich's retreat from the
issues of his times "to go in quest of pure beauty" is compared to the
position of Keats. But Moody identifies difficulties in the position:
"Since Keats's day, the wildness, the incoherence, the intellectual
turmoil of the age have steadily deepened. The wind has made short
work of most of the fragile harps set up to tame it to melody." Yet,
from such turmoil the work of Aldrich offers "a gracious febrifuge."
His objection to the texture of Aldrich's verse shows how Moody's
own taste had changed in three years. He finds Aldrich's muse is too
often "a wearer of gems" instead of a spirit. The consequence is verse
which "sometimes lacks the high nervous organization which the occasion demands." [69] Moody turns to identify Aldrich's major value for
American poetry in his "instinct for workmanship." In contrast to the
work of Aldrich, Stedman's volume, Moody found, "exhibits a deep
spiritual restlessness darkened by a sense of doubt and bafflement, but
refusing still to be hopeless or uncourageous." Warming to his theme,
Moody expanded in a passage that indicates the excesses of which his
public prose was still capable in 1898. Stedman, he wrote, "has watched
the wings of speculation fall crippled from the mysterious walls against
which they had flung themselves. He has marched with the armies of
belief when they beheld, beyond bristling defiles of thought manfully
stormed and taken, mountainous paradox rising stolidly inexpug-
nable." [70] Moody's letters indicate that he could write lively and controlled prose. He was here obviously writing in a style he thought
appropriate to public critical performance.

If he was doing little with his own poetry, Moody's contact with
friends who were writing grew closer by the end of 1897. He was in
touch with Richard Henry Savage, who was working in the Boston
Public Library. Since his *First Poems* in 1895, Savage had written
enough for a second volume, and Moody was reading his latest work

in manuscript. In his newest lyrics a quiet stream of disillusionment mingled with Savage's earlier transcendental faith.[71] He questioned Wordsworth: "Laurel, it may be, too early on his brow he set,/ And the thorn of life too lightly could forget." His themes had turned to those of death and decay; his imagery sought sources in the season of autumn rather than spring or summer. "The frost has walked across my world," he wrote in one poem. But his idiom had gained a new strength, directness, and simplicity that anticipated the work Robert Frost was to do. Moody was also following Trumbull Stickney's poetry with interest.[72] His friend was in Paris studying for a Sorbonne doctorate in classics. In the two and a half years since his graduation, Stickney had written even less poetry than Moody, but he was working with greater competence than earlier. In 1896 he wrote "Oneiropolos," a Browningesque dramatic monologue, and in January 1898 the *Harvard Monthly* published a series of seven new sonnets. His monologue presents the decadent sensuality and commercialism of fourth-century Athens from the perspective of a wandering Indian scholar, the speaker. Stickney's sonnets tend to a lush but sensitive rendering of *fin-de-siècle* moods and themes. In the well-known "Be still. The Hanging Gardens were a dream," Stickney presents the past as dead and man as a "frighted owl." "Live blindly and upon the hour" is a poem on the *carpe diem* theme, which asks the reader to give himself "to the lovely hours," and ends,

> Thou art divine, thou livest,—as of old
> Apollo springing naked to the light
> And all his island shivered into flowers.

Lines such as these represent Stickney's keen poetic sense at its best. His image, evocative yet clearly visualized and vigorous, shows the effect of a deeper response than Moody's to the stylistic qualities of French Symbolist poetry. But both Stickney and Savage were caught in the poetic forms and themes of the nineties and offered little that Moody found attractive. He sought a fuller rebellion from contemporary modes. Yet the work of both poets provided authentic voices of his own time and situation against which Moody could test his own.

In January good news came from a third poet. Moody aroused himself to enough spirit of Fellowship to greet Josephine Preston Peabody's announcement that Copeland and Day had accepted *The Wayfarers* for publication. "It is jolly that some of us are going to have a say," he wrote. "The elected one must be spokesman for the rejected, and say it with an air and a gesture!"[73] By March the *Atlantic* had taken his "Good Friday Night," and under this encouragement Moody felt he was ready to put out a small first volume of poems. He hoped to get it ready for press "before fall at latest."[74]

CHAPTER 5

THE HONIED
LUSTS OF LIFE

IN THE SPRING of 1898 an interlude of three months lay ahead
for Moody. His plans for it indicate an important shift of orientation.
Moody determined to go to New York, explaining to Mason, "I choose
New York rather than Boston in order not to be tempted beyond my
strength by the Social Whirl, and also because I think the atmosphere
of New York healthier for my especial mental constitution." [1] The
choice was wise. New York combined Chicago's attractive "crude juice
of life" with a cosmopolitan cultural scene. By the end of March,
Moody had established himself in a room on Waverley Place, just a
step from Washington Square. He explored lower Manhattan, stopping
into little Italian restaurants for something to eat. Evenings he spent
at Daly's Theatre and the Garrick, often setting off afterwards for a
long evening stroll. He explained in a letter to Herrick, "It is only after
midnight that I dare to expand my lungs and stretch my legs in that
superb sweep of Fifth Avenue, with the insolence which satisfies." [2]

Whenever he was in New York, Moody had dropped in at the
Harvard Club, and he maintained his contact with George Rice Carpenter, who was teaching at Columbia. Carpenter introduced him at
The Players, where the spirit of the theatre world captured him immediately. He wrote Mason energetically,

I have already met a number of capital chaps here at the Players . . .
chiefly playwrights, not very big ones I suspect, but full of enthusiasm and
practical expedient. The great thing about them is that they get their things
played, and that sort of thing begad, begins to appeal to me. Do not believe
me quite recreant to ideals; Cambridge and her elegiac airs seem still lovely
and of good report. But these chaps here, though very moderately elegaic

and of a dubious report, are splendidly American and contemporary; and I feel convinced that this is the place for young Americans who want to do something.[3]

Moody's romance with the practical commercial theatre, one he was never to feel was quite respectable, had begun. In addition to Carpenter, Norman Hapgood furnished Moody a card of entry. He had been one of a small group of men who left the *Evening Post* a year earlier to take over operation of the *Commercial-Advertiser*. They retained the name of their reorganized newspaper, though it belied their idealism. Lincoln Steffens became city editor, and Hapgood did general reporting and theatre reviews. Hutchins Hapgood, sharing the interest of his brother and Steffens in social problems, had given up teaching and joined the staff. He covered some of the reviewing and was prodding the subterranean life of the city, beginning the explorations which were to culminate in 1902 in his book, *The Spirit of the Ghetto*. Clearly there were lively possibilities here for a poet who wanted to make acquaintances and, as he said, "learn the ropes of New York life." [4] In mid-April Moody observed to Mason, "I am going in for people now, having made the discovery that the average man is among the most unexpected and absorbing of beings." [5]

The roar of Broadway, echoing in the talk at The Players, was in large part a roar of concern about the Syndicate's increasingly strong hold on American theatre. Nixon and Zimmerman in Philadelphia, Klaw and Erlanger, and Hayman and Fronman of New York had gained control of a network which included most of the first-class houses in the country. They guaranteed their houses a continuous flow of productions, reserving the crucial rights to determine matters of scheduling and to name specific productions themselves. Hapgood and Carpenter were unhappy about the ominous implications of the Syndicate for good theatre and experimentation. Hapgood saw the only hope for serious drama in the few independents and in stock companies which were holding out or forming in opposition to the power of the Syndicate.[6]

But Moody's central concern was for the world of the stage [7] itself. The glow of that world has faded for modern eyes, but it was lively if not distinguished. More than half of the Broadway plays in the late nineties were either adaptations from the French or were English imports. The quantity of plays from the French gave rise to one wag's remark that he had taken up French in order to read English plays in the original. Of the many English imports, the plays of Pinero and Henry Arthur Jones were most highly regarded. Both skillfully blended wit and sentiment in the guarded context of middle-class manners and morals. Shaw had just entered the arena, but *The Devil's Disciple* was his only American success in the nineties. The playgoer could count on two or three dramatizations of novels each year: Dumas, Stevenson, Dickens, Thackeray, and Hardy were frequently tapped sources. There were one or two productions of Shakespeare each season, and Ibsen was played from time to time to select audiences.[8] The productions of a German company in the Irving Place Theatre were attractive to Moody. Presenting the plays of Goethe, Schiller, Lessing, and certain moderns —among them, Hauptmann—they set a standard for good ensemble, somewhat rare in the star system which dominated American theatre then as now. Amid the roar, however, American playwrights were being heard from, either in adaptations from fiction or in original works. Clyde Fitch was becoming a popular playwright, but the two major producers of serious American drama in 1898 were James A. Herne and William Gillette. Both combined acting with playwriting.

Moody's writing plans were moving forward only slowly. He kept doggedly at work on his edition of Milton, and he worked on *The Masque of Judgment* as time permitted. But the time was all too brief. By the end of June, Moody was back in Chicago to spend the remainder of the year teaching.

Moody's sense of drudgery in teaching was maintained by impersonality and relieved by wit. Conscientiously, Moody fulfilled his responsibilities.[9] But his responses were characteristically excessive—the seething tensions of Moody's letters from Chicago are in marked contrast to the detached calm of his exterior personality. Rebellions of such strength as his against teaching required a countervailing resignation that shows its sharp edges in his emphasis on form and order, in the elaborate corrections in red ink Lovett noticed on student papers, and in the Job-like patience with which he met his students.[10] His students considered Moody's boredom a patient, sweet boredom, and they found no trace in his manner of impatience or exasperation.

Yet the establishment of a larger social life by the late nineties helped make life in Chicago bearable.[11] The return of the Lovetts after two years abroad helped considerably. And, in reaction against "the sterility" of the social soil, Herrick was prime mover in the creation of a dining club, The Windbag. Moody, Lovett, Schevill, Herrick, Adolph Miller, a political economist, and John M. Manly, newly arrived head of the English department, began meeting about every two weeks at members' homes for an evening of talk.[12] Or they would gather at Laubesheimer's Beer Garden, joined by Frank Tarbell and others, for afternoons of beer, food, and conversation. In the meetings of The Windbag, shop talk was outlawed to provide occasion for meeting on broader human and cultural grounds than day-to-day university business provided.[13] Moody was meeting more Chicagoans interested in literature and the arts, and small gatherings frequented by writers and artists occasionally attracted him. Of Chicago groups, the Little Room has become the best known and may serve as an example of one dimension of Moody's Chicago life. On Friday afternoons Ralph Clarkson's studio served as an informal meeting place for artists, journalists, writers, and others, who gathered around the samovar to talk and drink tea which was sometimes laced with rum. In such gatherings, Moody was meeting Hamlin Garland, Henry B. Fuller, *Dial* Editor William Morton Payne, and Harriet Monroe, among others.[14]

In addition to teaching a new course in Renaissance drama in the fall, Moody was working on his edition of Milton's poems. By December he had finished it. A major project, the book had engaged much of Moody's time for a year and a half. In addition to full introductions, textual work, and annotation, new prose translations of the Latin poems had been made. The critique of Milton's work, presented in the introductions, is a young man's critique. Moody deplores Milton's movement from youthful "idyllicism" to the "polemic sternness" of mid-career, finding the later Milton "gathering intensity and losing beauty." [15] He prefers the early poems, the sonnets, and *Samson* to Milton's epic poems, feeling that the former works "rest on more permanent human foundations" [16] than *Paradise Lost* and *Paradise Regained*. Of Moody's more specific interests and judgments, three can be identified as significant to his own work. Moody de-emphasizes Milton's theological position, preferring to focus on the formal skill with which Milton combined his materials. In treating "Lycidas," Moody stands in awe of the "wizardry" of the poet's imagination, listing the range of the materials —a range similar to that with which Moody himself was working in the masque. The treatment of "Comus" takes a similar course, and Moody notes "the peculiar fitness of the masque form for the conveyance of moral and philosophic truth." [17] A second interest may be found in Moody's comments on Milton's drama. He approves of the poet's disregard for problems of staging. Milton, he observes, moved beyond Ben Jonson to establish clearly the supremacy of the poet over "the musician and stage carpenter." And, commenting on *Samson*, Moody notes Milton's freedom from the "restrictions of the stage," identifying Milton's form as "epical drama." The Attendant Spirit and Sabrina in "Comus" served, Moody felt, "to enrich the arabesque of spectacle, to increase the opportunities for lyric embellishment, and to deepen the philosophic symbolism of the poem." [18] The views were to determine the nature of Moody's own earliest venture in the poetic drama.

The most interesting comments of many that Moody makes on rhythm and language come in treatments of "Lycidas" and *Samson*. He was struck by Milton's ability in "Lycidas" to prolong a single rhyme sound through a passage by means of near echoes. And he admired the poet's ability to create momentary dissonances in the flow. Moody was to experiment further with both effects in "Song-Flower and Poppy" and "The Daguerreotype." Particular attention given to the musical variety in *Samson* was also significant to the development of Moody's verse during the next few years. Moody cites approvingly Robert Bridges's work on the rhythms of *Samson*, identifying particular concerns of his own. Of interest were Milton's manipulation of line length, his use of feminine lines to reinforce moods of lassitude, his imaginative rhyme ("he lets it creep in, flicker lambently for a moment, then disappear, only to return again with the same faint-hearted insistence"), the ignoring of metric line by phrase and sentence structure, and the variation won "by preserving the fiction of the iambic iteration, and syncopating upon it intermittent half-lyric strains, which rise above the norm with a certain effort and sink back into it with relief." [19]

Moody had the casual opportunity to comment on another poet in December. Copeland and Day finally published Josephine's first volume, *The Wayfarers*. Moody wrote, expressing his delight with the book, finding that it justified his old enthusiasm. Yet the generous praise was tempered by Moody's old reservations. "Some things, which seemed to me less mature and less forthright," he wrote, "I could have wished away; and others I could have wished a little nearer to the everyday speech; but even for these the *Envoi* made *amende honorable*." [20] In her "Envoi," Josephine had written of her desire "to speak a common tongue," complaining, "Yet oftentimes, indeed, I seem/ To dream;—to dream. . . ." And she pleaded,

> Ah, Beautiful, be mild to teach
> This newcomer the household speech;
> So I some day with better grace
> May take the bounty of the place.

A fragile poetry of ideal dream and vision dominates the collection. Moody wrote that he hoped she would now "take hold of the common experience and the common idiom and glorify it [*sic*]." Confronted by Josephine's volume, against which he could only place his work as editor of Milton, Moody felt his deficiency and suggested that he was hardly one to offer advice. He closed his letter in melancholy: "I am one who has loved the Muses well, and hoped much from my friends, however I may seem to have forgotten both the one and the other."

The challenge inclined Moody more to activity than to idle nostalgia, however. He had made arrangements for alternating six months of teaching with six of writing, and by early January he was back in New York at work. He put his masque aside and returned to his plan for the play which was to become *The Faith Healer*. Moody's charge to Josephine to "take hold of the common experience and the common idiom" reflected his own determination. By mid-January he had made enough progress to write Mason of the new play:

It bids fair to be short (perhaps fifty minutes to an hour to act) but it's developing pretty well. I found myself embarrassed a good deal at first by the dull monochromatic medium of everyday speech, but am getting more used to it now and find that when you do get an effect in it it is more flooring than anything to be got with bright pigments. I am trying hard to give it scenic structure, for as I conceive it nearly half of it will be dumb show; at least a great deal of its effectiveness will depend on the acting.[21]

Clearly the play was to be totally different from anything Moody had done.

The first of a number of versions of *The Faith Healer* was in draft by February.[22] Moody had been working to construct a situation with a basis in psychological conflict, using the bare news reports on the disappearance of the New Mexico Messiah.[23] Sensitive to tensions of spirit and flesh, Moody put his faith healer, Schlatter, in a situation which set the call of human love against his divine call. Schlatter falls in love with a girl—Maggie in this version, later Rhoda—and a choice must be made. The healer chooses his spiritual mission, feeling it involves austere rejection of all human commitments. Schlatter leaves at the play's end, and Maggie goes back to her work. At least one problem in finishing the play rises from the significance of the issues to Moody's life. His view of the evil effects of domestic love had changed little from that expressed in "Wilding Flower." Nor had his work on Milton's life convinced him that he was wrong.[24] His own dedication was to poetry as a form of spiritual life, and he was sure that even a passionate involvement was inimical to it. He had come to this position in his relationships with both Grace Hurd and Josephine Peabody. Through idealization and withdrawal Moody guarded against the possibility of more mundane involvements while protecting a tenuous spiritual friendship. At the same time, he had explored imaginative and theoretical resolutions of his dilemma in such poems as "Ethics in a Gondola."

Mason visited for a week in February, and afternoons and evenings were spent roaming the city. Mason had tracked Edwin Arlington Robinson to the Harvard office in which Robinson began clerking in

January. He had become interested in Robinson's poetry and lost no
time in introducing him to Savage and Josephine in Boston. Moody
had seen none of Robinson's work but was eager to meet him.[25] Mason
brought the two poets together in New York. They saw enough of
each other to sense the value of a friendship. Moody talked of his
masque and play, and Robinson of *Captain Craig*, which was nearing
completion. Involved in his very different work, Robinson was thrown
off by the scheme of the masque and its eccentric, eclectic materials.
He was committed to "the breathing realities of common life" and felt
this was Moody's appropriate subject matter as well.[26] Perhaps thinking
of his own *Captain Craig*, Robinson told Moody he thought the
masque would be Moody's means of making his own poetical acquaintance rather than anything he would ultimately care about.[27] He was
at least half right. But Moody was hardly prepared to take the long
view of a work he was struggling with.

The confrontation of the two men who ushered American poetry
into the twentieth century affords an interesting contrast in personality
and dedication.[28] Born in the same year, both poets were soon to be
thirty, and there was impressive talent and high ambition on both
sides. Although Moody's home had dissolved in his teens with the
deaths of his parents, his emotional upheaval was very different from
the slow, grinding agony which marked for Robinson the disintegration
of his family in the nineties. Though given to a variety of moods,
Moody tended to meditation, broken by bursts of spontaneous exuberance when among friends. Robinson was usually quiet and generally
self-conscious.[29] Moody's attraction was to the grand and dramatic in
life, while Robinson responded to the potential misery and the quiet
ironies of human experience. These differences in personality permeate
their early poetic practice. Where Robinson understated, Moody overstated. Where Robinson found pathos or irony, Moody found passion or
rich sensuous materials. Where Robinson often relied on rhetoric in
structuring a poem, Moody relied on turns of mood or symbolic development.

Robinson had been as prolific as Moody—even more so—and had
more clearly identified the directions his best work was to take. He had
published two volumes: *The Torrent and the Night Before* (1896)
and *The Children of the Night* (1897), an expansion of the earlier
collection. The volumes give evidence of the community of interest
on which the friendship of the two poets rested in spite of vast differences in temperament. In them one finds the familiar ballades and
sonnets of the late Victorians, the occasional *fin-de-siècle* mood, some
use of Pre-Raphaelite symbolism, sharp tonal contrast, syntactical in-
versions, an addiction to the adjective, and a reliance on rhetoric rather

than image. There is often use of themes popular in the nineties. In "The Night Before," Robinson, somewhat unexpectedly, writes a passionate monologue. Other poems indicate his attraction to the large cultural syntheses of Herbert Spencer and his tendency to mysticism and idealism. Yet the strength of Robinson's early volumes is to be found in those poems which strike out in a new direction and indicate that he was finding the voice that most twentieth-century readers associate with him. He had already written a number of his best short poems in the nineties, a group including "The Clerks," "Richard Cory," "Cliff Klingenhagen," and "Zola." If he shared the curse of the nineties, Robinson was breaking his own path. The problem and Robinson's clear answer in "the courage to be where we are" are caught in an "Octave" he wrote in the nineties:

> We lack the courage to be where we are: —
> We love too much to travel on old roads,
> To triumph on old fields; we love too much
> To consecrate the magic of dead things,
> And yieldingly to linger by old walls
> Of ruin, where the ruinous moonlight
> That sheds a lying glory on old stones
> Befriends us with a wizard's enmity.[30]

In theory, if not in temperament and inclination, Will Moody was prepared to agree. And his growing interest in psychological problems together with his work in "the dull monochromatic medium of everyday speech" in *The Faith Healer* indicate his readiness to recognize Robinson's achievements. But he was not ready to seize upon either interest as the key to his own development.

2

In February Moody was dropping in at The Players, dining with friends, and savoring the range of New York life. His extensive excursions into the city both exalted and appalled the poet. Of one particularly strong impression Moody wrote Mason,

The valleys with their lights and business are tempting when night sets in, and too often betray me downward. My last excursion (from which I had not recovered when your letter came) was a horrible debacle of which only weeks of sober living will wash away the sordid recollections. However I am not sure that I want them washed away just yet, until I have got from them their grim lesson of pity for the spiritual castaways on this appalling globe.[31]

The strong and immediate social concern expressed here was coupled with a growing sense of the human debts Moody owed his friends. He thanked Mason for the "candour and spiritual grace" his friendship represented.

In this context of concern Moody had reworked the experience of his visit to Assisi in 1897 to achieve a major poem, "Song-Flower and Poppy," which treats largely of issues central to his life. In "Jetsam" the conflict introduced by the city environment heightened tensions and established motive, but it was rejected in favor of mystical union with the antithetical world of ideal beauty. Here the city becomes an element in a resolution that is philosophically more mature. In the first section, "In New York," the poet embarks on revery, stimulated by the song of a young Italian street singer. The voice is that of the casual, educated Easterner: "He plays the deuce with my writing time,/ For the penny my sixth-floor neighbor throws." The poet seeks the source of the street song: "Where did the boy find such a strain/ To make a dead heart beat?" Memory moves from Tuscany to Umbria, to Sorrento, to Venice, to the Dolomites, and to Tyrrhene vineyards before it stops at the portals of Assisi. Moody sets the suggestive landscape of memory against a vision of the city streets, and the message of the boy's song of life and love against the shouted headlines of New York's newsboys. The latter speak of time's repetitious cycle, fulfillment only of the planet's "gross destiny." The city's song is one of lust. It is "Too base of mood, too harsh of blood,/ . . . Too hungry after dust!" The poet turns to commit himself to the "song-flower" of the Italian street singer:

> O hark! how it blooms in the falling dark,
> That flower of mystical yearning song:
> Sad as a hermit thrush, as a lark
> Uplifted, glad, and strong.
> Heart, we have chosen the better part!
> Save sacred love and sacred art
> Nothing is good for long.

In the second part of the poem, "At Assisi," Moody returns to the experience of his Italian journey, referred to in the opening section of the poem. Here the bloom of a poppy on the hill flaunts the creed of St. Francis. It grows beside the walls of the church which medieval vision built. The poet develops the theme of death suggested earlier—

the death at the core of the city's vision of time is basic to the ascetic Christian position. Allusion is made to "the dead men" waiting at the Tiber's mouth in Dante's *Divine Comedy*. But Dante is a poet of the dead, and St. Francis too is death's representative, not life's:

> Gently he seems to welcome me:
> Knows he not I am quick, and he
> Is dead, and priest of the dead?

Turning back from the church to the poppies on the hillside, the poet rejects the vision of total spiritualization of life, as he had earlier rejected the modern city's mundane orientation:

> Too purged of earth's good glee and strife,
> Too drained of the honied lusts of life,
> Was the peace these old saints won!

Moody's treatment of Christianity is strikingly similar to that Wallace Stevens would later present in such poems as "Sunday Morning." In both sections of his poem there is curious metamorphosis as Moody reverses his contrasting sets of values. The suggested identification of the rose—the boy's "song-flower"—and the poppy anticipates the larger synthesis to which Moody reaches in the concluding stanzas:

> St. Francis sleeps upon his hill,
> And a poppy flower laughs down his creed;
> Triumphant light her petals spill,
> His shrines are dim indeed.
> Men build and plan, but the soul of man,
> Coming with haughty eyes to scan,
> Feels richer, wilder need.
>
> How long, old builder Time, wilt bide
> Till at thy thrilling word
> Life's crimson pride shall have to bride
> The spirit's white accord,
> Within that gate of good estate
> Which thou must build us soon or late,
> Hoar workman of the Lord?

The poem ends suspended in question, as Moody probes the dream of a synthesis of his conflicting value systems to be fulfilled in time through creative evolution. The major philosophical issue of Moody's later poetry has been raised.

Hints of Moody's creative method are present in the poem. The line, "Sunset crumbles, ragged, dire," which picks up the earlier line, "A rag of sunset crumbles grey," draws on a phrase from Moody's letter of 1896 to Mason—the letter which describes skating with a young girl in Chicago.[32] That experience was moving subterraneously in this poem. References to the city with its valleys of lights and its sordidness derive from the same context as Moody's comments to Mason in the letter of late February quoted above. The song-flower "blows like a rose by the iron wall/ Of the city loud and strong"—a merging of references in a passage of the journal of Moody's trip to Italy. He had contemplated the possible existence of a young poet "behind those old walls of Tarifa," asking, "Does the clay of his body not blossom mystically into soul beholding the sun come out of the East scattering impulses?" And he thought of his own youth. Without such a song-flower, he continued, "I would not give the iron mills, the muddy river, the common-place streets of New Albany, Indiana, for all the Alhambras and Vallombrosas in Christendom."[33] The combination of the blossom and the perplexing "iron walls" reference of the poem reaches through this entry to Moody's memory of the Ohio Falls Iron Works—his father's place of business—and of his youth in an ugly town. New Albany and Chicago stand behind the New York of the poem, as Moody's sense of his boyhood and the budding charm of a young Irish girl stand behind the song of the street singer.

Late in February Lewis Gates arrived in New York on his way to Europe. To Mason, Moody wrote, "I shall keep him from his narcotic —Europe—as long as I can manage it."[34] But the narcotic was Moody's as well, and the lure of Europe proved too strong. The Milton proofs were done and Moody could work on the masque anywhere. On March 11 Moody sailed on the S.S. *Mesaba* for London. London was active socially and culturally, and Gates drew Moody into the streams of the city's life. In spite of the distractions, however, Moody kept on writing—the masque doubled in length between January and the end of May. On May 18 he wrote Mason, announcing, "The Masque is done, all but the finishing touches and one song which won't get itself written."[35] The statement proved to be premature: the masque was to more than double again in size by the end of the year.

Moody's work selecting and revising his early poems for publication was agonizing. So much had Moody's taste and concerns altered since his Harvard years that he was torn between desire for a book and dissatisfaction with much of the poetry needed to bulk it out.[36] In preparation for the volume, Moody returned to "Jetsam" for major deletions and addition. He cut twenty-four lines and inserted a new section of fifty-two lines.[37] His addition makes of the poem a clearer self-interpreting lyric at some expense to the dramatic tension. In it the speaker of the poem declares that there are nobler ways than his *Liebestod* to achieve redemption: participation in God's strenuous battle of life, increase of wisdom through practice of love's "austerities," and "ripening of the blood in the weekday sun/ To make the full-orbed consecrated fruit." His own celebration of love, the speaker realizes, is not a mature offering. He has "stripped the boughs to make an April gaud." But he declares his "is not the failure God deplores," and he moves again toward his death in the moonlit waters. Moody's interpolation differs in tone from the rest of the poem and significantly alters our sense of the speaker's state of mind. His act is turned into a defensive, willfully self-conscious suicide. Moody has set his own changing values in clearer perspective, but the earlier version functions effectively in terms of its psychological consistency and its symbolic structure. If we linger too long over the interpolated passage, we wonder why the young man—so clear-headed about values—doesn't turn around and seek a riper life under the sun, as Moody indeed had done.

Toward the end of May, Moody left London to spend three weeks with Trumbull Stickney in Paris. With Stickney he strolled the streets and gardens of Paris, talked poetry in the sidewalk cafes, sampled the French theatre, and dropped in on Mrs. Toy, who was touring on the Continent.[38] But Moody's time was limited, for he had to return to Chicago for the summer term. In mid-June he was on his way back to New York. On the boat he received a telegram from Mason announcing Philip Henry Savage's sudden death. It was the first of the premature deaths in Moody's circle of poet friends. In the following decade death was to take Stickney, George Cabot Lodge, and finally Moody himself. Moody arrived in the United States to find his Milton edition in print and his "Road-Hymn" in the June issue of the *Atlantic*. He had assembled the poems for his volume and submitted them to Macmillan on his way through New York.[39] No record of the contents of the submitted volume remains, but it is not difficult to reconstruct. Moody had completed *The Masque of Judgment* to his satisfaction in Europe. To it he added the poems written since 1895, together with that small group of Harvard poems [40] which still seemed satisfactory. Such a volume, bulked out by the long title piece would have provided the conventional first volume of the nineties: *The Masque of Judgment, and Other Poems*. Moody had stripped his work of juvenilia and he aimed high in the choice of a first publisher. He was hopeful, but Macmillan sent word in late summer that it could not accept the volume for publication.

Moody took up his life in Chicago in July 1899 under the slower pace of the summer term. He returned to his old room with the Herricks, The Windbag met occasionally for an evening of conversation, and Moody frequented the Quadrangle Club, a faculty club where he could join friends for afternoon tea, billiards, and talk. There were cycling and walking excursions, and Moody was playing tennis and indulging in an occasional day of sailing on Lake Michigan. On the warm nights of Chicago's summer and early fall, Moody often set out on the long solitary walks through the city streets or along the lake that had become habitual. He sometimes slept out under the stars on the lake shore or in one of the parks, to be awakened by the sunrise over the lake. Casual about his nocturnal habits, he was often to be seen crossing the campus in the early morning with clothes and hair disheveled after a night out. Moody's stance as a poet, his minor extravagances of dress, the mysteries of his personality and his manner, all combined with his nightly wanderings to create gossip in the tight academic community. He gained a local reputation in conventional faculty circles as a Bohemian.[41]

Notice of the rejection of his volume of poems was discouraging, but little of Moody's reaction surfaced in the emotional upheaval that might have been expected. As an important sign of his new temper, Moody did not turn to Mason or to Josephine for comfort and reassurance. Instead he wrote Edwin Arlington Robinson. His respect for Robinson as a poet was high, and Moody had sampled the direct honesty of Robinson's unsugared criticism and comment. In writing, Moody sought the objectivity and clarity he felt his new friend would be able to offer. Moody's strange masque had been the major problem of the rejected volume, and he needed a new perspective. Moody had altered radically since his Harvard years, yet his closest friends and critics had not changed with him. He was finding limitations in the delicate sensitivity of Josephine Peabody, the youthful idealism of Mason, and the subtle but idiosyncratic impressionism of Lewis Gates. Not that Moody was prepared to do an abrupt about-face. But he was increasingly unhappy with himself. Continuing a discussion with Robinson that had already become intimate, Moody wrote,

I'm afraid you're not quite sincere. You know perfectly that your talk on the subject of "excessive self-respect" and the related problems of my particular life, was not in the least damn-fool. I know it too, and my chagrin at not having sooner chosen the path of real courage, is only made tolerable by the increasing prospect of something like liberty in the future.[42]

Moody suggested the artist's real need was "one convinced and weariless *Laudator* (or Laudatress), with a silver trumpet," and he begged for a word from his new friend.

Robinson answered immediately, sensing Moody's need. His long letter is open, intimate, and characteristically ironical. He knew of Moody's masque only through conversation, but he did not approve of its eclectic materials. He now bluntly suggested that the work was an apprentice piece, a perhaps necessary stage in Moody's development. Yet he directed his major attention to Moody's state of mind, pouncing on Moody's desire for a *"Laudator."* Moody had wanted praise, not criticism, as his friends well knew. Robinson now dismissed the whole issue as ultimately irrelevant to the mature poet. He wrote that he had been patient and was prepared to be patient for as long as necessary. He referred to his own circle of laudators in Gardiner, Maine, but he observed that he knew "a damned sight better" than they did what his problems were. He left them to "hug their delusions," he wrote, and he kept on with his "bloody sweat." [43]

Robinson's clear-sighted stoicism offered Moody the example he needed, and early in September he plunged into work on the masque. He returned to the work with determination to clarify its movement and develop its themes. But there was further stimulus. In a new friend, Elaine Dupree, he found the laudator he was seeking. She admired the masque and had great faith in it. Under her encouragement and enthusiasm, Moody worked through the fall to revise the poem. The friendship grew in quality and depth, and the importance of Elaine Dupree's sympathetic appreciation is recorded in Moody's ultimate dedication of the work to her. [44]

Moody had sent Josephine Peabody a copy of his edition of Milton. She wrote in September [45] to praise the book, but Moody's disappointment over the rejected poems flashed out in abrupt bitterness in his response. As for her praise, he wrote that she "ought to keep it for something that counts." Moody had not kept Josephine informed of his progress on *The Masque of Judgment;* perhaps he felt it alien to her personality in its scale and its bold heresies. But in answer to a request for some view of his work, [46] Moody sent the newly completed "A Dialogue in Purgatory," [47] together with a solemn and oblique letter which treated the problems of their Fellowship. Both poem and letter rest on a common central reference to Dante.

Written in the stanza of "Good Friday Night," "A Dialogue in Purgatory" is a low-keyed exchange between two of Dante's figures, Buonconte da Montefeltro and la Pia. They wander in Purgatory with a group of spirits who postponed repentance only to die suddenly and violently. Both misplaced their love on earth, binding themselves to spouses who did not return their devotion. The experience has destroyed them spiritually, for their passion was unredeemed and unredeeming. In a series of long, quiet speeches, the pair discuss their situation. They long to know the rich joys of love Dante will feel when he meets Beatrice. La Pia blames her own hasty sensuality for her failure to mate under "The solemn influence" of transfiguring love; "The weak hand stretched abroad in haste/ For gifts barely allowed/ The tacit, strong, and proud." As the poem moves quietly to its end, the focus is on Dante's human compassion and on la Pia's pathetic attempt to picture the meeting of Dante and Beatrice. The most to which she can rise is the negative vision of a meeting unmarred by the shame which fills her soul. The tone is a sustained pathos, which rises from the hollow echoes of the stanzaic pattern and from the quiet contemplation of loss in the passionless limbo of lost souls. The gestures are those of futility. The speakers are caught in apathy and self-pity. The poem, sophisticated and well controlled, is yet another variation on Moody's obsessive theme: the problem of reconciling earthly love with high spiritual mission.

Moody's personal stake in the poem becomes clear in the context of the letter to Josephine which accompanied the poem.[48] They are curious companion pieces. Moody's poem serves as an *exemplum* for the discourse he delivers in his letter. In spite of the efforts a man and a woman may make "to meet and understand each other on a sane and quiet upland of reflection," Moody observes, the force of gravity works against them, "urging them back into the insane and tropical valleys of personal emotion, as imperiously as the beast of the slope before which Dante gave back." What hope is there for higher spiritual fulfillment? Only full knowledge of self and of each other. But this mutual understanding cannot be granted or is not in this world. In making this observation Moody moves to more personal terms of discussion. If all depends on "a shared education," he asks, what then will happen to love in a world "when education is never shared, when men and women are taught different standards and live almost in different worlds from the cradle up to—well, up to Radcliffe college and somewhat further!" In such a world the poet must go his way alone, serving the ideal and envisioning such fulfillment as that la Pia suggests for Virgil in "A Dialogue in Purgatory." It is a fulfillment which is

> more and less
> Than woman's near-felt tenderness,
> A million voices dim
> Praising him, praising him.

Such individual search, Moody continues, necessarily and tragically involves being cruel to lovers who cannot share the poet's experience,

values, and visions. He adds, "You will not call me vague if I speak
of this a little veiledly, for I cannot so much as think of these things
without wincing and crying out—alone and in the waste night." Not
until the end of the long letter does Moody write directly of his relation
to Josephine and his desire "not to tangle it, not to confuse it with the
immediate and the personal" which always led to confusion and regret.
He pleads, "Do not make me too fond of you, in the easy futile way:
keep me from playing the kind of hide and seek and forfeits that is
in the end dust and ashes."

Moody sent "A Dialogue in Purgatory" to the *Harvard Monthly,*
which published it in December. In addition, his work on *The Masque
of Judgment* was proceeding with the free expansiveness that had
characterized Moody's work on "Jetsam." By the end of the autumn he
had written all but some five hundred lines of his projected additions.
He saw that it would make a volume itself, but was pessimistic about
finding a publisher for the strange work. Moody's sense of his masque
and the fact that he submitted his poetic dialogue to the *Monthly* give
indication that he knew the limitations of his poetry. While it was not
unusual for a graduate to publish in the Harvard literary magazine—
Santayana and Stickney were still using it as their major outlet—
Moody had not submitted any work to it for five years. He had aimed
for the national magazines, but with scant success. The *Atlantic* had
taken two of his poems, but neither "Jetsam" nor "Song-Flower and
Poppy," both substantial works, had been accepted anywhere. Moody's
rejection slips were to turn him to new themes and a new manner in
the next few months.

During the fall Moody had been making a determined effort to
secure a long span of time for writing. In November he made plans
to write a history of English literature to be used in the high schools.
He described the financial arrangement for which he was negotiating
in a letter to Mason:

It will bring me in five hundred plunks on delivery and if successful ought
to constitute a source of permanent though small income. If these negotiations turn out all right, and I get the percentage of royalty for which I am
stickling, I am going to apply for as long a leave of absence as the authori-
ties will allow me, perhaps a year and a half, as I think I can pull through
that period on what I have saved or can easily earn.[49]

Lovett agreed to share the project with Moody. According to their
arrangements, Moody would do two-thirds of the work for a similar
amount of the proceeds.[50] Moody thought to complete the book in a
year of free time, spending mornings on his own writing and after-

noons on the history. The contract was arranged with Scribner's in mid-December, and Moody made additional commitments for two more texts in the Lake Classics series. At the end of the term he left Chicago for what was to be the whole of the year 1900.

Moody went to Boston and settled into a room at the Hermitage on Beacon Hill, where Dan Mason was staying. He was primed for work and began immediately to complete the masque. Though there was an occasional evening of music, of talk, or of the theatre, Boston offered few distractions Moody could not resist. He kept his distance from Cambridge social life. Mason found Moody, when he had the temerity to intrude, "in a cloud of tobacco smoke, threading a labyrinth of emendations, surrounded by the carnage of previous encounters— burnt matches, scattered ashes, and discarded sheets." [51] On January 25, after two and a half years of work with it, he was willing to call the masque finished. Moody did not return it to Macmillan, nor did he try another of the larger publishers. Accepting its eccentricity and limited appeal, he took it to Small, Maynard and Company, friend to so many of the slim volumes of Moody's acquaintances. He was fairly certain of a favorable reception there, and within a month the work was accepted for publication in the fall.

3

From the sketch Moody had written in the Dolomites in 1897, *The Masque of Judgment* had expanded to a long poetic drama with a prologue and five acts. Moody wrote Herrick in February, describing the final stages of his revision. "Since you heard it," he wrote, "I have taken out some of the fustian, inserted large strips of the best broad-cloth, and generally made it clearer and (I hope you will think) more dignified." [52] The basic thrust of the masque had not changed in the innumerable expansions it had undergone. In a statement for the publisher's use in publicizing the work,[53] Moody called it "a lyrical drama . . . partly in apology for the daring and even extravagant symbolism by means of which the allegory is worked out." It represented, he maintained, "a vindication of individual will and passion as a means of salvation, and a humanistic attack upon the teaching that salvation is attainable only through the renunciation of the will." The dramatic action represents Moody's *reductio ad absurdum* of the Christian apocalyptic vision. A faulty metaphysician, God commits suicide in Moody's ironic treatment of the destructive nirvana wish which Nietzsche found at the heart of Christianity.

Moody's knowledge of the work of his contemporaries and his

immediate predecessors offered occasional suggestions to him. Romantic readings of *Paradise Lost* are basic to the theology of the masque, and the impact of Blake is especially strong in the work's powerful symbolic lyrics. But the deepest influences on the structure and method are Wagner and Milton. The poet's earliest conception of the play had been expressed in Wagnerian terms: he thought of the masque as a "Hebrew Götterdämmerung." In fact, Moody turns Wagner's characters into Christian and Hebrew figures. His God, like Wotan, is annoyed by human opposition and desires peace above all; but he is caught in the coils of a larger fate. At the end of the play the Lamps of God huddle like Valkyries around the celestial throne, awaiting death. The human figures of the masque are naïve, natural men, composed of will and passion, like Wagner's Siegfried. They lack both fear and understanding. Part of the celestial hierarchy, Raphael rebels against full allegiance to the world of spirit because of his common sympathy for man and his love of nature. Like Wagner's Brünnhilde, Raphael knows that strife is basic to the life of God. Raphael's final philosophical position is that of Brünnhilde: love alone can bless.

Milton is even more central to the masque than Wagner. Moody had been seriously studying the implications of Bunyan's Puritanism in 1896, and his recent work on Milton had plunged him into theology. The intellectual purpose of his masque, Moody told Lovett, was to provide a counterstatement to Milton's grim view of the relation of God and man.[54] The ultimate expression of Milton's deplorable Calvinism came for Moody in the inhuman presentation of the Last Judgment near the end of "On the Morning of Christ's Nativity." The passage, Moody felt, was "magnificent and flawless" in its art [55] and repulsive in its theology. Milton depicts the "happy day" when "at last our bliss/ Full and perfect is," as that on which the race of mortal men is destroyed together with the beautiful and passionate human world shaped by Greek mythology. Moody could not accept the way in which Milton's theological position takes precedence over his haunting evocation of the sorrowing natural and human world. In *The Masque of Judgment* Moody responds to Milton in that poet's own terms. The masque looks to Miltonic example in the dignity of its language, its intricate metrical patterns, its scenic emphasis, and its careful weaving of mythological materials. Moody hoped for the sort of effect he associated with Milton's "Comus." Its plot, he felt, afforded "just a touch of the fantastic mythological element needed for scenic display, yet leaving the main interest of the piece to center upon the rich, serious poetry." [56] This conception of the drama, with its extravagant de-emphasis of the role of action and character, indicates the strength of Moody's lyric commitment.

The Prelude of *The Masque of Judgment* is set first at dawn near
the sea and later in a mountain glade at midnight. The first scene is a
monologue by Raphael, the heavenly bard, followed by his dialogue
with Uriel, angel of the sun and the play's most perceptive theologian.
Raphael questions the value of heavenly peace, weighed in the scale
against the joys and pain of human passion. But Uriel warns him
against sympathy for man, reminding him of the dependent status of
creation in a passage developed in terms of the vine and rose symbolism
which is basic to the play's structure:

> Heaven rose
> As if from sleep, and, lo, through all the void
> Clambered and curled creation like a vine,
> Hanging the dark with clusters of young bloom.
> Then from the viewless ever-folded heart
> Of the mystic Rose, stole breath and pulse of change.

Creation is seen as a result of necessary conflict in the mind of God,
who acted in a compulsive "demand of joy" and "necessity of grief."
Raphael muses over his pleasure in watching the slow processes of
nature evolve human life:

> The strife of ripening suns and withering moons,
> Marching of ice-floes, and the nameless wars
> Of monster races laboring to be man.

But Uriel reminds him of man's terrible restlessness and profane pride.
In scene 2 Raphael and a shepherd contemplate an action reminiscent
of Euripides' *The Bacchae:* raging bacchantes tear a young poet to
pieces. The action prefigures the crucifixion to come.

In act 1, singing a hymn to nature's plenitude, Raphael climbs to
the cliffs overlooking the Valley of Judgment. There in half-clouded
vision he catches sight of the Lion and Eagle of the throne returning
weary and broken from battle with the Worm in Hell's pit. Angels
of the White Horse, the Pale Horse, and the Red Horse appear to
guard the path to Heaven. In a second scene in the garden of Heaven,
the Angel of the White Horse, the Eagle, and the Lion consider the
battle they have fought. The Angel of the Tree of Knowledge suggests
to them that the Worm is not God's greatest foe, but rather "The
searching and the scornful heart of Man." Act 2 is the crucifixion,
God's final offer of reconciliation to those obedient men who will break
"the thyrsus and the phallic sign,/ Put off the ivy and the violet." The
act ends in a false glow of hope, for in act 3 the Day of Judgment has
arrived. The first scene is a long lyric in which Raphael declares his

fellowship with humanity. Moody identified the song as central to his play:

> Darkly, but oh, for good, for good,
> The spirit infinite
> Was throned upon the perishable blood; . . .
> Not in vain, not in vain,
> The spirit hath its sanguine stain,
> And from its senses five doth peer
> As a fawn from the green windows of a wood; . . .
> Dust unto dust complains,
> Dust laugheth out to dust,
> Sod unto sod moves fellowship,
> And the soul utters, as she must,
> Her meanings with a loose and carnal lip;
> But deep in her ambiguous eyes
> Forever shine and slip
> Quenchless expectancies,
> And in a far-off day she seems to put her trust.

A second scene, set above the Valley of Judgment, contrasts Raphael with Michael, a Calvinist among the heavenly hosts, who exults in the splendid display of God's power and justice. Uriel arrives to re-affirm the view that the world is part of God's being. God's essence is will, he maintains, strengthened by the individual expressions of will in his universe. Raphael agrees that God is destroying man "With suicidal hand."

Act 4 presents Michael and Raphael listening to the voices of condemned humans in the Valley. The voices speak arrogantly in praise of life, of joy in strife and battle, and of the ecstasies of love and hate. A final human speaker declares that God is jealous because of man's knowledge that he is himself a god—the position is Emersonian. At the end of the act "the enormous swinging head of the Serpent blots out the scene." But the Worm moves out of the pit in act 5 and upward toward the heavens. The destruction of Heaven and of both God and "the Serpent of his [God's] sorrow" is imminent. Earlier, Uriel had maintained that human passion should be curbed, not destroyed. Here at the play's end, Raphael utters a nostalgic wish that God had been courageous enough to work out his fate in terms of Hegelian evolutionary process:

> Would He had dared
> To nerve each member of his mighty frame—
> Man, beast, and tree, and all the shapes of will

> That dream their darling ends in clod and star—
> To everlasting conflict, wringing peace
> From struggle, and from struggle peace again,
> Higher and sweeter and more passionate
> With every danger passed! Would He had spared
> That dark Antagonist whose enmity
> Gave him rejoicing sinews.

And he reiterates Uriel's earlier position, declaring, "Passion is power,/ And, kindly tempered, saves." In these passages Moody has moved to a synthesis of passionate humanism with evolutionary theory to present a new Christian theological vision.

The Masque of Judgment reveals the youth of its author. It is exuberant, a riot of opulent effects of vision and sound, and heavy with philosophical speculation and argument. Moody borrows freely where he wishes, bringing echoes of a number of English and classical poets into his context. His style ranges widely and experimentally from blank verse steeped in Miltonic artifice, to the lighter irregular odes of Raphael, to a series of tight lyrics which intersperse the dialogue. The masque is youthful as well in ready presentation of a vision of cosmic absurdity. The ironic force of the drama was not entirely intentional. Moody's conception of the work and his development of it through successive expansions made it less a progressive sequence of events than a gradual circling and elaboration of a static conception and situation. The play's thrust—the destruction of the Puritan ethic at the core of its legalistic, narrowly inhuman vision—resembles the moral disorientation at the base of absurd theatre. Powerful cosmic ironies build, as a limited, unseen God works out the terms of his suicide. And the masque's intellectuals, Raphael, Michael, and Uriel, discuss God's problems and errors down to the very edge of doom. But these effects are a deep function of Moody's lyrical orientation to the drama, his method of developing the work, and his own complex personality. They do not represent his reasoned intention. The masque merges the two sides of Moody's "double-vision": his sense of life's absurdity—usually reserved for his conversations and his letters to friends—expresses itself here in a powerful dramatic action which overwhelms the affirmation he more consciously sought. Moody was soon to be forced into elaborate defenses of the work's motives for his astonished friends.

CHAPTER 6 BILLIARD- WORK WITH THE WESTERN WORLD

MOODY'S ART had its roots in an intensely personal development of midwestern Protestant mysticism, the energies of which had been turned into literary channels in his young manhood. His egocentric, self-dramatizing genius had flowered in the luxuriant hothouse of *fin-de-siècle* art. He had cultivated the heights and depths of his moods as the source and essence of poetry—his environment was a personal landscape of powerful emotional conflicts. External stimuli were found in the literary materials accessible to his sensibility and in the imaginative provocations he sought out in Europe. In one sense Moody's romanticism, which combined the passion of private experience with an experimental eclecticism, resembles that of the young poet of any time and place. Yet its particular configuration—both in terms of the nature of Moody's private experience and of the traditions to which he turned —carried the distinguishing marks of his period. In further development of twentieth-century poetry, romantic internalization of a "personal tradition," selected with conscious care, has been a dominant characteristic.

The particular growth of Will Moody as a young man and poet was in many ways a narrow and restricting one. His stance had been one variety of the humanistic defensive reaction of the educated, middle-class Anglo-Saxon in the nineties. The pose struck by Matthew Arnold in the preceding generation had narrowed to a more restricted aesthetic rebellion against the massing technology as well as the moral posture of the Philistine in America. From the aestheticism of the early nineties, Moody had moved to an ethic that was basically the same as his society's, if directed to different ends. It can best be characterized as an ethic of intensity. Moody's habitual tendency to excess is a reflection of the ethic. Spiritual and emotional energies were compressed for more powerful response. Whether Moody was writing, climbing, cycling, tramping, or traveling, intensity was the goal and the guide for final evaluation. Moody's strenuous aestheticism finds its parallels in the energetic stances of Teddy Roosevelt, of America's "Captains of Industry," of the muckrakers, the tough-minded Social Darwinians, and the Nietzscheans. Henry and Brooks Adams's preoccupation with acceleration of force in history finds a counterpart in Raphael's vision of an ideal progression of spiritual and emotional intensities through human and divine history: God moves from struggle to peace to struggle, "Higher and sweeter and more passionate/ With every danger passed!" [1]

Such an ethic and aesthetic was clearly not without its grave limitations. It was too much a hasty, semi-intuitive response in kind to the sources of its conflict. While the effect of a criterion of intensity for art may be found in much of Moody's work in the nineties, there were important concomitants in Moody's life. Demanding the concentration of a medieval saint, his dedication to art helped to sustain a personality which offered little outward sign of human warmth and sympathy. Moody tended to fierce egocentricity. He responded casually to the misfortunes of his friends, but demanded full sympathetic response from them. Moody's unpredictable approaches and withdrawals, his ranging moods, his shallowness as a social being—in short, what Robinson and Josephine called his "Temperament"—were aspects of Moody's central ethical-aesthetic stance. The personality had found full expression in Moody's letter of October 1899 to Josephine Peabody. There, Moody's high idealistic aim becomes the justification for inhumane action—indeed, service to such an aim would seem to preclude all of the usual human virtues. Moody's youth was surely a factor in his egocentricity, and the calling of artist—at least of romantic artist—may demand more self-absorption than most. But the resulting tendency to shallowness and a restricted range of interest in human experience could not fail to limit his early range as man and as writer.

There had been important signs of a change of direction in Moody's life and work which must balance the partial portrait sketched above and which point toward the new poems Moody was to write in 1900. As writer he had broken from the enchantment of remote modes of Victorian practice long before—in the personal, symbolic poem, "Jetsam," of 1895. Nor had he returned to his earlier modes— the break was complete and dramatic. [2] From that point on, Moody had found most of his poetic impetus in immediate experiences, primarily in those of the Italian trip of 1897. He had developed a poetry of greater impact by experimenting broadly with sound and rhythm, with vivid contrast in theme and motif, and with complex symbolic organization. From the flaccid narrative of the longer poems of the Harvard years, Moody had turned to forms of lyric meditation, developed dramatically and psychologically.

While Moody's art had gained in technical maturity, it had gained in human strength and relevance. His letter to Josephine itself represents struggle with problems of human relationship at a new depth of sympathetic awareness, and Moody's most recent poems—"Song-Flower and Poppy" and "A Dialogue in Purgatory"—show increasing human concern. Most important, completion of his masque had helped Moody find a new voice. Wrestling with the work, he was confronting problems which were at once deeply personal and, in their intellectual formulations, central to his period. On both levels—the personal and psychological or the social and intellectual—*The Masque of Judgment* represents a first major stage of the mature poet's work with the issues central to his artistic life. While Moody relished the ironic suicide of God the father in the masque, he rose to the clarity, variety, and power of Raphael's fully achieved, if passive, commitment to life in nature and to human passion. Raphael's redefinition of his divine mission— his choice of role as spokesman for man, not God—represents a reinterpretation for Moody of the poet's task.

With the masque's completion Moody turned to new work. There was, of course, the long-term project to which he had committed himself in December. Moody immediately began work on the *History of English Literature*. By agreement with Lovett, the early literature and Chaucer fell to Moody, together with English drama, Shakespeare, and Milton. Lovett was to do the nondramatic literature of the Renaissance, much of Restoration and eighteenth-century literature, and the novel.[3] Moody began work on the Anglo-Saxon and Middle English periods in the Harvard library, brushing up his rusty skills in the language. In addition, Moody was completing two of the editing projects with which he had been supplementing his income. He edited Scott's *The Lady of the Lake,* and he wrote the introduction to a volume of selections of Pope's translation of *The Iliad.*

But the poet carefully balanced his work on the history with his writing of poetry. He picked up an idea that had struck him two and a half years earlier in Europe. Lovett's Boston *Weekly Transcript* of June 4, 1897, had described ceremonies held in conjunction with Memorial Day to mark the unveiling of Augustus St. Gaudens's monument to Colonel Robert Gould Shaw and his men. The sculpture stands on the Boston Common. Colonel of the first enlisted Negro regiment of the Civil War, Shaw had fallen, together with many of the men he led, in a charge on Fort Wagner, South Carolina. The

news account summarized a speech William James gave at the dedication. Fresh from completion of "Good Friday Night" in 1897,
Moody had been struck by the theme of brotherhood, emphasized
strongly in James's treatment of the event. Living a few blocks from
the Shaw Memorial, Moody began his "Ode in Time of Hesitation."

The issues of the Civil War had once again come alive in the
political contexts of 1900. Many had seen the Spanish-American War
as an idealistic protest against the corruption of Spanish imperialism.
Cuba and the Philippines had been liberated. But American troops
were still in Cuba, and Philippine fighters had turned to give battle
to their American liberators. The headlines of 1899 and early 1900
were filled with news of the fighting in the islands. There were appeals
for recognition of Philippine independence, reports of the barbarity
of American soldiers, and complaints of news correspondents about
censorship of their reports. Arguments for America's "Manifest Destiny" and annexation of the territories were strong. In response, an
Anti-Imperialist League had been formed, and it gained wide support
in both Chicago and Boston. In Chicago there were rallies in the
spring and fall of 1899, supported by most of Moody's friends—Paul
Shorey, William Morton Payne, and H. B. Fuller had publicly urged
attendance at one of them. William Jennings Bryan, who had roused
Moody's attention in 1896, spoke out against expansionism. Andrew
Carnegie supported the League, and Senator Hoar of Massachusetts
was an energetic spokesman against imperialism. A large contingent
of Harvard faculty, headed by President Eliot and William James,
ranged themselves on the side of the League.[4]

By late March Moody had finished his poem. He sent it to the
Atlantic, and Bliss Perry, the editor, accepted it for publication in the
May number. It was a first and dramatic indication of the fresh directions Moody's work was taking. For "An Ode in Time of Hesitation"
Moody drew on native traditions of the public poem as it had been
written by Lowell, Whittier, and Whitman. The ode's simple, direct
appeal to a single moral issue resembles Whittier's method. A sweeping
American panorama early in the poem, together with its celebration
of brotherhood and of the American soldier, recalls Walt Whitman.
And Moody follows Whitman's formal example in "When Lilacs Last
in the Dooryard Bloom'd," writing a public poem in the form of a
personal meditation.

The ode's nine sections vary in mood, building to a point near
the end of section 7 at which the speaker assumes the voice of the
American people. The psychological base is the set of attitudes and
values basic to the nineteenth-century genteel tradition. The approach
to causes and issues of American wars is single-mindedly moral, and

the speaker accepts "the white man's burden." He is a naïve patriot, assured through most of the ode of the moral impeccability of the nation's foreign involvements. Moody's handling of the dying tradition of the American public ode is distinguished by his subtle psychological development of the speaker's change of position, and by his treatment of theme in terms of rebirth ritual. The land is stirring to the rites of oncoming spring; war is presented in terms of a heightened rebirth cycle in which "infernal flowerage bloomed,/ Bloomed, burst, and scattered down its deadly seed. . . ." Shaw himself is described in terms appropriate to a god, and the American war dead are seen as victims sacrificed to a high ideal of national democratic purpose, sanctified by nature's processes:

> Now limb doth mingle with dissolvèd limb
> In nature's busy old democracy
> To flush the mountain laurel when she blows
> Sweet by the southern sea,
> And heart with crumbled heart climbs in the rose: —
> The untaught hearts with the high heart that knew
> This mountain fortress for no earthly hold
> Of temporal quarrel, but the bastion old
> Of spiritual wrong. . . .

The sacrifice becomes meaningful only in terms of the ritual love and rededication of the American people and their leaders to these men slain in spiritual warfare and to their ideals. The central motivation is established when the patriotic speaker asks, as he considers the ominous aftermath of the Spanish-American War,

> Must I be humble, then,
> Now when my heart hath need of pride?
> Wild love falls on me from these sculptured men;
> By loving much the land for which they died
> I would be justified.

The patriot moves through a series of denials and evasions of the issue, calling up past heroism as a defensive guarantee of similar motivation in the national leaders of his own time. Finally, however, he must confront the signs of moral turpitude in American leaders. In section 8 of the ode, the patriot turns to view the issues in their ironic perspective. He plays with possible metamorphosis of the "eagle nation Milton saw/ Mewing its mighty youth":

> Have we but the talons and the maw,
> And for the abject likeness of our heart
> Shall some less lordly bird be set apart? —
> Some gross-billed wader where the swamps are fat?
> Some gorger in the sun? Some prowler with the bat?

The patriot concludes, addressing the nation's leaders in the name of the American dead on San Juan Hill, charging them to remain true to the high moral cause. The people, he suggests, will rise to punish leaders who insult their ideals. Moody avoids flatulence by the psychological subtlety in which his conventional motif is developed: the outraged response will be that of a greedy people in an anguished fit of self-hatred, who will turn their anger and pain on their leader-scapegoats.

The speaker's shift in position embodies something of Moody's own increasing political awareness. Yet the poem's speaker is deliberately created for maximal effectiveness. The poem is a carefully constructed occasional piece, with exaggerations of attitude and with oversimplifications appropriate to its condensed psychological movement. That Moody was operating in normative contexts appropriate to his audience is clear from the public response to the poem. His liberal and idealistic readers shared the values of the speaker, and the ode was to thrust Moody into the range of vision of a small but powerful audience of national scope.

Robinson had marveled over the way Moody had "of making laddered music spring skyward from prophets' pillows and other kinds of music do things in a way on which he seems to have the God-given bulge, so to speak." [5] But when he received news that Moody had written an ode, he was sceptical, doubting that anyone in 1900 could be serious in calling a poem an ode. The result, which he saw in the May *Atlantic*, pleased him. He wrote on May 3, calling the ode "a stunning piece of work," done "in the spirit of the new age." Robinson's objections were two. He wondered if Moody had "not done rather too much billiard-work with the western world." And he objected to breaches in the decorum of the piece: "In two or three places you may have gone a little too far out of your way in your apparent determination to be common-place where the subject matter would hardly warrant such excursions." [6] A week later, however, even these objections were overcome. He was impressed by the restraint and control of the poem, writing, "The poem is big; and—which is the most important thing in any work of art—it leaves the reader with a confident feeling that the writer has not blown himself empty in producing it." [7]

In the social circles of Boston and Cambridge, Moody was able to gain some sense of the larger impact his "Ode in Time of Hesitation" was making and would continue to make during the year. The poem's political position was clear; it was an attack on McKinley's foreign policy, and that policy had already aroused considerable opposition. This had been enough to make Bliss Perry, editor of the *Atlantic*, hesitant about publishing it in an election year. But he was convinced finally by the quality of the ode, which he felt was the finest American political poem in thirty years. The ode was, predictably, joyously received by the strong anti-imperialist circles of Cambridge and elsewhere. The Spanish-American War had failed to bring forth poetry of any significance. The ode burst into the vacuum, and its spirit appealed to deep-seated American political and social idealism, even in such politically sophisticated men as Oswald Garrison Villard, editor of the *New York Evening Post* and the *Nation,* who later remembered the sensation it created in newspaper offices around the country.[8] Senator Hoar began citing the ode in support of his anti-imperialist position, declaring it "the strongest utterance since Lowell's 'Ode to Freedom.' "[9] And in the summer, Moody's ode was collected in a volume of poems published by the Anti-Imperialist League, *Liberty Poems Inspired by the Crisis of 1898–1900.* Edmund Stedman in New York, like Bliss Perry, was finding much to admire in the ode simply as a poem. In the final stage of compiling his *An American Anthology,* Stedman decided to include a large portion of it in the section of poems by America's new, young voices.

2

Most of Will Moody's life through the spring, summer, and fall of 1900 was spent at his desk; his significant life during these months is that of the poems he was writing. A new poem of the late spring came out of Moody's bemused contemplation of the menagerie of Adam Forepaugh.[10] The menagerie was well known, appearing in Madison Square Garden and other major arenas of the nation in the early nineties. And Adam Forepaugh was a name to conjure with. The speaker of "The Menagerie" is a well-educated drunk. On leaving the menagerie tent, he is suddenly struck by his kinship with the circus animals. He explores the relationship, seeing nature "forever groping, testing, passing on" through time "To find at last the shape and soul of Man." By his theory of a progressive evolution, the circus animals are nature's "vagrant births;/ Sick dreams she had, fierce projects she essayed," in her search. The animals, however, do not recognize man's preeminence. "But why should they, her botch-work, turn about/ And

stare disdain at me, her finished job?" the unnerved human asks. And
he confronts the ironies of his theory:

> Helpless I stood among those awful cages;
> The beasts were walking loose, and I was bagged!
> I, I, last product of the toiling ages,
> Goal of heroic feet that never lagged,—
> A little man in trousers, slightly jagged.

The drunken gentleman moves to consideration of the striving soul
"in everything that squirms," the omnipresent "Mystical hanker after
something higher." He recircles the issue from this new perspective,
trying to explain the animals' unfavorable attitude toward him. He
decides the problem lies in their desire for "Perfect Man," concluding
that they might well gaze "with mixed emotions" on him as the result
of all their striving. The poem ends in three overly slick stanzas of
flippant advice: various menagerie patrons are urged to shun ironic
juxtaposition with their animal counterparts.

At one point in the poem, the speaker sees his situation as a
judgment, observing, "The Judgment-day will be a picnic" compared
to judgment by a jury of such beasts. The motif affords a provocative
glimpse of the workings of Moody's mind. Here issues of judgment
appearing in the masque and issues of justification central to the ode
arise again. And he has taken Raphael's central expression of faith in
creative struggle to create a playful "anti-masque." Moody was per-
vasively questioning his positions through a wide range of contexts and
voices. A version of "The Menagerie" earlier than the published one
is of interest.[11] Longer than the finished poem discussed above, it ends
in a group of stanzas which treats nature's continuing search for perfect
man in sober seriousness. In omitting them in favor of his flippant
ending, Moody was motivated by interest in consistency of tone and
voice in the poem. But the stanzas help define Moody's social and religious commitments in 1900. These four, of the six stanzas, are
central.

> Well, *sursum corda,* as the preacher saith;
> We seek him as they sought him; night and day
> We struggle towards him past defeat and death.
> We do it in our own eccentric way,
> For God has made us of a peevish clay; . . .
>
> Some say he has been with us: here and there
> Along the world's worn high-road travellers tell

Of meeting him, a lonely way-farer;
And books record some scattered words that fell.
Perhaps so; it is barely credible.

But what we wait for is no single head
Ringed with a sad estranging aureole
From some unearthly source of radiance shed,
No uncompanioned and peculiar soul
Bearing its tragic burden to the goal.

No, but a morning host, a light-heart band
Of equal comrades, lovers, laborers,
Each with his reaper's sickle in his hand
To reap where, in the fields of pleasant years,
To song and laughter drop the ripened ears.

The ideal of the "light-heart band," one which would reappear in the young men's song to Apollo which ends *The Fire-Bringer,* is a more specific and socially oriented one than that presented by Raphael. Moody has moved beyond "Good Friday Night" to explicit rejection of a peculiar savior suffering in solitude. The vision is presented in terms of a utopian socialism as the unreached goal of social evolution.

By June Moody had rewritten his play on the faith healer. A poem was the by-product of Moody's revision. He had been unhappy with the play in December, yet he wrote Mason that he saw something in his first version worth saving.[12] It was the core of a long monologue, "Until the Troubling of the Waters." The speaker is a woman who waits with her small son for the healer's appearance. The situation had been appropriate to Moody's early emphasis on the healer's dedication to his mission. But in a change consistent with his rapidly changing views Moody now reversed himself: the healer rejects his calling and chooses human love instead. To create his focus, Moody had to set the opening scene in the household in which the healer was staying and de-emphasize his relation to the crowd seeking healing.[13] Even more significantly, Moody rewrote the early, pageantlike lyrical drama in prose and in terms of conventions of the realistic drama.

The poem created by the revision shows Moody concerned, as Frost would be, with psychological problems arising in the context of a simple Protestantism which leaned to superstition and spiritualism. The diction and rhythms of the poem are colloquial, but heightened at points by lyricism. The woman is paralyzed by fear that her crippled boy will recognize his disability and ask her about it. Her conflict is expressed in verse, with a rhythmic movement new for Moody:

The bitterest thought
Of all that plagued me when he came was this,
How some day he would see the difference,
And drag himself to me with puzzled eyes
To ask me why it was. He would have been
Cruel enough to do it, knowing not
That was the question my rebellious heart
Cried over and over one whole year to God,
And got no answer and no help at all.
If he had asked me, what could I have said?

By a series of visions the woman is aroused to hope her son may be
made whole by a healer. An annunciation, not of birth but of rebirth
for her son, came through nature and pervaded the atmosphere of the
mill where she worked. Moody's treatment of her vision is bold, a
passage that was to influence Hart Crane:

And all day long the noises of the mill
Were spun upon a core of golden sound,
Half-spoken words and interrupted songs
Of blessed promise, meant for all the world,
But most for me, because I suffered most.
The shooting spindles, the smooth-humming wheels,
The rocking webs, seemed toiling to some end
Beneficent and human known to them,
And duly brought to pass in power and love.

The mother is possessive, fearing alteration of her relation with the boy,
but a fuller, creative love arises from her struggle with her selfishness,
and she sets out on a journey to the healer. It functions as a ritual
ordeal through which her love is purified. The poems ends where it
began, as the mother awaits the coming of the healer. The situation
is existential. The mother's last words are the cry of suffering mankind
awaiting a redeeming answer from beyond itself: "Christ, I believe;
pity my unbelief!" Moody ignores the mundane problem—ultimate
cure of the boy. But the poem is fully developed. The mother's relation
to her child has changed; a genuine love has been established through
ritual suffering. The poet has created a viable contemporary vehicle
for the quest motif which dominates his early poetry.

Moody completed three minor poems in the course of the summer.
As a result of the success of his ode he was asked to read a poem on the
one-hundred-twenty-fifth anniversary of Washington's assumption of
command of the colonial troops on Cambridge Common. He wrote an
"Anniversary Ode," which he delivered before the Independence Day

throng gathered for the occasion. The poem is in the form of rhymed oratory. A brief heroic treatment of the ideal of liberty introduces a long consideration of the meaning of that ideal in 1900. Why do we continue to mouth the word "liberty," the poet asks. "Is it a mummery we make so long?" After some debate, the nation's dedication to human liberty is seen as minimal, and memorial ceremonies look like humbug in the context of illiberal political action. The shade of a revolutionary hero asks, "Where do their armies march this year?/ For what cause do they fight?" Of America in 1900, Moody concludes, "We know that she has failed and gone astray,/ O let us win her back into the way!" Moody's views had not changed in three months; in anger and frustration his strategy had turned to directness of approach. But the occasion did not encourage memorable poetic utterance, and Moody did not collect the poem in later volumes of his work.

Other poems of the summer drew on Moody's experience in Gloucester. They were "Gloucester Moors" and "A Grey Day." In the first, tension arises from the juxtaposition of the poet's peaceful, fruitful life on land against the struggle of life on the sea. In clear strokes Moody develops a central conventional emblem: the earth is a ship at sea. The sun is "her masthead light," the moon "a pinnacle frail," and so on. The ship's captains lack all sense of social responsibility, and the hold is filled with slaves. The poet asks whether the ship's course is directed by chance or by human purpose. While the smaller sails of Gloucester make port and gain their human rewards in comfort and in love, the ship of society does not move toward fulfillments. The poem's fluid rhythms, its emblematic method, and its adoption of other familiar conventions of the tradition of the American public poem mark the strength of Moody's desire to establish contact with a larger, general audience than his poems of the nineties could reach. Ironically, this uncharacteristic poem has become Moody's best-known work! "A Grey Day" is interesting primarily for the ambivalence of Moody's view of human endeavor. The poem's center is its second stanza:

> Unreal as insects that appall
> A drunkard's peevish brain,
> O'er the grey deep the dories crawl,
> Four-legged, with rowers twain:
> Midgets and minims of the earth
> Across old ocean's vasty girth
> Toiling—heroic, comical!

Heroic or comical? The response moves to the ironic mode of twentieth-century sensibility. But Moody ignores the temptation to explore the paradox, ending the poem in a statement of wonder at the sources of will and patience in the human heart. As in "Gloucester Moors," which ends in a stanza of questions, Moody was consciously inviting the insights potential to approaches of the utmost simplicity. The poems represent a gesture toward a passivity and an objectivity new to Moody's practice but central to his earlier poetic theory.

In the course of the fall in Boston, Moody's creative energies remained at full tide and he completed several more poems. Basic to the Gloucester poems and to the set of stanzas rejected for "The Menagerie" is the poet's deepening but far from doctrinaire interest in utopian socialism. Socialism had attracted Dan Mason as well. Mason's concern, developing out of his interest in Royce's large human sympathy and Thoreau's sharp social and political criticism, had been roused by the gathering movements of American protest. Through the spring and summer, Moody and Mason had a number of serious discussions of the means of social reform. In the course of a discussion of Edward Carpenter, Mason had suggested he might give up his music, feeling that it was less needed than work against social injustice. But Moody argued that while many could work for reform, there were few men who could reveal the spiritual reality of an industrial society and give the world "not a syllogism, but a song." [14] The argument involved issues to appear in Moody's "The Brute."

In tone "The Brute" is energetic and irreverent, owing something to the spirit of Truman H. Bartlett, a sculptor and Whitman enthusiast with whom Moody had spent much of August. Moody returns to the example of Kipling for his driving rhythms, and short, jabbing lines of the stanza's opening give way to sinuous, flowing lines of seven or eight metrical feet. The poem opens with a description of the machine—the Brute which man has caged to work his will. The Brute feeds on the limbs and brains of men, the hearts of women, and the souls of children. He destroys the land, uprooting the old, the quiet, and the beautiful. To human hopes for freedom from enslavement the Brute answers:

> "On the strong and cunning few
> Cynic favors I will strew;
> I will stuff their maw with overplus until their spirit dies;
> From the patient and the low
> I will take the joys they know;
> They shall hunger after vanities and still an-hungered go.
> Madness shall be on the people, ghastly jealousies arise;
> Brother's blood shall cry on brother up the dead and empty skies."

He laughs and hugs himself at the thought of God's unhappiness with the chaos created in his world.

But the Brute is akin to the Worm in Moody's masque, and Raphael's positive theology in the masque is operative in this poem. Even as the Brute roars his curse, "a still small Voice" speaks of neo-Emersonian compensations at work. Moody's biblical reference brings into the poem parallels with Elijah's sojourn in the wilderness and the renewal promised Israel by the still, small Voice of God. The Brute is destined to work out the people's salvation and muster in the millennium envisioned by those for whom and with whom he struggles. The vision Moody depicts involves the blooming of deserts, the destruction of strongholds built "For the powers of greed and guilt," the cleansing of the temples, the renovation of the lordly cities, the conquest of the weather, and the elimination of labor, hate, fear, and fruitless tears. The Brute shall give to each man his rightful portion and lift the lowly to a state of purity and grace. The sweeping vision is that of a new religion of the dynamo, seen in its larger role as necessary creative antagonist to man. The grounds for faith lie in the appeal of the vision itself and in the imaginative gusto and youthful vigor of the voice of the poem, a voice which suggests that the speaker can control the Brute. The poem ends in yet another scene of judgment. Man, brash and casual, presents the Brute to God in gestures appropriate to presentation of an old, faithful dog:

Then, perhaps, at the last day,
They will whistle him away,
Lay a hand upon his muzzle in the face of God, and say,
"Honor, Lord, the Thing we tamed!
Let him not be scourged or blamed,
Even through his wrath and fierceness was thy fierce wroth world reclaimed!
Honor Thou thy servants' servant; let thy justice now be shown."
Then the Lord will heed their saying, and the Brute come to his own,
'Twixt the Lion and the Eagle, by the armpost of the Throne.

Two lesser poems of the fall are the last political poems Moody wrote. Both are topical. Through allegorical narration, "The Quarry" celebrates a noble action in American foreign policy—intervention to moderate the rapaciousness of European powers set on despoiling China in the wake of the Boxer Rebellion. Moody's treatment of the event shows that he thought ancient Chinese lore might hold clues to the prehistoric chthonic rites he searched out in Western mythic materials. Instead of developing his theme, Moody weaves a tapestry of sensuous detail which merely presents the enigmatic confrontation of eagle and elephant, America and China, an energetic emerging nation and one frozen in ancient traditions and gestures. In his second political poem Moody turns to heavy sarcasm. In "On a Soldier Fallen in

the Philippines," the speaker urges his fellow Americans to cover their
guilty betrayal of a naïve dead soldier's idealistic motives with ceremony. Moody's tone is best articulated in the last stanza:

A flag for the soldier's bier
Who dies that his land may live;
O, banners, banners here,
That he doubt not nor misgive!
That he heed not from the tomb
The evil days draw near
When the nation, robed in gloom
With its faithless past shall strive.
Let him never dream that his bullet's scream went wide of its island mark,
Home to the heart of his darling land where she stumbled and sinned in
    the dark.

The poem is Moody's bitter farewell to the hope of influencing public
political action through poetry.

3

Moody had avoided New York City through the year, but in early
November the theatre season tempted him from New England. He
wrote Robinson of his plans, and Robinson found him a small room
in his own rooming house on Irving Place. The visit was a diversion
for Robinson, and he relished the difficulties Moody and "his Temperament" were having, trying to live together in cramped quarters.[15]
Robinson soon shifted to a room in Yonkers, in search of cheaper living.
Moody consoled himself for his friend's defection by frequenting The
Players and the Salmagundi Club. But on Sundays he went to Yonkers
to visit Robinson,[16] and the two poets spent their time in long walks
between Riverdale and Yonkers along the Hudson River. Moody's
personality particularly intrigued and perplexed Robinson, and the
tendency of both men to be reserved about personal matters filled the
spaces between their communication with tentative silences. Moody
veered to a cover of rich mystification, while Robinson habitually threw
out a net of anguishing qualification and requalification. But Robinson
was quick to feel that Moody was a "most agreeable addition" to his
social life.[17] Their mutual respect grew stronger by the end of two
months of association. Robinson's most balanced estimate of Moody is
given in a phrase that strikes cleanly to the heart of the problem of
Moody's work. Writing to an impartial friend in Gardiner, he observed,
"Moody, with all his predigested experiences is not yet more than half

so old as he thinks he is." But he balances judgment, characterizing his friend as also "one of the most human and attractive of mortals." [18]

Moody had come to New York for the theatre [19] and found it good. Frohman's production of Rostand's *L'Aiglon* was playing at the Knickerbocker Theatre, with Maude Adams in the lead, and Mansfield's *Henry V* was on Broadway. But what drew Moody to the city was the major event of several seasons—performances by Sarah Bernhardt and Constant Coquelin at the Garden Theatre. Before packed houses they played both of Rostand's newest plays, *Cyrano de Bergerac* and *L'Aiglon*, as well as Dumas's *La Dame aux Camélias*, emphasizing the poetry of the lines and situations. The French tradition seemed quiet, subtle, and assured compared to the histrionics of the American stage. These French performances, the sensitive production of Hauptmann by the German stock company of the Irving Place Theatre, and a successful showing of Browning's *In a Balcony* suggested strong possibilities for a revival of poetic drama in the theatre.[20]

Yet Moody was not in an exuberant mood. During the day, he was going over his work, preparing his long-delayed volume of poems for the press. Both the reconsideration of his work and the impending publication of his masque—Moody had received prepublication copies before leaving Boston at the end of October—involved him in the violent alternation of moods that oppressed him from time to time. Josephine had been unhappy with his aloofness in Boston, and Robinson found him bound in conflict—his references to Moody and his temperament were more than idle jest. His despondency is reflected in at least one letter he wrote to accompany a copy of his masque. Moody had sent the work to influential friends and critics: Payne in Chicago, Wendell and Norton at Harvard, and Stedman in New York, among others. To Stedman, he wrote abjectly, "Doubtless you are overwhelmed with tributes of this questionable kind, yet I am bold enough to hope you will read the book, even if it remains in your mind as a symbol of grotesquely ambitious 'first volumes.'" [21] The immediate reception of the book by his most sympathetic readers did little to relieve the poet's mood. Only Dan Mason's responses were encouraging, and Moody wrote to thank him, observing that he had been going through "a crisis of discouragement" which made the efforts of his year seem "pitiably futile." He continued,

I am alarmed about myself, when I notice that the fluctuations of heaven-scaling confidence and something very like despair, instead of decreasing as they ought to do, seem to increase with my years and knowledge. I don't understand it at all, nor do I see any way of combating it that promises much.[22]

Other responses, focused on the meaning and structure of the masque, deepened Moody's sense of failure. Robinson's reaction was especially discouraging. It wasn't that he disapproved of it. He told Moody that its scheme escaped him, and he was rightly worried that it would not be an easy thing for most readers to approach. He thought it showed great talent but could not think of it as an accomplished or fully mature achievement in terms of Moody's abilities and the requirements of the modern age. "Perhaps Moody's greatest trouble," he observed in a letter to Josephine, "lies in the fact that he has so many things to unlearn." [23] If Robinson's confusion was disturbing, letters from Mrs. Mason and Mrs. Toy convinced Moody of the problems of the masque as conceived and presented. These sensitive friends were horrified; they vehemently protested against Moody's God. Moody patiently reiterated his own view in explanatory letters. To Mrs. Mason he wrote that he had hoped Raphael's humanistic attitude and Uriel's philosophy would disengage them from the action, setting the tone and presenting as central theme "a brave love of life and faith in its issues." The rest of the play, Moody declared, "was only mythological machinery for exhibiting the opposite attitude and philosophy—that of the deniers of life." [24] To the upset Mrs. Toy he explained, "Of course I didn't intend my 'strangely unpleasant' God to be taken seriously." He again called attention to the positions of his heroes and declared the central thrust of the work was to be found in the view of "passion as a means of salvation everywhere latent." [25] Not yet a dramatist, Moody himself had miscalculated the effect of his compelling movement of plot and the power of its ironies. Nor did his audience want complexity and irony: it demanded affirmation.

Discouragement over the masque, together with the task of judging his poems for a volume, roused old nostalgias. The result was a poem which, like "Jetsam," concerns the nature of Moody's vocation as poet. But in spirit and form it is very different from the earlier work. In 1895 Moody had been an excessive young reveler, rejoicing in the riches of the language, passionately exploring the wild extremes of his moods. In "The Daguerreotype" we find a mature man and poet contemplating the sources and issues of his personal and poetic life. The poem is a meditation on a daguerreotype of his mother at seventeen. The meditation develops with psychological subtlety as it shifts from mood to mood through a variety of attitudes, insights, and memories. Moody creates a feminine ideal more appropriate to his commitments than the Virgin of "Good Friday Night" and less bizarre than the fin-de-siècle moon-virgin of "Jetsam." Moody's youthful mother is presented as a modern Eve, a suitable contemporary of Raphael and of Moody's Brute in the post-Darwinian garden of the twentieth century.

Moody's treatment anticipates the work of D. H. Lawrence in its balance of passion and objectivity, psychological complexity, and simple frankness.

"The Daguerreotype" begins as the poet searches the picture for its life. His apparent objectivity is established by an attitude of casual inquiry, by a careful series of descriptive distinctions, and by an open response to the sensual appeal of the girl depicted. But he is too casual, too careful, too quick to reach a depersonalized response. Moody recognizes his evasion of genuine involvement, an evasion of both the joy and the pain of recollection which the picture invites. Finally drawn to the "vehement peace" of the light of the portrait's eyes, the poet no longer shrinks but enters the pain and weeps as memory floods back upon him. "The sweet and heavy years" return—the times when he and his sisters gathered at Mrs. Moody's bedside to share a sense of beatitude that was "Holier and more mystical than prayer." As he remembers his mother's death, Moody relives his sense of anger and frustration, his impotent rage against an unfair God. The meditation turns as the poet contemplates the strange ways of time and of change, thinking of the "girl face, expectant, virginal" as his mother—"The flesh which caught my soul"—and considering that this was the body which nourished him in the womb.

Addressing the eyes of the picture, the poet clarifies the reaction he has hesitated to face:

> Here in this web of strangeness caught
> And prey to troubled thought
> Do I devise
> These foolish shifts and slight;
> Only to shield me from the afflicting sense
> Of some waste influence
> Which from this morning face and lustrous hair
> Breathes on me sudden ruin and despair.

The eyes have awakened the sense of his mother's early pride in him. It is defined in terms of high romance, and the definition is basic to Moody's sense of his mission as a poet. Though an "Earth-encumbered, blood-begotten, passionate man-child," the poet was to be "a trump of mighty call," "a sword of flame," and "a lyre/ Of high unquenchable desire/ In the day of little things." These hopes of the budding mother make mockery of the poet's work and overwhelm him with discouragement. Under the felt judgment of his mother's eyes, the wines of poetry he has stored turn to vinegar, to dry and mouldy dust. As the poet asks the eyes of the picture for their final judgment, or at least for a turning aside, he realizes that they do not judge, they aspire. The eyes are "younger than spring," calling to courageous life through their cleansing and reawakening power. The poet ends, accepting their challenge: "Let/ These eyes afflict me, cleanse me, keep me yet/ Brave eyes and true!"

Moody here comes to terms with the classical oedipal situation, fraught with tension. Without denying his open sensuality, he strikes through to the point at which it becomes subsumed by a deeper, primal concern for his relation to the very sources of his physical and spiritual existence. He confronts his sense of guilt, transcending fear of judgment by reaching to the values on which it is based—the promise found in love, struggle, and courage. The conflict treated in Moody's ode, in his masque, in "The Brute," and elsewhere—a conflict involving judgment and justification—finds its terms in the depths of the poet's inner life.

By the end of the year, when Moody returned to Chicago, a number of encouraging signs had appeared. Scribner's had accepted "Gloucester Moors," and "The Brute" and "On a Soldier Fallen in the Philippines" were accepted for publication in national magazines during the winter.[26] Most auspiciously, Houghton Mifflin quickly accepted Moody's new volume of poems for spring publication. His achievement during his year of freedom had been little short of phenomenal. He had completed A Masque of Judgment and had rewritten The Faith Healer in a prose version; he had written ten poems, at least half of which were of major importance. And to supplement his income he had done two minor editions for the Lake English Classics and had written almost half of a history of English literature.

By midwinter Moody's poems in Scribner's and the Atlantic were attracting attention. There had been a series of letters in the New York Times in December from readers who liked "Gloucester Moors," and one or two of them referred other readers to the "Ode in Time of Hesitation." Moody's admirers called attention to the combination of sensitivity to nature with "deep human interest," and they were attracted by the "lofty nobility" and "fearless strength" of the poet's work.[27] On January 2 the Boston Evening Transcript devoted a column to Moody, hailing him as "a new voice and a strong one," and citing the "inherent dignity, skill and devotion to beauty" of his poems. Again his combination of "the inspiration of nature and the aspiration of man" in "Gloucester Moors" was singled out for comment.[28] Moody had struck a rich vein of popular appeal in the merging motifs of "Gloucester Moors." At the end of January the poet had the pleasure of being attacked in the Chicago Inter-Ocean for his "On a Soldier Fallen in the Philippines." His attacker viewed the war as "the revolt of semi-savagery against civilization, and as such righteously put down in the general interest of humanity." Where, the writer demanded, was Moody's authority to write such a poem, and what reasons could be found for the production of this kind of "poetic sewage." [29]

But aside from a half-dozen early newspaper reviews toward the end of 1900, response to *The Masque of Judgment* was slow in developing.[30] Reviews, spaced through the winter and spring in the national publications, finally came in a limited number. They tended toward hesitant confusion. Reviewers called the masque "original" or "daring." Bliss Perry, who reviewed it for the *Atlantic,* observed that it was "not very easily understood," [31] and many felt that Moody's aim was "higher than his flight." One assured reviewer decided that the book had to be the product of a "disordered imagination." Several reviewers were horrified by the "blasphemy" they found, and there was frequent rebellion against the masque's "pessimism." It was "full of gloom and despair." Others ascribed the faults in the work to the materials, themes, and dramatis personae, joining company with the *Outlook* reviewer who found the play "too academic to inspire the imagination or give joy to the spirit." [32] Praise centered on Moody's construction or on characteristics of the poetry. The blank verse was approved as "stately and dignified," or "strong and sonorous." Attention was called to the beauty and free rhythms of the "exquisite lyrical movements." But the emphasis on technique which characterized many reviews was a defensive maneuver of reviewers unable to interpret the masque.

In two or three cases Moody's work aroused immediate enthusiasm. A Chicago *Times-Herald* reviewer included comment on Moody's ode and "Gloucester Moors" and told readers that "all lovers of good literature have their eyes upon him." [33] Mrs. Richard Hovey, young widow of the poet, was ecstatic about Moody's masque. In a fine symbolic gesture, she began the book on New Year's Eve and stayed up all night to finish it,[34] ushering in the twentieth century with Moody's rich ironies. George B. Rose was another enthusiast. Preparing an article which appeared in the *Sewanee Review* in July, he wrote Moody declaring the masque to be the greatest poem ever produced in America.[35]

Lewis Gates reviewed *The Masque of Judgment* for the *Nation* at the end of March. His piece is a qualified but positive review, which attempts to focus attention on the modernity of the themes. Gates, however, could not resist opening with barbed banter. He cites possible tags for the poem: "Prometheus Rebound," or "Decline and Fall of the Holy Cosmic Process." But he quickly denies the value of such foolery, finding the book's distinction in "its use of an elaborately finished and highly sophisticated literary form for the utterance of a genuinely democratic impulse." He expands on the observation, writing,

The poem is a brilliantly imaginative interpretation of the same modern impulses, of the same restless craving for richness and luxuriance of life, of the same audaciously optimistic belief in the worth of life, of the same strenuous and reckless pursuit of individual good, that are just now peculiarly characteristic of our youthfully sensuous and materialistic American nation, and that find their extreme and most picturesque expression in the raw splendor and the exultant and almost ferocious carnality of the pageant of life as the wayfarer encounters it in New York city.[36]

The passage offers an acute characterization of a major strain in the temper of the times, one to which Moody was especially responsive both in the masque and in his poetry. From this vantage point, as Moody would have desired, Gates focuses on the nature of the masque's moral affirmation. He declares it a plea "for the joy of life here and now, for the largesse of the senses, for the worth of passion, . . . for the rigor of the cosmic game, for the divine contradictions of actual life (its 'laughter and sorrow and brawl')." Gates fears this moral position tends to anarchy, but he cites as countervailing force the "noble and lofty idealism." Faults of the drama are found in its "over-ambitiousness" and in its language, "at times—not often—over-luxuriant, and languid." But these faults are, Gates observes, "the authentic faults for the first volumes of poets doomed to go far; they are the appropriate vices of the poetic temper."

CHAPTER 7

THE SUBSTANCE OF THINGS HOPED FOR

MOODY'S long-delayed volume of poetry appeared in early May 1901. A ten-year period of writing is covered, but the book gives little sense of Moody's poetic development. Fully half of the poems were written in 1900, and Moody's arrangement disregards chronology. The volume opens with "Gloucester Moors" and "Good Friday Night," sounding the theme of brotherhood in different contexts, social and religious. "Road-Hymn" follows, and then his three political poems are balanced against his long monologues, "Jetsam" and "Until the Troubling of the Waters." "The Brute" and "The Menagerie" appear, followed by a scatter of lesser work. Moody mixes short lyrics and early quest poems, framing the grouping by "The Golden Journey" at one end and the medieval quest poem, "The Ride Back," at the other. The poet's themes are love and art. In a final group Moody places poems which deal at greater depth with these issues: "Song-Flower and Poppy," "The Daguerreotype," "How the Mead-Slave Was Set Free," and "A Dialogue in Purgatory." The arrangement is designed dramatically, to identify major concerns by grouping parallel poems and to provide thematic chiaroscuro through darks and lights of tension and contrast.

In May and June reviews appeared in most of the major newspapers and literary journals, raising a chorus of excited praise for the volume and hailing William Vaughn Moody as an American poet of major significance. Hamilton Wright Mabie, editor of *Outlook*, commented in an unsigned review in his magazine, "It is not too much to say that no young poet of recent years has given more conclusive evidence of the possession of unusual gifts and of the spirit of sincerity and scrupulous regard for the high demands of his art." [1] William

Morton Payne, *Dial* editor, wrote that "with the possible exception
of what has been done by Professor Woodberry, no such note of high
and serious song has been sounded in our recent American poetry as is
now sounded in 'The Masque of Judgment' and the 'Poems' of Mr.
Moody." [2] In the *Atlantic*, Rollo Ogden stated his great pleasure "in
signalizing the rise of so bright a star upon our poetical horizon." [3]
The Chicago *Tribune*'s reviewer observed, "It would partake of the
nature of self-annihilation to deny that a new poet has arisen out at
the University of Chicago, and that there is something akin to great-
ness in his poetry." [4] Joseph B. Gilder wrote in the *Critic*, "We hold
this volume to contain more of promise, and of performance, too,
than any other first collection of verse in English that we have seen
for many a long day." And he rose to the occasion in an echo of
Emerson's reception of *Leaves of Grass*: "We greet the author at the
beginning of a brilliant career." [5] Jeannette L. Gilder, cofounder and
editor of the *Critic,* was even more positive:

We . . . wondered when the next great American poet was coming and
where he would come from. Now we know. He has come, and he has come
from out the West. There is no doubt in the minds of the best judges that
William Vaughn Moody is the poet for whom we have long waited.[6]

As Jeannette Gilder's comment suggests, critics everywhere in
America were ready to welcome a poet who might fill the place of the
poets of the nineteenth century. The nineties had witnessed the deaths
of Lowell, Whittier, and Whitman, but no poets of comparable stature
had risen to take their places. The delicate moods of the *fin de siècle*
caught little of the sense of life in an America which looked forward
to a mighty future in the new century. In a letter of mid-May, Hamilton Wright Mabie expressed to Moody the spirit with which so many
reviewers greeted his volume. Mabie found recent verse to be graceful
and fanciful but totally out of touch with the energetic spirit of life
in America. Moody's work, he felt, had finally caught that spirit.[7]

Poems most often selected by reviewers for acclaim were the social
and political poems of 1900, especially "The Brute" and "Gloucester
Moors." Of issues, treatment of labor and of the machine were most
often mentioned. Critics responded to the deep sense of humanity,
the voicing of democratic ideals (one critic found Moody's democracy
a good American counterbalance to Kipling's imperialism), the ethical
enthusiasms, the deep feeling for natural beauty, and the dedication
to idealism. But these were hardly unusual characteristics of the
poetry of the time. Of greatest interest to his critics is the voice of
Moody's poems. They draw attention to the "strength," "vigor," direct-

ness," "power," "vitality," "virility," "largeness," "nobility" of the voice. They rejoiced in Moody's "robust optimism." [8] Harriet Monroe, in an essay-review in the Chicago *Evening Post*, best captures the spirit in which Moody's poems were read. The social poems, she felt, were works which "strike to the heart of our life with an air of being big enough to cope with its violence, its roar, its brutality, its great outreachings, its passion of wild hope and unsatisfied love." [9]

Moody had sent Robinson a copy of the *Poems*, and it is instructive to compare his friend's response with those of the public critics. Robinson characteristically concerns himself with Moody's potential as revealed in the book. He writes, not that Moody had given voice to the twentieth century, but that he could, with his gift, "give American literature a new meaning for the new century."

From all that I can see, everything depends on what you choose to express. Perhaps there is too much color and not enough light in your work thus far, but I suppose I am an ass to suggest it. You know what life means to you and it is not likely that you will spend your days in the making of [a] book that will leave the souls of your readers unfed. The final note of hope and faith in the Daguerreotype—which is a great poem—makes me sure of all this.[10]

Like Moody's critics, Robinson calls attention to the "note of hope and faith" but with a vast difference. He is discussing Moody's personality and the psychological growth he finds in "The Daguerreotype." It is in the maturity of this poem that Moody is "big," not in the ring of voice. Robinson reiterated his praise in a letter to Mrs. Richards in Gardiner, adding comment on the virtues of "The Menagerie" and calling Moody "the pessimist man-child who branded himself the best of living poets with 'The Daguerreotype.' " [11]

Publication of *Poems* presents an opportunity to consider Moody's poetic development in perspective. His Harvard poems had been highly imitative of Victorian models—chiefly the poems of Browning, Morris, and Rossetti. In the later nineties (and throughout his career) Moody's poems and plays continue to exhibit intimate relationships with the work of other writers, but the nature of the relationships shifts. Moody's later "models" are evoked as a kind of total literary allusion through echoes of theme and style. "Jetsam" would probably not have been written without the example of Francis Thompson, "Road-Hymn for the Start" without Whitman, "Until the Troubling of the Waters" without Browning, or a much later poem like "The Moon-Moth" without Keats's "Ode to a Nightingale." But no reader would mistake one of these poems for a work—good or poor—by the writer to whom

Moody alludes. For example, any educated reader would think of Whitman when reading "Road-Hymn for the Start." But Moody's road, as has been shown, differs considerably from Whitman's; Moody develops his poem through narration and symbolist techniques, and the expansive, energetic rhythms are metrical in form. A contemporary creation is presented in a carefully identified traditional context.

Moody works in a variety of modes. His style in each case is not distinctively new or personal. Major characteristics of style may of course be identified, but they are always subordinated to the stylistic decorum of Victorian practice in the mode. Neither are Moody's allusions personal in the manner of twentieth-century modernism. A generation trained to respond to obscure, highly individualized versions of tradition has missed the point. Moody's method is not only that of a poet intimately at home in the Western literary tradition but his orientation to poetic creativity is almost neoclassical in its de-emphasis of originality of subject and style and uniqueness of form. Although of infinite variety, the Christian-humanist tradition was seen as a stable heritage, preserved in a limited number of great works accessible to all men. Like the great Victorians—but unlike the poets to come after him—Moody sought to regain the poet's diminishing contact with a large public of general readers. Moody's method of allusion conveys his sense of the permanence of a common heritage to be conserved, clarified, and elevated by the poets in succeeding periods. The nature of Moody's commitment to classicism as thesis in a Hegelian dialectic of culture is suggested by his idea that the mission of art in his time was to present romantic themes in the great classical forms.

In defining Moody's relationships to his models—the term *influences* seems imprecise and awkwardly implies Lockean psychology—a distinction between the surface model and what may be called the deep model should be made. A surface model can be identified and established on the basis of similar structures, parallel passages, and so forth. The impact is primarily technical and does not imply a sharing of deeper commitments in two writers. The impact of a deep model is both less particularized and more pervasive in a writer's work. It becomes a basic function of his personality and commitments. Moody's deep models were first, Browning, then Keats and Shelley, then Dante and Milton. Moody's surface models were almost always near-contemporaries or writers one generation removed. Early, Moody imitated Rossetti, like him in personality and commitment only tangentially. Moody's relation to Browning is quite different. In his early work, Moody occasionally imitated a Browningesque monologue; but by 1900 Browning had been fully absorbed, and it is more difficult to identify that poet's specific contribution to "Until the Troubling of

the Waters" than to, say, "Sister Angelica." Browning as craftsman
was of little interest to Moody after 1900, but Browning's work was
basic to Moody's whole vision of life, a foundation on which he built.
The impact, and incidentally that of Keats as well, is reaffirmed in
this passage from *A History of English Literature:*

The World is for him [Browning], in Keats's phrase, the "Valley of Soul-
making"; and every act, thought, and feeling of life is of concern only as it
hinders or determines the soul on its course. But he believes salvation to
lie, not, as does Tennyson, in the suppression of individual will and passion,
but in their strenuous exercise. It is the moments of high excitement in human life which interest him, because in such moments the great saving as-
sertions of will and passion are made.[12]

We are here at the heart of Moody's own faith in "passion as a means
of salvation everywhere latent."

The case of Milton is different, and it will be instructive to sketch
the outlines of the relationship. Milton emerges in 1897 as a deep
model, and his impact on the form, the thought, and the style of
Moody's masque has been treated. The unevenness of that work is
the result of Moody's impatience in rewriting and of writing in
Milton's shadow over a period of two and a half years. Moody's earliest
response to Miltonic blank verse, in a passage like this one from act 1,
was gross imitation:

> Each time when I stand
> Upon the borders of this monstrous place,
> I still must question wherefore it was flung
> Thus ruinous with toppled peak and scaur,
> Sheer from the morning cliffs that hold up Heaven
> To nether caverns where no foot of man
> Has clambered down, nor eye of angel dared
> To spy upon the sluggish denizens,
> If any dwell so deep.

But the passage is immediately preceded by one of the "strips of the
best broadcloth" that Moody had written Herrick he was inserting early
in 1900. This later passage deliberately echoes Milton, but with an
assuredness and grace which mark Moody's mature assimilation of
the style:

> The trees grow stunted in this keener air,
> And scarce the hardiest blossoms dare to take
> Assurance from the sun. Southward the rocks

Boast mosses and a poor increase of flowers,
But all the northern shelters hold their snow.
Such flowers as come, come not quite flower-like,
But smitten from their gracious habitudes
By some alarm, some vast and voiceless cry
That just has ceased to echo ere I came. . . .
Ages of looking on the scene beyond
Have worn the granite into shapes of woe
And old disaster.

Such assimilation signals the extent of Milton's impact. If Moody looked back to Milton through Blake, Milton's theology was a foundation from which he built. He shared Milton's synthetic approach to tradition and Milton's view of the nobility of poetic vocation; Milton's career became a model for his own. "An Ode in Time of Hesitation" affords a revealing example of levels of allusion to which Moody's poetry customarily reaches. Lowell and Whittier are surface models for the poem; they are not genuine influences on it. Moody's debt to Whitman goes much deeper, but the poem reaches beyond these models. And Moody deliberately evokes his tradition by direct reference to Whittier, Whitman, and Milton.

A third type of contextual relationship in Moody's work must be considered, partially because much of the small body of Moody criticism has operated, too often with little profit, from this perspective.[13] Here we are concerned with what might most accurately be considered influences. Moody was extremely sensitive to literary movements of his period and kept in close touch with what his contemporaries and immediate predecessors in the United States, Great Britain, and Europe were doing. Moody's contemporaries, however, seldom offered models Moody sought to imitate. The nature of influence in these cases has been suggested, usually simply by a reference in the appropriate context. Sometimes Moody's contemporaries suggested modes or subject matter which he worked independently. Edwin Arlington Robinson's example may well have influenced Moody to work in the style he developed for "Until the Troubling of the Waters." The style of Rudyard Kipling suggested techniques which Moody employed in "The Brute," but it was the popular success of Kipling as well as that of Edwin Markham—whose work did not influence Moody in other ways—which showed him how to reach a larger public. Similarly, the success in the theatre of the poetic drama of Stephen Phillips was to influence Moody to do The Fire-Bringer, but Phillips's work did not influence Moody's. A much more important kind of influence, but one more difficult to assess, is that of the complex tension provided by contemporary influences against which a mature poet defines himself and identifies his own path. For Moody the work of men like Robinson, Stickney, Maeterlinck, and later Yeats was of major and immediate importance, and these writers surface out of a sea of dozens of contemporaries whose work helped Moody focus his own. Moody learned little from any of them of direct importance to his poetry or drama, but the simple fact that their work was the cultural context for his own is as important as its exact effect in each case is difficult to establish, let alone define.

Poems represents a limited achievement. Discriminations above have been made to suggest that the limitations of Moody's poetry are not, as has been proposed, a result of tasteless imitation of poor models or pretentious imitation of masters whose influence Moody was unable to dominate. Moody possessed one of the best minds in American poetry, and he was a talented craftsman. He succeeded in writing poems distinctively his own. Working well within the bounds of the code of decorum of poets of the period, he reinvigorated his tradition through experiment with rhythm, symbolic patterning, and dramatic movement. Moody's work is a late, mature flowering of the Victorian poetic tradition. His conservative poetic was one central to the Christian-humanist tradition in nineteenth-century America, although it was not a poetic which provided a basis for the century's best poetry. To be sure, Moody's position was a function of his personality and it is difficult to separate the two. He was hardly a weak character, yet he lacked both the rare independence and still rarer genius with language through which Robinson and Yeats were more successful in transcending their time and place. The man makes a difference. But the more interesting problem of defining Moody's poetic achievement and its limitations remains. Both are to be found in the curious fact that the issues of his work shifted to their twentieth-century formulations before the strategies of a poetic style adequate to them had been developed.

Moody's sensitivity to problems central to twentieth-century experience is an important strength of his poems. Sharing little of the romantic writer's faith in the natural world as a manifestation of spiritual reality, Moody's constant theme was the psychic, social, and spiritual alienations of man. His poems rise out of the growing burden of individual guilt, the sense of moral failure and helplessness, which has been basic to much of twentieth-century literature. He is concerned with the debasement of human relationships and the perversion of love into lust or egocentricity, taking up a theme American poets, with the exception of Whitman and Dickinson, tended to ignore. As his sense of guilt deepens, there is an increasing interest in the nature

of innocence, which Moody explores and which remains at the base
of haunting images in his poetry. Perhaps most significant, Moody is
the first American poet to treat cultural materials in a modern way. In
his longer poems he developed his symbolism in the contexts of ritual-
istic or mythic patterns central to Western experience. He turned to
his materials in the spirit of comparative mythology and viewed them,
not as outworn science in the manner of the nineteenth century, but in
the new perspectives which James Frazer was codifying and which
were to influence later writers significantly. These cultural materials
and Europe itself were more than a source for suggestive settings or
standards of taste, as had been too often the case for America's earlier
intense but provincial writers. Like Henry James, Moody approaches
Europe as a landscape of cultural values to be explored, motivated by a
desperate need for self-definition in a context embodying viable values.
A spiritual expatriate in all but the political poems of 1900, Moody
takes a modern stance as a poet of Western Europe who happens to be
writing in America.

For all of its affinities with poetic practice of the last century,
Moody's was hailed by his contemporaries as a new poetic voice, and
so it was. Its individuality may be gauged by comparison with the
lesser voices of the nineties in England and America and with those of
earlier poets of Victorian England. In one sense, it creates a poetry of
the middle ground, moving in a range which could accommodate the
colloquial or rise to largeness of utterance according to the requirements of the poem. It is a poetry which best represents the nature of
American participation in the international symbolist movement of the
late nineteenth and early twentieth centuries. Yet it represents a
poetic tradition *in extremis*. Moody's ethic and his poetic were themselves grounded in a principle of tension. Intent on breaking through
to a contemporary vision, Moody developed old issues in a form new
to the tradition. But he tended to restate traditional values in greater
energy as countervailing force. When successful, he raised the tensions
of his time to a new power. Even then—or rather, most often then—
the voice is straining for a breadth impossible within the old decorums
and for affirmations of reconciliation impossible within the older value
structure. There is too little possible mediation of the tremendous gulfs
which lie between spirit and sense, ideal love and lust, the uncom-
monly high aspiration and the depths over which it soars and into
which it could fall. Confronted with chaos, Moody too often elaborates and re-elaborates his symbolic clusters and his rhetorical and
rhythmic patterns. Or he replaces old adjectives with more powerful
or suggestive ones. Confronted with corruption of ideals, he restates
them in a voice of greater dignity. Technically these strategies led

Moody into lapses of taste, and represent a failure of imagination.[14] Yet the situation required a kind of independent genius which might have leapt free of its time and place. All of these defensive gestures were typical of Moody's age. His audience, as shown by critical reactions to both the masque and the poems, turned a deaf ear to Moody's deepest grappling with his despair, happy to hear only the affirmations. In one of its dimensions Moody's poetry prefigures the American personality which World War I would collapse, and which would create out of strained idealism an ironic, nostalgic countertheme to its deepening disillusionment.

Will Moody was neither a fool, a naïve optimist, nor a popularity seeker. The demands he made of his poetry were the most stringent, nor was he willing to relax them. Was there insufficient confrontation with the problems he was tackling? Yes, clearly, from the perspective of seventy years. He was exploring and redefining issues on the basis of his own experience and inexperience and "predigested experience," although increasingly in 1900 he emphasized the sheer presentation itself. Moody was not always self-aware: "He is not half so old as he thinks he is," Robinson had written at the beginning of the year.[15] But Moody was hardly blind to his problems. The judgments of "The Daguerreotype" were honest ones, and Moody demanded not only affirmation, but affirmation in the midst of the most profound grasp of the issues of his age he could reach. His sense of his poems as a series of half-successes, his sense of unfulfilled search, is obvious from a curious fact about his *Poems*. With the possible exception of two or three of the short lyrics, each poem takes its own unique form. Of the two long dramatic monologues, one is worked in a realistic setting with near-colloquial rhythm and diction, while the other—"Jetsam"—turns to the techniques of expressionism and symbolism for a quest poem in a modern urban environment. The form of the loose ode finds very different uses in Moody's political ode and in "The Daguerreotype." The personal lyric is revitalized through sophistications of psychological and symbolic development, and Moody had briefly revived the public poem—writing it, too, in a variety of styles. The volume is that of a poet who has searched the tradition, bringing each mode to its potential fullness in terms of his period and his own personality, and then turning from it as if it were not enough, to try something else. Moody's volume is not a "promising" first book. It is fulfilled. There are no directions to pursue, no suggestions for further development. All he could do was to turn in the direction to which his interest had more and more inclined in the later nineties: to the drama for a form adequate to the demands of his experience.

2

In the spring of 1901 Moody began to consider the possibility of severing his connections with the University of Chicago. He was in a second term of teaching, and the catalogue listed him for courses in the summer, the fall, and the winter—a sequence mirroring his first years of teaching. He was in his sixth year as Instructor in English, and in March he had again been bypassed for promotion. Professor Manly wrote President Harper, suggesting a meeting, pointing out that Moody had recently attracted more favorable comment than any writer of serious verse in America.[16] He and Herrick united to support Moody's request for an assistant professorship on special appointment for six months of employment a year. The issues remained unresolved until early May. The delay irritated Moody and roused him to an uncommon aggressiveness by the time he finally met with President Harper. Harper offered a promotion to assistant professor with a salary increase to $1600 for two terms of work. Moody was still in doubt, balancing the offer against the uncertainties of supporting himself entirely by his writing. After mulling over the situation, he wrote on May 8 requesting a commitment for salary increases over the term of the appointment—a raise of $200 after the first year, and a similar amount after the third.[17] The matter rested in the inertias of academia until midsummer.

Though Moody's social life in Chicago had changed little on his return from the East in 1901, one addition to his circle was to be of major significance to his life. He picked up the threads of a friendship that had been established in the fall of 1899 with Harriet Brainard.[18] A woman in her forties, Harriet was tall and vigorous, blonde and blue-eyed. Her beauty was on the large scale: "personal splendor" was the phrase friends used to characterize Harriet's impact on others. As a successful teacher and businesswoman she was conversant with the ways of the world. Harriet's father, William Tilden, had made and lost several fortunes in the Chicago cattle market by the time of his death in the 1880s. She had been educated at a Friends' school in the East and at Cornell University. After graduating from Cornell in 1876, she entered Women's Medical College in Philadelphia to train as a doctor; but after a year she was called back into Chicago society by her parents. An unfortunate marriage to Edwin Brainard, a young man of wealth, ended in divorce. The divorce and her father's death made it necessary for Harriet to help support her mother, and she entered the University of Chicago as a graduate student in 1892 to prepare for high school teaching in English. She took a job in a Chicago school and maintained university connections both as an Honorary Fellow in English during the academic years 1893–94 and 1894–95 and as a close friend of Martha Foote Crow, a colleague of Moody's who introduced the poet to her. Harriet was an energetic teacher and her interest in students led her to set up a small printing press in her home to print the best of their work. But teaching was not totally absorbing. In the mid-nineties she began a catering service to Marshall Field's, and it gradually expanded to include all of the Pullman service on Chicago railroads. Flourishing as the Home Delicacies Association, the business was carried on from the top floor of Harriet's large home at 2970 Groveland Avenue.

Moody became one of the friends the successful cateress enjoyed entertaining for dinner and an evening of talk. He presented a copy of his masque, which immediately caught Harriet's interest, for in temperament, education, and commitment, she and Moody were much alike. Both were active and self-dramatizing human beings, approaching life with spiritual energy and physical gusto. Harriet shared Will's mystical orientation to spiritual values and his inclination to seek salvation through strength of will and passionate experience. At the same time, both were clearheaded and practical in planning their lives, in touch with the realities of their environment. Harriet was attracted to the vibrant depths of the younger man, and he responded to the strength and vitality of the dignified and attractive older woman—a model of the strong feminine ideal of the period. Through the winter and early spring Moody spent more and more of his time in Harriet's pleasant home on Groveland Avenue—"the Grove" to Harriet's large circle of friends.

Harriet Brainard rented a cottage at Lakeside on Chicago's north shore for the spring. There she gave weekend parties. Moody was a frequent guest, enjoying her companionship and that of her young protégés, Alice Corbin and Elizabeth O'Neill, who helped Harriet manage her extensive professional and social life. At the end of a house party on May 16, Harriet was injured. The group had picnicked beside the lake in the evening, and some of the guests lingered around the fire reading poetry until time for the late train back to Chicago. Will and Harriet left to escort Lorado Taft, the sculptor, and his wife to the train. The remainder of the party—a group including Ferdinand Schevill and Alice Corbin—were gathered around the fire when they were suddenly startled by cries for help. Returning just after midnight, joyously intent on the beauty of the spring sky and flinging her arms in the air to the stars, Harriet had stepped off an embankment near the lake's edge, shattering her ankle. Bones of the foot were

smashed, and the leg bone had been forced through the leather of the
high-laced cycling boot she was wearing. Schevill and Moody carried
Harriet back to the cottage, where the boot was cut off. A local doctor
immobilized the ankle. In the morning she was taken by train to St.
Luke's Hospital in Chicago for examination. The fracture was serious
and infection had set in, but Harriet refused the amputation of her
foot recommended by the doctors. The alternative was a painful and
experimental series of operations, and the danger of increasing infection in the course of treatment posed a serious threat to her life.
At Harriet's insistence, the surgeon proceeded, and afterwards she
remained in the hospital until the end of June.[19]

Harriet's friends were upset and anxious, and Moody had been
particularly affected. On May 20 he sent a note to Harriet at the
hospital, suggesting the impact that the accident and Harriet's suffering
had had on him:

What is it that I want to say, you will wonder. I hardly know myself. I only
know that your pain and danger have made your mind and character stand
out before me as if disengaged from the illusions and interruptions of this
world, and filled me with a sense of deep—bear with me if I say religious
—gratitude for the gift of your friendship. I feel that in knowing you I
have had a rich blessing—one which will enter for good into all that I do or
become.[20]

In June, finishing his spring-term course work, Moody visited
frequently at the hospital, and in early July he saw Harriet again in
her home on Groveland Avenue. A second operation was set for
August. She installed a large swing in the parlor from which she
received guests and resumed supervision of her catering business.
Moody began visiting every afternoon, watching over her progress,
reading with her or sitting in silent companionship. Ferd Schevill
sometimes joined them. By August Moody was willing to admit that
he was in love. The transmutation of friendship into love had come
with his sense of her danger, her undeniable need for help and attention. The scene was set for a love in the pattern of the late nineteenth-
century ideal, mirroring the legendary relationship of the Brownings
and recapturing to some degree the lost, bitterly cut-off relation of
Moody with his invalid mother.

During the spring and summer Moody continued to wrestle with
the question of his continued association with the university. In July
a new consideration complicated an already complex set of possibilities.
President Wheeler, who had met Moody the previous summer in
Cambridge, offered a position at the University of California. Wheeler's

offer was seductive. Moody would assume a full professorship at $3000, be responsible for a single semester of teaching each year, and be entirely free of responsibility in composition courses.[21] Moody was stunned, remembering his struggle for an assistant professorship won only belatedly a few months earlier and still unresolved as to salary. Chafing from those negotiations and assuming Harper's reaction, Moody asked Manly merely to inform the Chicago president that he was leaving for Berkeley. Interested in keeping Moody, Manly urged him to await Harper's response. Harper rose to the challenge from the West and negotiated a competitive offer. In position Moody would remain an assistant professor, but his contract met the California salary in terms of Chicago's calendar.[22] In addition, Moody requested and won another year free of teaching.[23]

In early August an opportunity arose for a trip to the Rockies. Hamlin Garland had aroused Moody's interest with talk of the West, and Moody made impulsive arrangements for a trip, promising Garland, "Any time you wire me, I will come." [24] The wire arrived, and on August 15, the day Harriet reentered the hospital, Moody left for the West. Harriet's courage was high and she urged Will off as she faced the outcome alone. On his side, Moody needed violent distraction and time to work his way through the events of the summer and to come to some sense of himself and of his future.

Moody met Garland in Wagon Wheel Gap, Colorado, and the two men set out, taking mountain ponies and a pack mule for equipment and food. Garland took pleasure in exposing the greenhorn to all the rigors of the trail at once. He set a hard and strenuous pace, designed to put the poet—out for impressions—on his mettle.[25] Moody's account of the trip indicates that he succeeded:

We tackled the stiffest proposition in reach—a country of great cañons narrowing up to strange green mountain meadows, overlooked by savage peaks of sheer rock. There was of course much exhausting labor involved, . . . so that as yet the physical difficulties of the trip almost obscure the aesthetic impressions (how I hate that phrase!).[26]

The expedition was broken short when Garland's horse fell on a sloping bank, crushing the rider's foot. Through freezing rain they rode thirty miles through what Garland said was "the wildest piece of country" he had seen. After putting Garland in good hands, with a sense of deep relief Moody spent his days in trips through the more settled regions around Ouray, usually finding a rancher's roof to sleep under at nightfall. He explored the upper Rio Grande and did some of the mountain passes on horseback, riding from thirty to fifty miles a

day. At the end of the first week of September a letter came from
Harriet.[27]

Recuperating from her operation, Harriet had decided to take a
house for a month on Mackinac Island, where her doctor was vacationing. She enlisted Moody's aid, and he joyfully joined her entourage,
a group which included Harriet's young helpers and one or two necessary servants. Schevill joined them to spend a week, lulled, Schevill
recalled, "by the peace of an Indian summer of unforgettable magnificence." [28] Moody, fresh from the West, with the assurance of a
bright future, was confident and settled in his feelings. He and Harriet
sat late before the flickering fire in the Mackinac house after the rest
of the household retired. Sunday evenings especially were reserved for
reading aloud of poetry by Harriet, and Moody reminded her of the
love recognized and pledged by the fire while the echoes of recited
poetry lingered. In November he wrote from Boston, reminding
Harriet of "the blessed expansion of these firelit hours, and how we
found each other in the wind of the poetry, and went down it together to the unguessed-at goal!"

Work with Lovett on *A History of English Literature* had drawn
Moody to Boston. He rebelled against the detailed coordination of
the manuscript, but his relationship with Harriet had been cemented
by several arrangements which provided a sense of communion. The
lovers were reading the Gospel of John together, one chapter each
evening. Harriet had embarked on a private course in music appreciation to pass her time, and she sent her listening programs to Will.
Mason, with whom he was staying, played through them for him.
Though as sceptical as ever of domesticated life, Moody began entertaining an Arcadian dream of a retreat in the country. The possibility
was to haunt his imagination for the rest of his life. He inquired about
Cornish on the upper Connecticut River, a fashionable summer center
for artists, writers, and theatre people. A small house there was for
sale. It was on a high hill outside the village, with a view of the river.
Moody wrote, asking, "Does it sound? Has it a flavor?"

Moody completed his final work on the manuscript in February,
and he joined Harriet, who was vacationing in an inn at Cape Henry,
Virginia. As proofs for the book arrived, they settled down to read
them, Moody making numerous changes in the already much revised
text. As weather improved, Moody took up his painting again for the
first time in years. Harriet's spirits improved with her physical condition, though she was still unable to walk. There were carriage excursions to favorite spots along the coast, and they talked while
Moody sketched.

Harriet's zest for experience corresponded to Moody's, and they
were both dedicated to a spiritual view of reality. Even more strongly

than Will, Harriet saw the visible world as illusion. She lavished praise on Moody's work, and together they strove to live free of the accidents of material existence, so painfully present to Harriet in her all-too-slowly healing foot. Suspicious of casual humor and irrelevant frivolity, as well as of excessive imaginative or sensuous indulgence, Harriet held herself to a stern but generous and humane spiritual dedication. Preferring life in "plain russet," she deplored Moody's tendency to rhapsodize over what she saw as mere "Scenery." Her dedication is expressed by a ring she gave Moody in Virginia, one of two she had made up for them. They bore mottos committing the lovers to spiritual warfare on the side of God.

As work on proofs for the history neared completion, Moody made plans for a trip to Greece to gather materials and impressions for new work. He was attracted to the potential of Greek dramatic forms for revival in the contemporary theatre. The success of Stephen Phillips's classically inspired plays may have stimulated Moody's interest, but such stimulus was hardly needed. It had been present since his Harvard years. Moody began considering the Prometheus legend as one embodying themes which might present dramatically the philosophical implications of his masque. By mid-April his proofreading was complete and Moody left the United States for Greece, in search of new dramatic material.

3

The Greece to which Moody was looking was not Arnold's land of sweetness, of proportion, and of the clear light of reason. It was the Dionysian Greece Nietzsche had celebrated.[29] Moody had brought along Homer's *Odyssey* and was reading a book of it a day, planning to begin on the more strenuous Greek drama when he arrived. But his initial impulse on arrival in the Piraeus was to embark on a tour of the islands.[30] He made his devotions at Melos to Venus, whom he recognized as Harriet's patron saint. He was entranced by the play of light "over the noble forms of shore-rock and upland and peak . . . as over the naked form of the goddess herself," in love at once with the light, the island, Venus, and Harriet. In Crete came a startling vision of Christ, this time in a spare Greek setting. Moody was casually watching a sailor caulking his boat on the distant beach. Speaking to the sailor was a man in a dark robe: "I took him for a Greek priest," Moody wrote Harriet. But, he continued,

There was something in the spare frame of the man, the slight stoop of the shoulders, and the calm intensity of the attitude, which made my heart stop beating. Presently he turned to look at me, and it was indeed He. This has happened to me twice now—once before at Sorrento seven years ago.

Moody later drew on the experience for his poem, "The Second Coming." The vision came, like the first at Sorrento, early in his trip and in the spring. It seems to have signalized for Moody a first imaginative involvement, a casting off of the layers of superficial personality, a communion with spiritual presences in the suggestive Mediterranean landscape.

On returning from his short tour, Moody found a pleasant room in a house kept by an Englishwoman in Athens. The room offered a view of the Acropolis and the Gulf of Aegina. Moody obtained access to the library of the American school and usually spent his mornings reading. Afternoons and evenings were reserved for short excursions to points of interest in and around Athens. Often Moody took along a play to read in some evocative setting.

In spite of his intent preparations, Moody had some difficulty breaking through to the sense of presence and place he sought. He found the site of Sophocles' *Oedipus at Colonus* "a dust-heap, inhabited by goats and dogs," though the play itself engrossed him. He disliked the presence of smokestacks in the Piraeus and of a steam tram to Eleusis—site of the Eleusian mysteries. But Moody had even less patience with the few hangers-on at the American school. The archeologists' approach to the past Moody thought was unimaginably pedantic. He wrote Harriet that they were making dust heaps of the old monuments, observing sardonically, "Archeology here attacks all human organisms, as the dry-rot; they would shovel Olympus into the sea in order to unearth a seventh century stew-pan, at least if there was a chance to quarrel over its date."

When evidence of modern civilization and historical research were out of sight and hearing, Moody found the stimulus he sought. He rented a bicycle and began to explore Attica with it. He came home from a ride to Eleusis by the old Sacred Way over the Pass of Daphne, returning at sunset to a glorious vision of the Attic plain as "a great pool of purple shadow, out of which Hymettos and Parnes rose up intense with the very spirit of light—living flame, and the ghost of flame." In the midst of the plain lay Athens, white and proud in the last rays of the sun. The experience was to play its part in the vision of the archetypal city of light, an important symbol of *The Fire-Bringer*.

After but a week Moody was restless once more, and his confidence in using modern Greek had picked up enough to allow him to strike out further afield. He took a trip to Delphi, traveling by boat to the coastal town of Itea. In the late afternoon he began his climb through the olive orchards and across the rocky ridges above the city toward the shrine of Apollo. At sunset Moody paused to sketch the valley. Then by the light of the moon he continued upward to the ruins above the town, where he thought to consult the god. He described the experience to Harriet:

The mornings and nights are delicious—still, still as the inmost heart of love, colored (the mornings) like the centre of an opal, and fragrant with all mysterious sweetness. When I came down from Delphi, . . . the light was making up over the sacred mountains behind me. It was a morning to remember for a hundred lives. You were with me, as always when the wonders of life most declare themselves. I seemed often to be walking, not through those mountain paths, but through the heights and morning splendors of your divine heart.

The dark and light of the mountain landscape were to provide the setting for Moody's play, and Pandora's lyric, "I stood within the heart of God," was inspired by Moody's sense of walking in the landscapes of the human heart.

Moody hired a guide in Itea for a climb of Parnassus, mountain of the Muses. They climbed in an icy wind to the snow line, where the cold and the prospect of night on the mountain halted them. Moody had hoped to go on to the summit, but his guide wrapped himself in his rug and went to sleep in the sun. Moody had little choice but to follow the example. Cold and stiff at dusk, they climbed down to Arachova, a little mountain village at the head of the valley above Delphi. The next day they crossed the valley to another village, arriving in the midst of wedding festivities. The little Greek town was in holiday dress, and the poet felt like a visiting hero: "I was never so feted and toasted and done grace to since I came home from Crusade with Barbarossa," he wrote Harriet. His hosts insisted that he remain overnight to participate in the torchlight dancing and celebration of the marriage. Moody observed that he learned "something about the gentilezza of the human heart when it is still innocent and primitive." The young couple of The Fire-Bringer owe something to the village wedding on Parnassus.

Coming down from the snow line on the mountain, Moody had injured his hip. Two additional days of walking and riding irritated it to the point that, when he returned to Athens, he was obliged to give himself over to complete rest.[31] He ignored the symbolic implications of a poet's fall while climbing Parnassus, observing instead, "I have drunk of Castaly and slept on Parnassus, so that henceforth in-

spiration is mine by right." In his enforced idleness Moody turned to
Aeschylus's *Prometheus Bound.* He thought it dry, except for the
grandeur of language and the choruses, which he studied with care.
The *Agamemnon* appealed more to his imagination. He felt it, like
Oedipus at Colonus, was primarily romantic in conception and effect.
Moody was wrestling as well with the mysteries of Greek religious cult
and ritual and finding the seeds of his own faith. He discovered in
the Orphic poets, the teachers of the cult of Dionysus, and the hiero-
phants of Demeter at Eleusis a similar somewhat vague doctrine which
appealed—one, he wrote, "of mystic regeneration, to be achieved
however not through denial of this life but by a complete entering
into it." Again the issue is basic to the theme of the play, still to take
form in Moody's thought and imagination.

Moody's pace in Greece, deliberate as it was, had been fatiguing
physically and emotionally. With an imaginative intensity unknown
to the casual traveler, he strove for total response to the landscape—a
landscape he worked to saturate with the spirit of classical Greek
experience. In the month he had been in the country, Moody had
made almost daily excursions into Athens and the surrounding territory. He had searched the library of the American school for hints of
early myth and ritual and for suggestions of sites he should visit. With
painstaking effort he had pressed his rusty college Greek into service
to read through ten plays,[32] working to unlock the secrets of the metrical
intricacies of the Greek chorus. In addition, his daily medium of communication had been modern Greek, a language with which he had
only the barest familiarity. In the restlessness of a sensibility heightened
by fatigue, and not yet recovered from his fall, Moody set off on June 7
for the Peloponnesus and a two-week trip through the splendors and
shades of Greek light, the heat of the summer sun, and the heady,
thin air of the Greek mountains.

He left Athens for Gytheion, where he stopped overnight. From
the coast Moody went through the country to Sparta; there, finding
mules and a boy to guide him, he began his journey. He left Sparta
in the starlight at four in the morning and welcomed the dawn breaking over the orange groves and vineyards through which he and his
guide traveled to the tinkle of mule bells toward the Langhada Pass. As
they climbed, the cultivated areas gave way to a trail walled by fern
and ivy, which offered glimpses of mountain springs and waterfalls.
Moody came out at last on the heights above the plain of Messenia, a
"tapestry of dyes," that seemed to him "a robe that Aphrodite had
dropped from her as she flew to her chosen island of Cythera." Moody
was living in the thought of the heroic life the area had nurtured as he
crossed Mt. Taygetos to Ithome to view the bare mountaintop on which

stood an altar to Zeus Ithomas—an altar on which human sacrifice had been performed in times almost beyond recorded history. Instead of the altar, he found a ruined chapel inhabited by an ancient hermit, who said he had spent exactly thirty-three years there—the span of Christ's life on earth and, indeed, of Moody's, for he was now thirty-three. The poet shared the hermit's bread and water as he pondered a mood of deep *Weltschmerz* in anguished concern for the meaning of his own life and of all life, questioning, "What are we? What do we here? Alas, alas!"

Moody climbed on upward across wild pastures and barren gorges, through oak forests to an ancient temple of Apollo which looked out across the mountain peaks, "so far from everywhere that for many centuries . . . it remained unknown except to the shepherds who drove their flocks into these upper reaches for summer pasture." He traveled by starlight but reveled in the sun, "scattering abroad his terrible glories." He pondered, "It seems to me that these suns are needed to reveal the central secret of that art and religion which once was here, and which by virtue of its truth and beauty is forever here." By the time Moody reached Andritzena, a mountain village, he was at the borders of Arcadia. He was now unable to sleep except for an hour at midday, feeling no need of rest in the light mountain air. He was in a high state of excitement, the scene peopled with the ancient Greeks and their dim gods whom his imagination summoned into life again. Night was especially precious. Then, he felt, "the earth-spirit seems most passionately awake and intent upon its own business."

Moody had been traveling most of the time by mule, but now, having nearly lamed his mule and exhausted his guide, he walked while the boy rode through the lonely valleys of Arcadia and Elis toward Olympia. He conjured up the mad pipes of Pan, feeling he understood for the first time "the listening, the brooding, the lonesome music, the sudden terror ('Panic terror'), the animal yet mystic mirth, and all the other attributes of that wonderful god that the Arcadian peasants dreamed out for themselves." The valleys and mountains spoke more eloquently than the ruined temples, monuments, and statues of Olympia, over which he lingered only briefly. Leaving his guide and mule behind in Olympia, he pushed quickly on for Corinth, where he found "all things on land and sea . . . merely varieties and shapes of flame, wonderful to look upon but not wholly good to be amongst." He made pilgrimage, like that to Delphi, to the ruins of the temple to Aphrodite above the city. He remained for the sunset and into the evening, meditating on the luxurious glory of ancient Corinth, on the old tales of Jason and Medea, and of Bellerophon. Held by the magnificent view across the isthmus to the sea and back toward the rugged country through which he had traveled, he pondered the rites and mysteries of love. Of the memory Moody was to write his poem, "The Moon-Moth," several years later.

The poet was ready to leave Greece by June 20, and friends were scattered through Italy and France. Trumbull Stickney had written him from Paris in the hope that Moody might join him there for the summer. The Lovetts were spending most of the summer in Grenoble, and Ferd Schevill and his sister were cycling in Normandy. Lewis Gates was in Sicily. Moody left to join Gates, and after a few days in Sicily they headed north to Naples and Rome.[33] Moody responded to the atmosphere of Rome enough to place two roses on Keats's grave and an ivy leaf on Shelley's. But he was exhausted by the experience of Greece and he was fretting over the strenuous perfections Harriet's love demanded. In the lush setting of Italy he gave way to "rebellion, and reckless grasping after life or what bore the semblance and wore the red flower of life, careless whether—nay, even glad if its heart were poisoned." Thus he described his activity later in a letter to Harriet. Moody had written her three or four times a week from Greece, but from Italy he wrote nothing. In Rome he took off her ring in joyous release from "its impossible summons and its intolerable reproach." Harriet's idealization of the poet had troubled him earlier, and he had written from Athens, "Sometimes I cannot bear to have you make so much of me, knowing how ordinary are the levels on which most of my life is led, how utterly unheroic I am in all the relations of life." Moody had been pressing himself to the limits of heroic imagination to capture the setting for his poem as well. And the emotion appropriate to his mingling of Dionysian and Promethean themes was clashing with Harriet's emphasis on spiritual values.

Moody made his way quickly to Florence and then north into the mountains, but a sense of his betrayal of himself and Harriet oppressed him. By July 13 he was in Paris; from there he finally wrote Harriet his first letter in almost a month. It was a letter of *Sturm und Drang*, telling a tale Moody characterized as one "of wasted—worse than wasted days, of that failure of will and courage which is the ultimate affliction, of defeat after defeat by the dark powers of unrighteousness and division of soul." He located the cause of his defection in creative frustration. It seems impossible that Moody should have felt his play would take shape so soon after the trip, yet his masque had fallen into place in Venice and work on it had gone swiftly in the summer of 1897.

Under the burden of his guilt and his nervous exhaustion,[34] Moody mused over the welcome given the Prodigal Son and the son's dazed reaction to generous treatment of his sins. He contemplated the

fiery onslaughts, "the implacable coils and swift-playing inescapable
fang of the Serpent," which should awake him from bemused torpor
and prepare him "to go down into the terrible waters of purification."
And he was driven into self-analysis by his mood:

All along my life I see how a too quick despair has hurled me out of the
path to which I had to struggle back with punishment and loss. It is this
too which has made my human history incoherent, has made me take and
cast away, claim hearts and deny them, handle the most precious gifts of
time like a fool and a spendthrift.[35]

Such alternations of hope and despair, of involvement and withdrawal,
of passion and indifference, provide a coherence of their own for
Moody's history. But he was acting out his conflict and despair, ridding
himself of the demons which haunted him.

Moody's vision of the Prodigal's welcome, his glance ahead to
purification, his intellectual arousal to self-analysis and castigation were
signs that a revival of spirits was not far off. On the morning of July 24
Moody awoke as if reborn to a clear, beautiful Paris day, rejoicing in
life, "when unfevered either by over-striving or by the sickness of
weariness which follows over-strife." But he immediately qualified the
remark in parenthetical explanation: "I am not preaching the 'golden
mean'; I am not preaching anything; we must be as we are." Moody
had drawn back from the rare atmosphere of strenuous moral idealism
to the fundamental position of the poet, that position which had informed his own best work and set it in a context of human conflict.
It was, to be sure, a moral position. But it was one in rebellion against
the heavily weighted dogmas of his period: "We must be as we are."
The fully human affirmation was central to Moody's view of the act
of Prometheus and its implications. It came, bringing with it—however
cloudily—the play.

Moody rested and absorbed the scene, walked the streets, and
spent hours sitting in the Luxembourg Gardens near the apartment of
Stickney, with whom he was staying. Stickney was at home in Paris
as he had not been in Cambridge. His wit and charm, his sensitivity
on questions of poetry, music, and art, and his ease of movement in
the language and ways of Paris contributed to Moody's growing sense
of well-being and his receptiveness to the virtues of a Paris summer.

Returned to his reading project, Moody picked up the plays of
Euripides and later turned to Pindar and Plato. He bolstered the background scholarship for his play with trips to the Bibliothèque Na-
tionale. Trumbull Stickney's personality and interests, however, were
of more important influence than these activities. Stickney had matured

as scholar and poet in the three years since Moody had last visited him. Like Moody he had become interested in the poetic drama and had published a one-act play, *Prometheus Pyrphoros,* in the *Harvard Monthly* two years before. Its appearance coincided with that of Moody's masque, and Stickney's work may well have offered the hint of a figure and a theme which were a more positive embodiment of Moody's concerns than the masque had provided. The play itself, together with Stickney's sophistication as a student of Greek drama,[36] was invaluable to Moody. In Paris Stickney became a sounding board for Moody's Promethean speculations.

By August 8 Moody was ready to leave Paris for a place where he could write. He chose to return to the Dolomites, the scene in which his masque had taken shape. Convincing himself that he was well again, Moody left Paris for Innsbruck. Though he had not replaced Harriet's ring on his finger, he wrote her that he felt he might soon be able to, though he declared,

It will have to be with a more human and less ethical conception of its meaning than before. I am not going to deny my nature, nor cramp it, for it and the natures of the sisters and brothers whose lives I see and share, is all that I know of God.

Moody settled down in an informal, inexpensive hotel in St. Vigil in the Tyrol, surrounded on three sides by high mountain peaks. He hiked and sketched up and down the valley, taking short trips and sometimes venturing up a mountain. But he still felt the effects of his overexertion, observing to Harriet that he hadn't managed yet to pull his nerves very firmly together. On August 20 he decided to wear Harriet's ring again, having come to the conclusion that it put him "under no constraint, involved no vow of life other than the knowledge of love and high thoughts in another heart must involve."

In the mountains an early sketch for *The Fire-Bringer* was taking shape. Two notebooks on his Promethean materials, gathered in Greece and in Paris, give some indication of the direction Moody's play was taking and the way in which he worked.[37] He noted treatments of the legend in Hesiod, Aeschylus, and Apollodorus; Prometheus's opposition to the destruction of man and the creation of a new race is commented on in its possible connection with the central theme of *The Masque of Judgment.* From the beginning Moody identified Promethean fire with the element of passion, stolen in a hollow fennel —the Wand of Dionysus. In Apollodorus Moody found supporting figures for the play: Deukalion, son of Prometheus, and his wife, daughter of Pandora, the Greek Eve. Deukalion's ark, settling on

Parnassus after the great flood, roused Moody to consider parallels in the Hebraic myth of Noah. Typhon, he felt, he could identify with the Worm of his masque. And Moody noted the possibility of representing the story of Abram's sacrifice and vision in the fifteenth chapter of Genesis as a dream of Deukalion's. The Greek trip had enriched Moody's sense of his material immeasurably. Not only did it provide a vivid sense of setting, but Moody's reading on the worship of Pan, of Dionysus, and of Demeter provided suggestive motifs for the play in early Greek ritual and possibilities for symbolic enrichment of which he took full advantage. Experiences as different as his visit to the site of ancient human sacrifice to Zeus and his participation in the marriage on Parnassus were to be worked into the complex texture of the play.

With the advent of September the mountains grew increasingly cold and rainy, and Moody left the Dolomites for Riva on Lake Garda. In the slow mails of 1902, Harriet was just responding to Moody's letters from Paris. She suggested that too much stimulus was not good, and urged her lover to return to America. In reply Moody maintained that his stimuli were neither overpowering nor excessively esoteric, and he pointed out that he was given to exaggeration. "True, I have been very, very restless," he wrote, "but I should have been so anywhere."

The next month and a half are a blank. Either Moody wrote no letters or the letters have been destroyed. He had intended to go on to Florence from Riva, and perhaps he did. But after his return he referred to having seen Maeterlinck's *Mona Vanna* in Munich.[38] Perhaps he decided to go to Germany and Austria for October and early November, seeking the theatre and music. In any case, the period is one in which Moody lost sight of his American life and was seriously considering remaining indefinitely in Europe, for he wrote Harriet from on board the *Ryndam*, November 21: "I got your letter three days ago in Vienna, and immediately started for Rotterdam, where I was fortunate enough to catch this boat. It was a case of coming home now or not at all, and I know that to remain abroad would have been a fatal mistake."

A severe cold developed as Moody took the train from Vienna for Rotterdam, and complications had set in by the time he embarked. The illness and fever were like those which afflicted him in Genoa five years earlier, and he remained in his berth for most of the voyage. He arrived in New York at the beginning of December and put himself in the hands of his sister, Charlotte, who nursed him through the illness.[39] Moody called his malady grippe in a shipboard letter, but Charlotte identified it as rheumatic fever. Until mid-December Moody rested, seeing only Charlotte and Dan Mason, to whom he read a por-

tion of his new play and explained the project. On Christmas Eve
Moody read Milton's "On the Morning of Christ's Nativity," but
without much enthusiasm. The reading was more than a sentimental
gesture. He was preparing his Milton course for the winter term, and
he found it difficult to readjust to academic demands. After a reference
in a Christmas note from Harriet, he reread it, however, and "found it
lifted up into its old place." Moody was back in Chicago for New
Year's Eve, which he spent before Harriet's comfortable fire at "the
Grove." The Prodigal had returned from his wanderings.

CHAPTER 8

THE FIRE-BRINGER

AFTER EIGHT MONTHS of separation, Moody was ready to return to Harriet, and she to receive him. He had rebelled against the ties of their relationship, striking out toward new definitions and a larger freedom. Harriet had remained courageous during the crisis in spite of the difficulties of her own situation. While Will was away, she had begun the slow process of trying to walk again. Her hopes for a rapid recovery were not to be fulfilled, and she moved awkwardly and with great pain. Already in her late forties, Harriet had been worried by Moody's restlessness. But with all her anxiety for him, for herself, and for their love, she recognized his claim of independence. Her admonitions were temperate and wise and her letters were vigorous, sparkling with her faith and hope. Harriet's love combined a direct, womanly love with a larger maternal love that was generously protective and substantially hopeful. Out of his own exhaustions and depressions, the talented young poet looked on Harriet's practical wisdom and "patient heroism" with admiration.

Moody had left his things with Harriet, and he returned to the room which had been prepared for him in her large house. He turned aside from his play and plunged back into the classroom, a world from which he had been away for eighteen months.[1] Under his new dispensation he was teaching only literature—one course in Milton and another in the drama from 1580 to 1642. Neither was new to him nor strenuous, though both seemed foreign to the creative interest closest to him at the moment. His social life was larger under Harriet's guidance, but old friends were included with the new. Schevill was often one of the company and Moody especially sought out Paul Shorey, Chicago's sensitive Greek scholar, for discussion of the materials which form the background of *The Fire-Bringer*. Shorey relished the association, and he willingly read the odes of Pindar and the choruses of Greek tragedy aloud with Moody, as the poet worked to catch their cadences and patterns of sound.[2] As Moody settled into his winter's work his restlessness disappeared. His life with Harriet fulfilled most of his desire, and his teaching routine filled his time. Immersed in the concerns of his Chicago life, Moody dropped all communication with his friends in the East.

Moody's Chicago contract put him in an exceptionally good position financially, in spite of his extended stay in Europe. His term of teaching represented his year's work, and Moody had begun to draw on his Chicago salary in July. It was large enough for him to save an impressive portion, and nine months of his year were free for writing. On the other hand, Moody's hopes for an income from the *History of English Literature* were slow in materializing. The Chicago school system, on which Moody had banked heavily, had not adopted it. In passing through New York, Moody found his publisher pessimistic. The book was stimulating interest in the colleges, but Moody and Lovett were advised to "recast the text on simpler lines" for the schools. While sales were respectable at the end of the first six months, royalties had barely made up the $500 advance to Moody, and Lovett had still received nothing. Longer term prospects seemed good, though the suggestion of revision did not please Moody: "I am in communication with a reliable anarchist whom I think competent to blow Scribner and his whole shooting-match at the moon, in case nothing else avails to save me."[3]

In the spring of 1903 Moody turned again to his Prometheus. The next six months were to see his dream of a quiet cottage retreat fulfilled. Harriet took a house on Mackinac Island for the indefinite future, and she and Will left for northern Michigan in May. Drawn by the demands of her business, Harriet returned to Chicago, leaving Moody in the care of a cook-housekeeper. During the late spring and summer she was able to join Will for a week or two from time to time. Moody drifted into the leisurely pace of island life with a quiet joy. If he engaged in violent extremes of emotion while working over his play, he did not tell Harriet of them, writing in her absence low-keyed letters, commenting on events of the day or on his reading. His moods were, in fact, no longer emotions wrought out of his inner struggles, but simple, clear reflection of nature as the weather changed and the days passed. He had bought a dog—fit companion for his new existence —whom he named Siegfried. But at Mackinac he usually called it, more humbly, Brother. With Brother he took short treks through the woods and fields of the island. There were excursions with Harriet.

She brought a book for identification of wild flowers and together they sought out Mackinac's varieties. Moody followed their spring and summer progress, sometimes discovering an unusual specimen with which to surprise Harriet on her visit. He spent many leisurely hours painting and sank into a domestic concern for the cottage and its appointments. They read together by the fire in the evenings when Harriet was there; at other times, Moody read alone. And Moody was slowly and carefully constructing the lines of *The Fire-Bringer*.

In May he worked on a study in oils of the meadow and finished a group of pastels. The play, he felt, was going well, though slowly. Working on the second act, Moody wrote: "I am not forcing it, for I feel that upon the success of this portion of the poem (the return of Prometheus) the success of the whole will largely depend." At the end of May Moody redid his oil sketch of the meadow, turning from brush to palette knife; he troweled the paint on "in everlasting chunks and shovelled until all of a sudden—*ecco!* the thing began to talk." Through June and July he worked slowly to the end of act 2 and into the final act. Casual reading of a volume of Howells's ghost stories provided material supporting his own distrust of literary realism. "How impressive it is to see," he observed in a letter to Harriet, "how almost all earnest minds, and exactly by reason of their earnestness, have sooner or later to abandon the realistic formula, or at least to so modify it that it ceases to have any meaning *qua* realism."

In July Harriet read the masque and the developing *Fire-Bringer* side by side. Moody had conceived the Prometheus play in relation to his masque, and he was considering the possibility of a trilogy. But Harriet's reading emphasized their differences in form and language, and Moody decided to give up the idea. Harriet suggested changing the masque to fit, but Moody thought he would let them "stand as companion poems, breathing different aspects of the same theme in different moods and with each its separate 'aura.'" But denying and redeeming in the same breath, he thought he might "add a scene to the *Masque* which will at once complete its own inherent idea and serve as a sufficient link of suggestion between the two."

Moody's emotions as he worked through the last act of his play, with its tragic exaltations and dark, flaming grandeurs, are traceable only through the changes in nature he records in his letters. There were days of "halcyon warmth and sunshine," and there were others like one at the end of August, when, "under the ban of the rain even painting has ceased," and "roads and woodpaths are so soft with the everlasting downpour that walking is difficult even if one has heart to brave the dogged leaden drench." September brought colder weather and wood fires through the day. Moody and Harriet were still reading

fiction, Moody relishing *The Pit,* a recent book by Frank Norris, the
American novelist with whom he had so much in common. He found
it "a good deal of a book," carrying "big sail" equal to "the breeze it
invokes and gets . . . through its unequivocal celebration of the Brute
and his worshippers." By the first of October, Moody had finished the
chorus to Apollo which ends *The Fire-Bringer.* Only some projected
songs for Pandora remained to be written.

With the coming of fall the pastoral idyll, together with his play,
was nearing its end, and Moody roused himself to plans for the future.
He quickly moved to reestablish contact with friends in the East. He
sent off an exuberant letter to Josephine, chiding her for publishing in
the magazines, barraging her with questions, and loosing his high
spirits on completion of the play—"a large and juicy stunt"—with
"Whoop la!" [4] Two weeks later he wrote Charlotte Moody, suggesting
he would be East in a month or so. Josephine had not responded to
Moody's missive and he turned to Mary Mason, filling his letter with
the same stream of questions.[5] Moody then wrote Dan Mason in New
York to ask him to get a room in the Benedick, pointing out that he
wanted to be downtown.

Harriet had been prevented from visiting in September and was
becoming restive in Chicago as Moody's letters became lighter in tone
and briefer. But she spent October on the island, where she and Will
took advantage of the autumnal beauty, driving through the woods on
good days and spending long hours before the fire reading and talking.
They returned to the idea for a trilogy. Harriet was taken with the
thought of a masterwork of size and dignity that would culminate in
bright hope and a gathering of the themes of the two plays in a powerful third, filled with faith and resolution. After discussion, Moody
agreed, waiving his earlier hesitations over the project. The seriousness
of his decision is clear from two letters of mid-October. "I have got my
book practically done," he wrote Charlotte, "but shall probably not
publish it this fall, as I have in mind to finish a companion book first."
He made the same comment to Mary Mason, referring to his third play
as "another still obscure as conclusion to the trilogy." [6] The play was
not merely obscure; Moody seems to have had no idea for its content!

There were a number of themes for prose plays, and discussion
turned to them. Moody was eager to establish contact with the theatre
—to write something for production. *The Fire-Bringer* had in fact been
written with the contemporary poetic theatre in view. Moody entered
one idea in his notebook merely by title, *The Fardel Bearers.*[7] The
play would have developed the theme Hamlet's best-known soliloquy
suggests. He entered a longer note for "a poorhouse play." In it two
outcasts from society were to gain strength for a normal and useful

life through their love for each other. A third idea for a play centered on the love of a cuckolded husband for the child of his wife and a bachelor friend. The superficial bachelor was to be brought to awareness of the values of human affection by the child's death.

Moody was contemplating ideas for poems as well. A subject listing of the fall includes the hymn to Apollo which he did write and incorporate as the final chorus of *The Fire-Bringer*. He also listed the Fountain of Youth, the Caryatides (which had intrigued him on his first European trip and of which he made symbolic use in his play), a poem on skating with the Irish girl six years earlier, and—most interesting—something on the wife of Hosea. The treatment would have centered in the prophet's necessary marriage to a whore in order to bring prophetic condemnation but also ultimate redemption to Israel. Moody was still troubled with the role of Pandora in *The Fire-Bringer* and had yet to suggest her full significance in the unwritten songs for the play. Hosea's wife raises the problem of Pandora. The thematic motif, which was to provide material for much of Moody's work of the next few years, has continued to attract twentieth-century writers, and poets as diverse as Hart Crane and William Carlos Williams were to follow Moody's lead.

Moody remained with Harriet on Mackinac Island a week longer than he had intended. On November 10 he finally left for New York City. By a stroke of luck he found a room available in the Studio Building on West Tenth Street. While there was no bathroom and no central heating, Moody responded to the place. It was swarming with artists, and the walls of the top-floor studio, well lighted by a skylight and two windows, were a medley of colors. Moody liked "the feeling of *bien-être* and homeliness, the sense of seclusion from the insistent New York rush-and-grab, and the atmosphere, subtly diffused from half-open doors and passing figures in the corridors, of the artistic life." The room was bare, and Moody bought a couch-bed and a stove. He telegraphed Harriet for his table, chairs, rug, easel, and anything else she wanted to send. Dan Mason offered some hangings, and the studio began to take on an air of friendly bohemian charm.

While the studio was taking shape, Moody spent most of his time regaining the feel of the city. Mason was available for dinner and introduced Will to his friends. Moody went to the theatre or the opera almost nightly, seeing Stephen Phillips's *Ulysses* and Barrie's *The Admirable Crichton*. But he found nothing he considered to be very important. Harriet was in his thoughts, and an evening of *Die Walküre* roused Moody's response to her at its deepest level—that of the archetype of the primal earth-mother. He wrote: "It is through music that I seem to come nearest to you, and nearest of all through this elemental

welter of Wagner's, this chaos of chords continually shaping themselves into divine form only to gaze about for an instant and melt back
once more into its primordial element."

After his months of solitude, Moody was seeking out people. He
began visiting the studio of Arthur Whiting, a composer and friend of
Mason's. He made casual acquaintance with his fellow tenants, among
whom were some artists of repute: John La Farge, Alden Weir, J. G.
Brown, and Thomas Dewing. Moody saw Robinson from time to time,
but Robinson had begun work as a subway-construction inspector and
was generally too tired and dispirited after his day's work to offer
much companionship. At dinner one evening, Robinson introduced
Ridgely Torrence to Moody, who was delighted.[8] Nearly thirty and a
graduate of Princeton, Torrence had already established close friendships with Josephine and Robinson. A native of Xenia, Ohio, he was
pursuing his fortune in the literary circles of New York. He haunted
The Players and was on good terms with a growing number of writers
and editors, among them Stedman and the Gilders. In 1900 Torrence
had published a first volume of poems, *The House of a Hundred
Lights*; the poems tend to lyrical moralizing on time, death, and love in
the accents of *fin de siècle*. When Moody met him, Torrence had completed his first verse play, *Eldorado*, and was at work on a second on
Héloïse and Abelard. But he was able to work only after his hours at
the copy desk of the *Critic*. The poets began meeting for dinner or
the theatre occasionally.

Moody found it difficult to settle down to work, and there had
been a recurrence of illness—"a severe cold . . . with grippe symptoms,
and . . . a sharp touch of that accursed pain in the hip," which he
supposed was rheumatism. In early December the theme of outcast
woman in her role as reconciler of man and God took a new turn,
and Moody began work on a blank verse narrative on the death of
Eve. For two or three weeks of December, Moody spent most of his
time on the new poem. But as the holidays approached, his work was
giving Moody the perspective he needed for the additional lyrics in
The Fire-Bringer. By the end of the year he had written half a dozen
songs, most of them for Pandora. One song, however, a by-product of
his work, was "Thammuz."

The poem is spoken by the Assyrian fertility god, whose death and
rebirth bring renewal of spring out of the death of winter. In "Thammuz" Moody weaves motifs of the rites to Adonis with the myth
of Orpheus, who was torn to pieces by Bacchantes. The victim's body
was thrown into the river, which runs red with his blood and with
the promise of spring. Moody had treated the Orpheus myth dramatically in his prelude to *The Masque of Judgment*, and the song may

have grown out of his interest in linking the two plays more closely. An economical dramatic lyric, the poem presents Thammuz's reappearance to his daughters, who have slain him. The god, reborn as a youth, accepts his daughters' passionate ecstasy, saying, "Such ye are; and be ye such!" Their own renewal is suggested by their hair, grey in stanza 2, but now raven and gold. These are the final stanzas:

> Mourners, mourn not overmuch
> That ye slew your lovely one.
> Such ye are; and be ye such!
> Lift your heads; the waters run
> Ruby bright in the climbing sun.
>
> Raven hair and hair of gold,
> Look who bendeth over you!
> This is not the shepherd old;
> This is Thammuz, whom ye slew,
> Radiant Thammuz, risen anew! [9]

Moody continued to work nervously with *The Fire-Bringer* in the early weeks of the new year. He tested his new lyrics against their contexts, considering rewriting them or juggling them in their places. Not until the end of the month was he ready to call a halt. He decided not to hold the play until a third part of the trilogy was written. Moody showed the play to Trumbull Stickney, asking his opinion and suggesting a prefatory statement of indebtedness to his friend. But the play proved "puzzling and baffling" to Stickney, at least on first reading.[10] On Stickney's advice Moody omitted his statement, citing instead the relevant passage from Apollodorus and presenting a brief announcement of his plan for a trilogy. Then he sent his play to Houghton Mifflin.

2

While *The Fire-Bringer* is modeled after the Greek drama, the impact of nineteenth-century operatic tradition on the play is particularly strong. Indeed, during the following winter Moody was to write Harriet of how little the contemporary theatre offered him, commenting, "There is more strong meat of suggestion for me as to what the stage ought to be, in one good opera than in all the plays I have seen this winter put together and raised to the *n*th. And I don't care much for the opera as such, either."[11] Like that of the Greeks, the theatre of

Wagner and Verdi offered a dramatic tradition both poetic and dignified, suited to Moody's themes and temperament. *The Fire-Bringer* is
heavy with scenic description, with narration of offstage event, and
with exposition of background myth and legend. Actors compose as in
tableau, and choral passages and lyrics slow the action while adding
perspective to the dialogue. Moody's relationship with Harriet, in both
its human and archetypal dimensions, contributed to his portrayals of
Prometheus and Pandora. The *Sturm und Drang* of the summer of
1902 rises out of its hackneyed expression in Moody's letters into art.
And the relationship of man and seasons in the pastoral letters from
Mackinac Island finds heroic parallel in the play's imagery, which
correlates a sublime cosmic landscape with the psychic contours of the
human heart.

The Fire-Bringer opens as the great flood has begun to recede and
the ark of Deukalion has settled on Parnassus. Some "dull, bewildered
beasts" survive the flood, together with a group of Deukalion's people,
who remain on the heights for fear the waters will mount again. Pyrrha
awakens from a dream and probes her husband's view of their desperate
situation. Time is dead. Zeus has destroyed most of his people and has
withdrawn "the seed of divine fire"—the fire of life, the fire of human
passion and will—from the world. Memory returns to events of the
flood and of their vain efforts to recreate life by throwing clods and
stones over their heads. They created only stone men and earth women,
mockeries of the human form. "The unwrought shapes, the unmoulded
attitudes" still haunt them, pleading for life. Deukalion rails at Pandora,
sent as a mockery to man, and at Prometheus, whose aid he sees as
unrealistic folly. As Pandora sings a lyric in praise of the soul, which,
when snared in "one sky of light," flies free and laughing in another
sky, Prometheus enters to tell of his frustrated attempts to find fire. To
the old king's suggestion that he assume humility to "bend Heaven
from its anger," Prometheus responds:

> Either now with violent hand
> We snatch salvation home, or here we sit
> Till Python, hissing softly up the dark,
> Dizzy our lapséd souls, and headlong down
> We drop into his jaws.

Pyrrha and Deukalion leave to search for roots and water, and Prometheus, alone, reveals his discouragement and despair. He longs to return to his deep source in the womb of creation, crying, in a gesture
of prayer to his mother, Clymene,

> One deep, deep hour!
> To drop ten thousand fathoms softly down

> Below the lowest heaving of life's sea,
> Till memory, sentience, will are all annulled,
> And the wild eyes of the must-be-answered Sphinx,
> Couchant at dusk upon the spirit's moor,
> Blocking at noon the highway of the soul,
> At morn and night a spectre in her gates,—
> For once, for one deep hour.

The wish is a wish for death. The Sphinx guards the paradoxical issues of life, combining in its riddling presence the enigma of woman, the godlike masculine lion will, and the aggressive bird of Zeus. The riddle and its embodiment in these symbols are central to the play. Prometheus's discouragement brings spectres of lower levels of being—the stone men and earth women—from the darkness. Pandora, speaking from among their shadowy forms, sings of weaving the means of triumph from defeat and weariness:

> Of wounds and sore defeat
> I made my battle stay;
> Wingéd sandals for my feet
> I wove of my delay . . .

Prometheus recognizes Pandora as his companion in "the high home and fortress of his soul," but Pandora does not recognize him in his discouragement. She gives him a hollow reed, used to fetch unpolluted fire in annual renewal ceremonies, and, crowned with "fir-cone and similax," associated with Dionysian revels. Prometheus revives, seeing the elemental urge to life represented by Pandora's challenge and by the stone men and earth women as the bases of life and human society. He is roused to desire, wishing

> Of these stones
> To build my rumoring city, baséd deep
> On elemental silence; in this earth
> To plant my cool vine and my shady tree
> Whose roots shall feed upon the central fire!

The desire is expressed in terms of symbols associated with Christ and basic to the play. Prometheus departs, echoing Pandora's song in stronger accents and images, resolving to

> Build all this anger into walls of war
> Not dreamed of, dung and fatten with this death

New fields of pleasant life, and make them teem
Strange corn, miraculous wine!

Act 2 of the play opens as Deukalion's people come to sacrifice
a girl, Alcyone, and Deukalion's son, Aeolus, to pacify Zeus. Roused
to angry resistance, Deukalion first rails and then claims the price is
too high. It is the price of their future as a people. But a storm breaks,
the men and women bow down in terror, and Deukalion, half-crazed,
places his son on the altar with Alcyone. As the priest advances with
knife ready to make the sacrifice, Pyrrha flings herself before the altar,
demanding that they wait for a sign from Prometheus before proceeding. From this point on, the action builds through hints and visions of
Prometheus's suffering and triumph. A chorus of men presents the
hero's fate in emblematic prevision of the Crucifixion:

The eagle tempest, gyring from its place,
Seized him, and whirled,
And hung him on the plunging prow of the world,
To shed the anguish of his face
Upon the reefs and shoals of space,
To lighten with the splendor of his pain
Earth's pathway through the main,
Though death was all her freightage, and the breath
That swelled her sails was death.

The passage is a dynamic reworking of the central image of "Gloucester
Moors," and an answer in Christian-humanist paradox to the issues
there posed over three years before.[12] The scene composes as a symbolic tableau as Deukalion, weak and sightless, rises from his swoon.
Pandora stands with her hands on the heads of kneeling male and female stone and earth people, and the would-be victims on the altar
raise themselves, looking at the sky and pointing. Light comes:

The dark
Gathers and flees, and the wide roof of night
Leans in as it would break; the mountainous gloom
Unmoors, and streameth on us like a sea.
O Earth, lift up thy gates! It is the stars!
It is the stars! It is the ancient stars!
It is the young and everlasting stars!

Pandora sings a strange song of the event. The confrontation of death
with song and of despair with hope has brought passionate bridal and

The writer's father and mother in 1883. Francis Burdette Moody was born in 1826 and for a time was a steamboat captain on the Mississippi. As a result of the Civil War, he left the river and ultimately became secretary to the Ohio Falls Iron Works at New Albany, Indiana. He died in 1886. Henrietta Stoy Moody was delicate and through much of Will's youth an invalid. She died in early 1884. —Torrence Papers, Princeton University Library

William Vaughn Moody was born in Spencer, Indiana, on July 8, 1869, and grew up in New Albany, Indiana. This is his grammar school graduation picture taken in June 1881.—Torrence Papers, Princeton University Library

The editors of the Harvard Monthly, *spring 1891. Moody entered
Harvard as a freshman in the fall of 1889 and, by joining the Monthly—
which was both an informal writers' club and a literary magazine—
formed several friendships that were to endure throughout his lifetime.
In this photograph, Moody is second from the left; Hugh McCulloch,
center; and Robert Morss Lovett, far right.—Torrence Papers,
Princeton University Library*

*Josephine Preston Peabody in 1895.
Miss Peabody was a student at
Radcliffe College (or the Annex
as it was then called) and was
highly esteemed by Moody and his
friends for her literary and critical
perceptions. She was herself a successful writer and first published
a poem at the age of fourteen.—The Schlesinger
Library, Radcliffe College*

Jetsam / 1st Version = +

letter about it

[The man whose body was found at W—— Point
this morning, was a resident of that neighborhood. He
is believed to have been drowned last night while
bathing.. — newspaper clipping.]

I wonder can this be the world it was
At day-shut. I remember the sky fell
Green as pale meadows, at the long street ends,
But overhead the smoke rack hugged the roofs.
Beneath the gas flare stolid faces passed,
Too dull for sin; loose lips set hard to drain
The last lees from the heavy cup of sense;
Or if a young face yearned from out the mist
Made of its own bright hair, the eyes were wan
With desolate fore-knowledge of the end.
My life lay waste before me; waste behind,
From the gross dark of unfrequented ways
The face of my own youth peered forth at me,
Struck white with pity at the thing I was;
And globed in ghostly fire, thrice virginal,
With lifted face star strong, went one who sang,
Far-heard and cricket-small and piercing dim,
Rich verses from my youth's gold canticle.

*Page 1 of the first version of "Jetsam" with objectionable phrases
underlined by Josephine Preston Peabody.—By permission of
the Harvard College Library*

*Daniel Gregory Mason in 1895.
Moody first met Mason in the
spring of 1894 in Cambridge and
formed a friendship that was to
endure for the rest of his life.
Mason, later a distinguished
professor of music at Columbia,
first introduced Moody and
Robinson and edited a collection
of Moody letters entitled* Some
Letters of William Vaughn
Moody *(1913).—By permission
of the Harvard College Library*

*Edwin Arlington Robinson in 1897. By the time
Robinson and Moody first met in the late
nineties, Robinson had already published* The
Torrent and the Night Before *(1896) and*
The Children of the Night *(1897).—By
permission of the Harvard College Library*

This is the photograph of Moody's mother at age seventeen that inspired "The Daguerreotype," a poem in which the author contemplates the sources and issues of his personal and poetic life. Henrietta Moody nourished her son's desires to excel, lent vistas to his cloudy dreams, encouraged his first movements toward painting and writing, and shared with him her tendency to mystical and aesthetic apprehension of experience.—Torrence Papers, Princeton University Library

Edmund Clarence Stedman, who befriended Moody and other young poets of the turn of the century, and included a large portion of Moody's anti-imperialistic "Ode in Time of Hesitation" in his An American Anthology. In early 1906 as president of the National Institute of Arts and Letters he was influential in securing Moody's election to that organization.—Torrence Papers, Princeton University Library

Harriet Moody in the 1890s. Moody first met this remarkable woman in the fall of 1899 while he was still affiliated with the University of Chicago. When she met Moody, she was a divorcée in her forties, a successful teacher, and a businesswoman who ran a catering service from the third floor of her home.—Torrence Papers, Princeton University Library

"The Grove." This was Harriet Moody's pleasant home in Chicago, at 2970 Groveland Avenue, a famous haven for writers visiting Chicago until Harriet's death in 1932.—Torrence Papers, Princeton University Library

Will Moody in 1902. This is the studio photograph upon which he based the self-portrait of 1903 used on the jacket of this book.—The University of Chicago Archives

Will Moody and Alice Corbin on a beach outing in 1902. Miss Corbin was one of Harriet Brainard's protégées who helped her manage her extensive professional and social life.—Torrence Papers, Princeton University Library

This snapshot of Moody in 1902 provides a vivid contrast to the formal studio portrait of the same year.—Torrence Papers, Princeton University Library

Harriet at Mackinac Island with Will's hat beside her, 1903. For several summers Harriet rented a house here, and Moody would often come to visit her. —Torrence Papers, Princeton University Library

One of Harriet Moody's house parties. Will Moody is at top, left; William Morton Payne, top row seventh from left; Harriet, top row second from right; and Harriet Monroe, seated on steps at center. — Torrence Papers, Princeton University Library

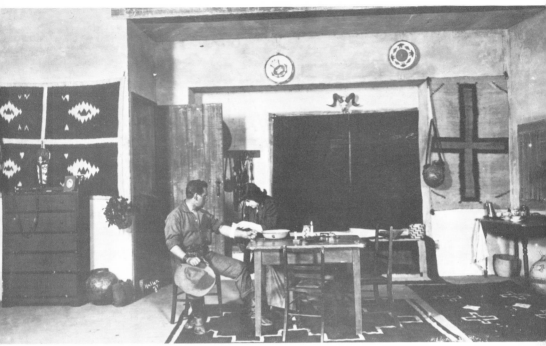

Henry Miller and Margaret Anglin in act 1 of the 1906 Broadway production of Moody's The Great Divide, which ran in New York City for two years. The author himself selected most of the decor for the Broadway set from items gathered on a trip to New Mexico.—Photograph by Hallen; Theatre Collection; The New York Public Library at Lincoln Center; Astor, Lenox and Tilden Foundations

Henry Miller and Margaret Anglin in a tense moment in act 2 of The Great Divide.—Photograph by Hallen; Theatre Collection; The New York Public Library at Lincoln Center; Astor, Lenox and Tilden Foundations

For several years Moody maintained a studio in New York City, in a building inhabited by a variety of artists including, among others, the sculptor Gutzon Borglum. This 1906 photograph shows Moody in his studio.—Torrence Papers, Princeton University Library

Ridgely Torrence in Moody's New York studio, 1906. Torrence was a contemporary playwright who wrote Abelard and Heloise *and* El Dorado.*—Torrence Papers, Princeton University Library*

Harriet, Moody, and Charlotte Moody (seated) in 1908. Charlotte was a trained nurse and the author's devoted sister.—Torrence Papers, Princeton University Library

Henry Miller and Jessie Bonstelle in
The Faith Healer (1910). Since this
Moody play questioned many popular
religious beliefs of the day, it was widely
attacked and misunderstood, much to the
author's disappointment.—Photograph by
Byron, by permission of the Harvard
College Library

Will Moody in California, February
1909. In this next-to-last year of his life
he and Harriet married in Quebec
on May 7. On October 17, 1910, in his
forty-first year he died.—Torrence Papers,
Princeton University Library

"A Group of Harvard Poets." This illustration is taken from the
Harvard Graduates Magazine for June 1909. Moody knew all the
writers depicted here. Upper left, George Cabot Lodge, '95; upper
right, Joseph Trumbull Stickney, '95; center, William Vaughn
Moody, '93; lower left, George Santayana, '86; lower right, Percy
MacKaye, '97.—Harvard University Archives

Applause. II

Under the chandeliers' blaze
See how they listen and gaze?
Listen, their eyes growing tender,
Gaze, while the magical splendor
Thy music spreads in their skies,
Flushes and darkles and dies.
I, who have wrought them the wonder,
What do I care for their cries,
Plaudits, and hand-clapping thunder?
All that I care for is yonder:—
A strip of brow in the dotted maze,
One loosened strand cutting through it, and under,
Blown by a rapture of gladness asunder,
Thrilling me through with an exquisite praise,
Her two eyes.

William Vaughn Moody.

Manuscript of "Applause," spring 1892. Moody's wrestling with problems of his public identity surfaces in the confusion over his signature.—The University of Chicago Archives

the birth of a "son"—the promise of the future and the ground for
reconciliation of spirit and matter. In her song, Prometheus is treated
as the crucified Christ, "Wounded with love in breast and side," who
revives life in the Dionysian pine cone and willow-rod, as in "tardy
stone" and "patient sod." Deukalion's men and women stir in terror
to the reawakening of will and passion. They turn from the coming
light, but Deukalion sees Prometheus returning in glory, rolling the
night on before him, bringing the day after him, in a Day of Judgment tableau Moody has converted to new purposes:

> The hours, the months, the seasons, and the times
> Acknowledge him; the waste calls to the sown;
> The islands and hoar places of the sea
> Sing, as the chief of them that are taught praises.
> About his torch shineth a dust of souls,
> Daughters and sons, who fly into the light
> With trembling, and emerge with prophecy;
> And round about goeth a wind of tongues,
> A wind as of the travailing of the nations;
> Vast sorrow, and the cry of desperate lives
> To God, and God to them crying or answering.—

With the vision of the new dispensation, the old king dies. The stone
men and earth women walk into the light which the humans are unable to face, as Pandora sings welcome to the God coming in triumph:

> *Pandora.*   Ye who from the stone and clay
>   Unto Godhood grope your way,
>   Hastening up the morning see
>   Yonder One in trinity!
> *The Earth Women.* Save us, flaming Three!
> *Pandora.*   Dionysus hath the wine,
>   Eros hath the rose divine,
>   Lord Apollo hath the lyre:
>   Three and one is the soul's desire.
> *The Stone Men.*   Save us, sons of fire!

Invisible in the light, Pandora is greeted by Prometheus, who says,
"Thou gavest me the vessel; it is filled." To which Pandora answers,
"I am the vessel, and with thee 'tis filled." Pandora's song and the exchange serve to define Prometheus, half-humanized Titan, as prophet
of a new trinity of fire gods, and his relationship with Pandora, the
mother of all earthly life, is reemphasized.

Prometheus gives the fire to Aeolus and Alcyone, and the two young people light the "altar of the world." The act ends as Pandora sings from below in fear of "the estranging dawn." The creative act is itself estranging and the final issue is not peace; instead, the act of love opens upon a new vision of deeper suffering and union on a different plane.

Act 3 opens as the funeral train of Deukalion comes up a steep path to an open tomb hewn into the rock wall at one side. The stranded ark of Deukalion is outlined in the background against peaks and a sunset cloud. A chorus of old men sings of a god mirrored in the paradoxes of the human condition:

> In one same breath
> Uttering life and death,
> Whatso his mouth seems darkly to ordain
> The darkling signal of his hand makes vain,
> And like a heart confused He sayeth and gainsaith.
> With himself He wrestles thus
> Or gives this wrestling unto us.

They accept the boon of conflict. Girls and young women sing of both Thanatos, "the dark peace-giver," and his winged opposite, Eros, while a parallel chorus of young men sings of Bacchus. The funeral train departs, leaving Pyrrha, Aeolus, and Rhodope, a handmaiden of Pyrrha, for the night watch by the tomb. As Pyrrha mourns Deukalion, Pandora comes, now for the first time in sorrow and pain. The shadow of Zeus's giant bird of wrath has darkened the earth as he searches for the fire-bringer. Prometheus enters, embraces Pandora, and answers Pyrrha's fear that light may be withdrawn. He invokes a vision of the permanent cycles of life and the dance and song of the spheres, rising to admonition based on man's microcosmic nature:

> The sun whose rising and whose going down
> Are joy and grief and wonder in the heart;
> The moon whose tides are passion, thought, and will;
> The signs and portents of the spirit year,—
> For these, if you would keep them, you must strive
> Morning and night against the jealous gods
> With anger, and with laughter, and with love;
> And no man hath them till he brings them down
> With love, and rage, and laughter from the heavens.

The individual man must himself become the whole of the cosmic order, his own "sun-thief" and "flaming reed/ That kindles new the beauty of the world." The savior of the race is also its exemplar. Prometheus draws Aeolus and Rhodope to him, praising the teeming, mysterious life of the breeding universe, producing "fantastic life" for their sakes. He hails the great joyous source of all life "In the sun's core . . ./ Where all things past and present and to come/ Ray out in fiery patterns, fading, changing,/ Forevermore unfaded and unchanged." He suggests the eventual coming of another "dim end of things," when again "In swoon and anguish" a cry shall ring out of the sun's core. Another end involves a new beginning, for the patterns of the sun are eternal. In a major shift of Moody's philosophical emphases, the Apollonian vision subsumes both Prometheus's own dream of creative evolution and the apocalyptic Christian vision. The universe is complete in the play's third act. All of existence is present, if unfathomed. The most significant process within the system is that of human realization, the renewal of spiritual and intellectual life in a world, forever ancient and forever young.

Pandora asks to be with Prometheus, and he answers in accents of her affirmation of act 1: "There where I go thou art; there, even now/ Thou cried'st me to thee, and I come, I come." He climbs to the ark, around which the stone men and earth women stand, outlined against the fiery sunset cloud. The scene suggests the possibilities in their groping evolution toward new grace. He pronounces the benediction which signaled his sense of mission in act 1: "Out of these stones/ I build my rumoring city; . . . in this soil/ I plant my cool vine." He disappears to wrestle with the bird of Zeus in an eternal triumph and an everlasting crucifixion. Pandora again sees Prometheus "nailed in pain/ On the blown world's plunging prow"; but as if in explanation of the raging vision, she sings of reconciliation and fulfillment:

> I stood within the heart of God;
> It seemed a place that I had known;
> (I was blood-sister to the clod,
> Blood-brother to the stone.)

> I found my love and labor there,
> My house, my raiment, meat and wine,
> My ancient rage, my old despair,—
> Yea, all things that were mine.

> I saw the spring and summer pass,
> The trees grow bare, and winter come;
> All was the same as once it was
> Upon my hills at home.

Pandora's environment is God's heart, yet she is kin to clod and stone.
The seasons of nature are the seasons of man's soul. Even as she finds
fulfillment in the life of God's heart, he finds his fulfillment in hers:

> Then suddenly in my own heart
> I felt God walk and gaze about;
> He spoke, his words seemed held apart
> With gladness and with doubt.
>
> "Here is my meat and wine," He said,
> "My love, my toil, my ancient care;
> Here is my cloak, my book, my bed,
> And here my old despair.
>
> "Here are my seasons: winter, spring,
> Summer the same, and autumn spills
> The fruits I look for; everything
> As on my heavenly hills.["]

The curtain falls on a chorus of young men, ascending the path into
the growing light, singing a hymn to Apollo, the third member of the
holy trinity and guide into spiritual adventure toward "the ultimate
stream/ Of vision and of dream."

The Fire-Bringer is a fuller treatment of the issues of Moody's
masque. In The Fire-Bringer, Moody's religious commitments are expressed in terms of the action. Moody's mature philosophical position,
here presented in terms of a mythic and symbolic system resembling
that of Blake, is complex. But its major outlines, as they appear in
the mythic action of the drama, may be sketched. The wasteland is
redeemed by ritual celebration of the creative act. Woman is the silent
waiting pool, desiring her fulfillment and quick to respond with hope
to the vibrations of annunciation which come to Pandora, as to women
and girls of the play. The masculine will, associated with the fire, the
wine of passion, the pine and the cones of Dionysus, is creative force,
whether acting on the level of Dionysus or on the spiritual level of
Apollo. The continuing battle of Prometheus and the bird of wrath is
not punishment but rather cosmic expression of the struggle which
continually renews life—a struggle to be engaged in "With love, and
rage, and laughter." Life is not finally located in any of the visions of
fulfillment which motivate Prometheus: the early desire for Nirvana,
the dream of the utopian society, or that of total sexual union. Life is
rather the cruel splendor, the wild passion, recognized by a male voice
of the play who, reawakened to its urges, cries out, "My soul is among

lions." Like him, though in the quieter tones of her song, Pandora finds in God's heart her "ancient rage," and her "old despair," not the peace often associated with a state of grace.

The relation of Prometheus and Pandora is repeated on the heroic, but natural, level in Deukalion and Pyrrha. She bears the redeeming vision, though he is discouraged. Deukalion is proud in his age, unaccustomed to the attitudes of abject humility which he is driven to advocate. He clings to his dream of a new society to be founded by Aeolus, and his deepest nature speaks when he refuses to sacrifice him. Like the great primal lovers, Deukalion and Pyrrha identify and reaffirm their love in moments of crisis and recognition. Earth-bound lovers, they are able to create shapes of human life in stone and clod, but the shapes lack the divine impregnation which gives birth to the human spirit. Prometheus brings them fiery souls. Confrontation with the fire brings death to Deukalion and suffering and struggle to Prometheus—parallels in natural and spiritual worlds. Alcyone and Aeolus, like the envisioned inhabitants of the city of peace, represent the motivating dreams of man. The same is true of the dedications to Eros, to Dionysus, and finally to Apollo: the young men and women express their hope, faith, and pride in their trinity of gods. In their songs it is the spirit of the quest, one aspect of which was expressed in "Road-Hymn for the Start," that is emphasized. But these songs are partial human visions,[18] and the play's larger resolution comes in the ultimate relationship of the pairs of lovers, in their tragic but heroic recognitions of their divinities and their humanities.

The play is a major achievement for Moody, not only in terms of the philosophical maturation it represents, but in terms of its art. The work is well constructed, effective in the context of theatrical requirements of the heroic tradition in which Moody was working. The slow-moving first act gathers in necessary expository materials and establishes mood and situation for the dramatic conflict of the second act, a theatrical tour de force. The third act is scenic but dramatic, a reversal in which the issues of the play reach to their complex depths. The language of *The Fire-Bringer*, though heightened by archaism of diction, inversion and complexity of syntax, and circling repetitions, troubles the eye more than the speaking voice. The rhythms shape themselves to the tongue, the lines move easily, and the syntactic units cling together. Blank verse dialogue is balanced by Pandora's graceful lyrics and the rhythmically subtle and variable odes—closer to dance and song than the lyrics of *The Masque of Judgment*. The play is most remarkable, however, for its kaleidoscopic blending of interpenetrating mythic motifs and symbols drawn from the Hebraic-Christian and the classical systems. And echoes of English and Greek literature are pervasive, as Moody gathers from history materials to suggest the timelessness of an eternal present. Powerful in the restrained simplicity and dignity of its action, and haunting in its suggestive symbolic structure, *The Fire-Bringer* is a better poetic drama than any that had yet been written in America. Indeed, it stands with some half-dozen poetic dramas in English, written between the Renaissance and the twentieth century, which retain interest for the modern reader.

3

While he was carefully polishing *The Fire-Bringer,* Moody continued to work on his narrative poem on Eve. The work went quickly, but Moody found it "getting rather crazy and raucous." In a burst of energy it completed itself, and Moody sent it to Harriet on January 18. Although Harriet praised the poem, Moody was dissatisfied, feeling that it was written in a period of excessive tension and that it lacked balance. He decided to set the poem aside and turned to other work. Once again in the world of Broadway, Moody began moving restlessly through ideas for a contemporary play. He picked up his projected bachelor play, blocked it out, and wrote a first scene. The surviving outline [14] gives an indication of Moody's early work in the prose drama. Elsa, Moody's heroine, though pursued by a number of admirers, is attracted most to Marcel Truman, a young cellist, and to Walter, an artist who is Marcel's friend and patron. A third admirer, Mr. Updike, is sketched as "a shy man, given to extravagant and obscure statement to cover his confusion." He, Lucy Dean, a friend of Elsa's, and Gregory Newell, Elsa's young cousin, provide vehicles for comedy and exposition. Scenes were blocked out to move from Elsa's birthday party, through exposition, to a scene in Walter's studio in which the sexual relationship of Elsa and Walter is established. An insult, however, motivates Elsa's choice of Marcel, not Walter, as husband. A fifth scene is sketched as "Dresden: meeting with Walter. The choice reaffirmed." The last scene was to involve the death of Walter's child, whom Marcel regards as his own. The play was to end with Walter's recognition of the values arising out of human love, values he had missed in life. Four pages of a first act survive, but either Moody lost interest at this point or the further development of the play is lost.

Among other ideas was one for a dream play. Moody had been reading Lindsay Swift's book on Brook Farm and was intrigued by the possibilities of the subject. He wanted to do a play "which should reveal the humorous in the unworldly, without any touch of satire or *parti pris,* and which should humanize to the materialistic and worldly average eye the mystic and otherworldly personality." [15] Moody decided to get Hawthorne's *Blithedale Romance* to see what Hawthorne had done with the subject, but the seed did not germinate into a play.

In early February Moody took up yet another idea, beginning a verse play on a modern theme Harriet had suggested. The new theme, perhaps that for the poorhouse play, took hold. After a few days of work, Moody felt he was about to strike through to a new kind of blank verse. He wrote Harriet that he wanted a verse medium "which has much of the unconventionality and unguided movement of prose, in the passages where the emotional level is low, and which yet is capable of gathering itself up, when needed, into the passion and splendor which prose is incapable of." [16] The search was to involve most of the major American poets of the next generation. Moody finished a first act of the play in nine days. By Valentine's Day, when two dozen lilies arrived from Harriet, he was already well into the second act.

Moody's playwriting received a boost from signs of change in the taste of the theatregoing public. The tide, he felt, was at last turning from the trite offerings of the Syndicate's "dramatized historical novels, their patched-up French farces, their pick-me-up Clydefitcheries." Outside the empire of Charles Frohman's Syndicate, the season boasted a production of *Candida*, still running to packed houses after seven weeks. Mrs. Fiske staged *Hedda Gabler*, and Ada Rehan and Otis Skinner, sensing the shift of theatrical winds, emerged from retirement to perform Shakespeare and Sheridan. Sidney Rosenfeld had organized the Century Players, and there was promise that the Everyman Company would invade the city for an undoctored performance of *Twelfth Night*. Three of Yeats's plays had packed the house, and people were turned away from the doors. Frohman's "remarks upon men and things," Moody observed, "are said to have the gloom and force of great tragic literature." [17]

Yeats was in the United States on a lecture tour and stopped in New York. While Moody did not meet him, the energetic Harriet greeted him in Chicago with enthusiasm.[18] She admired his work and was attracted to his spiritual force. Moody had been less interested. He was sceptical of Yeats's deep involvement in "folk-poetry and the folk-spirit," finding it "an artificial attitude" and "the undoing of Yeats and all his 'school.' " He wrote Harriet, "A self-conscious attempt to assimilate and reproduce what is itself of the very essence of naïveté, is bound to be a cancelling business; good old Bishop Percy over his port and his last find in broad-sheets, was nearer the heart of the matter." [19]

Robinson was still mired in his job in the subway, but Moody saw Mason occasionally and Ridgely Torrence frequently. Torrence was an

amusing and knowledgeable companion for Moody. He was pleased to
find Moody "as good as his poetry," but he quickly observed to their
mutual friend, Josephine Peabody, that Moody "certainly wears a large
mantle." [20] Moody was also becoming acquainted with his neighbors in
the Studio Building. He entered upon a stimulating friendship with
Gutzon Borglum, the sculptor and painter, spending an occasional afternoon or evening in his studio. They talked while the sculptor modeled
in clay, swiftly bringing his materials to life in a way Moody found
amazing. Moody recognized in Borglum "a big sane mind" and "altogether . . . the most powerful figure of an artist" he had ever encountered. Borglum's art, like Moody's, was heroic in style and proportion: he was to spend years sculpturing the presidential memorial at
Mount Rushmore. In February Borglum introduced Moody at the Arts
Club, where he began to dine from time to time.

Moody had been working on the proofs for *The Fire-Bringer* as
well as on his new verse play during February. By the end of the
month, having sustained himself on quantities of coffee and tobacco,
he completed the proofreading. He dropped off his work at Houghton
Mifflin in Boston and began "to loaf and lark a little" in his old haunts,
visiting Stickney who had taken a position as Instructor in Greek at
Harvard. On a visit to Charles Eliot Norton in Cambridge, Moody met
John Norton, the young painter, and his wife. They urged him to accompany them on a trip to Arizona to visit the Hopi reservation. Moody
jumped at the chance. He was able to obtain a free railway pass, and
the possibilities of Hopi myth and ritual for poetic drama attracted
him.[21] He was in Chicago by the middle of the month and quickly
convinced Ferd Schevill to join the party in the West when his teaching term was completed. He renegotiated his lease on his New York
studio through the good offices of Mason and turned the place over to
Robinson for the period of his absence.[22] Moody's reunion with Harriet
was brief, and on March 28 he set off from Chicago with the Nortons.

Moody's response to the Grand Canyon offers yet another revelation of the extent to which the quality and action of their mutual life
had taken on essentially mythic dimension. He wrote Harriet, "My love
and knowledge of you seems to grow vaster here in the face of these
silences and immensities, and the great drama of our lives to gain both
solemnity and mirthfulness from each day that it is projected against
this landscape of amazing light, primeval contour, and whimsical barbaric detail." [23] In Canyon Diablo the party outfitted for their trip.
Upon Schevill's arrival they set out for Oraibi, where they rented a
small adobe house. Moody reacted characteristically to both scene and
people, taking delight in the visual. He admired "groups of old women
weaving baskets on the borders of the 'Flute Well,' while waiting for

their water-jars to fill under the slow trickle, files of girls carrying jugs of water up the rocks, a distant line of dancers returning from Walpi to their home on the 'second mesa,' in ceremonial garb, four aged priests sprinkling sacred corn-meal to mark and hallow the path across the desert."

Although Moody was to use the scene at the well in his play, *The Death of Eve,* the picturesque life of the Indians and their rituals and myths were not to be of central importance to Moody's later work. His sense for character had matured. It was active as it had not been in his earlier trip, and the Oraibi scene was a mixed one. First of all, there were the young Nortons. Moody found Mrs. Norton "rather pretty and quite honest and unaffected." Norton himself had "a touch of rudeness," and was generally impatient about delays in their plans. Moody found him "a creature of much elemental unformed power." The couple stood in sharp contrast to the crowd, in which picturesque Hopis, Navajos, and straggling Mexican section hands mingled with Americans and Europeans in various stages of assimilation to the native culture. Among the latter group Moody and his friends found guides to Oraibi life. One was Louis Aiken, a New York painter, who after six months in the village, Moody observed, "dresses and looks more like an Indian than if he were the real thing." Another was a German who had spent twelve years studying the Hopis and told Moody some Hopi legends and folktales. A third guide was a certain Sawyer, "ostensibly a painter but really an irreclaimable tramp to whom adventure is as the breath of the nostrils." Moody felt he was " 'the West' in little." Moody was establishing contrasts in character and values which would provide a ready nest for the plot basic to *The Great Divide* when it presented itself a few months later. The scene was there, even to Aiken's high, mesa-based "adobe house, from the roof of which one can see all over creation."

By the time Moody returned to Chicago in May, *The Fire-Bringer* had been on the general market for a month, but the bulk of reviews of the volume did not appear until May and early June. The response was not that which welcomed Moody's *Poems,* yet the new volume was widely greeted as an important work by a major American poet. Moody was called "one of the greatest of American poets," and "one of the chief poets of his time." [24] But comment on the poetic drama was conditioned by the critical battle raging between the traditional critics, still in control of the major organs of comment in the country, and modernists, who demanded American materials and issues immediate to the times. An amusing minor controversy arose over William Morton Payne's casual identification of Moody and Woodberry as America's two greatest living poets. [25] A number of critics reacted not to

Payne's evaluation but in protest against the critical mentality which sought to number and rank poets in such terms. The most direct reaction to Moody's candidacy came in an article in the San Francisco *Argonaut,* entitled "Who Is the Greatest Living American Poet?" The writer felt undue compulsion under the task of reviewing so great a poet, commenting ironically that, if it were not for the reverence aroused by Payne's statement, he would be tempted to write of *The Fire-Bringer* that "while distinguished by imagination, while daring in conception, it lacked the quality of interest which Matthew Arnold said 'is demanded.' " And he might then judge the volume as "a rather superior book by a minor poet." [26]

A second, more central issue arose to affect and sometimes to distort response to the play: the question of the appropriateness of its subject matter for twentieth-century literature. The play was attacked for the same reasons that Moody's *Poems* had been welcomed so enthusiastically. Some reviewers, like Edwin L. Schuman of the Chicago *Record-Herald,* greeted *The Fire-Bringer* as "a fine, scholarly work, fully sustaining Mr. Moody's reputation as one of the greatest of American poets." [27] But more often there was dismay, confusion, or hostility, and the work was judged "academic" or "literary"—both damning terms. Tone of the attacks ranged widely. A reviewer for the Los Angeles *Express* found an "utter lack of human interest" in the drama. "The world is so busy nowadays," he commented, "the needs of her children so importunate, that it seems a waste of time to spend it on purely imaginary scenes and beings." [28] Another felt that Moody had "overlaid" his symbols "with such a multitude of classic references, and depended to such an extent upon the implied knowledge of the reader" that the book would be unintelligible to all but classical scholars. He found the play "steeped in the atmosphere of the library and class room." [29] A *New York Times* review commented, "A poet who is long and generally to be recognized as 'foremost' in the America of the twentieth century will not find his best themes in the Greek legends of the beginnings of humanity." [30] Others rose to virulence over the issue, one writing, "A poet who at this stirring moment in the world's history steers his bark back into the Brazen Age, and sings us of Stone Men and Earth Women, Prometheus, the stealer of fire, and Pandora, discloses in himself a certain moral cowardice. He evades the hour's issues, and sails on sterile seas." [31] Yet another put Moody in the same category with a modern lover who decided to "write his love letters in Assyrian on bricks." He proclaimed, "A Prometheus who discourses in post-Darwinian terms on man and the cosmos is an anachronism if he be not a fraud." [32]

No more than one or two critics touched on the work's viability as theatre, and then only to comment that it had little or no value from this point of view. Moody's characters seemed to many reviewers, as they had to Trumbull Stickney, not humanly convincing. He had rightly found the play "less dramatic in the human than in the symbolic order"—a view Moody had regarded as "most grievous." [33] When there was praise, it usually came in the observation that Moody "deals in masterly power with the primary emotions and experiences of the human heart, the bases upon which all imagination must build." [34] Moody's "artistic reserve" was admired, and critics, if not convinced that his goal was the appropriate one for the times, admired the diction of the play—"neither too familiar nor too remote," suggesting "grandeur" but escaping "pomposity." Rhythms of the blank verse were found to be "strong and individual," and Pandora's songs were highly praised.

If some comments on *The Fire-Bringer*, then, moved to side issues, others were well formulated and considered. The criticism of Thomas H. Briggs, Jr., writing in the Baltimore *Sun*, is thoughtful. Briggs looked back to *The Masque of Judgment*, observing that there "the excellence was uneven, the touch of the artist uncertain," although "wonderful passages of poetry and unforgettable lyrics" stood out from the context. In the new play Briggs was "not so often startled by unexpected pages of exaltation." He felt that "during the intervening three years the poet has learned that the drama is . . . a whole":

We are everywhere on a higher, firmer elevation, and care is taken that effects be gradually developed and then splendidly maintained. . . . This perfect adjustment of part to whole is seen nowhere better than in the songs, which are integral chorus passages that one may omit no more than he may an act.[35]

In spite of the wide and generally favorable reception of *The Fire-Bringer*, Moody was understandably unhappy with the direction so many reviews had taken. Like all writers, Moody desired full and positive praise. He needed "laudators" and bristled at instruction from his critics. But he had not anticipated becoming the fortuitous center of a battle between the critical establishment and its detractors, nor had he foreseen the problems his choice of subject and theme would raise. Moody had worked particularly and with considerable success to make his play self-sufficient. He had virtually thrown off his teaching role, and treatment of his work in terms of the library and classroom hit with the force of deep personal insult. Concerned with surfaces of the play, reviewers had seldom touched on the basic human problems to which *The Fire-Bringer* had given contemporary statement if not contemporary form. Moody asked Harriet to collect all the reviews she could find, so that he might test his allegiance to his craft.[36]

CHAPTER 9 REVISIONS

FOR THREE YEARS Moody's poetic impulse had been directed into his work on *The Fire-Bringer*. In spite of his growing interest in the theatre, Moody's major achievements of 1904 and 1905 were to be poetic, though his new work was to be very different in tone and concern from that of 1900. On his return from Arizona in May 1904, however, Chicago life engulfed him, and Moody remained in the Middle West until early August. Scribner's had continued to press Moody and Lovett for a simplified version of their history, and Moody reluctantly set aside his plans to sit down with his friend to the task. Planning occupied the early weeks of the summer. Moody joined the Lovetts for weekends at their summer cottage on Lake Zurich, forty miles from Chicago, and began the work of cutting and simplifying the history. Occasionally old friends gathered—members of the Chicago English department and participants in Windbag discussions of former years. But Moody's vigorous exercise in the West had aggravated the irritation in his hip, and when rest with Harriet at "the Grove" failed to make for any improvement, he decided to try a spa in Kramer, Indiana. Harriet had found the baths helpful for her foot. "Salubrious Mudlavia," as Moody dubbed the place, was as close as he had come in almost ten years to returning to his boyhood home in southern Indiana. He was dubious, but Indiana happily surprised him. A few days after arriving, he wrote Harriet,

I find the country surprisingly beautiful—surprising, because, although you praised it, I knew your tolerant affection for anything that haphazard Nature sees fit to do, and perhaps (unconsciously) minimized your report. It is a broad, homely, fruitful beauty which speaks home to me through old and all-but-forgotten associations.[1]

The local doctor said Moody had come just in time to save himself from an acute attack. Indeed, after only two baths, the poet found that his hip, which was swollen and painful before, was much improved. "I move with an ease and luxury," he observed, "which I have not known for more than a year." Harriet joined him in Kramer in mid-July, and they walked and rode together. The occasion and setting were later used in Moody's poem, "A Prairie Ride."

Though there were periods of restlessness and loneliness for both Will and Harriet under the constraints placed upon their love, they had agreed upon a relationship which involved long periods of separation. They talked earnestly of their arrangements, but the situation offered no viable alternative. Harriet was rooted in Chicago, and her life offered interest, activity, and security. Her business was thriving and she was a strong, proud woman, accustomed to the freedom her wide-ranging life in Chicago provided. Harriet's divorce was less the reason for her present caution than the sign of her independent spirit. She once said, laughing, "that she could love a dozen men at once and that no one man could completely respond to her in kind." [2] Beside her devotion to Moody and the commitments of her numerous, generous friendships, Harriet was exceptionally close to her mother. She paid her constant attentions and supported her mother in a state approaching luxury. When Harriet traveled, she left orders that a report on her mother's health be sent by telegraph daily. [3] Mrs. Tilden strongly disapproved of her daughter's relations with the poet, and a rumor later circulated among Moody's friends that she had forced Harriet to promise not to remarry during her lifetime. [4] But the tale was probably a convenient romantic fiction. Nor would a promise have been more compelling than the situation itself.

On his side, there was Moody's deep and instinctive aversion to the conditions of domesticity. He needed freedom and solitude. He had been convinced since the late nineties that his life as a writer had to center in New York, and Chicago had assumed the form of a personal nemesis. Nor would he have suggested marriage without an assured income. He was barely supporting himself in these years. He had not taught in over a year and the *History of English Literature* was making only slow, if respectable, headway in the marketplace. It alone hardly provided him enough to live on. [5] He shared Harriet's largesse when they were together, accepting her hospitality in Virginia, on Mackinac, and at "the Grove." Moody's continuing sense of responsibility for contributing to the support of his unmarried sister, Charlotte, mirrored Harriet's relationship with her mother. These considerations caused him to embark on the tedious, hitherto avoided, revision of the history. And he cautiously retained his university connection to fall back on in case of need. But neither he nor Harriet was prepared to suggest his return to teaching as a solution to the problems of their love.

The lovers again agreed to live as they must. True life and true love were spiritual realities, however crossed by the illusory problems presented by mundane existence. The agreement of November 1903 when Moody established himself in New York had been reaffirmed in Chicago in March when Moody wrote Mason asking him to renegotiate his studio lease for another year. Both Will and Harriet were strong and secure human beings, relatively indifferent to mores and judgments of the world, at least in theory. And Harriet, who might have been more vulnerable, was more indifferent than Moody in actual fact. They were however discreet. Moody had spoken of Harriet to none of his family and only to Mason among his friends. Although he was using "the Grove" as his Chicago address, he generally remained there for only brief periods. He met Harriet outside Chicago and New York, and Harriet always traveled with a companion or two. When they were apart, a constant stream of letters and telegrams kept them in communication and reaffirmed their sense of spiritual unity.

In early August Moody left Chicago once more to pick up the threads of his New York life. On one occasion he escaped the heat of the city in an excursion to Coney Island, where he enjoyed the perfections of what he called "that miracle of vulgarity." But he was lonely, writing Harriet, "Our months of dear companionship have spoiled my palate for the solitary life. Nevertheless I must lead it, and must relearn the lesson of leading it with contentment and inner exultation." Letters began to lose their power to communicate. On one occasion he wanted to write but had nothing to say. He missed the ordinary communications of daily life, observing,

If you and I could ever say Good-morning in such a manner as to really express our meaning, we should go straight on to glory, towing the astonished universe after us. "Is it not so?" "Good-morning," "Good night," "I am happy". . . —over what gulfs of meaning we walk on these little bridges, what loads of cosmic matter we lift and swing into place with these frail levers! [6]

Moody had immediately gone to work in New York. He quickly put the finishing touches on the new textbook, and when Lovett's sections arrived in mid-September the book went to press. His time was once more his own, and Moody turned to a listing in his notebook [7] of possible subjects for plays and poems. Play topics included Thammuz, probably considered as a possible subject for the third play of the trilogy, and the Hopi myth of "The Flute Hero." A third note reverts to Moody's dream play with the prophet of a new society as hero. He may have still been considering the Brook Farm theme, but he made notes on Rousseau and on Sanborn's treatment of French socialist thought. Moody listed several plots more clearly adaptable to the realistic theatre than these. One: "The tragedy of the unwilling & helpless betrayer, who visits punishment upon himself therefor." Another: "Her playwriting in hope to gain his respect & love. Contrast of two natures, one gifted humanly, the other intellectually. Defeat of the former." Yet another: "Of a woman who commits a crime in order to unite herself in sympathy with her criminal lover. His rejection of her."

None of the projects materialized, but Moody made preparations for the Hopi play which were as extensive as those for *The Fire-Bringer* had been. He assembled a bibliography of more than fifty entries on Hopi myth, almost all drawn from scholarly sources. He took detailed notes on the Walpi new-fire ceremony, which ritualized a myth involving Hopi equivalents to Orpheus and Eurydice. There are entries on Hopi creation myth, the Walpi flute ceremony, fertility rituals, male initiation rites, and the cult and dances dedicated to worship of the great plumed serpent [8] —materials which would later attract the interest of D. H. Lawrence.

Moody had several poems in unfinished form. The most important were the half-completed verse play and the narrative poem on Eve, set aside in January as a failure. In his August rereading Moody felt that the blank verse narrative stood up well, but he wrote a completely new song for Eve. The first one had been heavy and declamatory—it was the poem Moody later revised as "I Am the Woman." [9] The new song was genuinely lyrical, fulfilling its role in the poem. Moody observed to Harriet, "At least it embodies our great Idea—the Great Idea—that much you will be willing to grant, whether it seems to you to have the one thing needful, the 'float' and ecstacy [sic] of a real song, or not." [10] But he had only begun. By September 5 Moody completed a poem on the vision of Christ that had come to him in Crete in 1902.[11] After finishing it he launched into another. By the eighteenth he had finished it as well—a poem in blank verse on the theme of the fountain of youth. Its basic idea, he told Harriet, is "that there actually is such a thing and that some people find it." [12] Continuing to work at high pitch, Moody began yet a fourth poem before September ended. It was "Old Pourquoi," the treatment of an experience of the walking trip in Normandy that Moody and Mason had taken in 1895. Anxious over his unusually high level of productivity and sensing the breath of Harriet's disapproval, Moody observed to her, "I know that I am writing too fast, and that much of this stuff—or all of it—will have to go into the stove: but I can't seem to do anything about it." [13]

All of the new poems turn on contrasts between the naïve hope and enthusiasms of youth and the perspectives offered by maturity. The cause was not merely Moody's aging—he was thirty-five—but a deeper sense of his relationship with Harriet and of sobering changes in the lives of his closest friends. Though his grinding months of darkness in the subway were behind him, Robinson was depressed by a weight of family problems and by his own continuing failure to find anyone to take his poems.[14] His future seemed nonexistent, and he was again in need of a source of income. Torrence was not in the city. Having spent his days on the *Critic* reading and correcting manuscript, he had neglected his own work. He retired to Xenia, Ohio, in frustration to work on his play.[15] Dan Mason had been going through a period of agonized self-analysis, trying to come to some difficult decisions involving his family and his career. But even these problems faded into the distance when word came that Trumbull Stickney was dying. When Moody saw him in March, Stickney complained of headaches of increasing frequency and intensity and of problems with his eyesight. During the summer the headaches became worse and he was afflicted with periods of blindness. Doctors diagnosed brain tumor. By fall he was totally blind and on October 11 he was seized with convulsions and sank into a coma. The poet died without regaining consciousness and was buried October 15 in Hartford.[16] His death was both a deep shock and a responsibility. At his friend's request Moody had agreed to coedit Stickney's poetry with Stickney's friends, John and George Cabot Lodge.

After Stickney's death Moody continued to work, but to little immediate effect. He was impatient, aware of the passing of time and frustrated when "the abundance and overplus of vitality" which he needed to sustain the pitch of intensity he demanded of his poetry came capriciously or not at all. He tried to be philosophical about it, reminding himself that he could afford to be patient. Of greater help to him, however, was the new theatre season. "The theatre is my grand resource," he declared at the end of October. Among the multitude of things he saw, turning to Broadway almost nightly, were Pinero's *Letty*, Zangwill's *Serio-comic Governess*, Mrs. Gilbert on a farewell tour in *Granny*, Julia Marlowe and E. H. Sothern in *Romeo and Juliet*, David Warfield in *The Music-Master*, Nance O'Neill in Sudermann's *Johannisfeuer*, and *Parsifal* in both English and German. And he picked up some recent plays to read: Maeterlinck's *Double Garden*, Hauptmann's *Die Weber*, and Stephen Phillips's *Ulysses*.[17] This brief listing of theatregoing activity gives some sense of the extent to which Moody was in touch with the theatre of his time. His experiments in prose drama had not been the idle gestures of a closeted visionary.

His mood affected the spirit in which Moody viewed the November elections. Teddy Roosevelt was campaigning on the record of his efforts to restrain the corrupt use of economic power in the national life. He had intervened in support of labor in the disastrous Pennsylvania coal strike in 1903, and government regulation and control had tightened to meet challenges in a number of areas. Moody's position was strongly conservative. Hutchins Hapgood, working on the Chicago *Evening Post* and gathering the materials for his book of 1906, *The Spirit of Labor,* had joined Moody and his friends in Chicago occasionally during the previous summer. He was dismayed by the views of his old Harvard associates, Lovett, Moody, and Herrick. Though intelligent and concerned with social issues, they were totally untouched, Hapgood felt, by the labor movement's psychological and moral implications. Theirs were the perspectives and values of the Victorian era, the journalist observed.[18] Hapgood was clearly right: Moody's vantage point in the social structure admitted no point of genuine contact with the problems that concerned Hapgood, and earlier poems touching on such problems—"Gloucester Moors" and "A Grey Day," for example—are thin because of it. From Moody's point of view Roosevelt's actions posed a serious threat to American freedom, and his concern over Roosevelt's continuing willingness to exert national power in international affairs was as strong as ever. Moody's vague utopian socialism—a commitment not unlike the "Conservative-Christian-Anarchy" to which Stickney and George Cabot Lodge had introduced the intrigued Henry Adams—thus issued in support of the old conservative positions of laissez-faire government and nonintervention.[19] But Moody was not actively involved. He saw the election of 1904 from a distance, with nostalgic premonition that an old order was passing. Roosevelt's reelection he felt would be the sign that "the vision in the light of which our country was created and has grown great, will soon fade, and one more world-dream will have been found impossible to live out. . . . Our different destiny may be greater," he conceded, "but the America that we have known and passionately believed in, will be no more." [20] Moody watched the election returns until dawn with Robinson, whose mood did not lighten his own. Roosevelt's overwhelming victory added but a deeper shade to his nostalgia.

In November Moody revised "The Fountain," working primarily with the songs which interlace the narrative. He picked up the unfinished verse play of the previous winter and tried to continue with it, but "not to much purpose." Yet he wanted to finish it "just for luck," observing grimly, "When I bang it hard enough it wags its mouldy jaws in semblance of life." In October Moody had sent off "Old Pourquoi" to the *Reader,* and it was accepted for December publication.

The fee of $100 left Robinson wondering how the *Reader* could pay that amount for a poem to anyone, "even to Prometheus." [21] But the acceptance did not help; by early December it was clear to Moody that he was getting nowhere. Exhausted physically and emotionally, he left for Florida where he rested and checked his setting for "The Fountain" against the reality of the Florida landscape. By Christmas he was back at "the Grove" to spend the holidays with Harriet.

The question of Moody's relationship to the university had arisen again. Both Professor Manly and President Harper had written in November concerning his plans for the 1905–6 academic year, expressing the hope that he would teach for a quarter.[22] But Moody's dedication to laissez-faire dominated his view of this matter as well. He wrote President Harper,

I am anxious to retain my connection with the University, but, as I have just written Mr. Manly, I am unwilling to bind myself just now by an agreement to teach any specified quarter. When the work which I have now in hand is done, I shall be very glad indeed to teach, but until then, I would rather keep myself entirely free.[23]

Harper, in ill-health, responded with great understanding, agreeing that Moody was right. Perhaps it was in a talk with Manly at Christmas that Moody, arguing his position, said, "I cannot do it; I feel that at every lecture I slay a poet." [24] Moody never taught again, but he was listed in university registers through 1908 as an assistant professor "Absent on Leave."

2

Moody's unfinished verse play had not responded to his attempts at resuscitation, but he returned to Chicago at the end of 1904 with five new poems: "The Death of Eve," "The Fountain," "The Second Coming," "Old Pourquoi," and "The Counting Man." [25] In "The Death of Eve," Moody developed in depth the multiple meanings of Pandora. As the fire-bringer's source of regeneration she is a figure more basic to life than Prometheus himself. Moody had treated the role of archetypal female from male perspective in poems like "Jetsam," "The Daguerreotype," and the unpublished "Ethics in a Gondola." He may have been moved to consider the central event of the poem—Eve's death in the Garden of Eden—because of the parallel it offered to the situation in *Oedipus at Colonus,* a play he found compellingly romantic in tone and implication.[26]

Moody's narrative opens as Eve and Cain arrive at the river Hid-

dekel in search of Eden. In a narrative flashback Eve tells of her vain
appeals to Seth and Adam to accompany her back to the garden, and
of her flight eastward to "Nod, the land of violence," to find Cain.
Struck by "The savage misery of the sidelong eyes," Eve did not tell
her desire but remained "Until he seemed a young man in the house,/
A gold frontlet of pride and a green cedar." Then she spoke "as a
sovereign mother to her son/ Speaks simple destiny," kissing him on
the sign of God on his brow, and Cain agreed to return with her to
the garden.

The opening narrative is resumed. As Eve and Cain approach
Eden they find "its gates lay like a flower/ Afloat on the still waters of
the dawn." Cain sees an angel threatening in the sun, but Eve sees
only the open gates, which she says

> "Lie open to me as the gates to him,
> Thy father, when he entered in his rage,
> Calling thee from the dark, where of old days
> I kept thee folded, hidden, till he called."

As Cain waits at the gate, Eve enters Paradise. She goes to the Tree.
Putting off her age and grief she slowly circles the Tree, singing her
song to God.

The dignified blank verse narrative provides a focus of attention
for Eve's song and establishes Eve's initial need for Cain in order to
fulfill her own role. Eve's kiss recognizes and accepts the bond between
them. He is the "red first-born," archetypal lord of the wasteland,
doomed as "a fugitive and a vagabond" in the earth, unable to bring
his grain to fruition. But Cain has been touched by God, and the mark
is a sign that he, like Oedipus, is not to be slain by man. Cain represents the proud, self-aware male life implicit in God's creation but
crushed by the rebellious role he could not sustain alone. In returning
to Eden, Eve returns to her own fundamental identity at the heart of
the mystic lotus of being. The gates of Eden are the gates to creation,
gates of the womb of life, as Eve suggests. They are the gates Adam
entered, calling forth Cain in his virile rage. Eve circles the Tree, Tree
of Life and of Knowledge of Good and Evil: the two are a single tree
of inexhaustible life.

Eve's song is written in an elaborate stanza of slow, circling dignity, created by the cadenced pauses of the truncated third and seventh
lines. Eve presents herself as Bride of God, in spite of the will, word,
wrath, and warning of God himself. Her curse had been that she
should bring forth her issue in sorrow and be subservient to man. But
she declares that early she leapt the containing walls to taste of "many

a savage sweetness." She sings to a God who laughs in his ease, a lord
"of savage pleasures, savage pains." She displays the multiple meanings
of woman in her various roles: woman, wife, mother, child, sister,
and "Spirit that was and is and waits to be,/ Worm of the dust of life."
Eve explains the evolution of her own self-understanding, roused from
the narrow attempt to form herself to the loves of her husband and
sons:

> Still, still with prayer and ecstasy she strove
> To be the woman they did well approve,
> That, narrowed to their love,
> She might have done with bitterness and blame;
> But still along the yonder edge of prayer
> A spirit in a fiery whirlwind came—
> Eve's spirit, wild and fair—
> Crying with Eve's own voice the number of her name.
> Yea, turning in the whirlwind and the fire,
> Eve saw her own proud being all entire
> Made perfect by desire.

Eve knows God's own longing for fulfillment; and she sums up the
paradoxes of his nature, proclaiming her own role as his Bride, in
her final stanza:

> Far off, rebelliously, yet for thy sake,
> She gathered them, O Thou who lovest to break
> A thousand souls, and shake
> Their dust along the wind, but sleeplessly
> Searchest the Bride fulfilled in limb and feature,
> Ready and boon to be fulfilled of Thee,
> Thine ample, tameless creature,—
> Against thy will and word, behold, Lord, this is She!

A short final narrative section returns to Cain. Finally at evening
he steals through unguarded Eden to the Tree. He crouches above
"the shape that had been Eve," awaiting "the coming of the dawn."
Cain's attitude is that of a cautious beast, though his way to the Tree
has not been barred. Eve's self-awareness has not redeemed him. Only a
similar vision of his own rebellious role, Moody seems to imply, could
do so. The ending is reminiscent of the mood of suspended attentiveness which ends "Until the Troubling of the Waters." Cosmic dissonances are presented in a tension which affords no further resolution: the tension is that of life itself. Moody's view of the human
condition here takes on a new rigorous dimension, one implicit in the
tragic grandeurs of The Fire-Bringer.

"The Fountain" is a speech to his weary comrades by a would-be Prometheus who has grown old in his search for the Fountain of Youth. As "The Menagerie" turned to ironic reexamination of the philosophy of creative evolution central to *The Masque of Judgment,* "The Fountain" treats *The Fire-Bringer's* underlying motif of rebirth from the perspectives of despair. Moody had written Harriet of his idea in mid-September, and she responded, envisioning a joyous, positive approach to the theme. Moody's reply is a good indication of his own very different intention. He sent her the poem, observing,

I tried to write, as you see, from the point of view of one who had not found, was in fact almost despairingly far from finding, but who surmised wistfully from observation. I thought such an approach would be more poignant, or at least more conceivable and "convincing." [27]

Moody's seeker speaks in the empty accents of a purpose which has lost its motivating passion and long since fallen into rote gesture. His blank verse echoes the empty formal speech Shakespeare sometimes puts into the mouths of his kings. The tone is set immediately at the opening:

> Another evening falls, another leaf
> Drops from the withered bough. Here let us rest
> Till dawn, if still another dawn be ours,
> And these be not the limits of our hopes.
> This desert starlight seems to shale away
> The crust and rind of our disfigurement,
> And I can see us on the palm-fringed shore,
> Young, in a land of virgin miracle.

Under the influence of the desert starlight, the speaker recalls the youthful setting-out with "Light song which in the arrogance of joy/ Mocked all the shadowy issues of our search." But soon that vision is displaced by the memory of hunger, accident, disease, battle, and schism in the wilderness. Comrades had fallen away, lured by women, sloth, wildness, or ambition, leaving a small handful still ostensibly engaged in the quest:

> But we, who now out-tarry our own selves,
> Who are as our own spectres haunting us,
> Many a dim immemorable year
> We grope about, at hazard of our clue;
> . . . forgetting what we seek,
> Again remembering only to forget.

Moody has turned his vigorous "Road-Hymn for the Start" of seven
years earlier back upon itself.

The seekers, prefigurations of T. S. Eliot's "Hollow Men," are illuminated from time to time by a hint of their goal. They vaguely await
some "crisis" when "all the gates of life/ Swing wide, and there is access everywhere/ And mighty recognitions." The ghostly speaker calls
up in memory the series of guides whom they have followed and in
whom he still sees some vague gleam of hope missed. He recalls a
"dark-eyed leaf-crowned boy"—a native Dionysus—and a "tawny budding girl." Their song welled "like a fountain on the hills of dream."

> "Hasten, hasten, turn and twine
> Body mine, spirit mine,
> Spells behind me,
> Lest he follow me and find me!
> Never stay, but as we may
> Fleeing, fleeing, bar the way;
> To my love's delicious moan
> Make the air no thoroughfare,
> Lock the light to stone! . . ."

The song is a bright contrast to the blank verse monologue. Moody was
to explore the strong symbolism of the line, "Lock the light to stone!"
later in "The Moon-Moth." In a second song the young guides, like
their ancient followers, await a "heart-prophecied hour" when they can
pour the waters of the wild fountain on their "deathless child" and must
then set off in search of their "child that died." The paradox suggests
vistas of process, sorrow in a stasis however ideal, and fulfillment which
leads to renewed search, animated by the memory of the dead dream.
It is a complex vision presented at once in greater economy and complexity than it had been in Pandora's song at the end of act 2 of *The
Fire-Bringer*.

Other guides are summoned up, leaders to "mere household wells
and neighbor brooks," where they had "suffered the bright change."
But the waters had no virtue in them. Of old companions encountered, seven were "as old and worn" as the seekers, but two were "more
divine uplifted men" than at the outset of the quest. The wife of one
treats the source of her rejuvenation in a song. She had raged against
"death in life," crying, "What from our love God hidden hath/ Be
wrung from Him with strife!" But this is not the way to the Fountain.
Moody suggests a non-Promethean way in the song's culmination:

> All mutinous thought away I flung,
> And I, a risen woman, trod

> Those liberties where gushed and sung
> The living wells of God.

Of course, Pandora does not strive, but neither is she so specific about woman's way to transcendent life. Here the way is not found in self-restricting rebellion but in full acceptance of life and its issues. A second old comrade, who has accompanied the party, sings clearly of the male way to the Fountain:

> Not with searching, not with strife,
> . . . .
> But as the husband to the wife
> At evening thoughtless goes,
> And lo, about her careless head
> Twines terror like a flashing knife,
> Breathes wonder like a climbing rose,
> And dreams wherewith his youth was rife,
> The sorrowed-for, the long-since dead,
> He finds up-gathered in her eyes
> Beyond belief, beyond surprise—
> So shall ye find, not otherwise!
> For ere with striving you are come
> The fountain's singing heart is dumb,
> Faded its spell.

The "thoughtless" sexual act renews youth and redeems life, caught in time's process. If violent and passionate, the creative act is without strife—a turn from the Promethean theme, with its greater emphasis on conscious will and search.[28] But there too the way was one of "love, and rage, and laughter."

"The Fountain" concludes in weary dispirited continuation of the search. By the "peaceful desert men" the seeking ghosts are held in awe as "outlying gods." They proceed "Without search" and "without striving" with only a faint spark of hope that they shall find, perhaps in "pictured water-jars" placed along their path, perhaps among the rocks, perhaps in a desert mirage, or "Under the soft rain of a cataract/ Which leaps and scatters down the walls of Death." Both the landscape of the quest and the vision of fulfillment have been central to the life and literature of the century Moody's voice hailed at its rising. "The Fountain" is Moody's most mature, fully developed quest poem.

"Second Coming"[29] is a companion piece to "Good Friday Night." It opens in quiet reverie, as the speaker sits, an hour after the appearance of Christ, in ineffectual torpor. He cannot cope with the vision, making reference to his earlier experience in Italy, but sets perspective

with a parenthetical comment on it: "In pentecostal youth, too prone/
To visions such as these." The contrast of youth and maturity leads
to contrasts in the landscape of Crete—a point of meeting of Eastern
and Western power. The particular theme had briefly engaged Moody
in his "Ode in Time of Hesitation," and "The Quarry" dramatized another such confrontation of two civilizations. As he sits, unable to feel
anything but the uneasiness expressed in his reiterated comment, " 'Tis
strange," his mind drifts to recollection of Zeus's birthplace on Ida, to
the Corybants and Bacchus, and to the maze Daedalus built to house
the Minotaur. The poet returns to the event. He has seen from afar a
gowned figure leaning in speech over a sailor caulking his boat. As the
figure turned his eyes they burned with recognition, and the poet recognized Christ. But the scene has brought no genuine "recognition"—
it is hauntingly without significance for the poet.

The poem turns as the poet rises in protest against the unwel-
come vision, speaking directly to Christ. While he loves Christ, he
maintains, he also serves Dionysus; and he taunts Christ, asking where
he was when the Corybants reveled. And the poet invokes the larger
American response to the call of Christ:

> My glad, great land, which at the most
> Knows that its fathers knew thee; so
> Will spend for thee nor count the cost;
> But follow thee? Ah, no!

Christ's churches are seen as "empty shells," echoing a constant funeral
ceremony. But the poet reverts to uncertainty, asking at the end of the
poem if Christ has "yet more to say, that men/ Have heard not, and
must hear?" Moody's use of Christian symbolism in *The Fire-Bringer*
suggests what Christ did have further to say to Moody, at least. But
he is content here to end with the awkward question which has unsettled and angered the self-sufficient American traveler, to whom
Christ's unknown purposes have seemed totally irrelevant.

Of the poems of the fall, "Old Pourquoi" had been published.
Moody's first version of it was casual. His imagination was running
free, and he joyously welcomed the fun of doing the poem. But, as in
the case of "The Menagerie," it presented a problem of tone. Moody's
early version leaned to the deflating self-mockery and stylized parody
of the grand manner which his sense of humor so frequently took. He
had begun the poem as a verse letter to Mason, and he played with a
casual syntax and with slang in several passages. Finding it jarring, he
immediately revised, cutting some of the loose, slangy mannerism before submitting it to the *Reader*. But when he saw the poem in print,
Moody was struck by its weakness. His revision had not gone far

enough. Where, in the case of "The Menagerie," Moody had manfully excised passages diving to overly serious treatment of his issues, he returned to "Old Pourquoi" to excise the distracting playfulness. He cut his opening four stanzas entirely from the poem and extensively reworked three other passages. His final version is casual in tone, but it rises without destroying the mood to its exalted close.[30]

Like "Second Coming" and "The Fountain," "Old Pourquoi" sets up a contrast between the hopeful vision of youth and a vision altered by maturity and experience. The poem moves easily in a brisk stanza. The two young men on their summer holiday have reveled in the confident dreams of youth. Moody treats their discourse with light irony:

> All afternoon our minds had reveled
> In steep, skylarking enterprise;
> Our hearts had climbed a dozen skies,
> And fifty frowning strongholds leveled
> Of Life's old enemies.

But suspense and doubt enter the scene as afternoon darkens to twilight and the song of an old man who passes them on the road startles them. He sings only the word "Pourquoi?" but it is an "endless tale," dropping to dark anger or sweeping solemnly, "As if some great dishonoured dust/ Came crying its ancestral wrong,/ And found no listener just." Mason is interested only in the weird melody and disregards the text. Moody, outraged, expands upon its symbolic significance:

> *Pourquoi? Pourquoi?* Yes, that was all!
> Only the darkest cry that haunts
> The corridors of tragic chance,
> Couched in the sweet, satirical,
> Impudent tongue of France.

The confrontation of naïve youth with experience is an active one. The ancient French Diogenes had flung into their teeth "that iterant/ Enormous word he sung." In the editing of "Old Pourquoi" for 1912 publication, Moody's most suggestive implication—one basic to the poem—was thoughtlessly (or piously) ignored, for in both the *Reader* version of the poem and Moody's final revision of it, "Word" in the above quotation is capitalized. "Pourquoi?" is the creative Word at the heart of life. It combines, as the poem itself suggests, epistemological and teleological questions: for lost, pilotless worlds, "What?" is "the body of their doubt,/ And 'Why?' the quaking heart." In his final

stanza, the poet identifies Old Pourquoi's song as one "Calling young
hearts to war!" The youthful hope which had so easily disposed of
"Life's old enemies" at the poem's opening is here challenged to genuine battle. Moody catches the sense of youth's casual lightness as well
as its proclivity to indignant moralizing, finding an appropriate medium
for his ranging motifs in the tone of the poem.

"The Counting Man" is a very different work. In his notebook
Moody had jotted down references to books on children's games and
jingles. He entered, as subject for a poem, the game "Cross Tag." [31]
The children are numbered by a "counting man" and cross the street
when the count rests on one of them. Moody's poem consists of a set
of seven numbered stanzas, suggesting the poet himself is playing a
game of number magic. He elaborates on the simple four-line gib-
berish of his first stanza in variations through stanzas 2 through 6,
ending his poem by returning to the original rhyme: "Eeny, meeny,
miney, mo." The poem, which moves through a series of questions, is
a set of reactions to the counting man himself—a series of variations
on a theme. In one stanza the question concerns the identity of the
person solemnly counting out the children. In another the counting
man, muffled from head to feet, appears as "a shadow on the wall!" In
another he is "shiny" and we are asked if we perhaps don't hear him
counting. The speaker eagerly anticipates selection: "Maybe I might
be The One!" In yet another stanza the question is "where *will* his fin-
gers stop?" Moody's interest lies in the relation of the game and the
children's reactions to the game of life—the emotions it arouses and
the questions it presents. In the context of the work of the fall of 1905,
the poem is another, experimental treatment of the contrast between
unconscious youth and experienced maturity. But what would the *Atlantic Monthly* have done in 1905 with

> Eeny, meeny, miney, mo,—
> All the children in a row,
> Cracka feeny, who is he,
> Counting out so solemnly?

In the context of the children's magazine, *St. Nicholas,* in which it was
belatedly published in 1909,[32] "The Counting Man" is an exuberant,
nonsensical, children's game.

3

Moody had several projects on hand in the early months of 1905.
He returned to his New York studio in mid-January with the proofs

for *A First View of English Literature.* The revision would continue to
eat away at his time until early April. In addition, Stickney's papers
arrived in February, sent by George Cabot Lodge for Moody's reactions. The three editors of the posthumous *Poems* worked by mail, each
marking some items for definite inclusion, others for exclusion, and a
number for further consideration. The editing procedure invited mis-
understanding and paralysis of endeavor. It was to continue through
the spring and early summer. In their final decisions, however, the
editors decided to lean to inclusiveness and publish everything concerning which any of them had a conviction of worth.[33]

In spite of these commitments Moody continued to write poems,
though his relations with his muse were casual. On January 21 he
wrote, "Today, all unexpected and undeserved, the Muse walked in at
my window, and gave me a few blissful hours. With soiled hands I
took her, and she never minded them. Man is not saved by his works,
but by grace." And again four days later, he observed, "The Muse
seems inclined to give me about one good day in five. Perhaps that is
all one could expect from a person of her sex, and spoiled as she is by
too many lovers." The tenor of Moody's comments gives some indication of the themes of the two poems on which he was working. The
first was a short poem on the theme of the muse's "too many lovers" —
"Musa Meretrix"[34] — and the second was a Valentine's Day poem for
Harriet — "The Moon-Moth."

"Musa Meretrix" concerns the betrayal of a poet whose muse,
served by him in terms of the highest chivalry, has turned out to be a
flashy prostitute.

> I turn the last leaf down, and lay
> The flaunting rubbish in the grass;
> With folded arms across my face
> I shut the summer light away.
> On him too the old trick to play!
> Too dull, too base!
>
> I see again his dream-worn hand
> Shaken by my poor praise, his brow
> Flushed by the words I scarce knew how
> To speak at all, so shadowy grand
> He stalked there in Song's lonely land,
> Under the vow.
>
> So rare a spirit, and if frail —
> Curse thee! what should a spirit be
> That ate not, drank not, save for thee?

>Flat brothel-jestress, thing of sale,
>On his head too to pour the stale
>Indignity!

Moody did not show the poem to Harriet, perhaps because it was slight
and was not one with which her insights would have been of particular help. When it was finally published over a year later, he responded
to her inquiries about the poem's reference, saying that it "was written
about nobody in particular." [35] One motivating source of the poem, however, was Moody's reaction to Stephen Phillips's *Ulysses*. He had read
the play two months earlier and wrote Harriet in December that, while
it might be "honest in intention, it is not honest in result, in effect.
Quite dishonest." He added, " 'Good things about it,' of course, but let
us not do him the discourtesy to mention them, since nothing wounds
and impoverishes like such sorry amends made to failure. I speak who
know." [36] The dramatic scene of stanza 2 may well be a reworked
memory of the effect of Moody's praise on one of his friends—Robinson, Torrence, or Trumbull Stickney, who was in his thoughts. Moody
had considered writing an elegy on Stickney,[37] but "Musa Meretrix"
hardly represents his view of Stickney's work. He had been deeply
disappointed to find Stickney's volume of 1902, *Dramatic Lyrics*, "ex-
asperatingly, maddeningly" uneven. But he knew "the real stuff" was
there and had observed, "concerning how many books that come to
hand these days can one say that?" [38]

At the same time, Moody's own situation is the experience most
basic to the theme and tone of "Musa Meretrix," and it may have
merged with the ironic perspective that contemplation of Stickney's
career provided, representing the kind of ironic reversal of themes present in the poems of the fall. Moody had often risen in anger or dismay
at the irrelevance of his mood of exaltation in completing a poem to
any excellence in the work itself. The record of his sense of betrayal
is a full one, running through his work from the early poem, "The
Departure," to find major expression in "The Daguerreotype." Recent
events had reactivated that sense. Most immediate was Moody's unhappiness with "Old Pourquoi." He regarded its overhasty publication as
a major lapse of judgment, another effect of uncritical adoration of the
muse.[39]

Moody completed "The Moon-Moth" in February, dated it the
fourteenth,[40] and sent it to Harriet. The setting is Acrocorinthus.
Moody had climbed to the ruins of the temple to Aphrodite on the
mountain above the ancient city of Corinth during the trip of 1902.
The spirit of the poem is that of 1905, however, and patterns of youthful experience and quest are set against later, more mature attitudes.

"The Moon-Moth" is written in Moody's most complex stanza, a conscious variation on the stanza of Keats's "Ode to a Nightingale." The poem, employing gestures and structure of Keats's ode, forms a poetic comment on it and a reworking of its motifs. The experiment is almost foolhardy in its daring, but Moody's poetic voice is mature enough to control the poem.

In slowly circling stanzas, Moody sets an elaborate scene and establishes a mood of quiet reverie. The poet climbs a steep, winding path to the ancient temple at the summit. The scene is integral to Moody's themes. From the marketplace where old men talk of the passionate love of Medea, turned to hate, he has climbed to the pool where Bellerophon "Snared the winged horse and backed him in the moon." He moves symbolically from allusion to pure, uncontrolled passion up to Bellerophon's defeat of passion—the slaying of Medusa through the device of reflection. By Moody's interpretation, the backing of Pegasus, whose hoof called forth Hippocrene, into the moon involves defeat of the cheating fancy.[41] On the heights stands the ruin of the temple of love. At the summit, lying on a cornerstone of Aphrodite's temple, the poet contemplates the kind of aspiration it represented. Corinth raised it, he suggests,

> That in the intense zenith laughing free,
> Making inviolable light its screen,
> Passion might know a wilder secrecy,
> To an abandonment more wounding lean,
> More richly healing of a hurt more keen;
> That, high in prospect of all Hellene story,
> Love, which will gather power
> From all it sees of beauty and of glory,
> And on the top of every lifted hour
> Stand singing of itself as from a tower,
> Might stand and sing at ease from this bright promontory.

In suggesting passion's need of "an abandonment more wounding lean,/ More richly healing," Moody has moved beyond Bellerophon's negative response to passion—Moody's own in the late nineties—and introduced the theme to be developed in personal terms as the poem progresses.

His meditation leads to a state of suspension in dreamlike haze:

> Mountain and seas, cities and isles and capes,
> All frail as dream and painted like a dream,
> All swimming with the fairy light that drapes
> A bubble, when the colors curl and stream

And meet and flee asunder. I could deem
This earth, this air, my dizzy soul, the sky,
Time, knowledge, and the gods
Were lapsing, curling, streaming lazily
Down a great bubble's rondure, dye on dye,
To swell the perilous clinging drop that nods,
Gathers, and nods, and clings, through all eternity.

We cry with drowsy lips how life is strange,
And shadowy hands pour for us while we speak
Old bowls of slumber, that the stars may range
And the gods walk unhowled-at. . . . To my cheek
This stone feels blessèd cool. My heart could break
Of its long searching and its finding not,
But that it has forgot
What 't was it searched, and how it failed thereof.
—O soft, ye flute-players! No temple dove
Be fluttered! Soft, sing soft, ye lyric girls,
Till the shrine portals ope and the blue smoke outcurls!

The motif of search and forgetting is reminiscent of that in "The Fountain." Though the poet has conjured up the ancient dance, the temple's "jealous doors" remain closed. "Despair not," he reassures himself, "these delays/ We know are Paphian." The problem is time, but the poet's prayer does lead to a vision of sleeping lovers, perfected by the power of the goddess, in the temple and the grove.

As Moody asks for "some diviner secret" for himself, "half-atheist" in Aphrodite's hall, the vision is shattered in the familiar movement of the closing stanza of Keats's ode. It is not night. "Daylight is hardly touched with failure yet," the poet notices, though dew is on the stone, and the moon "sings up the world" and in his blood. With a sense of undeserved peace the poet welcomes the appearance of a moon-moth with rainbow wings. It is an emissary of Harriet, signaling the major turn of the poem. Moody describes its wings, gathering his symbols:

Rich as a pulse a worshiped head rests on,
The glimmering vans that time the trembling life
Open and close above the moon-washed stone.

The moon-moth's flame of pearl contains the power of Aphrodite risen from the sea—Harriet's patron saint, Moody had called the goddess in 1902—and of "sea-buried gems" that "give their color to the cup that dims/ Earth's piercing cry to music." In "The Fountain" the light,

locked to stone, was sunlight, symbolizing love's achieved perfection
in a unity of spirit and matter. Here the spiritual moonlight, the imaginative love, baptizes the stone, and Moody recalls his relationship
with Harriet and those occasions when he saw "A soft-winged splendor" about her and would say, "the moon-moth." In the metaphors of
Neoplatonism, Moody depicts their spiritual life. Their souls, reborn,
had been married in the illumination accompanying the moon-moth's
coming. The memory taxes his soul with gladness. It seems to wing
from the body, casting off the sense of "wasted days" in triumphant
bacchanalia, dancing like a faun in the moonlight. In his vision
Moody's soul escapes the bondage of "the ghostly power that . . ./
Did make as if the bolts of God were drawn/ Between her life and
me." A sense of Harriet's physical presence comes over him and he
greets her: "My love, my friend,/ My wild one, my soul's need, my
song of life!" Her hands are palpable—in fact, in comparison with earlier, actual physical contact, they are, he exclaims,

> More palpable, by that dark curtain wove
> And hung between us for Earth's lie of lies!
> Which these our meeting hands make nothing of
> And this thy happy bending-down denies,
> And these our clinging lips and closéd eyes
> And mating breasts have never, never known
> But for the cheat it was.

The "cheat" is not fancy, as in Keats's poem, but the illusion of
physical existence and physical separation.

As Harriet's presence fades "beyond passion's cry," Moody rises
to a vision of America, treating larger issues of his life raised by the
experience. He moves beyond grief to affirmation of love's freedom
from time, and he rejects the visions of the old world for the more
profitable visions of his own, new land:

> And my far country swims into the light.
> The seaboard states are up, the prairies stay
> But little longer now to make them bright.
> Westward the burning bugles of the day
> Are blowing strong across America.
> New laws, new arts, new gods, new souls of men,
> New hopes and charities!
> Why do I traffic where no profit is,
> Taking but one or two where they take ten
> Who trade to their own shores, and back again

To their own shores? O my beloved! Who replies
But thou, fled heart, who cling'st here close and true!
For us the future was, the past will be,
And all the holy human years are new,
And all are tasted of eternally,
And still the eaten fruit shines on the tree.
—Let us go down. There, in that naked glen,
Bellerophon played the thief.
Much lower lies the well where the old men
Sat murmuring at Medea, and at their chief
Spoused to the witch. Love, we'll not grieve again,
We ne'er shall grieve again, not what we could call grief!

The return to the level plain, to earth and physical reality, is return
to a union free of the dark barriers. The poem ends in paradoxes. Harriet, though fled, "cling'st here close and true." Past, present, future,
and grief exist, but all are transfigured by the affirmation of spiritual
love, stronger than the pale, forced vision of the ancient Greek goddess's spell. Affirmation of love for Harriet involves love for America —
its potential for fulfillment far beyond that offered by traffic with the
past.[42] As the ambiguous moon rises over a Mediterranean plunging
into twilight, day is dawning in America.

In the late winter Moody rewrote Eve's original song in "The
Death of Eve" as a separate piece, "I Am the Woman." Moody's reworking is an attempt to salvage the song without extensive change.
The original used, as challenge and refrain opening its stanzas, the
phrase, "Hearken to Eve." Moody changed this to "I Am the Woman."
And other revision was required. There were changes of word and
phrase, expansions, transposition of lines, omission of a stanza with
specific reference to Cain, Abel, Seth, and Jubal, and a new ending.[43]
"I Am the Woman" opens vigorously:

I am the Woman, ark of the law and its breaker,
Who chastened her step and taught her knees to be meek,
Bridled and bitted her heart and humbled her cheek,
Parceled her will, and cried, "Take more!" to the taker,
Shunned what they told her to shun, sought what they bade her to seek,
Locked up her mouth from scornful speaking: now it is open to speak.

Unlike Eve in the poem, woman here barely escapes the stance of the
strident feminist. She expounds her meanings. She was "Wrought in
God's perilous mood," and she proclaims kinship with the morning
star and the secret worm, her mother "in the ancient house." Her roles

span the range of "harlot and heavenly wife." She allures her "mad-
dened mate," paying him in his own currency, gold or "shining
dross," according to his lights. In her role as mother she creates and
nurtures unnumbered lives, comforting all. And she is mother of God.
A section of the poem in which she announces her role as spirit includes a long narrative which presents the biblical epoch "when the
sons of God came in unto the daughters of men, and they bare children to them." Woman is an Eve-Pandora, and her gift is treated in
the context of Moody's earlier Promethean vision rather than the
later one represented in "The Fountain."[44] The poem ends with woman's prayer to return to her ultimate source:

"Open to me, O sleeping mother! The gate is heavy and strong,
Open to me, I am come at last; be wroth with thy child no more.
Let me lie down with thee there in the dark, and be slothful with thee
    as before!"

An emanation of the earth-mother, woman returns from her active,
creative cycle and her high place as bride and mother of God to a
cycle of renewal in the earth's deep womb. The word *slothful* is deliberately chosen to suggest the latent potentiality of mere matter, the
antithesis of the masculine creative energy Moody located in the element of fire.[45]

The other two poems Moody completed in the spring of 1905 are,
like "The Moon-Moth," treatments of his love for Harriet. The first,
"A Prairie Ride,"[46] looks back to their Indiana sojourn of the previous
summer. In the poem Harriet becomes the good genius of the land,
reconciling the poet to his sources. The motif resembles that of "The
Death of Eve," now treated in a contemporary context. The poet, like
Cain, is alienated from the productive land, but Harriet's joyous acceptance brings a covenant of sunlight upon it:

> I never knew how good
> Were those fields and happy farms,
> Till, leaning from her horse, she stretched her arms
> To greet and to receive them; nor for all
> My knowing, did I know her womanhood
> Until I saw the gesture understood,
> And answer made, and amity begun.
> On the proud fields and on her proud bent head
> The sunlight like a covenant did fall;
> Then with a gesture rich and liberal
> She raised her hands with laughter to the sun, —

And it was done,
Never in life or death to be gainsaid!
And I, till then,
Home-come yet alien,
Held by some thwart and skeptic mind aloof
From nature's dear behoof,
Knelt down in heart and kissed the kindly earth.

They gallop through the fields, "Her body like a water-arum blade,/ Like a slanted gull for motion,/ And the blown corn like an ocean." And Moody rejoices in the fruitful land, crying, "land of mine, my mother's country!/ My heritage!" A final brief section reverts to the metaphors of the first. In a reminiscence of Wordsworth, Moody sees the memory redeeming the experience of the city:

And often here, above the weary feet
That pour along this fierce and jaded street,
As from a taintless source
Of power and grace,
Anxious and shrill and sweet
I hear her strong unblemished horse
Neigh to the pastured mothers of the race.

Like Moody's Eve, Harriet rises above the narrowing loves of woman to participate in her archetypal role. Moody's familiar motifs—woman as spirit of the fruitful earth and reconciler of alienated male to the sources of creative power—are presented economically and confidently.[47] The reconciliation to homeland on home grounds fulfills the theme Moody was moved to present in the more alien contexts of "Second Coming" and "The Moon-Moth." The poem's ease suggests the fullness of Moody's reconciliation, one which involves acceptance of the challenge of love:

But through her loosening hair
She has tossed me back the dare.
Drunken-hearted! shall it be a race indeed?
Then drink again, and drink again, to reeling drink the winy speed!

A second poem not as successful was written to commemorate the "sacred day" of Will and Harriet,[48] May 16, the day of her fall at the beach and the inauguration of their love. "The Three Angels" opens at dawn as Moody stands on the Lake Michigan shore below the "cliff-hung house" Harriet had rented for the spring of 1901. It is the morning after her serious accident. Dawn is introduced as an angel with burning wings and lifted hands, walking across the waters, and day lifts above its head a harp soon to be swept by the hands of light. Moody asks the "angel day" to sing of the new love that has risen, but then declares he will himself raise a song wilder than the angel's. Moody's song takes the high mode of romantic mysticism. He depicts the dawn of love as a scene of silent recognition under the threat of death. Even in the midst of physical suffering, the reborn hearts of the lovers play in childlike innocence. The last stanzas rise to sublime description and incantation. He and Harriet become angels on the "coasts of deathless light," raising golden lyres in song. Their souls are "plumed and whispering fires" which tower "from out the primal mist" to meet in rapture.

The poems written between August 1904 and June 1905 constitute a second major group, which matches those of 1900 in variety and surpasses them in interest. The issues are those of Moody's maturity: the poems probe the poet's disillusionment and rise to the affirmations of riper human experience. They represent Moody's best work, demonstrating a wide range of stylistic achievement as well as movement to a new spareness, dignity, and control. Paradox is skillfully employed, Moody relies more heavily than before on the bare, unfocused symbol, and there are several experiments in an elliptical lyric mode. Memory is a motif in all the poems, and their mood often tends to that of "emotion recollected in tranquillity." Perhaps it is this which tempts Moody into a defect common to most of the poems. In spite of a new complexity in his vision of life, there is an increasing lack of control in Moody's descriptive passages—a tendency to bemused and only partially relevant brushwork. Nor does Moody's medium offer him particular major challenges any longer. He is content with the forms he had developed earlier, bent on controlling and polishing them for his purposes.

In these poems poetry is becoming less a medium for exploration and dicovery than a means for placing transitory experience in a perspective of permanence, a medium for the banking of personal faith and spiritual vision. Moody seems not to have desired a fuller consideration of depths to which he was reaching in the best of these poems. Nor did the possibility of exploring a new poetic idiom attract him. At thirty-five, Moody had reached his poetic maturity and had already decided that the major hope and challenge for the poet lay in the drama. That interest operated both as cause and result of the closing of the circle on his lyric poetry. And "A Prairie Ride" signals the resolution of those major psychic conflicts which had shaped his work as a poet from the beginning. Moody had written his last poem.[49]

CHAPTER 10 NURSLINGS OF AMERICAN DRAMA

IN *A History of English Literature,* Moody had observed that the place of drama in literature had been largely usurped by fiction during the nineteenth century. But he predicted that it would again become the "great popular exponent of human life," writing,

There are good grounds for believing that the course of poetry in the next half-century will be in a dramatic direction; and that the tentative experiments of the last two generations, toward the presentation of modern life and thought in the noblest of literary forms, will bear fruit in accomplishment.[1]

The Fire-Bringer represents Moody's commitment as poet to this view. He was now to commit himself fully to the theatre and to work in drama, which brought the skills and perspectives of a poet to bear on the sluggish movement to realism in American drama.

While Moody was shaping the last of his poems in the early months of 1905, he and his friends [2] were becoming seriously involved in working toward a renaissance in the American theatre. The time was ripe. The New York theatre season of the fall, about which Moody had written Harriet, suggested that there was a new and growing audience for serious drama. The theatrical ferment of the Continent and England was encouraging as well. Plays of Yeats, Stephen Phillips, Maeterlinck, Hauptmann, and Rostand were being successfully produced, and a score of young English and Irish writers had turned to poetic drama. Outside of Moody's circle, a number of Americans had embarked on the writing of serious drama, much of it in verse and intended for the stage. Olive Dargan was in New York, working on her second volume. Vachel Lindsay had begun experimenting with his chants, and a Chicago lawyer, Edgar Lee Masters, had written and published several plays, among them *Maximilian*, in 1902. Richard Hovey had written four poetic dramas on Arthurian materials by the time of his death in 1900. And, in Massachusetts, Barrett Wendell had written two plays, George Santayana had published *Lucifer*, and George Cabot Lodge, having completed *Cain*, was soon to begin work on *Herakles*. Magazines like the *Atlantic Monthly, Poet-Lore, Forum, Critic*, and even the *North American Review* had opened their columns to articles hailing a new era in American theatre and welcoming the revival of the poetic drama.[3] The articles, as well as a flow of books on American drama, were being written by Brander Matthews, Richard Burton, William Archer, Edmund Clarence Stedman, William Dean Howells, H. W. Boynton, Norman Hapgood, and others.

Robinson had left New York for a job in Boston, but Ridgely Torrence had returned from Xenia in January of 1905. Robinson's antithesis in personality and taste, Torrence took his friend's place as Moody's occasional companion about town. They dined together almost nightly, frequenting Moody's favorite spots—Guffanti's or Bossi's restaurant on McDougal Street. Then they usually set out for a social engagement or for the theatre. Torrence's literary acquaintance was broad, and he was a mine of rumor and information. He was staying with Stedman in Bronxville, and in late January Moody went for a visit. He found Stedman a remarkable human being, observing, "His excitement over things, his immense flow of spirits and of talk, in the midst of manifest physical weakness, filled me with humility before the wonderful little man, which his pathos and humanity turned into complete surrender."[4] Torrence knew Edwin Markham, who had recently written a poem on the Fountain of Youth theme that Moody wanted to see.[5] A visit to the poet on Staten Island was planned. Stedman had introduced Torrence to Percy MacKaye, a Harvard playwright of thirty and the son of Steele MacKaye, the actor-producer. The two poetic dramatists hit it off immediately, and Torrence took MacKaye to Moody's studio for a meeting.[6] MacKaye had connections in the theatre world and was not reluctant to use them. An energetic entrepreneur and a prolific writer, he was ready to start bandwagons moving. He had already written five or six plays by 1905. On commission from E. H. Sothern, a leading producer-actor, he had written *The Canterbury Pilgrims*, published in 1903, and he had just completed *Fenris the Wolf*, a second commissioned play. MacKaye had met Josephine Peabody briefly several years earlier, when she submitted *Fortune and Men's Eyes* to Sothern for consideration.[7] Now, under the stimulus of Torrence and Moody, he began a correspondence with her.

Josephine's response combined her sense of discouragement with her vital interest:

Tell me of things dramatic and poetic, and what you are doing, and what I *ought* to be doing, and what hope—or fear—there is for all of us who are growing pale and thin watching for signs of American drama.[8]

But, as usual, Josephine knew what she should be doing and was making arrangements for a production of her play in Cambridge.[9] Robinson's interest had finally been aroused as well. In addition to the poems he was writing for a new volume, he began work on a three-act prose play. It may well have been *Van Zorn,* tentatively titled *Ferguson's Ivory Tower.*[10] The sense of isolation and loneliness that had drawn together Josephine, Robinson, Torrence, and Moody—all so different in taste and temperament—began to lift.[11]

They were young writers, interested in the poetic drama. While this alone guaranteed Moody's involvement with his friends' work, in those moments when he was free from partisanship, he recognized the extent to which they were all caught in nearly moribund forms of the drama. Their plays tended to delicate fantasy or ponderous pageantry, and they worked in terms of conventions of dialogue and theatre which were rooted in the seventeenth century. Josephine's two plays had been pictorial and lyrical in tendency, treating themes drawn from the English Renaissance in the style of drama of the period.[12] Torrence's *El Dorado* and *Abelard and Heloise*—he was at work on the latter in 1905—represent a revival of the heroic drama of the Restoration. His characters are addicted to lengthy analyses of their psychological and emotional states in soliloquy and conversation. The plays [13] balance startling melodramatic raving with gentle idealism. Both the fanciful lyricism of Josephine and the grand passion of Torrence are present in the drama of Percy MacKaye. He was fond of theatrical spectacle, and he wrote masques, heavy with allegory. *Fenris,* which draws upon Norse myth for its plot, centers in conflicts of heroic love. *The Canterbury Pilgrims,* when finally produced in Gloucester in 1909, boasted a supporting cast that included 1500 citizens, a large orchestra, and men and ships of the United States Navy. When Moody met MacKaye, he was collaborating with Louis E. Shipman of the Cornish Colony on the *St. Gaudens Masque.* It was presented at Cornish in June with forty artists and writers in the roles of Greek deities and demigods; members of the Boston Symphony provided music.[14]

It is ironic that, during this period when Moody was turning from poetry to the theatre, his poetry was taken up and promoted energetically by the New York literary establishment. Stedman had been consistently interested and warmly hospitable to Moody and his friends, but during the winter of 1905 the powerful Gilder family took interest. In December Joseph B. Gilder's article, "The Poetry of a Poet," appeared in the *Critic*, which he and his sister edited. Jeannette Gilder had already greeted Moody as "the next great American poet." [15] Her brother now observed, "No American poet of the younger generation is doing work of equal importance with that of this native of Indiana." [16] He went on to defend the un-American subject matter of *The Fire-Bringer* from its critics. In January Stedman informed Moody that he had nominated Moody to the National Institute of Arts and Letters. [17] The nomination was supported by Richard Watson Gilder and Robert Underwood Johnson, Gilder's associate on the *Century*. [18] Stedman, president of the organization, observed that he nominated Moody so that the Institute might include the man he regarded as the most promising younger writer of the new century. The absence of youth in the Institute was conspicuous—most of the members had been young men during the Civil War. Stedman and Gilder agreed that Moody was their choice to represent new American writing. He was elected at the annual meeting at the end of February. [19]

Moody visited with Richard Watson Gilder once or twice in the late winter. As if to seal the action of the Institute, Gilder wrote a poem in mid-March, hailing Moody as "A master voice." His poem proclaims that at last "A right true note is struck" which rises above the "pretty songs," the "phantom rush" for gold and fame, and the dust and emptiness of the times. Gilder advises his friends to "stop babbling" and listen, for "a poet's coming is the old world's judgment day!" [20] The tribute pleased Moody as a sign that generous impulses could survive in men even after thirty years of magazine editing. [21] But his pleasure was considerably weakened a month later when Gilder asked permission to publish the poem in the *Atlantic*, printing Moody's initials under the title. Perhaps considering the effect of Payne's praise on the critics of *The Fire-Bringer*, Moody wrote Gilder, "At the risk of seeming ungracious, and insensible of the honor which you have planned to do me, I am going to ask you to publish the poem in the *Atlantic* without my initials." [22] And so it appeared in June.

Moody's unfinished verse play of a year earlier had irrevocably faded away, but he turned to new projects. A scenario for the first act of a prose play which Moody was contemplating [23] gives an idea of one direction his thought was taking. The play concerns the relations of two families—the Trumans and the Blairs—who are involved in an ancient feud. On a base of native materials and a motif drawn from the melodrama of the period, Moody was working with the problems of unfulfilled love. He set up three couples in his exposition of the plot: a pair of young lovers; a pair whose love had been frustrated by the feuding families and who, at forty, are embittered; and a hero and heroine. The romantic leads are a poetic young man and a young woman, a relative of the Blairs from the city, whose love was to resolve tensions of the feud. The existence of the scenario for a first act only—Moody was not to write the play—suggests he was having trouble with plot development. The problem was to beset him in working on *The Great Divide*.

Moody was already thinking about that play. In November, Harriet began to send news clippings which were to provide the action of act 1.[24] An educated young woman of Harriet's acquaintance, left alone in a cabin in the Southwest, had been attacked by three men. She appealed to one of them to save her, promising to marry him. She was saved, but the marriage ended in the divorce treated in the newspapers. The story intrigued Moody, and he asked Harriet to send him everything she could find out about it. He was hesitant to commit himself to a play on the materials, however, observing, "The kind of play I itch to write is something quite different from anything that could be made out of that story."[25] Moody's strongest inclination had been to some kind of dream play, one involving an idealistic social reformer as central figure. But the unexpected arrival in February of old friends from Arizona helped bring to life the materials for *The Great Divide*. The artist, Louis Aiken, had doffed his Hopi garb and exchanged his mountain adobe hut for a New York studio. In addition, Volz, the Indian trader from Canyon Diablo, arrived to taste the pleasures of civilization. Moody and Aiken were delighted and planned a grand tour for him. "With vineleaves in their hair and saturnalia in their eyes," they explored Chinatown, the Bowery, and block after block of Broadway.[26]

During the month of March, Moody's new play was taking form in his imagination. He was encouraged but found himself in no condition to begin a large project. The pain in his hip, increasingly severe through the winter, drove him in early April to seek medical advice. Cautious consultation with doctors indicated the existence of a growth that required surgery. On April 21 Dr. William T. Bull removed a tumor from the spot injured in Moody's fall from Parnassus three years earlier.[27] Moody spent three weeks recuperating in Dr. Bull's private hospital. Robinson wrote from Boston to inquire; Moody reassured him, describing his bout with postoperative reactions:

For the first few days after they sliced me I had a squeak for it; temperature anything in the shade and pulse hopping like a jack-rabbit who descries Teddy [Roosevelt] on the horizon. However, Nature soon decided that I was of more use to her in an organized state than as phosphates, and since then I have made a rapid recovery.[28]

He spent his time probing the new perspectives to be gained from a hospital bed. The city outside his window seemed unusually fresh, and its sounds more exhilarating and rhythmical than he had noticed. "It is wonderful," he noted, "how the diminution of physical energy and of egotistic purpose which sickness brings, vivifies and clarifies the finer senses. It seems almost to amount to a demonstration of the ascetic doctrines which I have spent a large part of my time detesting as false and mischievous." [29] He welcomed his callers eagerly, finding illness to be very humanizing. Torrence was Moody's most faithful caller, with the exception of Charlotte Moody, who had participated in the discussions preceding the operation and had kept a daily vigil over her brother. To Josephine's request from Cambridge for news of the "God-gifted Mule," [30] Torrence responded, "He smokes tons of black cigars and out of the cloud he speaks from time to time declaring how hollow this life is." [31]

Moody left the hospital May 11 with the help of a crutch and a cane. The first evening out he spent at Guffanti's with Torrence, finding that a bowl of minestrone was more effective in establishing his sense of reality than was really decent in a person of high spiritual purpose. His incision was slow in closing, throwing out granulations, a process that called for burning, scraping, and clipping with shears. Charlotte watched over him closely, keeping him from the overexertion to which he was naturally inclined. But Moody soon began seeing people again. He visited the Masons, warning Mary Mason, "You must not look to find me the picture of grace—the pardlike spirit beautiful and swift—that I once was." [32] Gilder asked for a view of some of Moody's latest work, and the poet spent an evening with him. Gilder took both "Second Coming" and "The Death of Eve" for publication in the Century.[33] And Moody collected his honors, taking dinner with the writers of the National Institute, where he was decorated with a purple ribbon. He found it dull. Of greater interest was a social settlement dinner in late May. Moody finally met Markham, whose reading of his poems Moody found impressive. He delighted in Markham's simplicity and youthfulness and was pleased with Markham's praise of Moody's poetic dramas as the best things in their mode since Shelley's.[34]

In early June Robinson was back in New York, "engaged in the prevention of smuggling," Moody happily told Dan and Mary Mason.[35] It was true; Robinson was now a special agent of the United States Treasury, assigned to the New York Customs House. Moody had

played a part in the metamorphosis of Robinson, writing him in the
spring of the plot he and Gilder had set in motion. Moody's letter gives
a revealing glimpse of the easy relationship that had been established
between the poets:

It may interest you to know that you have been discovered by the national
administration. Roosevelt is said to stop cabinet discussion to ask Hay, "Do
you know Robinson?" and upon receiving a negative reply, to spend the rest
of the session reading *Captain Craig* aloud. R. W. Gilder, who told me this,
stands in with Teddy, and has promised at my suggestion to tell him you
ought to have a nice lazy berth in the consular service in England. If this
seems to you officious on my part, write a bad name on a postcard and mail
it to me, whereupon I will call off the genial Gilder. . . . P.S.—O he
(Gilder) won't say "lazy" to Teddy! [36]

Roosevelt himself opened correspondence with the startled, reticent
Robinson, who was writing advertisements in Boston for ten dollars
a week. The president was convinced that life abroad was bad for
American writers, and the result of communications and consultation,
in which Robinson decided against inspecting immigrants entering
the country from Canada or Mexico, was the customs position. It offered Robinson free time for his own work and a salary of $2,000 a
year.[37] Torrence and Moody were jubilant at Robinson's state of confused good fortune and the ironic perspectives the new post offered.[38]

Moody had hoped to head for New England early in June, and he
had excellent reasons. A visit to his relatives in Newton was long over-
due, the Stickneys insisted that he visit them in Dublin, New Hampshire, Gilder had invited him to his summer home in the Berkshires,
Josephine Peabody's *Marlowe* was to be staged in Cambridge with
George Pierce Baker in the title role, and MacKaye's *St. Gaudens
Masque* was set for June at the Cornish colony.[39] Perhaps the sheer
weight of invitations was overwhelming; Moody turned his back on
them all. The incision in his hip was not healed and exertion presented
difficulties. In mid-June he set out for Chicago and further recuperation at "the Grove."

2

Moody spent the summer of 1905 in easy exercise, rehabilitating
his hip. He had been giving thought to his new play, stimulated in
part by what he finally decided was the problem in MacKaye's *Fenris
the Wolf*. Rereading it during his convalescence, Moody felt MacKaye
had evaded his theme: "Fenris, instead of working out his regenera-

tion and achieving a new plane of being, through his first fierce appropriation of Frejya's love, never really comes to grapple with her.
The relation between them remains intellectual, hortatory, and renun-
ciative." [40] The theme was that of the materials for *The Great Divide*,
and the problem was that involved in development of the second and
third acts. In July Moody began writing *The Great Divide* and by
August was well into the first act.[41]

Donald Robertson's plans for an independent theatre were going
well, though it would be another year before the new theatre in Chicago opened. Robertson had found backers for the project and had already leased a hall.[42] Harriet was closely involved in the plans for the
new theatre, and Moody sat down with Robertson in Chicago for discussion of his own plays. The would-be producer was interested in both
The Fire-Bringer and the draft of *The Faith Healer* which Moody
showed him.[43] Moody was encouraged to hope that the staging of his
work might be near realization.

Aside from minor revision of one or two pieces, Moody let his
poetry go. There were several good reasons. While he had been seriously considering a new volume of poems for submission in the fall or
winter, his experience with "Old Pourquoi," together with his desire
to present only time-tested work to the public, led him to move slowly.
He had compunctions about publishing the poems that drew closely
on his love for Harriet, and Gilder was holding two others for publication in the *Century*. The money was good—Moody's fee for "The
Death of Eve" was $150—and such disposition of his poetry was more
profitable financially than a book. Moody's finances were in a precarious condition. Dr. Bull's charges for the operation and care were $650.
Of the bill, Moody observed, "I shall pay what I can, and leave the
rest as a pious obligation to my heirs, as I am in the mind to write
him." [44] He paid nothing on the bill until January 1906, when he
finally made an initial payment of $150.[45]

None of these reasons, however, adequately explains why Moody
had stopped work on his poetry. His notebook makes it clear that he
had ideas for new work, but either the stimulus of the new play and
the hope for production were overriding, or the ideas he jotted down
were not as compelling as those of the preceding fall.[46] Of his ideas for
poems, Moody listed three that reverted to the sociopolitical themes of
1900. He considered doing one on the election day of 1904, which he
had spent with Robinson. A second is listed as "The Barker," with a
note: "Satirico-symbolic gird at the modern advertising spirit in general." A third, "The Minotaur," was to be concerned with "the modern
sacrifice to the commercial spirit." Also listed are "The Shells," a projected reworking of his undergraduate poem; "The Peace of Frodi";

and a poem on Johnny Appleseed. Obviously, Moody was considering
a mixed volume very like that of *Poems,* 1901. None of them was ever
written.

In September, Harriet took a cottage near Grand Haven, Michigan, across the lake from Chicago. Moody remained there for two
months, visited from time to time by Harriet. He was still recuperating. "I find myself in a golden drowse," he wrote Harriet on September 24. "Effort, accomplishment, even the least strenuous entering into
one's self to behold and possess, are far too strident to be thought of."
But he did work on his new prose play; for by the end of October,
when he returned to his New York studio, the first act of *The Great
Divide* was in draft. In November he blocked the second act and entered upon the "trance-like routine without visible punctuation of incident or hours" involved in writing it. He was still unsure of the development, but it seemed to be taking form.[47] He wondered if he could
justify the time he was spending on it, but by early December the play
was going so well that Moody thought he could complete it by the beginning of the year.

Moody's routine did not inhibit his social life. He dined with
Torrence or Robinson, often with both, almost nightly, and Torrence
drew his more reticent friends into a swirl of New York activity. They
met the poet Madison Cawein and his wife, and occasionally saw the
Gilders and Laura Stedman.[48] Moody and Torrence attended a lunch-
eon given by one of the city's literary lion-hunters in honor of Louise
Chandler Moulton. Moody firmly resolved to avoid such occasions in
the future, finding the tone of literary high society both vulgar and
vapid. A major source of interest and amusement was provided by the
British novelist, May Sinclair, who arrived to survey the poetic scene
in America. In mid-November Torrence took his friends to meet her
at a tea given in her honor by the Holts, and she immediately found
them fine material for her pen. Having written a novel called *The
Divine Fire,* she was dubbed "the Lady of the Divine Fire." Robinson
found her both magical and monstrous,[49] but Moody saw her more
objectively as "a queer little papery, prim, cricket-piping yet beguiling
old maid," and "without a single feather to flaunt, meek-spoken, naive,
wholly unworldly and without guile, *habitat* Cranford." [50] She let the
poets know she found them fascinating, telling Torrence that he was
the living image of Rickman, the poet-hero of her novel.[51] As for
Moody, his work was like what she had imagined Rickman's to be.[52]
Moody thought of Miss Sinclair's ideal poet as a "somewhat dubiously
starry youth," but her portrait [53] unintentionally captures traits and
ideals of Moody, Torrence, and Robinson in startling caricature. Rickman, a slender, nervous dreamer with "the shy, savage beauty of an

animal untamed," is marked by a refusal to compromise his high sense
of honor or his dedication to art. This creates problems: his duty to his
father and his promise to marry his ailing beloved (she is dying of
grief) conflict with the raging fury of the Divine Fire in his veins. He
starves himself to pay a debt of honor and turns to drink under the
pressure of his conflicts. Rickman's poetry is described as strong and
virile. He stamps nature with the impress of his powerful soul. And
from his early lyric poetry he has turned to the Greek drama for model,
finding it the highest and most human form of literary creation. Even
so bare an indication of Rickman's character and commitments suggests the complex way in which Moody's own contours had been
molded to those of the idealized stereotype.

Miss Sinclair was found to be interesting. Moody thought her
conversation meaningful and charming. He observed that she had
taken up Robinson, who faithfully attended gatherings in her honor.[54]
Moody and Torrence circulated the story that Miss Sinclair and Robinson had been seen late one evening leaning on the railing in the middle of Brooklyn Bridge in silent communion.[55] But the impressions were
not all on one side. Miss Sinclair was taking notes for an article she
was eventually to publish in the *Atlantic Monthly*.[56] She rightly observed that Moody and his friends, unlike Whitman, felt that "existence needs a deal of editing." Noting the aversion of Moody and Robinson to the "sublime egotists" of the nineteenth-century tradition, she
shrewdly identified their tendency to impersonality as a means of providing a much needed distance and objectivity in poetry. It was a
problem Pound and Eliot, in another ten years, were to come to terms
with through stylistic revolution. Surface characteristics of Moody's
work—its "tumultuous splendor of things pagan and spiritual"—struck
her, but she went deeper to identify Moody's as a revolt from the techniques of realism and a conservative movement toward "reconciliation
and reconstruction" within the tradition.

The sharp autumn air of New York was full of hopeful signs for
Moody and his friends. The *Atlantic* had accepted some of Torrence's
work, a new group of poems by Josephine appeared in the December
Harper's, and Moody's "Second Coming" emerged with illustrations
from the *Century's* Christmas number. Robinson's poetic reputation
was at an amazing new high. In the spring Gilder had taken his
"Uncle Ananias." The acceptance was his first by a national magazine
in eight years.[57] Robinson's "Bon Voyage" [58] was scheduled for *Scribner's* in January and the publishing house, prodded by the poet's presidential patron, was prepared to support him strongly.[59] MacKaye made
an exuberant entrance from Cornish with "plays up both sleeves." He
"shakes them out of his boots when he goes upstairs," [60] Moody wrote

Harriet. E. H. Sothern was planning production of MacKaye's *Fenris the Wolf,* and costumes and music were being prepared. The opening had been postponed for a series of Shakespeare productions Sothern had undertaken with Julia Marlowe. Torrence, with the aid of Mac-Kaye's introduction, was paying court to the actress, and she was reading one of his scenarios.[61] On November 23 the group of dramatists dined together and then met in Moody's studio to hear MacKaye read his newest play, *Jeanne d'Arc.*[62] It was an impressive event, and they parted walking on air. They were ready to welcome signs of achievement, and Moody's comments on the play to Harriet are winged with their common hope:

It is superb, far and away ahead of the *Fenris*—a kind of miracle-play on an epic scale, full of exquisite poetry and showing a stage-craft—a "technique" —which quite takes the breath away for its audacity and verve. . . . While the rest of us have been dawdling and mooning he has done the thing—or something precious near it.[63]

Moody paused to offer several criticisms, rather damaging to the play. He felt it was "a bit over-spectacular, a little bit over-ingenious, and that it falls down rather badly at the end." But all the same it was "a magnificent start for the goal toward which we are all striving," and Moody, liking MacKaye better all the time, decided he had "the goods to the *n*th in *alt.*"

Moody was fully involved, and there was further cause. Only three days earlier Torrence had told him that the manager of the theatre in Prague had written *Cosmopolitan* magazine to inquire about them. The European producer had heard of a revival of poetic drama in America and wanted to see Josephine's *Marlowe,* Torrence's *El Dorado,* Moody's *The Fire-Bringer,* and Hovey's *Taliessen.* He wanted at least one play translated into Czech for presentation on his stage. Moody's reaction was more indicative of his own high hopes than of reality. "There is no time to be lost," he wrote Harriet, "for our fame is spreading." [64]

Will had intended to go to Chicago for the holidays, according to his custom, but he cancelled his plans, wanting to see his new play through while it was fluid in his mind. Characteristically, it was not until he knew that the play would work itself out that Moody told his friends what he was doing. MacKaye knew nothing of it, and Robinson thought Moody had been working all fall on the third part of his trilogy.[65] On New Year's Day Moody finally showed Torrence one of the news clippings from which the play's impetus had come. To Torrence's noncommittal reaction, Moody responded excitedly,

"Well, indeed! Don't you see *it's a play?*" [66] By January 24 Moody's
first draft of *The Great Divide* was completed, but not in three weeks
of frantic work, as Torrence believed and was later to remark.[67] Mac-
Kaye had been urging his friends to visit Cornish, and Moody was
ready for some exercise. He also wanted to prospect for a summer
home in the area. Early in February Moody and Torrence set off. They
met the Cornish winter colony, and the welcome was a royal one. A
small party and supper at Saint-Gaudens's was held for them, and
Maxfield Parrish gave a dinner, where they met a larger group. A
snowshoe and sleighing party was held at MacKaye's small studio in
the woods, and supper was cooked over bonfires. Afterwards, the three
playwrights held a round robin reading of their work. Torrence read
from *Abelard and Heloise,* on which he was still working, and Mac-
Kaye read *The Scarecrow,* an early play he was thinking of revising.
Moody read his draft of *The Great Divide,* which he had tentatively
titled *A Sabine Woman.*[68] An excited group sleighed back to the Mac-
Kaye house in Cornish after midnight. When the roan stumbled in a
large drift in the road, nearly overturning the sleigh, Moody, a young
Alexander at the reins, cried "Whoa, Bucephalus!" and warned the
old horse that "the nurslings of American Drama" should be treated
with more consideration.[69] They hoped to conquer the world.

3

Promotion of Moody's new play began immediately, as friends
arose to lend a hand. Jeannette Gilder asked to read it with a view to
helping find a producer,[70] and Richard Watson Gilder, misjudging the
nature of the play, suggested Moody might wish to stage it at the Mac-
Dowell Club. In response to Gilder, Moody suggested that the play
was "'realism' of a rather grim and uncompromising type," and observed, "I am anxious to get it produced on the professional stage, by
a professional troupe." [71] But there were more promising possibilities
as well. With MacKaye's aid, *A Sabine Woman* came to the attention
of Sothern, who read it as a possible vehicle for his wife, Virginia
Harned. Harriet told Donald Robertson about the play; he too was
eager to read it, so Moody sent him a copy. Robertson responded immediately and enthusiastically by telegram. Virginia Harned, however, returned the play, protesting that she thought it "very interesting
and dramatic, but alas! it is a problem play." She was afraid of problem
plays. "*Is* it a problem play?" Moody queried Harriet. "Perhaps." [72]

At the end of February Moody was afflicted by one of the periodic
attacks of what he called "cosmic depression." As often occurred, how-

ever, the depression brought with it a new inspiration, "an idea for a
play—but a play of a kind that there never was yet." [73] It was the
original idea for his play on the death of Eve, the third in his trilogy.
In his notebook Moody wrote: "The Death in the Garden. (Eve &
Adam.) miracle play, with mediaeval setting interwoven with play
itself." [74] The entry suggests that Moody was taken by MacKaye's interests in color and spectacle in the drama. Again in March Moody
was ill, having headaches of increasing severity. Of one which affected his vision, he wrote Harriet that "For about twenty minutes in
the middle of it I was really scared, beholding myself on the Avernian
slope." Moody's knowledge that similar symptoms had announced
Stickney's brain tumor added to his tension. When the doctor reported
him well but in need of exercise and fresh air, Moody decided on a
short trip to Spain. Indeed, such a trip after finishing a major piece
of work had become a pattern in his life, and he hoped it might furnish atmosphere and background for the Eve play. He bought a Spanish grammar, a history of Spain, and a guidebook. He tried to persuade
Schevill to go too, and Harriet offered the money for Torrence to make
the trip; but Schevill could not get away and Torrence did not dare
give up his means of support. Moody therefore made plans to sail alone
on April 10. He decided to give up his New York studio, feeling that
the $600 a year for rent was too much in view of the trip and his
lengthy absences from the city. Some of his things he sent to Charlotte
and the remainder were stored. As Moody's sailing date approached,
the old spectre of guilt arose. Moody began feeling "colossally hog-
gish," writing Harriet as he had written Charlotte before a trip some
years before:

I know that your view of this aspect of the question is the only large and
right one, but I could act upon it with more zest and grace if it didn't seem
always to point out to exactly me the flowery path and to just you (and incidentally one or two others in a minor sense) the dusty one! [75]

On April 8 Moody received a telegram from Chicago which
changed his plans abruptly. He cancelled his trip and left precipitously
for Chicago. Donald Robertson had given a copy of *A Sabine Woman*
to Margaret Anglin, a star who was in Chicago playing in her road
company production of *Zira*. On Thursday night, unable to sleep, she
began to read Moody's play. Usually such an activity was immediately
soporific, but Miss Anglin was intrigued and read the play to the end. [76]
She decided she wanted to try it out at once. She telephoned Henry
Miller, her associate, got his approval, and began to rehearse *A Sabine
Woman* on Saturday morning. Harriet and Percy MacKaye, who was

giving a series of lectures in Chicago on the theatre of the future,[77] assisted in the preparations for production. Three typists were put to work immediately on parts for the actors. Moody arrived on Tuesday [78] to find A Sabine Woman announced for performance in two days. On Wednesday, amid the confusion, the cast objected to the ending, an abruptly violent scene in which the hero was shot, leaving the audience to decide whether he would live or die. On Wednesday night Moody revised the scene to eliminate the shooting.[79] In spite of the confusion, he was careful to attend to problems of copyright, and the typists turned to producing a fair copy of the play for filing.

Hastily-mounted trial performances of new plays by road companies were not unusual, and problems of production did not interfere with Miss Anglin's plans. A Sabine Woman opened as announced on Thursday, April 12, in Chicago's Garrick Theatre. The audience was a good one and there were well-wishers, among them Robertson, MacKaye, Hamlin Garland, and possibly Harriet Monroe, Edgar Lee Masters, and Robert Morss Lovett.[80] The first two acts went well, and the appreciative applause following act 1 was heavy and prolonged at the end of act 2. After a number of curtain calls, Miss Anglin summoned Moody to the stage for a bow. He made a short statement to the audience, remarking on the speed with which the production had been mounted.[81] He was then called to the box office, where the Garrick's business manager told him that Miller and Lee Shubert were on the telephone to demand a contract before the company would proceed to the third act. A lawyer presented him with a contract of over a dozen articles. Moody had agreed that Margaret Anglin should have an option on his play, but the agreement had not been in writing nor had there been detailed discussion of possible terms of an intricate contract. From her dressing room the star insisted that she wanted Moody's signature before she would continue, but apparently she did not know Moody was being asked to sign a full contract. Confused by what he felt was an outrageous holdup, Moody called Robertson, MacKaye, and a lawyer from the audience into consultation.[82] After almost an hour of negotiation, during which Moody insisted on at least one change in the contract, he signed the document under protest and the play went on.[83] The third act was disastrous. Both the audience and the company had cooled, and the male lead garbled his lines, omitting a portion of the act. The curtain dropped well after midnight to perfunctory applause. MacKaye later called the evening "hallucinatic," and Moody was to declare that he had got ten years of experience in three days.[84]

In the morning the Chicago newspapers suggested that Moody and Miss Anglin, seeing the play a success, had kept the audience waiting while they disputed over royalties. An account in the Evening Post

referred to lawyers in conference "behind the scenes" and declared that
the principals were entertaining "thoughts which had to do with commercialism" rather than with art.[85] Nor did the story remain a local
one; a brasher account in the New York *Globe* presented Moody in
these terms:

> William Vaughn Moody, poet and writer of spiritual dramas, reached
> out last night to grasp the full measure of prosperity which he suddenly
> felt should be his. . . .
>   After two acts [of *A Sabine Woman*] had been given and the cheering
> had convinced Mr. Moody that the production was a success he demanded
> higher royalties. Margaret Anglin, who presented the play, refused to yield
> to the terms of the ultimatum. She issued an ultimatum of her own. For
> nearly an hour she held out, threatening to stop the show then and there,
> while the audience on the other side of the curtain wondered what was the
> cause of the hitch. Then Mr. Moody, in terms more practical than poetical,
> "came to time." [86]

Josephine Peabody saved a copy of the clipping, mounted in a cluster
of dollar signs and annotated, apparently by Moody himself, "Rockefeller at the yard arm/ Morgan marooned/ Clyde Fitch off the plank's
end."

But immediately and publicly, both Moody and Margaret Anglin
were offended by such treatments of the play's premiere. Moody was
to compare the reception in Chicago to the "brutal and blackguardly
onslaught" on the play and performers that fall in Washington, D. C.[87]
They prepared a joint statement for the press, declaring that at no
time had there been any misunderstanding or difference between
them concerning royalties. To it Moody appended a statement of his
own, explaining the seriousness of the matter to him and defending
Miss Anglin's dedication to art against the imputation of "commercialism."

In addition to the above statement, I should like to add that the regrettable
delay between the 2nd & 3rd [*sic*] acts in the opening performance of A Sabine Woman on Thursday was due to the fact that, in the hurry of preparation, I had failed to reduce to writing our verbal agreement, as it had
been understood between us that I should do. After the close of the second
act, Miss Anglin, knowing better than I the necessities of the case, and
calling to mind my omission, requested me to supply it before the play proceeded. I did so, as promptly as possible in view of the necessity for the
consideration of minor details and legal phrasing in a document which was
to determine our permanent business relations, in the event of acceptance
by her of the option offered. It transpired later that Miss Anglin desired no
detailed agreement, the mistake having been made by her representatives.

I deeply regret that Miss Anglin, whose whole-hearted zeal for the artistic aspects of her calling is indisputable, should have been subjected to the annoyance of public misinterpretation of the incident.[88]

The manuscript of this statement is a tortured series of false starts and revisions. This fact, together with the curiously uncharacteristic style of the final statement, reveals the tension Moody was under and suggests his desire for extreme caution. Miss Anglin's statement that a mistake had been made by her representatives is presented by Moody, but the full contract Moody signed was not returned to him.[89] There had, indeed, been no disagreement over royalties offered on American production by that contract, but Moody later told Mason that in the document he had given over practically all other rights in his play.[90]

A Sabine Woman continued before audiences of moderate size until the end of Miss Anglin's Chicago engagement a few days later. On the first of May, Moody returned to New York for a series of conferences on the play and the contract. Margaret Anglin's company had returned to the East for the end of her run in Zira. Not knowing what to expect after his rough encounter with the business ways of the theatrical world, Moody sent the star a note, couched in phrases he characterized as "too soft to sit up on a plate without gelatine." [91] Over tea they discussed the play. Miss Anglin was interested primarily in its possibilities as a starring vehicle for her. She gave Moody tickets for Zira, which he saw with Charlotte. Margaret Anglin was a popular star, trained in the overstated conventions of the American theatre, and Moody was not pleased with the constant pitch of intensity she brought to her roles, finding lack of pacing and variety annoying.[92] He was further initiated into the atmosphere of the star system at dinner with her after the performance, when, amid talk of how his play should be revised, there was much talk of the amount of audience response in Chicago to individual speeches or situations. Moody observed grimly to Harriet, "Applause is the actor's currency and abacus by which all is reckoned."

But Henry Miller soon entered the discussions, and it became clear that the final arrangements were in his hands. He and Moody embarked on a strenuous week of nightly discussion of business arrangements and plans for revision. The meetings inaugurated a partnership and friendship with the dynamic actor-producer that was basic to Moody's career in the professional theatre. Moody liked Miller immediately, finding him not only a gentleman but a man unselfishly interested in professional excellence.[93] Miller was flattering and encouraging about the play, and he declared his major interest was in "a thoroughly well-rounded and self-sufficing piece of dramatic art,

without regard to his own *particular role.*" Moody was overjoyed, after
the apprehensions aroused by Miss Anglin. The contract was rewritten,
and while negotiations were delicate, Miller generously stood between
Moody and the producer, Shubert, who remained in the wings.[94] The
business restored Moody to his trust in humanity—a trust which he
said had been "somewhat impaired by the Chicago mix-up." The contract was signed May 8, with agreement for a revision of the play in
the early summer, a series of forfeits for failure to produce the play
within a reasonable period, and royalties of 5 to 10 percent, depend-
ing on the weekly receipts. Moody reserved publication rights and authority over his text. And a host of minor details were settled in the
eighteen clauses of the legal agreement.[95]

CHAPTER II THE
GREAT DIVIDE

MOODY HAD AGREED to complete his revision of *A Sabine Woman* by mid-July. After rounding up Robinson and Torrence for a celebration, he set off for Cornish, New Hampshire, where he had decided to work. Cornish was in the first flush of spring, and the little colony was beginning to awaken from the quiet winter sleep Moody had admired on his visit to Percy MacKaye in February. He found a room in a farmhouse near the MacKayes and settled down to work on his play in the mornings. He reserved part of the afternoon for a walk through the New Hampshire countryside, which soon captivated him. He walked along Blow-me-down Brook, enjoying the apple trees in flower, the clumps of yellow willow, the song of the spring birds, and the rolling landscape. Perhaps because of the insistent beauty, Moody was writing without particular enthusiasm, but he finished revising his first act before May ended. Both Miller and Miss Anglin had suggested organic changes in the play, but Moody resisted the temptation to make them. His own interest was in stripping and strengthening his dialogue, which the Chicago staging had convinced him was "too suggestive and elliptical for the stage." [1]

By the end of May, Cornish was in the throes of preparation for the summer. Moody helped the MacKayes move into a house on the outskirts of Cornish. The Norman Hapgoods arrived and a call on them quickened Moody's desire for a summer retreat of his own. Their home and its setting reminded him, characteristically, of Tuscany, but there was some good Yankee flavor about it as well. Lovett came through, escorting the Herricks, and Moody helped them get settled. Ethel Barrymore arrived on June 2, and Moody was invited to dine on the evening of her arrival. He wrote Harriet that she was "the same

person over the soup as over the footlights, voice between a drawl and
a coo, eyes *gamin* and questing, attitudes free-ish and piquant, no 'conversation' (as Jane Austen would say) but amusing little jabs at the
passing subject, cigarettes ad lib.—inhaled." With the arrival of Ethel
Barrymore a lively social life began, and there were more opportunities
than Moody desired or could use. By the end of the month Moody
was accepting only dinner invitations, but they filled most of his evenings. While he suggested to Harriet that Ethel Barrymore was "on
the whole formidable . . . only to the *Weltmensch* or the fermenting
boy," Moody responded to her beguiling hospitality. He was attracted
to her unpretentious heartiness and became a member of the small
group of her friends who joined her in the afternoon for tennis or swim-
ming. They followed exercise with highballs on her big stone-flagged
porch.[2]

Cornish's social life offered an immersion in theatre talk. Sothern
was preparing to stage *Jeanne d'Arc* in the fall and MacKaye was deep
in elaborate preparations which involved creation of a number of complex stage illusions. Moody thought it all somewhat vulgar and decided
that the excitement over staging was "a kind of dramatic measles . . .
which everybody must have after his kind." Torrence had begun a new
tragedy in blank verse. He and Moody had discussed it in early May,
and Moody was giving comment and suggestion in response to Torrence's cries for help.[3] Harriet Monroe, visiting in Cornish, also showed
Moody her play, *The Happy Isles*. And Moody gave aid and encouragement.[4] Even the stage itself beckoned, in a small way. Ethel decided she wanted to produce and act in one of MacKaye's one-act plays,
and she selected Moody for the role of a Maine sea captain. But both
Moody and MacKaye were heavily involved with their work, and the
performance, which Moody thought would have provided great fun,
did not materialize.[5]

In mid-June Moody stopped work on *A Sabine Woman* long
enough to go to Cambridge. Two events drew him: a massive performance of *Agamemnon* in the Harvard stadium and Josephine Peabody's
marriage to Lionel Marks, a professor of engineering at Harvard. He
went with the MacKayes, and Torrence came from New York. Robinson joined his friends in presenting a mutual wedding gift to the fifth
member of the reconstituted Fellowship. It was a silver loving-cup,
engraved with the appropriate line from Theocritus: "May there always be concord in the house of the Muses." [6] Though confined to
New York, Robinson observed the occasion by writing "The White
Lights," a poem in which he anticipates the new glory about to de-
scend on Broadway. He wrote Josephine, observing that in view of his
labors on the poem she, Moody, Torrence, and MacKaye now had to
make good.[7]

On returning to Cornish, Moody found a letter from Miller, who announced his intention to open the season with Moody's play. He urged speed, and Moody set to work on the final copy. In addition to careful major revision of the script, Moody changed the title from *A Sabine Woman* to *The Great Divide,* substituting a more familiar allusion and one more appropriate thematically than the obscure first title.[8] The heroine's name was changed from Zona to Ruth, inviting relevant comparison with her biblical counterpart. In mid-July Moody left Cornish for New York and three strenuous days of conference with Miller and Anglin on the new version. Miller was enthusiastic, observing, "It may not *make a dollar,* but if they want good drama, there it is!"[9] Margaret Anglin was more guarded, balking because Moody had cut several of her scenes; but the role was a good one and she capitulated. There was nothing to keep *The Great Divide* from going into rehearsal.

Moody had been ready for a vacation trip in March, and the feverish and unfamiliar negotiations for the play together with rewriting under pressure left him exhausted. His headaches had recurred from time to time and he resolved to loaf a bit before undertaking anything new. When he returned to Cornish he picked up Gilbert Murray's new translation of Euripides and took it to read in pleasant spots along the route of his walks. The Cornish social life was as insistent as ever. He dined out and played tennis at the Barrymore court, occasionally teaming with Harry Fuller against Richard Harding Davis and his wife.[10] Intensifying his search for a New England retreat, he sought out abandoned places around Cornish in his walks. As he searched, his letters to Harriet returned more and more frequently to the theme of marriage. *The Great Divide* was scheduled for pre-Broadway opening—the first in a series of road trials—in Albany in early September. Moody suggested they might marry quietly there or in Quebec.[11] But Harriet was no more ready to consent than she had been on earlier occasions.

Moody was unable to devote himself entirely to relaxation for very long. On July 26, five days after deciding to loaf a bit, he returned to his plan for a play on the Eve theme. He had had little time to think of any work other than *The Great Divide* for months, but he had been considering the Eve play by indirection during the summer. A remark of a friend of Harriet's about the "discovery" of old age intrigued him, and he observed that the modern emphasis on youth had reversed the classical focus of psychological interest.[12] Moving against the tide that would result in the new century's unique emphasis on youth, he began mulling over his new topic under Harriet's encouragement. The projected play on Eve's return to the garden was clearly appropriate for such concerns.

In late August Moody made a quick trip to New Mexico to gather
properties needed to give authentic color to the first and second act
settings of his play. He returned a few days before the Albany dress
rehearsal on September 10.[13] Feeling that minor changes would be
necessary, Miller urged Moody to travel with the company for its
month on the road. Moody had had a baptism in the theatre, but the
month to follow provided a thorough immersion. The dress rehearsal
threw him into despair; it lasted from seven until five in the morning
and Moody thought the Albany theatre resembled "nothing so much as
a stock exchange except a skating-rink." The company itself looked
"indescribably bad, the vulgarizing process sickeningly complete." [14]
He thought Miller unable to play the role, and observed, "The minor
parts have been mis-mated to their would-be interpreters until the
unholy cohabitation cries to heaven." Moreover, the set was poorer
than that improvised in Chicago in the spring. He was ready to swear
never again to write a line for the commercial theatre. But the opening
amazed him. The company pulled itself together in a way that astonished him, and the house was large and enthusiastic. The nightmare
dress rehearsal was forgotten and Moody began to warm to the idea
of the strolling players' existence. The company set out for a week of
one-night stands which took them to Amsterdam, New York, across
New England to New Haven, and then to Atlantic City. In Washington the play settled down for a week's run in the Belasco Theatre.
Moody was lightheaded from the tension of performances and rehearsals, rushing to and from hotels and trains, bickering over details
of the text and interpretations of audience reaction, and drinking at
the impromptu champagne suppers Miss Anglin liked after the performance. In Atlantic City Moody finally met Shubert, whom he
characterized as "the Czar of all the theatrical Russians." Shubert
warned Moody against premature enthusiasms, observing that " 'Proad-
way' [sic] was a monster of great incalculability of taste, wont to eat
alive a playwright a day." [15]

Hopes were running high, for the company had been playing to
large and responsive audiences. But their Washington reception dashed
cold water over their spirits. An oppressive heat wave in addition to
an abusive review in the Washington *Star* reduced audiences to a
handful. The company moved on to Pittsburgh for a second full week,
to find itself "still in the critical storm-belt." [16] All the morning papers
but one attacked the play as disgustingly immoral. Moody observed:

To them it means an attempted rape, a revolting case of forced marriage,
and the final surrender of the woman to a moral monster. *Eheu!* I guess the
meat we are trying to get them to taste is too strong for them. I feel pretty
thoroughly convinced that they won't have the play on any terms.[17]

The reviews had been so devastating and the Washington box-office receipts so low that Lee Shubert arrived to suggest that Miller and Miss Anglin drop the play. But the Pittsburgh attacks did not hurt receipts, and the costars decided to go on to Broadway. Moody was uneasy and he began to think he should rewrite the entire play, but on September 26 he wrote Harriet, "unless something quite cataclysmic occurs we shall open as brash as you please in New York on Wednesday of next week." He urged her to plan to attend with him.

The company settled into the Princess Theatre in New York. The pre-Broadway dress rehearsal began at sunset and ended in chaos at dawn, as Henry Miller seized one of the huge Indian jars Moody had brought from New Mexico and smashed it on the stage, shouting one of his lines, " 'Smashed to hell is smashed to hell!' – There will *be* no 'Great Divide'!" [18] But that evening, October 3, he radiated confidence as he greeted Moody in his dressing room before the performance. The theatre was sold out, everything was going smoothly, and the smell of success was in the air. Moody returned to his seat beside Harriet in exhausted excitement to see what the unpredictable New York audience and critics would think of *The Great Divide*.

2

The Great Divide opens on a group of young Easterners in a cabin in Arizona.[19] It is spring. Philip Jordan, his wife Polly, and his nineteen-year-old sister Ruth have come West to revive the family fortunes. Philip has invested in land and formed a company, Cactus Fibre, which he and Ruth hope will, with work, make money. Winthrop Newbury, a young doctor in love with Ruth, is helping out. Polly, a sharp-tongued young woman, surveys her barbarous surroundings with disdain. She is about to leave for San Francisco, and Philip is furious but sullen over her defection. A greenhorn, Winthrop is enthusiastically trying on western manners for size, while Ruth responds romantically to the great, rude scene. She is the American ingenue, inclined to a genteel sauciness—a sister to Henry James's heroines. Characters and situation are established economically. Major themes are suggested in exchanges between Ruth and Polly. Polly denounces Ruth's fear that she will be "punished for being so happy" in the West, observing, "There's your simon-pure New-Englander." She lightly offers her own neo-Dionysian ethic: "Happiness is its own justification, and it's the sacreder the more unreasonable it is." Polly probes Ruth's relationship with the young doctor, and Ruth explains that he is finished, "all rounded off, a complete product." She wants someone rough and unformed, like the western country she loves. A series of unforeseen

events makes it necessary for Ruth to remain alone, and the rest of the
company leaves to accompany Polly to her train.

A lyrical scene follows in which Ruth prepares for bed. In rap-
turous response to the desert landscape, rife with cactus bloom, she
sings a delicate song that provides the deep, subconscious motivation
for the action which follows. As she retires, three drunken men break
into the cabin. There are muttered curses, a light is lit, and Ruth attempts to fire a shotgun amid some scuffling. The men proceed to throw
dice for Ruth; one man, Stephen Ghent, is attracted by her grace. She
appeals to him for aid, promising him her "life," that she will stick to
him "on the square." Ghent is dazed but stirred by the promise. He
eliminates his rivals, buying off a Mexican with a string of gold nuggets and disabling the other in an offstage shoot-out. A long exchange
between Ruth and Ghent follows. He plans to take her off to the
Cordilleras where he has a rich claim. Ruth attempts to rise to the
convention called for by her situation. She knows she should kill herself, but when Ghent questions her, she cries, "I cannot, I cannot! I
love my life, I must live. In torment, in darkness—it doesn't matter.
I want my life. I will have it!" The rigid conventions of melodrama
embody the rigid Philistine ethic against which Ghent's life-oriented
pragmatic ethic is set in the play. Ghent gives Ruth the opportunity
to shoot him as well—perhaps a desperate test of the unbelievable
dream to which he has succumbed. But Ruth does not shoot. She begs
him to go, in despair at her bargain and foreseeing nothing but "hatred,
and misery, and horror." But Ghent has found something he wants
and Ruth's view hardens his determination. The act ends in a show of
tenderness, for as Ruth gathers a few things to take along, she notices
he has been wounded in the gunfight and washes and binds his arm.
He appeals to her for help, promising success:

Make this bad business over into something good for both of us! You'll never
regret it! I'm a strong man. I used to feel sometimes, before I went to the
bad, that I could take the world like that and tilt her over. And I can do
it, too, if you say the word! I'll put you where you can look down on the
proudest. I'll give you the kingdoms of the world and all the glory of 'em.
Give me a chance, and I'll make good.

But the appeal, with its echo of Satan tempting Christ, merely increases
Ruth's conflict. She remembers the gold nuggets with which Ghent
bought off the Mexican, and she cries that he is trying to buy her soul
with a mining claim. Bewildered, Ghent can merely mutter, "Well, I
guess we'll blunder through." Ruth leaves a brief note suggesting that
she has left by her own volition.

The second act is set eight months later on the terrace of an adobe cabin high in the Cordilleras. Ghent's claim has proved a good one. He owns the rich Rio Verde mine, though litigation threatens his rights. Two miners open the act discussing Ruth's secretive weaving and selling of Indian baskets in the new "Buny Visty" hotel across the canyon. The miners' exchange reveals the flexibility with which Moody adapted his language to the requirements of a new genre:

Burt. Funny hitch-up—this here one—I think.
Lon. [After a pause.] How much you gittin' a day now?
Burt. Same little smilin' helpless three and six-bits.
Lon. Anything extry for thinkin'?
Burt. Nope! Throwed in.

Ghent enters with an architect and a contractor to discuss plans for a house. Ghent's good-hearted roughness, his eagerness to please Ruth, and his uneducated taste become obvious in the exchange. As the visitors leave, Ruth enters. She is pale and partially deranged. She rejects the gifts Ghent has brought and ignores the plans for the house, laughing jarringly, "My price has risen! My price has risen!"

At the hotel Ruth has been seen by Winthrop, who has begun work in the area; he arrives on the scene with Philip and Polly, who are visiting him. They had found the record of Ruth's marriage to Ghent in San Jacinto but could not trace her. She had not written. Ruth puts a bold face on the unexpected meeting, explaining nothing. To Winthrop's question as to her unexpected departure months before, she answers, "It was half accident, half wild impulse. Phil left me at the ranch alone. My lover came, impatient, importunate, and I—went with him." Symbolic dimensions of the relationship are suggested in Ruth's response to "How long had you known him" with "All my life! And for aeons before." Polly treats the situation casually, admiring Ruth's air of mystery and adventure and praising her action as courageous, exclaiming, "You are not good, you are merely magnificent. I want to be magnificent! I want to live on the roof of the world and own a gold mine!" Ruth's brother, Philip, bound by the conventions in which he operates throughout the play, regards the situation as disgraceful, the marriage as hardly valid, and Ghent as despicable. He speaks in stagy accents appropriate to the wronged man of melodrama. Philip's behavior and action suggest that his aggressive bitterness is founded on semi-incestuous love for Ruth. In an excess of self-pity, he claims Ruth's "desertion" is the main cause of the failure of Cactus Fibre and his ruin. The group leaves, begging Ruth to return with them to her true home.

In a final scene between Ruth and Ghent, Ruth reveals that she has spent none of his money but has paid for everything herself, keeping strict account of every penny. Bewildered by Ruth's defense of their life before her relatives, Ghent questions her. Reaching through her confusion to her basic love, Ruth cites the splendors of her first days with Ghent: "It seemed as if you were leading me out of a world of little codes and customs into a great new world." But in despair she recognizes that they are strangers, and she fears Ghent's rough sexuality, hating "The human beast, that goes to its horrible pleasure as not even a wild animal will go—*in pack, in pack!*" She has worked to buy back the necklace of nuggets from the Mexican, and she gives it to Ghent, buying back herself. He refuses it and becomes even more possessive when she reveals that she is pregnant, saying she is his "by blind chance and the hell in a man's veins," his "by almighty Nature." Philip appears and Ruth, turning from Ghent in exhaustion, asks her brother to take her home. The final scene inverts the situation of the first act. There Ghent's Darwinian ethic operated in terms of "buying" Ruth from his companions. Her moral rectitude expressed itself in standing by her promise, though she viewed it as a bargain with the Devil. Here Ghent enunciates the Darwinian ethic, claiming Ruth by Nature's great law. Ruth's Puritanism is expressed in financial terms and she pays the wages of her sin in self-chosen suffering, tallied in terms of strict accounting, buying her freedom from a human relationship.

The dialogue and detail of act 3 are realistic, but the action is patterned after nineteenth-century melodrama. It takes place six months later in the sitting room of Mrs. Jordan's house in New England. Ruth has lost all interest in life and her care for her baby boy is meticulous but heartless. Polly says the cure is Ruth's husband, and she has sent for Ghent. Her view of the situation is a preparation for the eventual reconciliation. The problem is the conflict of Eastern culture and Western freedom. She suggests that the cleavage in Ruth's life—her romantic attraction to the primitive and her civilized abhorrence of brute nature—has paralyzed Ruth, but that her dedication to Ghent is permanent. As Philip leaves in frustrated rage, Polly reveals her own situation to Mrs. Jordan: Philip has been "too much wrapped up in Ruth" to think of her; and Ghent and Ruth are "predestined lovers," who represent what she and Philip have missed. Ghent unexpectedly arrives, on his way West to try to save his mine from the connivance of his partner. The discussion reveals that, under Mrs. Jordan's cover of a benevolent uncle abroad, he has enabled the Jordans to retain their home, which was threatened by Philip's failure. In addition, Ghent has bought the stock of Cactus Fibre, put the project on its

feet, and the company is now worth a fortune. He wants Ruth to
have it to pay off what she conceives as her moral debt to her brother.

Ruth enters and refuses to meet Ghent. Her mother angrily reveals
Ghent's support of the family, whereupon Ruth wants to leave the
tainted house at once. Finally, she tells her mother the story of how
she became Ghent's wife; her stunned mother's reaction is that she
ought to have died first. Philip abruptly enters and the scene threatens
to end in violence, but the women force him out.

Alone with Ghent, Ruth apologizes for revealing their secret, but
Ghent rationalizes her action. It is a prelude to mutual understanding.
Ruth presses him to reveal what he sees as the truth between them.
Referring to a New England sermon, Ghent says love for her has been
his rebirth, that their love "burned away all that was bad in our meet-
ing." Ruth maintains that regeneration comes only with suffering, but
Ghent preaches a new code:

What have we got to do with suffering and sacrifice? That may be the law
for some, and I've tried hard to see it as our law, and thought I had succeeded. But I haven't! Our law is joy, and selfishness; the curve of your
shoulder and the light on your hair as you sit there says that as plain as
preaching.—Does it gall you the way we came together? You asked me that
night what brought me, and I told you whiskey, and sun, and the devil.
Well, I tell you now I'm thankful on my knees for all three! Does it rankle
in your mind that I took you when I could get you, by main strength and
fraud? I guess most good women are taken that way, if they only knew it.
Don't you want to be paid for? I guess every wife is paid for in some good
coin or other.

But he too has suffered, and now he is willing to sacrifice the mine by
not fighting, if she agrees. When Ruth does not respond, Ghent is
moved to express the fatalistic despair potential to Calvinism: "Done
is done, and lost is lost, and smashed to hell is smashed to hell. We
fuss and potter and patch up. You might as well try to batter down
the Rocky Mountains with a rabbit's heart-beat." But Ruth wants
Ghent's assurance that she would have loved him without struggle if
she could, and that her real motive was always love. She sees that her
tradition has trapped her into seeking salvation "by wretchedness, by
self-torture." As she puts the string of gold nuggets around her neck—
Ghent has brought them back as a memento for his son—she says,
"You have taken the good of our life and grown strong. I have taken
the evil and grown weak, weak unto death. Teach me to live as you
do!" Ghent is bewildered, but Ruth's face is joyous as she asks him to
help make a new life for her and their child.

Unrevised, *A Sabine Woman* [20] might have had a brief Broadway

success, but no more. Moody's astonishingly authoritative revision provided the coherence of structure and tone, the skillfully economic
dialogue, and the thematic significance by which *The Great Divide*
became a major event in the history of American theatre. During the
summer the play had been cut by a third; scenes omitted include
several in the first two acts between Ruth and Winthrop—scenes which
depicted their relationship in irrelevant fullness. In act 2 the Mexican
with his necklace of nuggets had reappeared, threatening Ruth with
blackmail—the scene was unnecessary and obscured the heroine's moti-
vational consistency. Tone was falsified in the earlier version by comic
business in act 1 and by excessive expansion of Polly's role in the first
two acts. Acts 2 and 3 included lengthy explanations by Ruth of her
motives and position, and in act 3 both the doctor and Philip discussed
her psychological state at some length. In revision much of this material was properly omitted. More remarkable than excision of these
passages, however, is Moody's sensitive stripping away of excess verbiage
inappropriate to the requirements of theatrical dialogue. Passage after
passage throughout the play is condensed to sharp, simple statement,
brief exclamation, or fragmented utterance. Such revision moved both
diction and speech patterns toward colloquial realism.

While Moody's authoritative cutting, together with some shifting
and integration of scene in acts 2 and 3, clarified the play's central
action significantly, Moody made important changes and additions to
strengthen psychological probability or focus thematic issues. Changes
in act 1 make Ruth's remaining alone seem more unavoidable. The
close of the act is altered to focus clearly on Ruth's objection to being
"bought." In act 2 Ruth's nearly psychotic state is more clearly projected by Moody's omissions. She, rather than Ghent, describes the
beauty of their early weeks together, a better preparation for her act 3
reversal. Her revelation of pregnancy is an addition which strengthens
Ghent's assertion of claim to her, and his statement of the natural ethic
by which he claims her is new—a major contribution to the development of the philosophical issues. Philip is wisely moved from foreground into background of the action in act 3. Polly indicates clearly
her anguish over the failure of her marriage, a change lending depth
to what might have been a superficial characterization. Finally, Moody's
new ending is strong and right. In *A Sabine Woman*, Philip, having
learned the facts of Ruth's being raped, is roused to shoot Ghent,
wounding him critically. The play had ended in grotesque irresolution
with an immediate overflow of love from Ruth, with distracting business about papers relating to the gold mine, and with young Winthrop
returning to the scene to say that he might be able to save Ghent's
life with Ruth's help! In the revision, Ruth's movement to reconcilia-

tion is sounder psychologically and her conversion to Ghent's vision of life brings the play's themes to final resolution.

For years Moody had followed carefully both the American and the European theatre and had been attracted to the possibilities of avant-garde drama. While he had reservations about the work of Maeterlinck and of Yeats, his interest had been in doing a dream play in the symbolist style, and he had considered Brook Farm a congenial subject. But the *donnée* of *The Great Divide,* if sensational and easily turned into melodrama, invited a realistic treatment for which Ibsen was Moody's best reference. A love triangle is a ubiquitous situation in drama, but Moody followed Ibsen, grounding psychological and thematic development in a struggle of elemental human passion against narrow social conventions.[21] Though plotting tricks of American melodrama help provide the structure of the third act, the play's original ending shows how much Moody was thinking in terms of continental realism. He had himself described *A Sabine Woman* to Gilder as " 'realism' of a rather grim and uncompromising type." [22] In revision Moody had been strongly tempted to retain his ending, though the movement and tone of the play insufficiently foreshadow such a resolution. In addition, Moody had resorted to sentimental business at the end of *A Sabine Woman.* A series of tragic recognitions would have been required for the play to attain a final focus as effective as that of *The Great Divide.*

Moody's achievement in *The Great Divide* is difficult to understand apart from the context of American theatre in the early years of the century. In the grip of a strong provincial tradition and dominated by actor-playwrights, it had been much less responsive than fiction and poetry to new currents in the arts. Even by 1906 the impact on American drama of European movements to realism and symbolism had been surprisingly slight. In the nineties James A. Herne's *Shore Acres* moved toward realism by the adoption of surface techniques that local colorists had been working with since the Civil War. And character is developed with some psychological sophistication in his *Margaret Fleming.* Bronson Howard and Augustus Thomas had taken important steps toward realism in the drama. But serious theatre was still trapped in the plot patterns and gestures of the sentimental, melodramatic traditions of the Victorian stage. The big money-makers of Moody's period had been the powerful showpieces of David Belasco and the facile, clever plays of Clyde Fitch. American theatre had remained practically untouched by the renaissance of European drama manifest in the work of Ibsen, Strindberg, Chekhov, Rostand, Hauptmann, Sudermann, Maeterlinck, Shaw, and others.

Yet if the example of continental drama provided points of refer-

ence for Moody, his experience as poet and poetic dramatist was of
major importance. He was accomplished in the complex thematic
development of an action and was sophisticated in the use of symbolic
and lyric techniques for enriching and universalizing an event. In his
poetry he had approached human problems at a depth unknown in
the American theatre of his time. *The Great Divide* is not the abrupt
reversal of Moody's creative career it might seem to be. The theme of
salvation through masculine strength of will and the power of passion
is central to Moody's earlier work. Ghent is an active, less articulate
Raphael, a Prometheus in the garb of Western American miner,
battling the same restrictive, legalistic code found in different form in
the earlier plays. In its contemporary setting, however, the theme sets
Eastern codes against vigorous Western freedoms—a conflict central to
Moody's Chicago years and to his friendship with Josephine Peabody.
In his relationship with Harriet, Moody had been the restricted one,
trying to force their relationship into narrow ethical patterns instead of
accepting the freedom and joy of the love she offered; Ruth's struggle
owes something to the moral tensions which beset Moody in 1902 in
Europe. Thematic development also comes in more narrowly American
terms than earlier. As in Henry James's later work, money is the great
metaphor of *The Great Divide*. Human relationships are treated in
financial terms of souls bought and sold, of ruin threatened and redeemed. The sign of Ghent's redemption is his successful development
of a gold mine, as the sign of Ruth's "fall" is the necklace of nuggets.
But the characters rise above these terms in Ghent's love and easy
generosity and in Ruth's final freedom to accept him.

In *The Great Divide* Moody had once again taken a traditional
form and raised it to a new power. In developing his themes he skillfully employs dramatic techniques of the earlier poetic plays. Ruth's
song in act 1 is integral, setting her mood and providing a new dimension of meaning. Other simple symbolic techniques are employed. The
settings suggest thematic conflicts, the gold necklace assumes central
importance, and through symbol and allusion Stephen is identified with
the devil, tempter of the self-righteous Ruth, and with Dionysus in the
significant if undeveloped vine and liquor symbols. Moody's choice of
names—Ruth, with biblical overtones, and Stephen, with suggestion of
the saint martyred for exalting a new dispensation over the Mosaic
code—is further evidence of his abiding interest in enriching allusion.
In contrast to earlier plays, however, dialogue in *The Great Divide* is
free and sharp, moving economically and rapidly. It is clearly the result
of Moody's remarkably swift adjustment to the theatrical requirements
which became evident in his experience with production of the play.
It usually avoids stereotype successfully as well—a rare achievement

for drama over fifty years old. Only in exchanges involving conflict of honor and principle—most markedly in Philip's speeches throughout the play, and in speeches of Ruth and her mother in shock situations—is there a sense of empty rhetorical convention. And there it is deliberately used to identify and discredit the hollow vision of life the play attacks.

Perhaps the most startling achievement of the play is the force and precision with which Moody's characters are presented. Set beside the stereotypes to be found in contemporary analogues like Belasco's *Girl of the Golden West* and Thomas's *Arizona,* Moody's characterizations are both fresh and realistic. Winthrop's minor contrastive role is conventional, but Moody provides opportunity for interesting rounded portrayals of Philip, Polly, and Mrs. Jordan. Once the possibility of Ghent's regeneration is accepted—and first act attitudes should prepare for it—his character, if simple, is dramatically and psychologically convincing. Ruth's character is much more complex, for both her deep response to Ghent and her moral recoil from him are operative in her personality through most of the play. Her dramatic self-recognition in act 3 is triggered by her violent revelation to her mother and brother of the sources of her conflict. The humility which follows prepares for final acceptance. If she could not accept Ghent's ethic earlier, she can now, even in her own terms, for she has fulfilled her obligation to suffer. But Ruth's movement to reconciliation begins in a series of questions which seek justification in terms of Ghent's natural ethic. Though the result of her narrow training, her actions, she declares, were motivated by her love. It is Ghent's ethic which she finally embraces.

The achievement of the play in the context of American theatrical tradition is, then, to be found in three areas. *The Great Divide* introduced a new, fresh realism to the drama, one expressed less in ponderous representational detailing of scene and dialogue than in serious characterization and genuine character conflict. There is an openness, a swiftness, an American angularity in the variety of realism the play represents. As important, Moody characteristically lifts the play into a larger realm of reference through the application of simple techniques of symbolism and lyricism which he learned, not from Ibsen, Maeterlinck, or Hauptmann, but from his own work as a poet. He domesticated these techniques in the American drama, extending its range and drawing it significantly closer to the spirit of his time. Finally, Moody developed the themes implicit in his action in a fullness new to the American theatre. *The Great Divide* brought realism and symbolism in an effective combination into the American theatre, offering a native model on which dramatists might build.

3

Miller's high hopes for the New York reception of *The Great Divide* were fully justified. The large audience was enthusiastic. Moody wrote Mason describing the response: "At the end of the first act, it looked like a go, and still more when, after the second, the audience rose like a sea in storm and thundered its approval." [23] In the papers the next morning, the critics seconded the audience's approval.[24] By the end of the week the house had been oversold every night, and tickets were placed on sale for three months in advance. Plans were already in motion for a Weber and Fields burlesque of the play, a sure sign of success. Shubert talked of sending the company to London in the spring, and he considered putting another company on the road while the original cast continued the New York run that clearly lay before it.[25] To MacKaye, who had returned to Philadelphia to work on the pre-Broadway trials of his *Jeanne d'Arc,* Moody observed: "Broadway the formidable has indeed roared us as any sucking dove, for this once. It's like taking candy from a child." [26] Henry Miller was exuberant, declaring that he did not remember a reception so promising in all his years in the theatre.[27] When Moody timidly suggested at the end of the first week that he had found further room for improvement in the play and wished to make a few changes, Miller threw up his hands and declared his playwright "a Nihilist, a man of no bowels, and a damn fool who didn't know when he'd got a good thing." [28] But Moody, unable to resist the temptation to revise, decided to make his changes anyway and spring them on Miller when the occasion presented itself.

Critics and friends responded to the strength, the freshness, and the sense of human reality in the play. The *New York Times* review is representative. After discussing tendencies to melodrama in the American theatre and melodramatic moments in the play itself, the critic observed:

As a whole . . . the play rises far above that class. Its characterizations are splendidly real, there is an undercurrent of subtle thought, its human contrasts are bold, strong, powerful and convincing, and . . . it moves forward with a steady, insistent, and absorbing grip upon the attention and the sympathy.[29]

Norman Hapgood wrote, praising the play in much the same terms, pleased that his friend had done something so strong and fresh, combining the poetic and the dramatic so convincingly.[30] Though there were rumblings of earlier attacks on the play's morality, they were overridden by the New York response to the image of modern man in Ghent. Speculation turned to psychological probabilities. The action and issues afforded possibility of a spectrum of opinion on Ruth and Ghent.

Much of the praise for the play was directed to the acting and staging. Two experienced stars were in the leading roles, and both brought to their parts great energy and stage presence. Miller played his role in the monumental American style with great flair. He was exceptionally well-suited to the role of the rough, dynamic miner. Margaret Anglin's habitual intensity, though it de-emphasized some aspects of the character of Ruth, projected the conflict of Moody's heroine. The staging, too, was expert and effective and the production smoothly professional after the month of road trials.[31]

Basic to audience response was the fact that *The Great Divide* was not a startling break with theatrical tradition. It represented a new treatment of that tradition and so was acceptably new. In addition, the play stirred roots of uncelebrated codes, vindicating American romantic morality in its exaltation of will and passion and its pragmatic stance. Perhaps most important to its popular success was the fact that the play succeeded simply as an exciting action with strong emotional appeal. And it was well written. William Archer, looking back at *The Great Divide* the next spring, thought it a unique first play for a man of letters to have written. But having granted the anomaly, he observed that there had been "no first play of so much practical validity" since *Lady Windermere's Fan.*[32]

Had it failed, *The Great Divide* would have been of significance to the development of American drama. But the tremendous commercial success of a serious and dramatically sophisticated American play gave incalculable encouragement to those who were working for a distinguished American theatre. It quickened the interests of producers in good native drama and contributed to the movement whereby professional dramatists were to replace almost completely the actor-writer-producers of the nineteenth century. The play's reception and the long Broadway run that was to follow provided a strong impetus to Moody and his friends, the most significant group of young dramatists writing in America. Percy MacKaye spoke for them when he proclaimed Moody's play had "riven/ Our specious theatre from its roof-beam . . . Unto the pit of smugness."[33] Robinson's poetic prophecy was coming true: the tide of American theatre had finally begun to turn "splendidly homeward."

Moody's success thrust him into a period of unfamiliar activity. There were publicity pictures to be taken, reporters and cartoonists eager for a moment of his time, and a constant round of well-wishers besieging him. It seemed to Moody that he had become the man of the hour, and as the play's popularity held he found "managers and dramatic agents waiting under every lamppost with contracts in their hands." [34] Daniel Frohman offered excellent terms for a new play for his wife, Margaret Illington. An agent of Charles Frohman, the power of the Syndicate, approached him with an offer of a $1500 advance and royalties twice what he was collecting for an option on his next play.[35] In addition, at least four publishers made Moody offers ranging from $25,000 to $50,000 to turn the play into a novel. Moody rejected all advances, feeling that writing under contract would be paralyzing for him and that translating the play into a different genre would be essentially inartistic.[36]

In early November Henry Miller gave a dinner for Moody at The Players. The menu was headed with a caption from Shakespeare's *The Tempest*: "How, now—moody?" [37] The dinner began at midnight and Moody finally left just before dawn, although a cluster of enthusiasts was still caught in discussion over the walnuts and wine. The British playwright, Henry Arthur Jones, was in New York to supervise the production of *Mrs. Dane's Defence,* and Moody attended a dinner he gave for American dramatists. Moody was amazed to find there were hundreds of them, but with a few exceptions he recognized no one. One exception was Bronson Howard, with whom Moody had a talk. Three weeks of notoriety were enough for Moody; the excitement was fatiguing, and being famous gave him little chance to think or read and none at all to embark on a new project.

Having given up his studio months before, Moody had been living in hotels since September. His search for a farm to buy continued in a disorganized way, and he took an occasional trip out of town to escape the city and to survey possibilities. But he wanted a place in New York as well. In mid-November he finally found an intriguing possibility on Waverly Place near Washington Square. The apartment spread over the top floor of an old house, its six rooms offered the luxury of space, and the rent was reasonable. Paperhangers, carpet-layers, plumbers, and other workmen began to make the necessary alterations and improvements, and as the days passed with no visible signs of progress Moody resigned himself to the situation and returned to Chicago for the remainder of the year.

New York had been bright with success, but the theatre outlook in Chicago was gloomy. Robertson's New Theatre had been launched in the fall over great obstacles. His backers, a group of which Harriet was one, met opposition from doubters of the viability of the plan and from the Chicago theatre establishment. In spite of problems they went ahead, but the financing was inadequate and by December it was in desperate straits.[38] Concessions had been made to popular taste, vitiating the experimental thrust of the venture without adding to box-office receipts. Robertson was interested in stimulating and producing native American drama, and he considered poetic drama a strong possibility. He had first call on a number of unproduced American works, among them *The Fire-Bringer* and *The Faith Healer*. But the New Theatre opened with a commonplace import, *Engaged,* and then turned to an American adaptation, a dramatization of Rex Beach's *The Spoilers*. The first was a financial failure; the run-of-the-mill American play was the New Theatre's only success, and a modest one at that. Moody offered to do anything he could, even to giving some public talks if Robertson thought it might help.[39] The project, however, was already too near failure to be revived by anything short of major financial backing.

By the end of 1906 Moody's commitment to the drama was complete. The success of his play definitely allowed him to put teaching aside forever. And there were signs of further renunciations. "Thammuz" had appeared in the October *Scribner's,* and Gilder published "The Death of Eve" in the *Century's* Christmas number. But Moody was neither writing new poems nor submitting still unpublished ones to the magazines. In the early fall there had been opportunities. After the appearance of May Sinclair's article on her triumvirate of American poets in the *Atlantic,* Moody had been invited to contribute something.[40] And Charles Eliot Norton asked him to share a Harvard platform with William Dean Howells and President Eliot to read a poem commemorating the hundredth anniversary of Longfellow's birth.[41] Moody refused both invitations, as well as one to lecture in a University of Chicago series on "Poetry and Life." Moody was not tempted; [42] having fulfilled a personal responsibility in his article-review of Stickney's poetry, he determined that he was through with criticism and literary history forever. The determination was confirmed in a letter of January 1907 to M. A. De Wolfe Howe. Howe had offered a commission for a treatment of Edgar Allan Poe, to appear in a series he was editing. Moody's refusal stated, not quite accurately,

Since leaving the University I have given up writing criticism altogether, and I have got so far away from the essay mood and point of view that I don't feel like taking up a task of the kind you suggest. . . . We live in strata, as you know, and I happen to find myself in an uncritical stratum.[43]

It was all perfectly simple and perfectly final, the casual observance of what Moody could now regard as existential fact.

CHAPTER 12 MOODY AND HIS CIRCLE

WHEN WILL MOODY returned to New York in early January 1907, he turned his attention immediately to *The Faith Healer*, having decided to recast the play. It proved "stodgy and sullen," but Moody felt something was "going on 'inside'" and reverted to a passive view of creativity, observing to Harriet,

It is clearer to me every day that the greater part of any real work of the imagination is done in the subterranean regions of one's personality, and that the part of wisdom is absolute passivity and patience. This is a hard lesson to learn, and a thrice hard method to put in practice, especially for one so impatient and faithless as I am. Doubtless the inability to sustain the period of incubation, the heathen yielding to the demand for something to exercise the surface faculties upon, is the secret of many tragic failures in this way of life.[1]

By the end of January there was some slow progress, but Moody found the difficulties were greater than those which might have been posed by a new work.

Seeking a new perspective on his theme, Moody picked up William James's *Varieties of Religious Experience*. He felt the book offered inescapable evidence for the work of a divine spirit in the world. Though not pressing a thesis, James offered masses of evidence supporting Moody's conviction that man neglected his spiritual dimension only at the cost of his own power to realize life's greatest and only real values.[2] His interest quickened, Moody attended a New York lecture in which James outlined pragmatism. Moody recognized his own working faith in James's view, which Moody found explosive. He hoped it would clear away "all the century-old lumber by which our lives are encumbered." [3] The idea was central to the spirit of the work of Moody's final creative period. The ethical structure suggested by the third-act resolutions of *The Great Divide* is pragmatic in essence — the play's final morality is that with "working value" in the large humanistic terms of James and Moody. And *The Faith Healer* was to draw on both James's work on religious experience and on the pragmatic philosophy. From the traditional commitments and the nostalgias, wistful and energetic, of the nineties, Moody had come a long way into the new century.

In the winter of 1907 Moody was more closely involved with his friends than he had ever been. They were clustered within easy reach of each other around Washington Square. Torrence and Robinson had moved into the Judson on the square, a few blocks from Moody's apartment at 107 Waverly Place, and the Masons had taken up winter quarters there. Gatherings were casual and frequent. Robinson was a working dynamo, eager for a taste of success. But his aloofness was marked. He was as charily self-deprecating as ever and his irony had lost none of its edge. MacKaye added his touch of entrepreneurial enthusiasm as he dashed between his Cornish workshop, appointments with theatrical managers and actors, speaking engagements, and evenings spent with his comrades in New York. But the central tone of the group was provided by Ridgely Torrence. Free in conversation and with inexhaustible resources of imaginative funmaking, his mood and talk filled the silences. With talk of literature and the theatre, of people and events, Torrence enjoyed mimicry. One of his roles was often enough repeated to have been developed into an elaborate routine. It was a monologue of the sort that Sinclair Lewis was later to relish — the speech of a missionary recently returned from the field to a congregation of the brethren. [4] Even Torrence's moods of discouragement tended to take the form of light comedy. A year before, Robinson had been inspired to write Torrence's epitaph, the poem "Bon Voyage." It characterized Torrence as a young Pan, "Vivid and always new/ And always wrong," a "Mocker of all degrees/ And always gay,/ Child of the Cyclades/ And of Broadway." Torrence accepted the premature and dubious honor of the poem with customary glee. [5]

Like Robinson, Moody was sometimes aloof. He spoke with sharp impatience when absorbed in his work or bored. But at other times, his sympathies and conversation flowed freely. There were moments, perhaps his most characteristic, when as MacKaye remembered, "his shy fancy, like an elfin ship,/ On foam of pipe-smoke spread elusive wings," [6] and he cast forth on a stream of metaphor and imaginative play. Moody's social concern remained strong, and he was sometimes roused to passionate expression. One evening, walking from dinner with MacKaye, the two writers stopped beside a lighted factory window, drawn by the sight of the work of women and children at their machines. In a sudden burst of wrath, Moody cried out for a bomb to wipe out the makers of the oppressive poverty of the slums.[7] The simple, casual but powerful outburst, was characteristic. MacKaye always remembered Moody as "the great, quick-hearted man." [8]

There were readings of plays and rumors of more plays in the winter and spring of 1907. Both Torrence and Robinson had succumbed to the dramatic fever, stimulated by the successes of Moody and MacKaye.[9] Robinson's poem, "The White Lights," catches the spirit which animated the fellowship of poet-playwrights. There was "triumph in the air," and for comparisons Robinson looked grandly back to Shakespearean England and Periclean Athens.[10] Robinson had little to lose by committing his time to the drama. He had completed "An Island" the previous fall, and by late winter the poem had been turned down successively by *Scribner's*, the *Atlantic*, and the *Century*.[11] Dan Mason, noting in his journal for January, "We are certainly a nest of the arts here," commented on Robinson's involvement. Moody asked Robinson if he had a one-act play, as Miller wanted one for an approaching benefit. Robinson took up the project and by the end of January had written a new play, *Terra Firma*.[12] It was his second curtain raiser. In addition, he was soon to begin *The Porcupine* and had already reworked his early three-act play, *Ferguson's Ivory Tower*, retitling it *Van Zorn*.[13]

Torrence had been writing through the summer and fall. With aid and advice from Moody, he finished a new play, *The Madstone*, in early January. For the play, he followed Moody's lead in using native American materials. The madstone was a property in the folklore of Xenia, Ohio. A small, porous stone, it was said to be effective in extracting poison from an envenomed wound. In the play, the stone becomes a symbol of woman, redeemer and ennobling influence on man.[14] Moody arranged for Torrence to read the play to Henry Miller. Both of them felt it might be an appropriate vehicle for Madam Nazimova, who had been playing Ibsen on Broadway, and Miller took it to the star.[15] Even Dan Mason became a fellow conspirator. He wished to do something in light opera and encouraged Torrence, among others, to write him a libretto. He brought MacKaye, Moody, and Torrence into contact with several musicians, hoping to stimulate fruitful collaboration.[16]

MacKaye's *Jeanne d'Arc* gave the writer and his friends solid grounds for hope. It opened at the end of January at the Lyric Theatre and was well received by audience and critics. By the end of the winter its successful run seemed to show there was a place for poetic drama in the commercial theatre.[17] MacKaye set about helping Torrence place his *Abelard and Heloise,* and he helped Robinson put *Van Zorn* into Frohman's hands for consideration.[18] From Cambridge came the encouraging news that Josephine Peabody was at work on *The Piper,* which had been commissioned by Otis Skinner;[19] and there was jubilance when Nazimova accepted *The Madstone* for production in the fall.[20] Most important, however, Moody's *The Great Divide* was proving to be a phenomenal attraction. Ticket sales had fallen off during the holidays, but the box office was active in January and February. Miller decided against taking the play immediately to London; the reception was doubtful and a London failure would threaten the coming American season. The New York run was extended for another four months, and things looked so bright that Miller completed negotiations to open the play the following fall at Daly's, a larger theatre than the Princess.[21] Then the company could go on the road with a solid New York reputation. Moody wrote Harriet, hopefully observing, "I believe we have got the ball rolling, and that the next ten years, if nothing happens to interfere, will see something done."[22]

As a successful playwright, Moody was welcome in New York drama circles. He was elected to The Players in mid-January, proposed by Adolphe E. Borie and Gutzon Borglum.[23] Now an insider, he continued to enjoy his associations there. But he was less pleased by the annual dinner held at Delmonico's for the Dramatists of America. The ceremonies included two and a half hours of after-dinner speechmaking which seemed to Moody nothing more than a mindless ritual performed to the goddess Success.[24] Moody was acutely embarrassed by his own success and felt morally implicated in the ceremonies. He cringed at the blatant playbills which announced that *The Great Divide* would remain on the boards because of the pressing demand for tickets by diplomats, statesmen, and other exalted personages.[25] But the play's financial rewards were welcome. Moody's texts provided an increasingly solid base for his needs, but his aid to his sister was now assured. By early March he was able to encourage Charlotte to give up her work as a nurse. He had already made $5,000 on *The Great Divide,* and he estimated that this sum would more than double by summer.[26] He began to invest the money and arranged to have the income paid to Charlotte.

In the spring of 1907, a few months before his death, Edmund Stedman, who had befriended Moody, MacKaye, Robinson, and Torrence, wrote Percy MacKaye, expressing the hope that he and Moody would find American themes for American drama and that they would provide the leadership for a poetic renaissance in America.[27]

While neither Moody nor his friends would have disagreed with
Stedman's view, Stedman's primary interest was in the poetic drama.
They were more and more committed to revival of serious American
drama itself, and most of their current work was in prose. In *The
Great Divide* and *The Faith Healer* Moody had turned to treatment
of American themes in contemporary dramatic modes, and the new
plays of Torrence and Robinson took a similar direction. Nor was
MacKaye unaffected. He rewrote and expanded an early poetic drama
based on a motif in Hawthorne's *Mosses from an Old Manse*. It was to
be his best-known work, *The Scarecrow*. In the next few months he
wrote *Mater*, which Henry Miller would produce in 1908. His theme
was the comedy of contemporary politics. The shift of direction and
aim was significant and decisive, if not entirely in accord with the
theoretical dedications of any of the writers. They maintained a hierarchy of literary values which reached up through prose to poetry.
And they continued to assert the supremacy of traditional themes and
plots over the local and immediate. Almost in spite of these views and
of their fondest wishes, the work of Moody, Robinson, MacKaye,
Josephine Peabody, and Torrence was the prelude to a later generation's massive achievement in the American drama.

As the end of winter approached, Ridgely Torrence's doctor advised a milder climate. It was an opportunity for Torrence's first trip
to Europe, and he urged Will to accompany him. Moody had been
working at high pitch for a long time and was feeling unsettled as
well as tired. He was getting nowhere with *The Faith Healer*. After
communicating by telegram with Harriet, Moody decided to accompany
Torrence. Catching wind of the plan, Donald Robertson wrote, pleading with Moody to complete his revision of the play for production in
a summer season at Ravinia on Chicago's north shore. But Moody did
not think the summer circuit appropriate, and the request was impossible in any case. Ten days after Moody began to consider the trip, he
stood on the deck of the *Romantic,* bound for Gibraltar.

Torrence was eager to see as much as possible, and the travelers
packed their days with activity.[28] They began in North Africa, where
Moorish life gave Moody an insight into the spareness of Old Testament settings—or so he felt. He was thinking of his play on the death
of Eve, half seeking whatever stimulus the setting might afford. As the
travelers moved into Spain, Moody found himself dull and unrespon-
sive. He was not sure how to interpret his reaction. Was his detachment from the passing panorama of "half-alien beauties and diversions"
a sign he was in a rut, or the effect of a shift of his attention from
scenic surfaces to life? Even Italy failed to work its charm. For both
Moody and Torrence the trip became a kind of duty to be completed,

and Torrence was glad to be seeing everything so that he would not have to do it all again.[29] Moody's failure to regain a sense of well-being troubled him most. Ominously, the pain in Moody's hip returned while he was climbing the hill of Posillippo overlooking Naples.[30] The recurrence threw him into a despair he could not shake off. He knew it meant the tumor had begun to grow again, a sign of its malignancy. Moody felt another operation was inevitable and the outlook for the future grim.[31] He wrote Harriet that his inability "to strike a rational balance" was the most awful thing in his life. "It is the suggestress of suicide and the mother of dead dogs," he wrote. "It lies at the root of all our pitiful bungling and waste, with regard to the real issues of our lives." [32]

Yet, on a sunlit day in Florence, Moody caught the vision for the third part of his trilogy—a vision he had been tracking in Europe. It was "plain as print and as perfect as the atomic structure of a jewel." He described it as a "rushing into organic relation" of several old things.[33] The landscapes of North Africa and Spain had reactivated the Eve play, which Moody felt he could write as a development of the theme of judgment treated in his masque. And he thought he would rework the last act of *The Fire-Bringer* to create a coherent trilogy. The remainder of the trip took Moody and Torrence briefly to Paris and London. But both men were tired of travel and with immeasurable relief, after only a week in England, they sailed for home.

Moody hurried from New York back to Chicago, where his doctors satisfied him that his symptoms were negligible. Relieved, he spent most of July and August at Mackinac Island with Harriet, working his way into the new play on the death of Eve.[34] His schedule was strenuous. Fears for his health had increased his sense of the onrush of time, and the dispensation of the doctors, while encouraging, was only for the immediate future. He wanted to get well into the play while his ideas were fresh in his mind, but by September he was restless and ready to return to the East. Moody briefly entertained the possibility of Gloucester or the Maine coast for isolated work on the play, but the lure of New York was too attractive. He returned to find his rooms buried in a summer's dust. In spite of his desire to move ahead on *The Death of Eve*, he put the play aside and took up his balky revision of *The Faith Healer*. The pattern is a familiar one. When with Harriet in Chicago or at Mackinac Island, Moody worked in the poetic drama, but New York always drew him to the contemporary theatre. He intended to return to his trilogy eventually, but he was never to do so. As much of the play as he would write had been completed.

2

While Moody's absorption in the stage was visceral, his articulated commitment was to poetic drama as the major hope for rejuvenating the American theatre. He had expressed his dedication clearly several years before in a letter to Stedman. Reacting against the critics' attack on the subject matter of *The Fire-Bringer*, Moody stated his belief that "a literary Americanism" was "false in theory and barren in practice." [35] In a communication with Percy MacKaye he observed, "It is true that I am heart and soul dedicated to the conviction that modern life can be presented on the stage in the poetic mediums, and adequately presented only in that way." [36] Moody saw his projected play on Eve as relevant and wholly modern in theme, but he aimed at universality in treatment and setting. After the success of *The Great Divide* he discussed the new play with Mrs. Le Moine, the actress. She expressed interest but asked why he didn't transfer the story to modern life. Moody has described his response: "I told her that's just where it was already, and I didn't intend to expose it to cobwebs and museum shelves by putting Adam in creased trousers and Eve into glove-fitting etcetera." [37] The play, conceived as a third part for the masterwork of which Will and Harriet dreamed, was to be a full expression of their faith, their optimistic apprehension of life and its issues. In spite of Moody's close attention to his prose plays, they represented for Moody a concession to the mediocrity of the theatre of his period.[38] They were caught in the accidents of place and time, but Moody's trilogy employed eternally viable forms and materials. He considered it as his major claim to the attention of posterity.

Moody's actual work in the drama was much more pragmatically oriented than this basic commitment would suggest. Into his prose drama he had introduced poetic techniques for handling language and scene. He had written his first version of *The Faith Healer* in a blank verse molded to the spoken language, searching for an idiom that might be appropriate to stage treatment of contemporary themes. And he had worked to create a prose medium flexible enough for realistic dialogue yet capable of rising into lyrical expression at moments of heightened vision or passion. Moody had early considered adaptations of the Greek chorus which might be appropriate to contemporary theatre.[39] In a discussion of his Eve play with Mason, he expressed a desire to make "music and drama interplay in a different way from Wagner's." He felt Wagner's music-drama submerged the language, and he was considering ways in which music might function as the Greek chorus had, entering the action when an appropriate movement

reached culmination to heighten and universalize incident.[40] Moody
was to experiment more broadly with a multileveled language in *The
Death of Eve* and *The Faith Healer,* just as he was to use music more
fully in them than in his earlier plays. The effect Moody desired was
to be found nowhere in drama, he told Mason. The language of Shakespeare's history plays provided the closest approximation to what he
had in mind.

Moody's work on *The Death of Eve* during the summer of 1907
had been extensive. The scenario was planned in some detail and he
had completed his first act, with the exception of a group of lyrics he
intended to insert.[41] He gave up his idea for a miracle play and returned to the Greek mode of *The Fire-Bringer.* But he returned with
a difference. The new play catches a sense of the vastness, the archaic
dignity of the drama of Aeschylus and of the Hebrew myth. The
actions are simple and primal, the motifs archetypal. The setting owes
something to Moody's experience in North Africa and Spain and in
the American West. There is fuller psychological development than
in earlier plays, for Moody's major concern here is character rather
than scenic display or action. The act [42] is a development and a dramatization of the first three narrative sections of Moody's poem on the
subject. His dialogue is even more formal than that of *The Fire-
Bringer.* It moves with slow dignity in frequent archaism, inversion,
repetition, and parallelism. Characters speak to each other using the
third person, and they often refer to themselves in that person. At the
same time, the verse is usually stark, there is increased fragmentation
of utterance, and more genuine exchange in the dialogue than before.
The medium is appropriate to epic drama.

The scene is a rocky mountain slope. Rude steps lead up through
a stone gateway toward Cain's stronghold in Nod. Eve and Jubal, her
grandson, rest near "the Strangers' Well," awaiting the arrival of
Cain. Vague about her purposes, Eve feels somehow "changed/ From
all I was," wondering, "Or am I back-returned/ Through life's deep
changes to my changeless self?" Jubal observes, "Thou are Eve, not
that bowed soul we knew,/ Not that great worn and patient majesty;/
But like an angel going on an errand/ Not for his lord but for his
longing self. . . ." He finds the height of her purposes in Eve's hands,
which look ". . . as if they seized the hands of God,/ And dragged
Him with her through his holy mountain/ Unwillingly to do her
glorious will." Their exchange establishes context and helps project
dimensions of Eve's character more fully. She is tempted to blame Seth
for his refusal to accompany her back to Eden, but she draws back
from judgment to the larger acceptance of all nature which is basic to
her role as the mother of life, crying,

O would 't were by with blame!
When has the oak been proud against the willow?
Or the light aspen shook her jeweled hands
In scorn of the removeless mountain pine?
To every soul his stature, girth, and grain,
Each sovereign to its end: the use is all. —

Jubal identifies Eve as woman "Who loves as wide as life, though deep as death."

Water-bearers approach the well, singing of the Lord, the hunter who makes women blessed when he slays them. In departing they taunt the hunter, proclaiming that they evade the Lord's snare and prohibition, luring their lovers to them. Their song is that of woman, rebel to a Lord who both loves and slays at once, but they play their roles without self-recognition and seek to taunt Eve before leaving. A young slave, Abdera, remains behind to ask Eve if she may be her daughter. Eve wonders if Jubal feels the vine of jealousy beginning to grow in his heart, but the vine seeded by Abdera's request is that of love. Again Eve's acceptance of the contradictions of life is full as she cries, "Winds of the world,/ Blow as ye will and blow what seeds ye will/ If this kind mingle in." Questioned by Eve, Abdera describes Cain as old, a king who, "as he grows more weak he grows more cruel." She sees that "in his withered blood a poison works,/ Distilling wrath and panic." Eve struggles with the image, attempting to reconcile it with her memory of young Cain. As Eve sinks into a reverie, Jubal embraces Abdera and they express their love for each other.

As an old, broken Cain approaches, Eve asks if she is being mocked, not believing this can be her son. Finally convinced, she unveils her face. Cain is terrified, but dismisses his attendants. He and Eve revive memories of their relation as mother and child from the dim past. The verse becomes lyrical as Cain recalls the birth of his male pride:

There was a day when winter held the hills
And all the lower places looking sunward
Knew that the spring was near. Until that day
I had but walked in a boy's dream and dazzle,
And in soft darkness folded on herself
My soul had spun her blind and silken house.
It was my birthday, for at earliest dawn
You had crept to me in the outer tent,
Kissed me with tears and laughter, whispering low
That I was born, and that the world was there,
A gift you had imagined and made for me.

> Now, as I climbed the morning hills, behold,
> I walked, and on my shoulders and my reins
> Strength rang like armor; I sat, and in my belly
> Strength gnawed like a new vinegar; I ran
> And strength was on me like superfluous wings.

But Cain says that Eve has come too late, demanding, "Look on me; look once. Is this crazed frame/ The thing Eve bare in joy?" He has heard tales, including those of her death—conflicting tales every wandering man told "after his heart." For Eve is all things to all men. When he learns that Adam lives as well, however, Cain's bitterness breaks out and he rejects his mother in angry, jealous rage, saying, "I know you not,/ Unclasp my knees.—I thought you were yourself/ Yours, therefore mine at last. It is not so." As Cain and Eve slowly mount the steps to the city, Eve sees Azrael, the Death Angel, descending. Cain does not see him. As he looks in the direction Eve points, he sees instead the figures of Jubal and Abdera approaching from the sheep wells. The difference in vision suggests the metamorphosis in which young life and love rise from death. Eve knows her death is near and pleads with Cain to "hold against Jehovah!" She has come for a son "Who questioned his own wrath . . ./ And seeing where his will went, followed it." Eve discloses her desire to return to her source, the eternal bright garden. She needs Cain, the strong male will "Whose soul is as a torch blown back for speed" to guide her. When Cain rejects the plea in terror, Eve claims her right as source of his life. Uncovering the sign on his forehead, she kisses it, taking upon herself Cain's rebellious wrath and his curse. The action brings Cain peace and he agrees to accompany her. As they enter the city gate together, Jubal and Abdera appear and move up the steps. The act ends as Jubal turns to exclaim, "O Abdera, the strangeness of the world." But his companion rises to the larger womanly acceptance of it: "Not strange.—Strange, strange before; no longer so." They live and move within the larger reconciliation of Eve and Cain.

The act dramatizes the central motifs of Moody's poem on Eve. The tree of life, Eve moves toward her ultimate self-realization, accepting the contradictions of experience and freely embracing the rebellious human will and the strife it engenders. Her full acceptance of Cain's primal curse is an act which redeems hatreds and forbidden loves— human urges to incest, to fratricide and patricide—which are an inextricable part of the fabric of life. Motifs of "The Daguerreotype" appear in the relation of Cain and Eve—in Eve's hope for her son, in Cain's memory of his boyhood and of his awakening to manhood. The intimacy of the connection is suggested with clarity in Moody's scenario. Cain, he writes, "goes through a struggle similar to hers [Eve's], in his attempt to connect her with the young mother whose picture he has preserved in his mind, which has been to him unconsciously the rallying point out of his despair and world-hatred,— though not sufficing to save him from these." [43] Like Moody's mother in the poem, Eve does not judge. She accepts with joy and faith. The poet's perennial theme finds expression in the context of the ancient myth.

Songs and music are indicated at certain points in the text. Moody's scenario describes the projected songs for Jubal and Abdera as "lyric outbursts of their new-found love, forming a little Song of Songs woven naïvely into the tissue of their impersonal talk." The scenario had also included a minor motif omitted in the writing of act 1. One of Cain's warriors was to claim Abdera as his, and the act was to end with Jubal in despair. Moody intended either to excise this concession to conventional romantic plotting or to develop it slightly in his second act. Moody's writing method had obviously altered with maturity. He simplifies the action projected in his early sketch rather than elaborating upon it. His experience in the theatre makes itself felt in the movement and structure of the dialogue and gesture. The work is skillfully constructed, and symbolic motifs are used economically and dramatically. The greatest virtue of act 1, however, is the psychological depth of Moody's characterizations and the dramatic power with which conflicts are projected.

The unwritten act 2 would have taken place at the gate of the Garden of Eden, a structure of vast plinths of which only the bases were to be visible.[44] It opens as Azrael turns the guarding angels away from the gates. The action suggests that Eve's desire to return to the garden is unopposed by higher powers. Eve and Cain enter. There is an exchange in which Eve argues basic human values against Cain's fear of losing his closely guarded kingdom by his action. Eve enters the gates. Jubal and Abdera approach Cain. They have joined a caravan of the ancient Adam, who has come to find Eve. As Cain leaves to greet his father, Jubal and Abdera talk of their love. Though free in spirit, Abdera is bound by respect for the "iron formulas of the East." The cause of her conflict was to be her obligation to the warrior omitted from act 1. Adam approaches, but when Cain finally reveals his identity to his father, Adam is enraged. He curses his son and enters the garden with Jubal. Abdera urges a reluctant Cain to follow, and they enter the gates.

Act 3 was to be set at the Tree, which spreads its boughs to form an arbor. The effect of the setting, Moody felt, should be that "of the tropical luxuriance and savage vigor of the jungle abandoned to

itself and exulting in its own fierce and secret life." [45] As indication
of that life, the act begins in a dumb show in which a satyr wakes
the dryad of the Tree by playing on a syrinx. As they are about to
draw into the shade of the Tree in savage embrace, Eve approaches
and they move off stealthily. The dumb show was to include the plucking, offering and eating of the fruit of the Tree, and it called for a
musical setting. After a prayer in which Eve treats her assumption of
Cain's guilt, Adam and Abdera enter. Adam is fearful and angered,
but Eve urges his reconciliation with Cain. Still not totally aware of
herself, she is outwardly penitent before her husband, but she instinctively expresses from time to time "her irrepressible love of life
as it is, with all its tragedy, suffering, and incompleteness." Cain then
enters. After argument with his father, he dies. Softened, Adam
blesses his dead son and there is a sense of peaceful unity before
Adam too dies. Eve chants over Adam and then tells Abdera to pluck
a fruit from the Tree and give it to Jubal. During Abdera's action,
Jubal sings. Eve then sings her death lyric. As she too sinks and dies,
the angels reappear to look upon the dead. The music fades to a
single harp as Jubal sings a passionate lyric of "the mysterious love-
life" into which he and Abdera have entered. His song ends the play.

Moody's scenario suggests his completed play would have been
closer to a music-drama than anything he had previously done. Through
a set of parallel rituals Moody's third act develops his vision of a death
which blooms in new life as the cycle begins again for the young
lovers. The play's reconciliations come in terms of human recognitions
and acceptances. Nature is not changed, nor is a transcendent God
turned into a gentle and forgiving father. There is nothing to forgive.
Passion and strife are part of the natural and supernatural order.
Moody's projected treatment of the Eve theme clarifies issues left in
suspension at the end of his poem, "The Death of Eve." But his major
vision has not shifted from his earlier position, defined by *The Fire-
Bringer* and elaborated in the poems of 1904 and 1905.

3

Moody returned to *The Faith Healer* in October 1907, desiring
to capitalize quickly on the success of *The Great Divide*. He hoped to
have it ready for the stage by the following fall.[46] After several weeks
of work, however, the old play continued to resist change, and he
felt he should probably throw it away and start afresh. But he could
not. He continued to work at it through the fall. *The Great Divide*
had reopened at Daly's Theatre in September. Miller thought to take

the company on the road in October, but business held up so well he decided to stay on until Christmas. Moody thought his theory probably was that "a plum pudding cuts richer the longer it is kept." He wondered, "Do plum puddings ever spoil?" [47]

Moody's circle of New York friends was an important factor in his decision to work in the city, and he immediately became involved in their plans. Torrence had spent the summer in Xenia gathering materials for a new play, but the expected production of *The Madstone* had been delayed. Moody found MacKaye in a flurry of activity, consulting on the production of his *Sappho and Phaon*, scheduled for Broadway opening later in the month. Robinson had finished *The Porcupine* and was planning yet another play. Torrence totaled five plays to his friend's credit, two curtain raisers and three full plays.[48] Moody was immediately recruited to hear *The Porcupine*. He found it a "Robinsonian imbroglio" but "a very strong play, and handled with a wonderful deftness and lightness of touch." [49] He took it to Charles Frohman, who received Moody in the private office from which he ruled the Syndicate. Frohman seemed receptive as Moody poured into his ear the crusading plans of the small group of writers. He promised to read Robinson's play immediately and offered the crusaders for serious American drama free tickets to all his theatres. Moody hoped the promising reception would furnish Robinson the encouragement he needed, but in a few days Frohman returned the play with a note, "Not available for stage." [50]

Another event dampened the spirits of the group even more—the failure of MacKaye's *Sappho and Phaon*.[51] It had been written as a commission for Sothern and Marlowe, but Harrison Fiske finally produced it. The published version had been well received the previous spring, and its pre-Broadway trial in Providence had been encouraging. But the opening was ominous, although the dramatist and his friends, seated together in the orchestra, tried to applaud it into success. Among a host of minor catastrophes, a cat strayed on stage and sat down in the middle of a love scene between Phaon and Sappho. Though the audience was responsive, the acting was poor—Moody pronounced it "hopeless." [52] Gathering afterward at the Arena restaurant, MacKaye's friends happily toasted the author, but Norman Hapgood correctly predicted the negative critical response the play would receive. It was withdrawn at the end of the week.

Moody was enjoying the hospitality of Mrs. Clara Davidge, a widow who had a home on Washington Square and who spent her summers in Cornish. The daughter of an Episcopal bishop, she was a rebel. Her religious inclinations were to strenuous mysticism and Christian Science. She took pleasure in extending aid and comfort to the young writers and artists of the Washington Square area, giving frequent dinners which they sometimes reciprocated.[53] At Hallowe'en she gathered in Will, Robinson, Torrence, and Mason, who twined grape leaves around their brows to celebrate in true pagan style. Mason thought Will especially in character, "half faun and half Greek god, flushed with punch and genius." [54] In early November Robert Herrick and his sister arrived in New York, members of a party which swept Moody off on a two-day automobile tour up the Hudson River and into the Connecticut hills, an experience Moody relished. Herrick too had a play on his hands, and Moody arranged for a reading by the actress, Grace Elliston.[55] As the autumn grew cooler Moody took up dining occasionally at The Players or the Century Club. There were also occasional formal dinners where he saw old friends, among them Hamlin Garland. Garland found Moody growing "more taciturn, more introspective" each year. He observed, "At luncheons, even when guest of honor, he sat in silence, almost Oriental in his abstracted calm, his bearded face a mask, his eyes, roving from face to face, with no more expression of interest than the lens of a camera." [56]

If the tendency to introspective withdrawal was deepening, among friends Moody's old exuberance still shone through in an occasional explosive laugh or a revelry of wit and good spirits. Public celebration of his success bored him, but it brought a mellowing of his personality and deepened his sense of humility.[57] Both MacKaye and Torrence later felt the key to the character of the Will Moody they knew was human kindness, and they praised his "innate capacity for deep friendship." [58] Moody freely extended the aid that flows from friendship to Torrence, to Robinson, and to MacKaye. In addition to his informal and casual gestures, Moody had the pleasure of sponsoring his three friends for the National Institute of Arts and Letters.[59] They were elected to membership in February.

Moody's human concern sometimes expressed itself in unique ways. He told Harriet a curious tale of his pleasure in helping a man who had begged some change from him. Struck by the beggar's gentility of manner, Moody helped him retrieve his belongings from the pawnshops. The beggar was a Canadian who had come to New York seeking work and had fallen ill with typhoid. After recuperation in the hospital, he was left weak and without resources. Moody found the man basically pure of heart and thought that when he got a job and could see the world as "not-too-savage," the fellow might tell him more of his experience.[60] Moody joined Robinson as occasional patron to Joseph Lewis French, a free-lance writer always in need of money. French opened his association with Moody by borrowing his only overcoat. Moody made plans for getting it back before deciding that

French needed it more than he. French continued to show up through the years to borrow a dollar or two from Moody, Torrence, Robinson, or Mason.[61]

Moody finished two acts of *The Faith Healer* by early winter and was deep in the crucial third act, bludgeoning the play into new form. He thought it would be interesting to read but wondered if any producer would touch the strange work.[62] Though the third act seemed full of soft places, by the end of January Moody felt confident enough to read his manuscript to his friends. The result was startling. Only one person—probably Torrence—liked the play.[63] The group's responsibility for mutual encouragement evaporated in a series of responses either negative or actively hostile. Mrs. Davidge, a devotée of divine healing, was especially outraged. Moody's New Mexico Messiah had fallen passionately in love with a "wicked woman," and Moody's treatment of the issues was unforgivable. Moody saw human love as the power which raised the faith healer to a larger religious faith—a good neoplatonic position. But such proceedings, Mrs. Davidge maintained, smacked of "Mariolatry." Love of woman and love of God are irreconcilable and conflicting emotions, she argued, and she viewed the play as one which might hold back the spread of faith healing for years. She declared herself prepared to lay down her life at the doors of the theatre to prevent people from seeing *The Faith Healer*.[64] Her response was a harbinger of the virulence the play would arouse, for it was fraught with controversial treatment of a variety of popular stances on the battlefield of science and religion. But Moody did not believe Mrs. Davidge's reaction would be representative. He wrote blandly to Harriet, "The passion of her attack amazed and staggered me. It shows at any rate how vital the whole field of thought is to our generation." [65]

In February Moody read *The Faith Healer* to Henry Miller, who was playing *The Great Divide* in Boston. Miller was unsure about chances for the play's commercial success, but he thought it would add to his and Moody's prestige and was inclined to consider that justification enough for trying it.[66] They planned for production in the fall, and Miller arranged for Moody to see a variety of actors he thought might be right for the demanding male role. Moody was distracted, feeling the play still contained too much of his old material. He decided it should be rewritten once more, but he was tired. Spring surprised him, bursting in upon the technical problems that absorbed him. "I thought spring was a legend," he wrote Harriet, "an invention . . . of poets. . . . I thought I recollected inventing it myself, when I was a poet." [67]

In early March Harriet's mother died, leaving her daughter in a state of shock and deep despair. Moody was about to leave immediately for Chicago, but Harriet wanted to get away. At her suggestion they met in New Orleans. They remained for several weeks, but their spirits were low and Moody himself was ill.[68] Back in New York by March 20, he put himself in Charlotte's care. His illness turned into a severe attack of typhoid fever, and he lay in his apartment for the next two months, nursed by Charlotte and Harriet, who came East to help. Not until the end of May was Moody sufficiently strong to be transferred to Port Chester, where his doctor had a small house. Moody's back was weak and his nerves shaky. Writing was forbidden and collapse threatened if he attempted the slightest unusual exertion. In June Mrs. Davidge took quarters at Cos Cob, and Torrence was a houseguest. Eager to get away from his nurses, Moody appealed to his friends for aid. Mrs. Davidge inaugurated a round of easy outings — auto rides, picnics, motor and sailing boat excursions.[69]

Though Torrence found his friend weak and haggard, Moody was restless under the months of constant confinement. Yale University invited him to receive an honorary degree at commencement in late June and Moody took the lure eagerly, convincing himself and his doctor that he was getting stronger. Unable to travel alone, he induced Torrence to accompany him to New Haven, and he planned to extend the expedition to Maine to look at country homes. On June 24 Moody received an honorary degree of Doctor of Letters from Yale. Presenting the honor, Professor Perrin noted of the poet, "He never speaks without a message." In Moody, he observed, "We believe the major poet has at last appeared for whom we have watched and waited since the passing of the great Victorians." [70]

Moody was still forced to be careful, and by doctor's orders he rested in bed until noon every day. In spite of his condition, however, he and Torrence went to Portsmouth, New Hampshire, and then to Monhegan Island off the Maine coast. He saw it as "Mackinac unspoiled" and thought of buying a piece of ground to build on some day. But not now. Harriet took the old place on Mackinac Island, Moody returned to New York for a few things, and by mid-July they were comfortably settled in their old haunts. Full recuperation came slowly, interrupted by setbacks which profoundly discouraged and irritated Moody. Under Mrs. Davidge's insistent faith, both he and Torrence became interested in practical faith healing. Vastly intrigued, Torrence had taken to *Science and Health* and began consulting a healer.[71] Moody remained somewhat sceptical, though he felt his mental attitude was important to his nervous condition. In late August he wrote, with some surprise, to Harriet, "I am feeling much better . . . having lifted myself by the scruff of the neck out of a slough

of invalidism, which was daily increasing, and decided to try a little
faith-cure on myself, with amazing results. There is really something
in it."

The writer spent most of his mornings in bed, but the cool weather
agreed with him and he was doing some driving about the island and
some painting. The movement to greater starkness in *The Death of
Eve* was reflected in his growing taste for fewer colors in painting.
And he devoted less time to landscapes and more to portraits of Harriet.
Moody was also able to return to *The Faith Healer*. Writing with
dogged determination, he had revised the third act by the end of
September.[72] Miller did not plan to put the play into rehearsal for
another month, however, and Moody decided to stay at Mackinac as
long as he could.

The New York scene to which Moody returned in November was
enlivened by the arrival of Isadora Duncan. Moody, MacKaye, and
George Grey Barnard, the sculptor, were enthusiastic after seeing her
first recital at the Metropolitan Opera House.[73] Fresh from a triumphant European tour, she danced Beethoven's Seventh Symphony.
After the performance Barnard invited his friends to accompany him
to the dancer's studio. They arrived to be greeted by a scene of bacchanalia. The flamboyant Isadora in Greek costume appeared in the
corridor at the head of a chain of guests in a wild variety of dance
postures. Through the coming weeks Torrence, Robinson, and Moody
haunted her performances, and she gathered them in for celebrations.
Isadora took immediately to the writers, dubbing them the "young
revolutionists." On one occasion she danced tributes to each of them,
amazing them by the appropriateness of her motifs. For Moody her
dance was one of slow, classic dignity, resembling the awakening of
a figure on a Grecian urn.[74] MacKaye began writing poems as dance
figures for Isadora.

It was something like old times, in spite of discouragement and
Moody's illness. He was elected to the recently organized American
Academy of Arts and Letters and had high hopes for the success of his
new play. MacKaye had spent part of the summer in San Francisco,
where Miller produced *Mater*. The play had opened in New York at
the Savoy Theatre near the end of September, enjoying a short run
before good crowds. Robinson, however, was in low spirits. Even
Torrence had been worried in the spring, observing that his friend
was in the grip of an unusual kind of despair—one which did not
rouse him to his usual edge of sharp irony.[75] He had invested a great
deal of emotional capital in his plays without success, in spite of the
efforts of MacKaye and Moody to help him place them. Robinson had
even tried the publishers, finding, he observed to Moody, that "a play

is about thirty-seven times more difficult to place than an epic poem founded on the life of Wan McAllister." [76] He decided to pin his hopes on the plans for a New Theatre in New York, and Moody gave him an introduction to John Corbin, who had been selected as literary director.[77] Moody's faith in his old friend did not waver. When Torrence expressed concern about Robinson's growing gloom, Moody told him that Robinson was in a better position than any of them. "When we're all dead and buried," he said, "EA will go thundering down the ages." [78] Torrence himself was discouraged as well. His hopes for production of *The Madstone* had dwindled to nothing. He began to write short stories on his Ohio materials, but the magazines to which he submitted were slow in responding.[79] Having given up editorial work to devote himself to writing, he was forced to turn to Moody and others for loans.

Much of Moody's time in November was taken up with plans for *The Faith Healer*. He began working closely with Miller in assembling a cast and advising on the staging. Feeling the title role was not suited to his age and personality, Miller enlisted Tyrone Power for the lead. At the end of the month rehearsals began, and a tryout was advertised for early December in Boston. Moody was as pleased as ever with Miller's courtesy and his intelligent work on the play. But at the end of November the production became entangled in red tape. For copyright protection in England, submission of the play in printed form was required. The tryout was postponed at the loss of a number of members of the cast, including Power, whom Moody liked in the role. Moody retraced his steps to Chicago, where *The Faith Healer* was quickly prepared for token publication in order to fulfill copyright requirements.[80] In addition, Moody was working on a fair copy of *The Great Divide* for the printer. But the playwright's difficulty was compounded by the two-year stage history of the play and the inevitable corruption of the text Miller was using. Publication also offered Moody the chance he wanted to make further revisions of the original play. *The Faith Healer* [81] was shipped off quickly, but Moody was not satisfied with *The Great Divide* until nearly the end of January 1909, when he sent his manuscript to Houghton Mifflin for publication. His final revision omitted references to marriage in act 1 of the early play, shifting the issue to a more elemental one in Ruth's offer to "stick to" Ghent "for good." He also heightened the clash between Ghent and Philip in act 3.[82] Necessary work on old projects was finally completed, and the future seemed to lie open before him.

CHAPTER 13 ON THE RAGGED EDGE

HIS PROSE PLAYS were in the hands of the printer, but the state of Moody's health was precarious. He had pushed himself beyond his limits in the aborted preparations for staging *The Faith Healer*. The quieter environment of Chicago did not seem to aid him, and he had not recovered from typhoid with the ease he had come to expect. By the end of January he needed complete relaxation. Moody left Chicago in early February with William Wendt, the painter, for some outdoor life and sketching in southern California.[1] It was a prescription for health that had always worked.

Moody had been free of a university environment now for almost six years, but his audience continued to think of him as an academic poet, and critics often referred to his connections with the University of Chicago. Sometimes, in an excess of respect, they called him Professor Moody. The image was one Moody had disliked from the beginning; teaching had been little more than a means of support for his life as a writer.[2] Especially after the reception of *The Fire-Bringer*, he had struggled to throw off the stigmata of the writer in academia. The image had become increasingly inappropriate. Moody's character and tastes had changed so significantly over the years that Percy MacKaye was unable to believe Will Moody knew enough to have written the lion's share of a book of literary history.[3] Willard H. Wright, talking with Moody about his plays in Los Angeles, had expected to meet a professor and man of letters.[4] Moody frustrated his expectations. The writer was dressed for the out-of-doors in leather leggings and rawhide shoes. His beard and hair showed signs of neglect, and his necktie was loosely knotted. Moody talked without restraint from a cloud of cigar smoke. He moved freely about on a sprawling davenport, sometimes bringing his feet up and hugging his knees. After his initial shock, Wright was charmed by the writer who had long ago begun to move to a neo-Whitmanic stance in reaction against Harvard in the nineties.

In San Dimas Moody tried to devote himself to sketching, but he was distracted by thoughts of his work. He longed to set off for Egypt and Palestine, he wrote Charlotte, in search of renewed inspiration for the unfinished play on Eve.[5] He wrote Mrs. Toy, the old friend of his undergraduate years at Harvard, observing that *The Death of Eve* was the thing he now had most at heart. But he was torn "between the ideal aspect of the theme and the stage necessities—the old, old problem." [6] He declared that he was tempted to write the play as a closet drama, yet his dedication to the theatre was too strong. Only in his daydreams did he long "for that justly lighted and managed stage of the mind, where there are no bad actors and where the peanut-eating of the public is reduced to a discreet minimum." [7]

A second distraction was more compelling: Henry Miller's plans for the postponed trial of *The Faith Healer*. Miller's company was in St. Louis, and he wanted to try out the new play there in preparation for a Broadway opening in the fall. He scheduled a week of rehearsals and a second week of performances for early March. The temptation to help with the production was too great to resist, and Moody arrived in St. Louis on March 8. The company was a makeshift one. Miller and Mary Lawton, latest of a series of Ruths in *The Great Divide*, took the leads, and other members of the company adapted themselves to roles as best they could. The chaotic rehearsals were exhausting for Moody, who insisted on sitting in the darkened playhouse day after day for consultations on staging and performance. Schevill came from Chicago to help and was shocked at Moody's condition. The usually energetic writer was nearly in a state of nervous exhaustion. He was plagued with severe headaches which were almost continuous. It was, Schevill later recognized, the beginning of the end.[8] Nor did the situation change during the week of performances which followed. The cast was mediocre and ill-rehearsed, and the audience restless and noisy. But this did not preclude powerful reactions to the play. Although reviews were mixed, several reviewers were either openly hostile or horrified, and St. Louis clergymen were roused to protest. "The audiences," Moody wrote Charlotte, ". . . were simply *flabbergasted,* and didn't know whether to be pleased, shocked, or merely eternally puzzled. In other words they didn't understand the play *at all.*" [9] He thought the difficulty was that he had condensed too much and that therefore the motive of the play was unclear to the average mind. Moody had lived so long with his materials that their

uniqueness and the singularity of his treatment were unapparent to
him. Thinking in terms of the symbolic issues of the action, Moody
continued to underestimate the impact of the play on its simple, realistic level. Nor did he react when one paper billed the play throughout
the week as a "Weird and absorbing drama but appalling in its sacri-
legious handling of sacred things." [10]

Will returned to Chicago, where, somehow, he began strenuous
revision of the play. The work took five or six weeks of steady application.[11] He revamped the basic structure, reducing four acts to three by
combining the first two acts of his St. Louis version.[12] Innumerable
transpositions of passages of dialogue were made in order to reduce a
sense of scatter in the earlier version. Acts were restructured to move
more decisively to climaxes basic to themes of the play. Individual
scenes and speeches were revised. Several long, descriptive speeches
by the hero, Michaelis, and some scenes between the healer and his
companion, Lazarus, an Indian boy, were omitted. Moody also strengthened the symbolism and reinforced the love motif. Act 3 conflict now
culminated in a direct confrontation of the healer and Rhoda's first
lover. The improvement in clarity, swiftness, and coherence of the
action was significant, but Moody made no concessions to those who
had greeted the play in St. Louis with outrage and indignation. Nor
did he alter the central theme; indeed, he clarified the healer's final
dedication to fulfillment of spiritual vision through earthly love.

Moody took the play to Henry Miller at Sky Meadows, the actor's
country place not far from New York. While conferring with Miller,
Moody did some riding and driving about, but he was not relaxing.
"I am on the ragged edge," he noted casually in a letter to Charlotte.[13]
As Miller's plans for production took shape, Moody was able to make
some arrangements of his own. Miller had incurred losses in the
theatre and hoped to recover his financial position by taking *The Great
Divide* to London. The production schedule for *The Faith Healer*
hinged on the outcome of the London negotiations. A number of plans
meshed; Moody desperately needed a vacation trip, and he wanted to
be in England for the production of his play there. Also, Harriet was
considering the establishment of a branch of the Home Delicacies
in London and was corresponding with Selfridge's. A year had passed
since her mother's death, and Will had reopened the question of their
marriage. Many of the old problems remained, but the most compelling had receded. On April 24 Moody wrote Harriet from New
York. He was significantly brief: "The less we talk and the more
promptly we act, the better now." [14] By early May it was clear that
The Great Divide would appear in London, and production of *The
Faith Healer* was postponed until early winter.

Moody quietly made plans for immediate marriage and a trip abroad with Harriet. He wired her, and the lovers, having postponed decision for so many years, met in Quebec. They were married there on May 7 and sailed for Liverpool. They settled in London for a few weeks and Harriet began negotiations with Selfridge's. In June, hoping that sea air might benefit Will, he and Harriet went to the Channel Islands. But his condition seemed to worsen rather than improve. His nervous system was unstable, he had a great deal of pain in the back, the head, the eyes, and his vision was clouding. An island doctor, who began to call daily, diagnosed neuritis. At the end of June the ill-fated lovers went to Winchester, from which Will went on to Salisbury and Stonehenge; but Harriet began urging that they seek a quiet, country environment for recuperation. They had found a charming cottage on the Isle of Wight overlooking the sea. It was everything they sought, but when confronted with the reality, they realized that neither of them wanted the idyllic pastoral existence it represented. The cottage seemed merely remote, a place of exile.[15] In July Moody's restlessness took them to Jersey for a few days and then on a tour of the Lake District—Windermere, Ambleside, Bowness. Nothing helped.

Moody's despair grew, but he let little of it show in his letters to America. In August he answered Josephine Peabody's letter of congratulation upon his marriage, writing, "The solemn and gracious words which you speak find a clear echo in my heart. Life grows larger, if we let it; that is the great and joyous truth." [16] He accepted the diagnosis of neuritis, considered his pain an effect of the typhoid. To Charlotte, to Josephine, to MacKaye and others, he observed only that his health was "wretched" and that he had broken down badly as a result of overwork. He wrote, more with vague hope than with reference to reality, that he was "crawling up again." [17] There were periods in which all that could be done was for Moody to remain on his back as Harriet read book after book to him to distract his mind. As his vision was more and more affected, Moody tried oculists and osteopaths in London, vainly hoping for some relief. By sheer strength of will he held on until September 15 when The Great Divide opened in London's Adelphi Theatre.

In the three years since that first night in Albany, Miller's American companies had given over one thousand performances of the play from coast to coast. The English company contained a number of the American cast. Miller and Edith Wynne Matthison, who had joined the New York company in February 1908, took the leading roles. Moody had the pleasure of seeing his play a London hit, and the English-born Miller relished his triumphal return to London. The Great Divide was hailed as an "emphatic victory" by more than one reviewer.[18] The London Sunday *Times* responded to the flamboyant billings of the play as an "American sensation," calling it "American melodrama with a vengeance." The *Times* suggested that it was written "in the sensational style of bold advertisement." The effect was not reduced by Miller's grandiose style, which was declared to be "very impressive." [19] The acting and production were widely admired, and most reviewers liked the play's emotional power. One writer commented on its "earnestness," finding a concern for "real men and women" which he thought lacking in the English drama of the time. Occasionally a critic maintained his composure to demur from the general praise. One decided the play was "ferocious" in sentimentality, "preposterous" in artificiality, and "enormous" in ingeniousness.[20]

Harriet and Will had little time for rejoicing. They sailed immediately, and upon arriving in Chicago, Moody put himself in the hands of a neurologist.[21] A diagnosis of suspected brain tumor was made. Moody was urged to consult Dr. Harvey Cushing, the eminent brain surgeon at Johns Hopkins. By October 6 Moody had entered the Baltimore hospital for observation. Both Harriet and Charlotte accompanied him. Dr. Cushing's examination confirmed the diagnosis, and two exploratory operations were performed in October and November.[22] On November 25, after a week of recuperation, Moody reentered the hospital. He was weak, in severe pain, and almost totally blind. The surgeons were not yet sure the diagnosis of tumor was correct. Harriet was confronted with the question of a third operation. Chances for success seemed slight and the operation posed a serious threat to Moody's life.[23] Harriet telegraphed Percy MacKaye, pleading for advice.[24] He arrived quickly from Boston and helped Harriet and Charlotte decide against another operation. They thought to seek possible recovery in rest for the patient. Leaving the hospital, Harriet asked Will whether he wanted to take the elevator. The broken man decided for the stairs: "I'd feel nobler to walk." [25] He had not known MacKaye was present to help him out of the hospital and into a train.

Harriet set out immediately for southern California. There a long period of anxious watching and waiting began. The reading aloud of a stream of books was varied by short walks and drives along the Santa Barbara coast. Harriet stoically and painstakingly noted every change of mood and physical condition in Will, finding in the activity a refuge from the overwhelming confrontation with tragedy. In mid-December she felt Will's state was worse, carefully noting a decline in vision, speech, memory, extent of pain, nervousness, and sluggishness of response.[26]

In January a telegram from Henry Miller arrived announcing plans for the imminent staging of *The Faith Healer*. Moody was excited and several telegrams were exchanged. He proposed that Harriet set off for New York to sit in on the rehearsals, but she quietly refused. On January 19 the play opened at the Savoy Theatre on Broadway.

2

The problem of *The Faith Healer*—the conflict of spirit and flesh —had been central to Moody's life and a recurring theme in his work. He had become interested in doing the play when he was twenty-six and had worked intermittently on it for almost fourteen years. Like his healer, Moody felt a sense of spiritual mission as a writer. For him that call meant intense concentration of all his energies in his work. It also meant the freedom of movement provided by absence of other duties. In the nineties he had viewed the ties of love as restricting. They represented distractions of sense and passion which made spiritual conquest an impossibility. Eventually they involved bondage to the dullnesses of domesticity. The complex history of his play's revisions is the history of Moody's spiritual life. He had moved from the exclusive spiritual dedication of the late nineties to a willingness to give all to love early in the new century. Finally, Will's love for Harriet opened out upon a vision of life in which the formerly antagonistic values of love and art became mutually strengthening.

Moody's materials were anxiety-arousing. The play was laden with stuff of his own childhood which reached into the depths of his psychic life. The scene of *The Faith Healer*[27] is a farmhouse near a small midwestern town. Like the Moody house in New Albany, it is the ancestral home of an invalid who has not walked or used her right hand for almost five years. The invalid, Mary Beeler, is a Bible-belt mystic, given to visions. Her husband is a hardheaded, practical man. He keeps his small library of scientific books in the living room and displays the pictures of his heroes, Darwin and Spencer, on the wall. Like Moody's parents, the Beelers look back to the earlier, more prosperous and joyous period of their young married life. Beeler's sister, Martha, a member of the household, is reminiscent of Grandmother Stoy in her bustling activity and her sharp-tongued practicality. There are younger women in the home: Rhoda, a twenty-year-old niece of Mary Beeler's and Annie, Mary's young daughter. Uncle Abe, an old Negro who sometimes does odd jobs around the house, is reminiscent of a Negro retainer of the Moody family. Ulrich Michaelis is a wandering religious worker—a man like those Grandmother Stoy often sheltered. He is an inspired and poetic man, who will raise Mrs. Beeler from her wheelchair to new wholeness of life. He redeems the mother and marries her youthful counterpart, the passionate Rhoda. In one of its biographical dimensions, *The Faith Healer* is a reconstruction and a redemption in art of Will Moody's lost youth, a fulfillment of his deepest desires.

The play's mode seems to be realism, and its three acts are set in the living-dining room of the Beeler home. But the play itself is a rewriting of Christian myth. It takes place in twenty-four hours between dawn Saturday and dawn on Easter Sunday. Beeler's name is Matthew, suggesting strictness of the law and a materialistic orientation. Mary and Martha invoke their New Testament counterparts in character, and the healer fills the messianic role of Jesus. The first sign of his powers had come in raising from the dead an Indian boy who calls himself Lazarus. Rhoda—a rose—is a passionate woman, awaiting fulfillment, and the names of the representatives of church and medicine, Reverend Culpepper and Dr. Littlefield, suggest the limitations of their vision and their ministrations.

The structure of *The Faith Healer* is complex. Moody's cast is large and the numerous casual entrances and exits create an openness of form more appropriate to realistic drama than the economical structure of scenes in *The Great Divide*. But Moody's symbolism is more complex and his treatment of setting and minor characters is genuinely expressionistic. Changes in lighting reflect shifts in Michaelis's spiritual state as the play moves from the heavy fog surrounding the house in act 1, through darkness, toward the full, brilliant dawn of Easter morning at the play's end. We are also aware of the shifting moods of an offstage audience which begins to gather in act 1, grows to several hundred by act 2, and becomes a multitude representing all humanity at the end of the play. Annie, a sensitive child, and superstitious Uncle Abe function as choral figures setting a tone of terror and suspense: they are dimly aware of the battle of demonic and divine forces in which Michaelis is engaged. Mrs. Beeler and a child in a coma are objective correlatives to Michaelis's spiritual states, moving toward paralysis and death in periods of his despair and toward life when his faith is strong. Beeler helps focus issues of Michaelis's struggle, but he too responds to the action on its spiritual level.

In act 1 the tone of the Beeler household is set by Beeler's embittered scientific scepticism and Martha's practical empiricism. Michaelis's role and conflict are established by his own speeches and clarified by Beeler's interpretation of them. Discussion of the new Beeler boarder creates a mood of mystery and suspicion which prepares for Michaelis's entry. The nature of his role is presented in an allusion which reappears in the play. Beeler calls Michaelis "a fakir," and Rhoda explains to Annie that a fakir leaves the earth to climb a rope to heaven by spiritual power. Michaelis's relation to Christ is established by his gentle manner, his simple workingman's garb and his tales of early life as a shepherd, of his visions and voices, and of his miraculous raising of the son of an Indian chief from the dead. Conflict in his sense of mission is presented when he half welcomes Rhoda's suggestion that the Indian boy might have been in a state of trance. The center of Michaelis's conflict is established in a statement to Rhoda that he feels strangely reborn when he is with her. Beeler focuses the issue by pinning on the wall a newsprint of a medieval palmer who meets Pan in a forest. Beeler approves of Pan, a god who stands up for "Natural things, with plenty of sap and mischief in 'em," foreseeing that the palmer with "religion on the brain" will be diverted from his mission. Moody's theme, once again, lies in apparently antithetical Christian and Dionysian visions of life. The act ends as an exalted Mary Beeler, who has been talking with Michaelis, enters walking. As the gathering crowd outside begins to sing, Michaelis accepts the knowledge that his hour is at hand. The curtain falls as he admonishes himself, "I must not fail. I must not fail."

Act 2 introduces Michaelis's antagonist. The scientific scepticism of Beeler—presented in his small library, his portraits of Darwin and Spencer, and his identification of his wife's state as "pathological"—reappears in the figure of Dr. Littlefield. A blustering, self-seeking young man, Littlefield has been Rhoda's lover. She has been deeply disturbed by her loveless, casual introduction to sex, but he takes the matter lightly, taunting her. He has given up a sick baby, whose desperate mother enters, appealing to Michaelis for aid. Sensing the challenge, he becomes aggressive. He denies that God has had a hand in Mary Beeler's recovery, observing to Michaelis, "You gave her a jog" in the mind and heart and she did the rest. But to affect a baby's psyche is impossible, he suggests. When the healer challenges Littlefield to save the child, the doctor shrugs, observing that failure would not be good for his reputation. Watching the nervous Michaelis with interest, the doctor diagnoses the case:

Nervously speaking, you are a high power machine. The dynamo that runs you is what is called "faith," "religious inspiration," or what-not. It's a dynamo which nowadays easily gets out of order. Well, my friend, as a doctor, I warn you that your little dynamo is out of order.—In other words, you've lost your grip. You're in a funk.

Annie and Uncle Abe continue to supply the action with a margin of mystery. Annie shares Abe's ominous fear of Beeler's Pan as an incarnation of "de Black Man," but in moments when faith is ascendant she sings the refrain of a spiritual: "Mary an' a' Martha's jes' gone along,/ Ring dem charmin' bells." Earlier suggestions that Rhoda has cast a spell over Michaelis are verified. In a reinforcement of the Dionysian motif, Michaelis has told Rhoda that his failure, if it came, would come through "The wine of this world! The wine-bowl that crowns the feasting table of the children of this world. . . . The cups of passion and of love." At the end of act 2 Michaelis declares his love to Rhoda, saying, "Before creation, before time, God not yet risen from His sleep, you stand and call to me, and I listen in a dream that I dreamed before Eden." He has known her—the primal female, body of the natural world—and has fled, defying her with "the sign of God's power" in his gift and mission. The healer's language here, as at other significant points in the action, shifts its reference from the realistic to the mythic level of the plot.

As the lovers embrace and Michaelis suggests they leave together for some earthly Eden in the West, the world of the play shudders and collapses. The child's mother proclaims that her child is dead, Littlefield and Uncle Abe rush in shouting that Lazarus has disappeared, and the crowd presses through the door, aroused by a rumor of the healer's disappearance. Michaelis cries out, "As a whirlwind He has scattered me and taken my strength from me forever." Mrs. Beeler sinks weakly into a chair, an invalid once more, as Michaelis mutters in a tragic whisper, "Broken! Broken! Broken!"

Act 3 opens just before sunrise on Easter morning. Michaelis enters with his knapsack, prepared to leave the community. When Annie asks if he is going up on the rope, like the fakir, he says no, the rope must be used "By some one who can climb up, toward the sun and the stars, and yet never leave the earth, the cities, and the people." The speech establishes a base for a new vision. Michaelis urges Rhoda to leave with him, but she sees that their life would be rooted in failure. She believes in the value of Michaelis's work. In order to restore his strength, she reveals that his love for her has been misplaced and that she is "a *wicked* woman."

Littlefield enters to threaten Rhoda and urge her to join him in a western retreat, offering the materialist's equivalent of Eden. Moody's implication is that both visions offer fake heavens detached from true life. Roused to anger, Michaelis tells Littlefield he is spiritually dead and accuses him of the wanton murder of Rhoda's innocent love. The confrontation, like that in the third act of *The Great Divide,* takes the pattern of melodrama, but Moody has invigorated the convention by using it to develop his theme and inaugurate the final movement. Michaelis has risen to active love through participation in Rhoda's desperate struggle. He tells Mrs. Beeler, "I have shaken off my burden. Do you shake off yours. What is pain but a kind of selfishness? What is disease but a kind of sin?" Mary rises from her wheelchair and walks again, for good this time. Taking a lily from the vase on the table, she goes out to sunlight and the waiting crowd.

Michaelis turns to Rhoda to explain his rebirth. He had believed love was denied to those doing the Lord's work. He now understands "that God does not deny love to any of his children, but gives it as a beautiful and simple gift to them all." Love for Rhoda is not his curse but his ultimate blessing and salvation. He has shared the depths of her anguish and humiliation, sensing her desperate need of him. The genuine existential miracle has occurred: "Out of those depths arose new-born happiness and new-risen hope." The voices of the crowd rise in a great hymn as Michaelis says he and Rhoda will seek spiritual victory "On the good human earth, which I never possessed till now!" The prisoned souls waiting outside shall be delivered by faith "which makes all things possible, which brings all things to pass." The young mother enters breathlessly, speaking of her revived child, saying, "I believe—I do believe—," and Rhoda echoes her fragmentary statement with positive conviction as the final curtain falls.

The play is well constructed. Moody skillfully handles a more complex action than in earlier works. Dialogue moves with a new ease and there is a stronger sense of staging and gesture than in *The Great Divide*. *The Faith Healer* brings to culmination several of Moody's earlier concerns. It represents a reinterpretation of Christ and Christianity, one which D. H. Lawrence and others were later to popularize. Moody's dual dedications to Dionysus and Jesus find synthesis in Michaelis's newfound vision; and the theme of Hosea's marriage, which intrigued Moody earlier, is here given form in a contemporary setting. The prophet weds the harlot—a passionate, if contrite, Pandora-Eve—taking unto himself life's suffering, anguish, and sin. In doing so he finds life's passionate, creative joys. The act of love redeems society, represented by the gathering multitudes who await rebirth.[28]

The play is of much greater interest than *The Great Divide*. In realistic detailing and in fluidity of structure it represents a significant extension of the realism of the former play: Moody conveys the genuine sense of a midwestern household and community caught in an unusual situation. But the play's real interest lies in Moody's daring attempt to domesticate a mythic action in a realistic context. His materials are not those of fairy tale and folklore which were being explored in other American and continental dramas of the period, but he leaps forward to the concerns of the theatre of Eugene O'Neill and beyond that toward the synthesis of realism and symbolic action to be found in

Edward Albee's *Who's Afraid of Virginia Woolf?* and *A Delicate Balance*. Moody has also identified the theatrical mode necessary to his synthesis in an expressionistic rendering of scene. The play's theatrical success rests on a subtle and skillful staging, and it demands a male actor of charismatic power, capable of taking on the mythic dimension of Michaelis's role effectively. Once *The Faith Healer* is seen as a mythic action, the extent of the influence of Greek drama on it becomes obvious. The play's world becomes a function of the action of Michaelis and it is redeemed by him. The greater world of spectators is expected to participate in the drama as an involving and cleansing ritual: its third act is an Easter sunrise service. Moody is attempting, in a modern context, to return to the very roots of the drama, and his play anticipates the view of the nature of drama which is basic to contemporary experiments in participatory drama.

But is the play even possible as twentieth-century theatre? Miller had been hopeful during rehearsals for the Broadway opening of *The Faith Healer*, finding Moody's changes had made for immense improvement.[29] The opening-night audience seemed cordial, and actors took many curtain calls. Percy MacKaye immediately sent an enthusiastic telegram to Will and Harriet in Santa Barbara: "A glorious play, gloriously acted, and the audience rose to it gloriously." [30] But MacKaye's enthusiasm did not accurately represent the response of audience and critics. *The Faith Healer* activated the deep-seated conflict of science and religion in the cultural life of Moody's time without serving the commitments of any significant portion of his audience. Viewed as realism, the play offends. Moody treats scientific materialism in the persons of Beeler and Dr. Littlefield in bitter caricature. Christianity takes forms in Uncle Abe, Mary Beeler, Reverend Culpepper, and finally in Michaelis, which were equally repugnant to the American middle class. On its symbolic level the play aroused powerful dissonances: to see Michaelis as Christ was an invitation to confusion and blasphemy. The critics were generally satisfied to object that *The Faith Healer* was simply unclear in meaning and intent.[31] But several objected specifically to the issues. The drama critic of the New York *Press*, for example, launched a vigorous attack. Mother Eddy, he wrote, had been "out-Eddyed," and he felt the play pandered to a credulity that was inappropriate to the scientific twentieth century. Michaelis was seen as a monstrous charlatan.[32]

A more immediate problem was presented by the production itself. The set and staging reached Miller's customary high level of excellence, but even those critics sympathetic to the play descended upon the acting in almost unanimous disapproval. Both Miss Bonstelle and Miller were attacked. The *Times* found a stiffness and lack of passion in their love scenes, and Miss Bonstelle was not as beautiful as she should have been.[33] Miller came in for the strongest criticism, however. He played the role sanctimoniously, his makeup was "pasty-faced," and he looked "merely stout and middle-aged." One critic observed, "He posed like a stained glass window saint and intoned his lines like a melodeon." [34] Miller was unlike Michaelis both in age and personality. He had taken a somewhat similar role in Henry Arthur Jones's *Michael and His Lost Angel,* and had gone down in a defeat which New York critics had cheerfully referred to as "Mike and his Lost Box Office Receipts." [35] The New York *Evening Sun* succinctly observed, "the role of a he vestal is not his metier." [36]

Friends who saw the play discreetly echoed the critics. Garland commented in a letter to Moody that the play was big and original. But he objected to Miller in the part, feeling the need for a more passionate and poetic personality for Michaelis.[37] E. K. Rand was equally responsive to the play, finding its resolution strikingly effective. But he too found Miller clumsy and brittle and his delivery painfully pompous.[38] At the end of the week Miller withdrew the play and took it to the Sanders Theatre at Harvard for a final one-night invitational performance. The audience responded well. Miller sent Moody a telegram citing his belief that the play would endure in spite of its reception.[39]

3

The passing months were months of waiting, punctuated with brief hours of hope or of depression. There were occasions on which Will seemed once more himself and Harriet could observe, "His old personality spoke forth fully and his whole aspect seemed changed." [40] On February 9 he was well enough to dictate a letter to Dan Mason, expressing pleasure in his friend's appointment to a teaching position at Columbia University and his hopes for Mason's future as a composer. "I have not heard from you for so long," he wrote, "that I felt as though I should never hear again." [41] Proofs for the new edition of *The Faith Healer* arrived, and Will dictated corrections with clarity and assurance. But the slow, agonizing trend was downward.

As summer approached, Will and Harriet returned to the Grove in Chicago. Once again Will seemed to rally, and there were brief visits from old friends—Torrence, MacKaye, and Schevill. MacKaye was as busy as ever. His early play, *The Canterbury Pilgrims,* had been produced, once in Georgia and later as *The Gloucester Pageant* in Massachusetts. During the winter *The Scarecrow* had been presented at Harvard and a new, contemporary comedy, *Anti-Matrimony*, was scheduled to open on Broadway in the fall. MacKaye had collected and organized his speeches and published them as *The Playhouse and the Play*. The volume gave voice to the interests of the "young revolutionists" of the American theatre. MacKaye decried the commercial theatre's emphasis on box-office receipts and its hesitation to produce the works of native dramatists. He hoped for the establishment of endowed civic theatres as a force to vitalize the American drama.[42] Josephine Peabody scored a major success. She had submitted her play, *The Piper*, in a prize competition for a work with which to inaugurate the new Stratford Shakespeare Memorial Theatre in England. Her poetic drama was chosen over those of three hundred competing writers, and it was produced at Stratford in July. The New Theatre in New York, which had earlier rejected the play, was to give the American premiere in the winter.[43] Robinson, vacationing with Bartlett in New Hampshire, sent Moody notes on life with the grand old man, which aroused pleasant memories. In discouragement over his plays, Robinson had begun to convert them into unsuccessful novels, but there was a glimmer of hope. A new book of poems was in the press.[44]

As for Moody himself, the last of his work had been done. The prose plays were published, and the uncompleted Eve play, together with many of the poems of 1904 and 1905, were in manuscript, to be edited in 1912 by John M. Manly in consultation with Moody's friends —Josephine, MacKaye, Torrence, Robinson, and Mason.[45] Characteristically, Moody was far from satisfied. To his old friend Schevill he spoke of his regret at having given so much of his time to prose— "the work of my left hand," he called it. "It is perhaps a judgment," he felt, "that this confusion has come upon me."[46] Though a hierophant of Dionysus and Phoebus Apollo, Will Moody still saw the issues of life in terms of final judgment. In a letter of 1895 to Daniel Gregory Mason he had written a premature epitaph for himself and his friends: "The twentieth century dates from yesterday, and we are its chosen; if not as signs set in the heavens of its glory, at least as morning birds that carolled to it, mindless of the seductive and quite palpable worm—."[47] His prediction is not completely wide of the mark, though Moody was soon to find the carol of a morning bird inadequate to the challenges of the new century. In the cultural dilemmas central to his society Moody had identified correlatives to the psychological and philosophical problems of his adolescent trauma. In his poetry and drama he had slowly worked his way through them to a vision remarkable in his time for its breadth and coherence. Based in romantic reformulations of the Christian-humanist tradition, Moody's work interprets that tradition in the contexts of the social and theological implications of Darwinian, Hegelian, and Nietzschean thought. He found his appropriate medium in the great myths which lie at the heart of Western experience, and in drama which reaches through ritual back to them. Concerned with a range of modern alienations and stirred by the vision of life under the aspect of eternity, Moody was an avatar of American transcendentalism. But Moody's identification of the ultimate source of creative affirmation reaching beyond good and evil, joy and sorrow, in the human sexual act itself is at once ancient and contemporary. In the problems he identified and in his discovery of the potential of myth and the drama for their exploration, Moody is most clearly one of the "chosen" of the twentieth century.

Yet as a literary craftsman he was not uniquely inventive, nor was he willing to renounce communication with a present audience to develop an idiosyncratic art. He was unwilling to follow Robinson into what has been called "strategic retreat," and he was too much a cultural democrat to turn to the avant-garde conservative elitism Eliot and Pound were to find attractive. Instead, Moody developed a wide range of poetic and dramatic modes from the point at which he found them to their limits in terms of Victorian styles. As successive forms and styles revealed themselves as insufficient to the burdens of experience and vision he placed on them, Moody turned to others. Much of the interest of his development lies in this quest, one which almost necessarily led from dramatic lyrics to poetic drama and public poetry into the world of American theatre. Moody's achievement is distinctly limited by the fact that there was little potential for creative development of the styles in which he worked, and the imaginative vigor and precision of his personal letters suggest that Moody's view of the nature of art was itself debilitating to his work. In the prose drama alone he finally found a medium with vast unexplored potential for fresh stylistic development.

Moody's achievements were in many ways conclusive: he clearly identified the dead ends of a style. For this reason his work has served primarily as a negative example to both traditionalists and modernists. Yet Moody helped pioneer a significant movement in expressionism in twentieth-century American literature. Expansive and passionate in spirit, traditional in its lexical range and its metered rhythms, structured in terms of evocative symbolic clusters and by mythic motifs, oriented to metaphysical issues, the work of Moody like that of Hart Crane and Eugene O'Neill creates a world bent to the needs of human passion and faith. There were and are, of course, others who have shared the commitments basic to the style most fully defined in the work of these men, both of whom were indebted to Moody in minor ways. Harriet Moody gave encouragement and guidance in his art to the young Hart Crane,[48] who was to share Moody's transcendental orientation to experience, his ultimate dedication to domestication of myth in American materials, and his love of richness, energy, and emotional power in language. With similar tendencies, Eugene O'Neill was to look to the forms of Greek drama and the possibilities for symbolic enrichment of dramatic language under the guidance of Moody's friend and admirer, George Pierce Baker.[49] With a field brushed clearer of the rubbish of nineteenth-century American theatre, he was to write *The Hairy Ape, The Fountain, The Great God Brown*, and *Lazarus Laughed* for the new theatre of the twentieth century. Their themes are those which had most concerned Will Moody.

In October 1910, at Will's insistence, he and Harriet left Chicago for the Rocky Mountains. They stopped at Colorado Springs, where Will could still faintly see the rugged peaks which loomed out of the hazy blur of his vision.[50] Robinson sent a copy of his new volume, *The Town Down the River*, expressing to Will his hope "that it may not be bad enough to interfere with your rapid recovery." [51] But Moody had passed beyond the reach of the hope or humor of his friends. He died on October 17, in his forty-first year. For Will and Harriet, whom Schevill later called "the two greatest souls I have known or shall ever know," [52] the long ordeal testing the strength of their spiritual dedication was over. On hearing of the event, Dan and Mary Mason began rereading the poet's letters, struck afresh by "their big views, alert sensitiveness to all sensuous and spiritual beauty." Mason wrote Torrence, "Do you remember the explosive shout of his laughter and what depth of well-being sounded in it?" [53] "Thank God he lived to do his work," Robinson wrote generously to Harriet, "—or enough of it to place him among the immortals." [54]

On October 28 Harriet Moody, en route to Europe, stopped briefly in New York City.[55] She carried an urn, wrapped in her scarf, that contained the handful of Will Moody's ashes. With Charlotte Moody, Ferd Schevill, and Ridgely Torrence, she went to Far Rockaway Beach on Long Island, where there was a stretch of low sand dunes and the sea met the beach in long, low, rolling waves. Taking turns, they read aloud the whole of *The Fire-Bringer*, ending with the final lines of Moody's song to Apollo:

> O thou alone art he
> Who settest the prisoned spirit free,
> And sometimes leadest the rapt soul on
> Where never mortal thought has gone;
> Till by the ultimate stream

Of vision and of dream
She stands
With startled eyes and outstretched hands,
Looking where other suns rise over other lands,
And rends the lonely skies with her prophetic scream.

A fire was lit, and when the setting sun touched the edge of the water, beckoning in a shimmering path across the waves, Schevill scattered the contents of the urn on the waters of the Atlantic Ocean. They knelt as Harriet read aloud the Ninety-first Psalm: "He that dwelleth in the secret place of the most High shall abide under the shadow of the Almighty." Will Moody's ashes tossed in the tumbling surf.

SOURCES   NOTES   INDEX

SOURCES

IN SPITE of its errors, omissions, and numerous fragmentary entries, the standard bibliography of the works of William Vaughn Moody (1869–1910) has long been that in David D. Henry, *William Vaughn Moody: A Study* (Boston, 1934), pp. 263–65. Errors are corrected below and thirteen items have been added: six poems, two short stories, and five critical reviews. Two of Henry's entries have been omitted. No corroborative evidence exists in published or unpublished Moody materials that "Clouds," a poem ascribed to him in an Indianapolis *Sentinel* article, February 2, 1908, was written by Moody. "We Dying Hail Thee, Caesar," a poem accepted by Henry and treated by him and other Moody critics, was not written by Moody but by a classmate, Mortimer O. Wilcox. The sonnet appeared in the *Harvard Advocate*, 48 (1890), 159, following Moody's short story, "Baptisto." It was reprinted as Moody's in a *New York Times* review of *Poems*, June 8, 1901. The hoax has blurred the fact that Moody's early commitments were to Greek literature and experience, not Roman. Two genuine Moody poems have been published by Daniel Gregory Mason in *Some Letters of William Vaughn Moody* (Boston & New York, 1913): "Dawn Parley" (pp. 71–72) and "Wilding Flower" (pp. 57–60), an early version of "Heart's Wild-Flower." Moody occasionally retitled his work. Titles of periodical publications, as changed by Moody for inclusion in *Poems*, are entered in Section 2 below in square brackets. It should be noted that a generous number of Moody's early poems have been collected as Appendix B in Henry's volume, but there are a number of errors in transcription.

1. POEMS, PLAYS, AND LETTERS

The Faith Healer; A Play in Four Acts. Boston & New York, 1909.
The Faith Healer; A Play in Three Acts. New York, 1910.
The Fire-Bringer. Boston & New York, 1904.
Four Hitherto Unpublished Letters of William Vaughn Moody. Ed.
    Thomas H. Dickinson. Madison, Wisc., 1915.
The Great Divide; A Play in Three Acts. New York, 1909.
Letters to Harriet. Ed. Percy MacKaye. Boston & New York, 1935.
The Masque of Judgment. Boston, 1900; rpt. Boston, 1902.
Poems. Boston & New York, 1901. Rpt. Boston, n.d. [1912?] as
    Gloucester Moors and Other Poems.
The Poems and Plays of William Vaughn Moody. Ed. John M. Manly.
    2 vols. Boston & New York, 1912.
Selected Poems of William Vaughn Moody. Ed. Robert Morss Lovett.
    Boston & New York, 1931.
Some Letters of William Vaughn Moody. Ed. Daniel Gregory Mason.
    Boston & New York, 1913.

2. POEMS IN PERIODICALS

"The Amber Witch." *Harvard Monthly,* 14 (March 1892), 22–23.
"Angelle." *Harvard Monthly,* 13 (December 1891), 102–8.
"Anniversary Ode." *Harvard Monthly,* 31 (October 1900), 1–5.
"The Answer." *Harvard Monthly,* 13 (November 1891), 50–51.
"Applause." *Harvard Monthly,* 14 (July 1892), 213.
"A Ballade of Death-Beds" ["The Ride Back"]. *Chap-Book,* 1 (June 15,
    1894), 51–53.
"The Briar Rose." *Harvard Monthly,* 18 (May 1894), 100–103.
"The Brute." *Atlantic Monthly,* 87 (January 1901), 88–90.
"By the Evening Sea" ["The Departure"]. *Harvard Monthly,* 15 (Janu-
    ary 1893), 154.
"A Chorus of Wagner." *Harvard Monthly,* 10 (April 1890), 51.
"The Counting Man." *St. Nicholas,* 36 (August 1909), 882.
"Daffodils." *Harvard Monthly,* 10 (June 1890), 151.
"Dance Music." *Harvard Monthly,* 12 (April 1891), 57–59.
"The Death of Eve." *Century,* 73 (December 1906), 270–77.
"Dolorosa." *Scribner's,* 10 (November 1891), 620.
"Dux Vitae" ["The Golden Journey"]. *Harvard Monthly,* 20 (April
    1895), 41–43.
"Faded Pictures." *Scribner's,* 12 (August 1892), 148.

"Gloucester Moors." *Scribner's*, 28 (December 1900), 727–28.

"Good Friday Night." *Atlantic Monthly*, 81 (May 1898), 700–701.

"Harmonics." *Harvard Monthly*, 13 (October 1891), 31.

"The Hawthorne Bush." *Harvard Monthly*, 17 (October 1893), 32–33.

"How the Mead-Slave Was Set Free." *Harvard Monthly*, 13 (February 1892), 197–99.

"I Am the Woman." *Poetry*, 1 (October 1912), 3–6.

"The Lady of the Fountain." *Harvard Monthly*, 14 (May 1892), 100–104.

"Love and Death." *Harvard Monthly*, 10 (May 1890), 110.

"Musa Meretrix." *Reader*, 7 (May 1906), 573.

"An Ode in Time of Hesitation." *Atlantic Monthly*, 85 (May 1900), 593–98.

"Old Pourquoi." *Reader*, 5 (December 1904), 101–4.

"On a Soldier Fallen in the Philippines." *Atlantic Monthly*, 87 (February 1901), 288.

"Parting." *Harvard Advocate*, 48 (December 21, 1889), 94.

"The Picture." *Harvard Monthly*, 11 (January 1891), 149–50.

"The Picture and the Bird." *Harvard Monthly*, 18 (July 1894), 212–17.

"A Prelude in Purgatory" ["A Dialogue in Purgatory"]. *Harvard Monthly*, 24 (December 1899), 102–8.

"Road-Hymn for the Start." *Atlantic Monthly*, 83 (June 1899), 840.

"Sea Shells." *Harvard Monthly*, 14 (June 1892), 167.

"Second Coming." *Century*, 71 (December 1905), 310–12.

"The Serf's Secret." *Harvard Monthly*, 11 (November 1890), 47.

"A Sick-Room Fancy." *Harvard Monthly*, 12 (July 1891), 173–74.

"A Song." *Harvard Advocate*, 48 (November 1, 1889), 21.

"The Song of the Elder Brothers." *Harvard Advocate*, 55 (June 23, 1893), 136–39.

"Sonnet—To the Niké of Paionios." *Harvard Monthly*, 11 (December 1890), 96.

"The Sun Virgin." *Harvard Monthly*, 11 (February 1891), 185–86.

"Thammuz." *Scribner's*, 40 (October 1906), 405.

3. SHORT STORIES

"Baptisto." *Harvard Advocate*, 48 (February 21, 1890), 157–59.

"The Joyless Asphodel." *Harvard Monthly*, 17 (December 1893), 116–23.

4. CRITICAL REVIEWS AND ESSAYS

Review of *Christopher Columbus,* by Justin Winsor. *Harvard Monthly,*
    14 (March 1892), 44.
Review of *The Divine Comedy of Dante,* trans. Charles Eliot Norton.
    Harvard Monthly, 13 (January 1892), 171.
"Eugene Field and His Work." *Atlantic Monthly,* 77 (August 1896),
    265–69. Unsigned. See *Atlantic Index Supplement, 1889–1901*
    (Boston & New York, 1903) for Moody's authorship.
"On the Introduction of the Chorus into Modern Drama." *Harvard
    Monthly,* 14 (June 1892), 142–51.
"Our Two Most Honored Poets." *Atlantic Monthly,* 81 (January
    1898), 136–39. Unsigned. See *Atlantic Index Supplement, 1889–
    1901* for Moody's authorship.
Review of *The Perfume Holder, A Persian Love Poem,* by Craven
    Langsworth Betts." *Harvard Monthly,* 13 (January 1892), 174.
"The Poems of Trumbull Stickney." *North American Review,* 183
    (November 16, 1906), 1005–18.

5. EDITIONS AND LITERARY HISTORIES

The Complete Poetical Works of John Milton. With a Life of Milton.
    Boston & New York, 1899.
A First View of English Literature. New York, 1905. With Robert
    Morss Lovett.
A History of English Literature. New York, 1902. With Robert Morss
    Lovett.
The Iliad of Homer, Books I, VI, XXII, XXIV. Trans. Alexander
    Pope. With Introduction. Chicago, 1900. Coeditor W. W. Cressy.
The Lady of the Lake, by Sir Walter Scott. With Introduction and
    Notes. Chicago, 1900.
The Lay of the Last Minstrel, by Sir Walter Scott. With Introduction
    and Notes. Chicago, 1899.
Marmion, by Sir Walter Scott. With Introduction and Notes. Chicago,
    1899.
The Pilgrim's Progress, by John Bunyan. With Introduction and Notes.
    Boston, 1897.
The Poems of Trumbull Stickney. Boston & New York, 1905. Co-
    editors George Cabot Lodge and John Ellerton Lodge.
The Rime of the Ancient Mariner and The Vision of Sir Launfal.
    With Introduction and Notes. Chicago, 1898.

Selections from DeQuincey. With Introduction and Notes. Chicago,
1909.

Much of Moody's published work has been preserved in manuscript or typescript draft. Newly discovered unpublished poems are
these: "To Julia," Moody's gift of the spring of 1887 to his sister. The
manuscript volume contains eleven poems in Moody's hand. The poem,
"Sister Angelica," written in Poughkeepsie, is entered in Julia's hand
together with transcriptions of her brother's early Harvard poems. This
volume and a double sonnet, "I would I were a poet," included in a
letter to Grace Hurd in the fall of 1889, are in the Princeton University
Library. "Song's sorcery" and "Ethics in a Gondola," poems of the
spring of 1895, are in the Josephine Preston Peabody Papers at Harvard. In the case of drafts for and variant versions of published work, I
have tried to exercise restraint. A wealth of materials makes a detailed
study of Moody's revisions possible. Such a study is beyond the scope
of this biography; yet when the creative history of a poem has seemed
particularly rich in documentation and suggestive of Moody's writing
methods or of changes in his thought and taste, I have made fuller
comment. See especially the treatments of "Jetsam," "Heart's Wild-
Flower," "The Menagerie," and "Old Pourquoi."

Of unpublished prose documents, I cite passages from Moody's
high school essays in the Moody Papers in the Princeton University
Library, and from Moody's undergraduate themes in the University
of Chicago Library; from Moody's unpublished Master's thesis, "An
Inquiry into the Sources of *Sir Philip Sidney's Arcadia*" (Harvard,
1894), in the Harvard University Archives; from the draft of the
fragmentary Truman-Blair play at Chicago; and from the scenario for
The Death of Eve. The manuscript of *A Sabine Woman* in the Princeton University Library is my source for discussion of that play and its
revision as *The Great Divide*.

A large number of unpublished letters by Moody and his friends
have been consulted. While the majority of Moody's extant correspondence with Harriet Moody has been published in Percy MacKaye, ed.,
Letters to Harriet (Boston & New York, 1935), much of his correspondence with Robert Morss Lovett, Robert Herrick, Daniel
Gregory Mason, and Josephine Preston Peabody remains unpublished.
Two large and significant collections—Moody's letters to Grace Hurd
and to his sister, Charlotte Moody—are here used and cited. Full documentation of all manuscript materials is given in the notes.

Some comment on my handling of text may be useful. In presenting passages from Moody's letters I follow the published text of *Letters*

to Harriet for that correspondence. Other letters are quoted from their manuscript versions where possible. I have corrected one idiosyncrasy of the letters: Moody often punctuates the contraction *n't* with the apostrophe before the *n*, and he usually omits the apostrophe from *it's*. I standardize in both cases. In presenting passages from Moody's poems and plays written after 1897 I follow texts in the standard two-volume work edited by John M. Manly, *Poems and Plays of William Vaughn Moody* (Boston & New York, 1912), as most readily available to readers. For uncollected works I have followed the texts of the versions printed in the *Harvard Monthly, Scribner's,* and elsewhere. Many of the texts of Moody's uncollected poems have been reprinted by David D. Henry in his *William Vaughn Moody: A Study*. When Moody changed the title of a poem or play between its first version and its publication, or between publications, I consistently refer to the work by the last title used, the title in the final edition of his works. Thus, *The Faith Healer* is so named long before Moody settled on the play's title, and *The Great Divide* appears in my text in a period when Moody was calling it "the Zona play."

NOTES

THE following abbreviations are used in the footnotes for convenient identification of major collections of source materials:

PPH   Papers of Josephine Preston Peabody [Marks], Houghton Library, Harvard University.

MPH   A portion of the above collection, consisting of Moody's letters to Miss Peabody and documents filed with them.

MPC   Papers of William Vaughn Moody, University of Chicago Library. They have been sorted and arranged in six boxes. A descriptive list of contents is available.

MPP   Those Moody materials in the Princeton University Library that are catalogued, principally letters to Percy MacKaye, Daniel Gregory Mason, and Mrs. Mary Mason, together with some manuscripts.

TPP   Papers of Ridgely Torrence, Princeton University Library.

TPPM   A portion of the above collection, consisting of six boxes of papers of and relating to William Vaughn Moody. The collection has been partially arranged.

LH   Percy MacKaye, ed., *Letters to Harriet* (Boston & New York, 1935).

CHAPTER I: THE SWEET AND HEAVY YEARS

1.   For information on Francis Burdette Moody's father and mother and on his New York years, I am indebted to Julia Moody Schmaltz, "Background and Early Years of William Vaughn Moody," I, pp. 1–25, typescript draft, TPPM. Mrs. Schmaltz presents a Moody genealogy. The work is a discursive family memoir in two volumes. It breaks off at the poet's graduation from Harvard in 1893.

     There is conflicting evidence as to the date of Burdette Moody's birth. I follow the date as given for the census of 1860. See entry 493, Francis B. Moody household, Fifth Ward, City of New Albany, Floyd County, Census of 1860, Indiana Historical Society.

2. Schmaltz, "Background and Early Years," I, p. 24.

3. Two letters held for Burdette Moody beginning in January 1849 were picked up at the New Albany Post Office shortly before the March 31, 1849, issue of the *New Albany Democrat*.

4. Betty Lou Armster, *New Albany on the Ohio, 1813–1963* (New Albany, 1963), pp. 29–31. Other useful sources for information on Moody's life in New Albany have been these: State of Indiana Census, 1850–1880; State of Indiana registers of deaths and marriages; *New Albany Democrat*, 1847–49; *New Albany Ledger*, 1849–86; C. W. Cottom, *New Albany, Indiana* (New Albany, 1873); *Advantages and Surroundings of New Albany, Indiana* (New Albany, 1892); *Souvenir History. The New Albany Centennial Celebration* (New Albany, 1913).

5. On September 21, 1852. WPA Records, Vols. IV and V: Marriages 1845–1920 record this marriage and others of the Moody and Stoy families. This useful source is in the library of the Indiana Historical Society.

6. For a record of this household see entries 14–15, recorded July 24, household of Peter R. Stoy, City of New Albany, Floyd County, Census of 1850, Indiana Historical Society.

7. Captain Moody's New Albany career is treated in his obituary, *New Albany Ledger*, May 31, 1886. For the composition of his household in 1860, see census entry, n. 1 above. In that entry Burdette's occupation is given as Steamboat Captain. For tax purposes he lists his real estate and his personal estate at $500 each. Mrs. Stoy lists $10,000 in real estate and $2,000 in personal estate.

8. Francis B. Moody and Noah Allison households, recorded August 4, Owen Township, Owen County, Census of 1870, Indiana Historical Society.

9. Mrs. Schmaltz uses the title, and Burdette Moody is referred to throughout his obituary as Captain Moody. *New Albany Ledger*, May 31, 1886.

10. Moody's portrait of his father in "The Daguerreotype." See John M. Manly, ed., *The Poems and Plays of William Vaughn Moody* (Boston & New York, 1912), 2 vols. All passages quoted from Moody's poetry and drama, except as noted below, are drawn from this edition.

11. On Mary Stoy and her background, see Schmaltz, "Background and Early Years," I, pp. 50–78.

12. Henrietta Moody shows herself to have been lively and witty as a younger woman. In a letter of September 21, 1859, to her younger brother, William Vaughn Stoy, she turns her attention to a certain Mr. Douglass, a Louisville teacher, who was said to beat his recalcitrant scholars regularly. He is, she wrote, "a perfect heathen and ought to be tarred and feathered, then burnt in effigy." She continued, sweetly,

"I am, as you know, in favor of persuasion, rather than compulsion."
A transcription of the letter appears in Schmaltz, "Background and
Early Years," I, p. 98. The original letter has been lost (see ch. 2,
n. 46, below).

13. Schmaltz, "Background and Early Years," I, p. 113.

14. Ibid., p. 273.

15. Ibid., pp. 274–75.

16. Ridgely Torrence visited the house in New Albany and has left
notes which corroborate Mrs. Schmaltz's memory. Torrence Notebook Three. TPP.

17. Entry 405, recorded July 2, Mary A. Stoy household, Fifth Ward,
City of New Albany, Floyd County, Census of 1870, Indiana Historical Society.

18. Francis B. Moody household, recorded August 4, Owen Township,
Owen County, Census of 1870, Indiana Historical Society. For the
composition of the Moody household in 1880, see entry 144, recorded June 1, Fifth Ward, City of New Albany, Floyd County,
Census of 1880, Indiana Historical Society.

19. In 1873 the Ohio Falls Iron Works, capitalized at $300,000, em-
ployed 170 hands and paid $135,000 annually in wages. Cottom,
New Albany, Indiana, p. 24.

20. For business and religious activities of the Stoys, the New Albany
histories listed in n. 4 above have been useful, together with *The
Beginning of Methodism and a History of Wesley Chapel Church,
1816–1954* (New Albany, 1954). Harriet Moody much later was to
maintain that "there was nothing Puritanic in his [Moody's] background and early training" in a communication to David D. Henry.
He accepted her incorrect assertion as basic to his interpretation of
Moody. See David D. Henry, *William Vaughn Moody: A Study*
(Boston, 1934), p. 69.

21. Schmaltz, "Background and Early Years," I, pp. 192–94, et passim.

22. Information on Moody's personality as a schoolboy is drawn from a
description by Harvey Peake, a boyhood friend, as cited by Henry,
Moody, pp. 11–13.

23. Armster, *New Albany*, pp. 60–61.

24. *The Minute Man*, 1 (April 14, 1884), 1. A photostat appears in
Schmaltz, "Background and Early Years," I, p. 226.

25. As quoted in Schmaltz, "Background and Early Years," I, p. 216.

26. Armster, *New Albany*, p. 54.

27. Schmaltz, "Background and Early Years," I, p. 163.

28. Henrietta Moody's obituary, *New Albany Ledger*, January 18, 1884.

29. Schmaltz, "Background and Early Years," I, p. 289.

30. Ibid., p. [290].

31. For the obituary, see *New Albany Ledger*, May 31, 1886. A "Resolution of Condolence" by employees of the Ohio Falls Iron Works appeared in the newspaper on June 5, 1886.

32. Schmaltz, "Background and Early Years," I, p. 347.

33. This detail and others in my treatment of Will Moody's last year in New Albany are drawn from ibid., pp. 320–43. She gathered information from Elizabeth and Armon Stoy.

34. Ibid., pp. 330 and 333.

35. "To Julia" is a collection of eleven unpublished poems in Moody's hand. TPPM. Copies of "Angelica" and of twelve of Moody's Harvard poems were entered later in Julia Moody Schmaltz's hand.

36. For details of Moody's life at Riverview Academy I draw on Schmaltz, "Background and Early Years," I, pp. 356–64. Mrs. Schmaltz cites communications from Harlan P. Amen, Murray Bartlett, Fred Morgan, and Charles Rowley.

37. Robert Morss Lovett, ed., Introduction, *Selected Poems of William Vaughn Moody* (Boston & New York, 1931), p. xiii.

38. Schmaltz, "Background and Early Years," I, p. 363.

39. "To Julia." TPPM.

40. Daniel Gregory Mason, ed., Introduction, *Some Letters of William Vaughn Moody* (Boston & New York, 1913), p. vi.

CHAPTER 2: SUBTLE THREADS THAT BIND

1. The following sources on the Harvard of the period have been particularly useful: Harvard College catalogues and class books, 1880–95; Harvard *Crimson*; Harvard *Advocate*; Harvard *Monthly*; Samuel Eliot Morison, ed., *The Development of Harvard University, 1869–1929* (Cambridge, 1930); William C. Lane, *The University During the Past Six Years* (Cambridge, 1887); and *The University During the Past Seven Years* (Boston, 1898); Rollo Walter Brown, *Harvard Yard in the Golden Age* (New York, 1948); and Edward S. Martin, "Undergraduate Life at Harvard," *Scribner's*, 21 (1897), 531–33. For information on George Santayana and the Harvard intellectual and literary scene in the nineties, see my "Santayana's American Roots," *New England Quarterly*, 33 (1960), 147–63; and "Santayana's Necessary Angel," *New England Quarterly*, 36 (1963), 435–51.

2. That the Harvard of Moody's time provided an exciting educational experience is attested by a number of Moody's closest friends. See Hutchins Hapgood, *A Victorian in the Modern World* (New York, 1939), pp. 66–67; Norman Hapgood, *The Changing Years* (New York, 1930), p. 46; Robert Morss Lovett, *All Our Years* (New York, 1948), p. 33; and Daniel Gregory Mason, *Music in My Time, and Other Reminiscences* (New York, 1938), p. 46.

3. See Moody's transcript of courses, Harvard University Archives. The statements on Moody's undergraduate curriculum by Henry, who follows Lovett, are erroneous. Henry, *Moody*, p. 17.

4. Schmaltz, "Background and Early Years," II, p. 3. While Moody was hardly affluent, Moody's statement to Mason that he entered Harvard with a total capital of $25.00 is misleading. See Mason, *Some Letters*, p. 3.

5. Lovett, *All Our Years,* p. 40.

6. Moody to Grace Hurd [September 1889], TPPM. This collection of seventy unpublished letters, written between summer 1889 and winter 1894, offers valuable information on Moody's Harvard years.

7. Moody to Grace Hurd [fall 1889], TPPM.

8. For information on the undergraduate literary renaissance, see my "Harvard Poetic Renaissance: 1885–1910," Ph.D. diss. (Harvard, 1958).

9. The first version of this poem appears in "To Julia." I quote below in my text from Moody's second version, *Harvard Monthly,* 10 (April 1890), 51.

10. "Aspects of Walt Whitman," *Harvard Monthly,* 14 (1892), 123.

11. Theme for English Five. MPC. All references to Moody's undergraduate themes are to this collection.

12. See especially Charles M. Flandrau, *Diary of a Freshman* (New York, 1901), and *Harvard Episodes* (Boston, 1897); Elbert Hubbard, *Forbes of Harvard* (Boston, 1894); Waldron K. Post, *Harvard Stories* (New York, 1893); and Owen Wister, *Philosophy Four* (New York, 1903).

13. *Harvard Advocate,* 55 (1893), 19.

14. *Harvard Monthly,* 14 (1892), 99. In an earlier article Santayana found it necessary to point out that Spinoza's rejection of Epicureanism did not imply that he was a Philistine. See his "The Ethical Doctrine of Spinoza," *Harvard Monthly,* 2 (1886), 144–52.

15. Moody to Grace Hurd [November 1889], TPPM.

16. Moody to Grace Hurd [October 1890], TPPM.

17. According to information collected by Mrs. Schmaltz from Mr. Brandt, quoted in her "Background and Early Years," II, p. 45.

18. For Lovett on Morris, see *Harvard Monthly,* 12 (1891), 150 ff.; on Newman, 15 (1892), 99–113 and 137–46; and on Mark Pattison, 13 (1891), 205–11.

19. Lovett, *All Our Years,* p. 43.

20. "The Student as Child," *Harvard Monthly,* 15 (1892), 13.

21. *Harvard Monthly,* 13 (1891), 143.

22. Ibid., 11 (1890), 70.

23. Moody to Grace Hurd [December 1890].

24. *Harvard Monthly,* 11 (1890), 136.

25. Ibid., 14 (1892), 160–66.

26. William Bryce Cohen, "The Discouragement of Horace Tennant," *Harvard Monthly,* 12 (1891), 139–49.

27. A. Kimball, "The Progression of Altman: A Study," *Harvard Monthly,* 14 (1892), 188–204.

28. *Harvard Monthly,* 12 (1891), 173–74.

29. Introduction, *Selected Poems,* p. xviii.

30. English Five themes, MPC.

31. Moody to Grace Hurd [November 1891], TPPM.

32. Moody to Grace Hurd [September 1891], TPPM.

33. Introduction, *Selected Poems,* p. lxv.

34. Schmaltz, "Background and Early Years," II, p. 30, quoting a communication from Philip B. Goetz.
35. Lovett, *All Our Years*, p. 40, quoting Norman Hapgood.
36. Introduction, *Selected Poems*, p. lxv.
37. Ibid., p. xvii.
38. H. Hapgood, *A Victorian in the Modern World*, p. 81.
39. English Five themes, MPC.
40. H. Hapgood, *A Victorian in the Modern World*, p. 81.
41. *Harvard Monthly*, 14 (1892), 142–51.
42. See N. Hapgood's account of the event in his *The Changing Years*, pp. 78–81.
43. *Harvard Monthly*, 14 (1892), 167.
44. This passage and others quoted in this section of ch. 2 without citation are drawn from letters to Grace Hurd, written between June 1892 and June 1893.
45. N. Hapgood, *The Changing Years*, p. 75.
46. Moody to Charlotte Moody, August 8, 1892, TPPM. I quote from a collection of sixty-two typed transcripts of Moody's letters to Charlotte, transcribed by Julia Moody Schmaltz as *Letters to Charlotte*. It was apparently conceived as a companion volume to MacKaye's *Letters to Harriet*. A portion of this correspondence has been published in Introduction and Notes, *LH*. The originals, together with early family correspondence, were probably in the collection of memorabilia Charlotte Moody deposited in the Boston safe of her brother-in-law, Fred Fawcett, in 1934 (see Charlotte Moody to Ridgely Torrence, November 4, 1934, TPP). This collection of papers has been lost.
47. See Lovett's account of the climb in his *All Our Years*, p. 44.
48. Moody to Lovett, [September 5, 1892], MPC. Portions of this correspondence have been published in Mason, *Some Letters*.
49. Moody described his Paris day in a letter to Grace Hurd [November 1892], TPPM. Observations made to Lovett are in a letter of [November 22, 1892], MPC.

CHAPTER 3: LASSITUDES OF *Fin de Siècle*

1. Moody to Lovett, September 17, 1893, MPC. In a letter of August 23 [1893], Moody suggested to Grace Hurd that his major interest in the exposition was in the collection of European art works. America, he wrote, is "so 'nude of art, and mute of song.' " TPPM.
2. February 5, 1894, MPC.
3. Ibid.
4. Ibid. Among local scholars involved in the study of comparative mythology and related matters were John Fiske, Louis Dyer, Crawford H. Toy, Charles Eliot Norton, Frederick W. Putnam, Frederic D. Allen, John H. Wright, Charles R. Lanman, George Lyman Kittredge, David G. Lyon, W. Sturgis Bigelow, and George Santayana.

Harvard College catalogues for Moody's first two years of college, 1889–91, list eleven public lectures in the area, including several on the Upanishads, one on ancient religious rites in the Ohio Valley, and a third on the Delphian Apollo. In the first decade of this century, central concerns of the movement were passed on to Wallace Stevens and T. S. Eliot by their teachers, George Santayana and Charles R. Lanman.

5. [October 1893], TPPM.
6. *Forum*, 14 (1893), 768.
7. Triggs, "Literature and the Scientific Spirit," *Poet-Lore*, 6 (1894), 113; and see William James Rolfe, "The Poets in School," ibid., 596. For a broad survey of the American poetic scene in the 1890s, see Carlin T. Kindilien, *American Poetry in the Eighteen-Nineties* (Providence, 1956).
8. Moody to Lovett, February 5, 1894, MPC.
9. Moody to H. S. Stone, February 26, 1895, MPP.
10. Actually, two records exist. The first appears in *Some Letters*, p. vii. Mason revised this passage, tempering his contrasts and presenting a mellower portrait, for *Music in My Time*, p. 21. I quote from the latter passage.
11. *Music in My Time*, p. 23.
12. Ibid.
13. *Harvard Monthly*, 15 (1893), 154. Moody collected this poem in his *Poems* (Boston & New York, 1901), and it appears in the standard two-volume collection of his work, *Poems and Plays*, I, with the following changes: (line 2) for joy of one faint/ to greet the evening; (line 5) great/ slow; (line 7) purple/ uncertain; (line 10) "Once all/ "All these; (line 13) My/ One. In three of his five punctuation changes, a comma was omitted.
14. *Harvard Monthly*, 18 (1894), 100–103.
15. In the spring of 1894, in addition to these poems Moody wrote a song, "My Love Is Gone into the East." It treats the situation of "The Ride Back" from the woman's point of view. Mason set it to music in 1895 and revised it later for publication. The original setting is in the Mason Papers, Columbia University Library. Mason, Introduction, *Some Letters*, p. xxv; and see Moody's reference to Pierre La Rose in a letter of 1896 (*Some Letters*, p. 70). The lyric was not published as a poem until 1912, when it appeared in *Poems and Plays* under the title "Song." The dating of the poem some eight years later in Martin Halpern, *William Vaughn Moody* (New York, 1964), is in error and his comment on the poem (pp. 136 and 139) should be ignored.
16. "An Inquiry into the Sources of *Sir Philip Sidney's Arcadia*," Master's thesis (Harvard, 1894), Harvard University Archives, p. 1.
17. Ibid., p. 52.
18. Ibid., p. 2.
19. Ibid., p. 1.

20. Ibid., p. 3.
21. I am indebted to Olivia Howard Dunbar who gathered this information for her "William Vaughn Moody" (typescript, TPPM), pp. 110–11. The 202-page typescript is based on her research for *A House in Chicago* (Chicago, 1947), a life of Harriet Moody, and on the materials given her by Julia Moody Schmaltz. The period from 1901 to 1910 is treated in a scant final fifty pages of the typescript. (Dunbar, the wife of Ridgely Torrence, published under her maiden name.)
22. Moody to Mason, [July 21, 1894], MPP. Mason's side of the correspondence is in MPC. A selection from Moody's letters appears in Mason, *Some Letters.*
23. Mason, *Some Letters*, p. 21.
24. Mason, *Music in My Time*, p. 22.
25. Gates's teaching and criticism, with special consideration of his impact on Frank Norris, are treated in John S. Coolidge, "Lewis E. Gates: Romanticism in America," *New England Quarterly*, 30 (March 1957), 23–38.
26. "Romantic Elements in Alfred Tennyson," *Harvard Monthly*, 15 (1892), 92–98.
27. *Harvard Monthly*, 20 (1895), 138.
28. For Lovett's revealing description of Gates in the nineties, see his *All Our Years*, p. 46.
29. Christina Hopkinson Baker, ed., *Diary and Letters of Josephine Preston Peabody* (Boston & New York, 1925), p. 40. I have relied on this work for information on the poet's early years. For the period of her friendship with Moody, I have consulted her diaries and letters in the Josephine Preston Peabody [Marks] Papers, Harvard University Library. Only a small fraction of Moody's letters to her were published in Mason, *Some Letters.*
30. Baker, *Diary and Letters*, p. 40.
31. Entered on that date in her diary, PPH.
32. Diary, May 20, 1895, PPH.
33. Mason, *Some Letters*, p. 35.
34. Introduction, ibid., p. x.
35. *Sketch for a Self-Portrait* (New York, 1949), pp. 138–39.
36. In a letter to Mrs. Mary Mason; Baker, *Diary and Letters*, p. 147.
37. October 5, 1895, MPH.
38. Moody to Miss Peabody, [late spring 1895]; the poem exists as an undated, unsigned manuscript of five pages in Moody's hand, MPH.
39. The narration which follows in the text represents a synthesis of information in letters of Moody to Herrick, April–June 1895; of Professor George Herbert Palmer to Herrick in the same period; and of Moody to Lovett, May–June 1895. Letters to Herrick are in the Herrick Papers, and those to Lovett are in the Moody Papers, University of Chicago Library.
40. Moody to Lovett, May 18, 1895, MPC.

41. Moody to Herrick, May 22, 1895, Herrick Papers, Chicago.
42. Diary, July 4, 1895, PPH.
43. [Late June 1895], MPH.
44. For much of the detail I am indebted to Mason's treatment of this trip in his *Music in My Time*, pp. 24–32.
45. Moody in conversation about his summer with Miss Peabody. Recorded in her diary, September 18, 1895, PPH.
46. Moody to Miss Peabody, October 5, 1895, MPH.
47. Diary, September 18, 1895, PPH.
48. As quoted by Mason to Moody in a letter of September 27, 1895, MPC.
49. [Fall 1895], PPH.
50. Moody to Mason, [October 2, 1895], MPP.

CHAPTER 4: CHICAGO'S ALCHEMICAL POWER

1. For the contexts of Moody's life in Chicago the relevant passages in Lovett, *All Our Years* and in Harriet Monroe, *A Poet's Life* (New York, 1938), have been helpful. Early novels by H. B. Fuller and Robert Herrick have been consulted, and Herrick's later novel, *Chimes* (New York, 1925), is suggestive. Factual detail and a larger context for my treatment of Moody's professional life at the University of Chicago and his relationships with his colleagues have been provided by consultation of relevant portions of the following: The President's Papers: President Harper, University of Chicago Library; Annual Register of the University of Chicago, 1895–1910; *General Register 1892–1902* (Chicago, 1903); and the correspondence of Herrick, Lovett, Moody, and Manly.
2. September 22, 1895, MPH.
3. To Josephine Preston Peabody, October 27, 1895, MPH.
4. Lovett, Introduction, *Selected Poems*, pp. lxviii–lxix. Lovett describes the "life *en ménage*," pp. xxxv–xxxvi.
5. Lovett, *All Our Years*, p. 70.
6. To Mason, [October 23, 1895], MPP.
7. Both Mason and Lovett comment on this trait of Moody's. See Mason, *Some Letters*, p. 3; and Lovett, Introduction, *Selected Poems*, p. xiii.
8. October 27, 1895, MPH.
9. Moody to Miss Peabody, November 28, 1895, MPH. For Mason's description of circumstances of the poem's inception, see his *Some Letters*, p. 27.
10. The strongest of the influences on the poem is that of Francis Thompson's poetry. René Taupin finds Moody's poetic dramas symbolic in form and, on occasion, lyrical in technique. But the dominance of allegorical form and the reliance on rhetoric in poems like "The Brute" are not *symboliste*. And he finds little direct influence of French symbolism on Moody (*L'Influence du Symbolisme français sur la Poésie américaine* [Paris, 1927], pp. 53–56). Martin Halpern identi-

fies the symbolist influence in "Jetsam" and, fully acquainted with
Moody's work, he recognizes the extent to which Moody adopted
symbolist techniques to his own purposes (see *William Vaughn
Moody*, pp. 33–34). Still the best treatment is Charleton M. Lewis,
"William Vaughn Moody," *Yale Review*, 2 (1913), 688–703. Lewis
considers Moody the most successful poet of his time in assimilating
the essential qualities of symbolist poetry. Identifying Moody's mature style as a synthesis of symbolist delicacy and American robustness, he defines Moody's position in literary history through comparison with a number of writers, including Browning, Yeats, and Thompson.

11. "Jetsam I" is a manuscript of six numbered pages in Moody's hand,
dated "Thanksgiving Day, 1895," and signed "William Vaughn
Moody." "Jetsam II" is a manuscript of eight unnumbered pages in
Moody's hand, dated "December 12/1895," and signed as above.
Both "Jetsam I" and "Jetsam II" are filed with Moody's letters to
Miss Peabody, MPH. I quote here from "Jetsam II," the more fully
conceived version, feeling that few readers will be interested in an
intricate discussion of differences in these two manuscript poems.
"Jetsam III" is the poem as published in *Poems*. Here a new passage
of fifty-two lines is interpolated near the end. The passage begins,
"For all my spirit's soilure is put by," and ends with repetition of the
line at which Moody had entered his insertion, "Of silver on the
brown grope of the flood." The addition seeks to answer objections to
the poem made by Lewis E. Gates in a letter to Moody of May 29,
1896, MPC. Moody probably made his changes in the poem and
added this section in a number of work periods extending from summer 1896 to as late, perhaps, as winter 1899. Since the interpolated
passage represents the addition of a man who is philosophically and
psychologically at some distance from the poem of 1895, I treat it
separately (see ch. 5, sec. 2). For indicative tabulations of changes
Moody made in two sections of "Jetsam II" for the final publication,
see nn. 20 and 21 below.

12. In the thirty-eight-line passage I quote from "Jetsam II," aside from
minor changes in punctuation, Moody changed four words for "Jetsam III," the final version: (line 17), "Ghostly youth/ risen youth";
(line 18), "the/ her"; (line 20), "Would/ Might"; (line 33),
"looked/ gazed." His major change represents a vast improvement of
lines 24–26. He expanded them as follows:

> Faun-shapes in goatish dance, young witches' eyes
> Slanting deep invitation, whinnying calls
> Ambiguous, shocks and whirlwinds of wild mirth,—
> They had undone me in the darkness there, . . .

13. This passage is quoted from "Jetsam II." Moody had changed only
one word in "Jetsam I": (line 3), "alone/ apart." Changes made for
"Jetsam III" were: line 2 was omitted entirely; (line 4), "Wild bell-
towers/ Bright rivers; strong hills/ low hills"; (line 5), "Vineyards/

Forests"; (line 7), "folded/ opening": and (line 11), "horns of herald silver surgent/ herald trumpets softly lifted."

14. Moody to Mason, December 1, 1895, MPP.
15. November 28, 1895, MPH.
16. Her letter has been destroyed, but she noted her reactions to the poem in her diary, December 2, 1895, PPH.
17. Moody to Miss Peabody, November 28, 1895, MPH.
18. A group of articles on the healer's disappearance appeared in the *New York Times* between November 15 and December 30, 1895. My treatment is based on these eight articles.
19. Moody to Mason, December 1, 1895, MPP.
20. January 4, 1896, MPH.
21. Diary, January 6, 1896, and February 11, 1896, PPH.
22. [January 1896], MPH.
23. Ibid.
24. Moody to Miss Peabody, [January 1896], MPH.
25. Moody to Mason, February 16, 1896, MPP.
26. Recorded in Josephine's diary, March 17, 1896, PPH. Cf. Lovett's recollection of Moody's geniality in 1895–96, Introduction, *Selected Poems,* p. xxxvi.
27. April 11, 1896, MPP.
28. May 9, [1896], MPH.
29. Moody to Mason, May 16, 1896, MPP.
30. The dates of these letters are: Mason's critique, May 21, 1896, MPC; Moody's first response, May 24, 1896, MPP; Moody's second response [June 1896], MPP; Gates's critique, May 29, 1896, MPC. Mason printed the poem in *Some Letters,* pp. 57–60. The manuscript, dated May 1896, is in the Moody Papers, Princeton.
31. The revised draft of this poem, dated June 6, 1896, is in MPC.
32. Moody to Mason, [June 6, 1896], MPP.
33. Typed transcript, Moody to Charlotte Moody, July 1, 1896, TPPM.
34. Moody to Lovett, July 14, 1896, MPC.
35. [June 1896], MPH. This letter is misdated "[probably Autumn, 1895]" in Mason, *Some Letters,* pp. 38–39.
36. Moody to Miss Peabody, [June 1896], MPH. Mark Van Doren, who does not like Moody's poetry, finds his letters "brilliant," commenting, "The genius which is lacking in the poems is abundantly present in the letters." See *The Private Reader* (New York, 1942), pp. 225–28.
37. Moody to Miss Peabody, [June 1896], MPH.
38. Moody to Mason, [August 1896], MPP.
39. "The Present Conditions of Literary Production," *Atlantic Monthly,* 78 (1896), 156–68.
40. The issues dominate the discussions of poetry and drama in the literary magazines of the mid-nineties. *Poet-Lore,* 7 (1895) furnishes some fine examples. Specific phrases quoted in this paragraph in the text are from the following articles: Helen Abbott Michael, "The Drama in Relation to Truth," *Poet-Lore,* 7 (1895), 149 ff.; Livings-

ton Hunt, "The Decay of Spirituality in Our Literature," *Critic*, 27 (November 9, 1895), 297 ff.; J. S. Tunison, "The Coming Literary Revival," *Atlantic Monthly*, 80 (1897), 694 ff.; and Calvin Thomas, "Have We Still Need of Poetry?" *Forum*, 25 (1898), 503–12.

41. [June 1896], MPP.

42. Mason prints the poem, "Dawn Parley," in *Some Letters*, pp. 71–72. The manuscript is dated July 18, 1896, MPP.

43. Introduction, *The Pilgrim's Progress* (Boston, 1897), p. vi.

44. Ibid., p. ix.

45. Ibid., p. viii. In addition, Moody had worked his way through the ten volumes of the recently published *The Writings of Eugene Field* for an essay-review, "Eugene Field and His Work," *Atlantic Monthly*, 78 (1896), 265–69. The review is unsigned. See *Atlantic Index Supplement, 1889–1901* (Boston & New York, 1903) for identification of Moody's authorship.

46. Moody to Miss Peabody, [June 1896], MPH.

47. William Vaughn Moody and Robert Morss Lovett, *A History of English Literature* (New York, 1902), p. 330.

48. Ibid., p. 290.

49. Ibid., pp. 265–66.

50. *The Gospel of Freedom* (New York, 1898), p. 265.

51. Grace Neahr Veeder, *Concerning William Vaughn Moody* (Waukesha, Wisc., 1941), 19 pp., MPC.

52. [February 1897], MPP.

53. Neither lyric exists in manuscript, and both were first published in *Poems*. From this point on, unless otherwise noted, I print the texts of Moody's poems and plays from Manly's edition, *Poems and Plays*. Moody did not revise *Poems* for this edition, published after his death. He did publish poems in national magazines before collecting them for book publication, but in most cases he reprinted the poems with few substantial changes. When Moody changed the title of a poem between its first and later publication, I have used the title as it appears in *Poems and Plays*.

54. Moody to Charlotte Moody, [March 25, 1897], typed transcript, TPPM.

55. Diary, April 2–May 17, 1897, MPC.

56. See Moody to Herrick, April 16, [1897], Herrick Papers, Chicago; and Moody to Charlotte Moody, April 9, 1897, typed transcript, TPPM.

57. Moody made a pilgrimage to the home of the prolific young Italian writer, returning with autographs and a note in Italian quoting from the passage in Dante that Moody was to turn to for "A Dialogue in Purgatory": "Sempre, sempre, ricordati [sic] di me." Lovett, Introduction, *Selected Poems*, p. xlii.

58. Diary, April 2–May 17, 1897, MPC.

59. Lovett, Introduction, *Selected Poems*, p. xxxix.

60. See Moody to Herrick, May 28, 1897, Herrick Papers, Chicago. Much

of the detail on Moody's travel in company with the Lovetts is
drawn from Lovett, Introduction, *Selected Poems,* pp. xxxviii–xliv,
and Lovett, *All Our Years,* pp. 74–77. Where the accounts are con-
tradictory, I have followed the earlier source.

61. Mason, *Some Letters,* p. 87.
62. Moody to Miss Peabody, July 15, 1897, MPH.
63. Moody to Mason, August 1, 1897, MPP.
64. Moody wrote Miss Peabody that he had contracted for this edition,
    July 15, 1897, MPH. He informed Herrick of his plans in a letter of
    August 3, 1897, Herrick Papers, Chicago.
65. Moody read these three works to Miss Peabody in Boston (see her
    Diary, September 19, 1897, PPH).
66. Moody to Miss Peabody, October 31, 1897, MPH.
67. In addition, Moody drew on his work on Milton for a paper, "The
    Pastoral Idea in Later Renaissance Literature," announced for de-
    livery December 7, 1897. See *Register of the University of Chicago,*
    1897–1898. The paper does not survive.
68. *Atlantic Monthly,* 81 (January 1898), 136–39.
69. *Atlantic Monthly,* 81 (January 1898), 137.
70. Ibid., 138–39.
71. Passages of Savage's poetry cited below in the text are quoted from
    Daniel Gregory Mason, ed., *Poems of Philip Henry Savage* (Boston,
    1901).
72. Stickney spent the summer of 1897 with his mother and sister in
    Engelberg, Switzerland, and Moody may have visited him briefly
    after leaving Lovett at Innsbruck, but there is no record of a meeting.
    Their continuing contact is attested in a letter of October 1897, in
    which Stickney wrote Lovett, "Will is getting on properly; quite dis-
    couraged, he yet seems to be guessing at truth of some sort. No doubt
    he will clamber out onto some city roof, where the prospect is—not
    beautiful, of course, but clear." Seán Haldane, *The Fright of Time*
    (Ladysmith, Quebec, 1970), p. 91. Haldane's valuable life of Stick-
    ney is the only full treatment of Stickney as man and writer in print.
    It makes available for the first time the complete texts of Stickney's
    extant letters, most of them written to his sister, Lucy. The majority
    of Stickney's letters to friends and personal papers have been de-
    stroyed (see Haldane, *The Fright of Time,* p. 1). Thomas Riggs, Jr.,
    "The Life of Trumbull Stickney," Ph.D. diss. (Princeton, 1947), is
    a useful, pioneering treatment of Stickney, and I am indebted to it
    as well.
73. [December 1897], MPH.
74. Moody to Lovett, February 21, 1898, MPC.

CHAPTER 5: THE HONIED LUSTS OF LIFE

1. March 13, 1898, MPP.
2. March 29, 1898, Herrick Papers, Chicago.
3. April 8, 1898, MPP.

4. Moody to Mason, April 8, 1898, MPP.
5. April 13, 1898, MPP.
6. Norman Hapgood's discussion of the Syndicate may be found in *The Stage in America 1897–1900* (New York, 1901), pp. 6–38.
7. For New York theatre in the period, in addition to Hapgood's book and information in the letters of Moody and his friends, I have used Arthur Hobson Quinn, *The American Drama from the Civil War to the Present Day* (New York, 1927), 2 vols. For periods during which Moody was in New York, the *New York Times* has been consulted.
8. Moody probably saw Elizabeth Robins as Hedda in *Hedda Gabler*, and Mrs. Fiske in Margaret Merington's adaptation of *Love Finds a Way*. The latter play concerns the restoration to health of a crippled woman when her egocentricity gives way to unselfish love. It may have influenced Moody's depiction of Mrs. Beeler in *The Faith Healer*.
9. See Charlotte Wilson [Baker], "The Gift," six-page typescript, MPC; and Lovett, Introduction, *Selected Poems*, p. xxxiv.
10. See Lovett's description of Moody as teacher, Lovett, Introduction, *Selected Poems*, p. lxiv.
11. Moody was living with the Herricks in this period. He paid $12.50 a month for room, $7.00 a week for board, $0.50 a week for laundry, and was responsible for the cost of the gas he used. Moody to Herrick, April 11, 1898, Herrick Papers, Chicago.
12. Lovett, *All Our Years*, pp. 97–98.
13. Blake Nevius, *Robert Herrick* (Berkeley, 1962), p. 293. See Moody to Herrick, August 26, 1900, for an inquiry about the "club." Herrick Papers, Chicago.
14. Harriet Monroe describes the Little Room in *A Poet's Life*, p. 197; and Lovett treats Moody's visits, Introduction, *Selected Poems*, p. xxxv.
15. William Vaughn Moody, *The Complete Poetical Works of John Milton* (Boston & New York, 1899), p. xiv.
16. Ibid., p. 252.
17. Ibid., p. 34.
18. Ibid., p. 37.
19. Ibid., pp. 288–90, for Moody's discussion.
20. January 8, 1899, MPH.
21. January 17, 1899, MPP.
22. Lovett distinguishes among three versions of the play, Introduction, *Selected Poems*, p. lix; and Mason refers to the version he has just heard read, in a letter to Moody of February 24, 1899, MPC.
23. These reports are discussed in ch. 4, sec. 1. And see ch. 4, n. 18.
24. See his treatment of the effects of Milton's marriage on his work in *Complete Poetical Works of John Milton*, p. xiv.
25. As a special student at Harvard in the early nineties, Robinson had been awed by Moody's position in the inner circle of the Harvard literati and by his local reputation as a poet. In a letter to Harry

de Forest Smith, he wrote of his experience watching the Harvard class games: "It was good fun at first, but I soon sickened of [it]. Men like W. V. Moody and R. M. Lovett seemed to enjoy it, however, so I am probably at fault." Denham Sutcliffe, ed., *Untriangulated Stars* (Cambridge, 1947), pp. 62–63. The men did not meet, and even as late as 1898 Moody had no knowledge of Robinson's poetry. Mason saw Robinson's "Richard Cory," published belatedly in the *Harvard Monthly* in February 1898. He sent an admiring comment on his new find to Moody, who responded: "Note what you say of Robinson with interest. Do not know his work. Wish you could get me a line of introduction from some friends." Moody to Mason, May 8, 1898, MPP. If Moody and Robinson met briefly during Moody's attendance at the Harvard commencement in late June, there is no record of the meeting; it was probably delayed until the New York meeting of February 1899. See my "Moody and Robinson," *Colby Library Quarterly,* 5 (1960), 185–94, and Richard Cary, "Robinson on Moody," *Colby Library Quarterly,* 6 (1962), 176–83, for differing treatments of the relationship of these poets.

26. See Robinson to Moody, August 27, 1899, in Edwin S. Fussell, "Robinson to Moody: Ten Unpublished Letters," *American Literature,* 23 (1951), 175. Robinson's reference in this letter to the poets' New York meeting suggests that Emery Neff's statement that the poets met in Cambridge must be corrected. See his *Edwin Arlington Robinson* (New York, 1948), p. 100.

27. Fussell, "Robinson to Moody," p. 175.

28. Of the fine work that Robinson's editors and biographers have done, and of which I have made use, two studies should be specifically mentioned. I have worked with many of the same unpublished sources used by Hermann Hagedorn in his early *Edwin Arlington Robinson: A Biography* (New York, 1938), and have a new respect for the careful work which went into that deceptively "popular" biography. Peter Dechert's "Edwin Arlington Robinson and Alanson Tucker Schumann: A Study in Influences," Ph.D. diss. (University of Pennsylvania, 1955), has added useful information on Robinson's early poetic experience in his circle of Gardiner friends.

29. See Mason's comparison of the personalities of his two very different friends in his *Music in My Time,* p. 84.

30. Edwin Arlington Robinson, *Collected Poems* (New York, 1934), p. 105.

31. February 26, 1899, MPP.

32. See ch. 4, sec. 1.

33. Diary, April 2–May 17, 1897, MPC.

34. February 26, 1899, MPP.

35. May 13, 1899, MPP.

36. Moody attempted revision of a number of early poems for the projected volume. For example, as late as the fall of 1898 a poem of 1892, "The Amber Witch," was revised and read in a new version to

Manly in Chicago. The poem was finally discarded. Manly, Introduction, *Poems and Plays,* I, p. xvi.

37. See ch. 3, n. 21, above.

38. Moody to Mason, July 5, 1899, MPP.

39. Ibid.

40. It is possible that Moody had included a somewhat larger selection from his early poems than the group which appears in *Poems.* If so, his Macmillan readers might have objected to some of them, but Moody's major concern of the fall was the revision of the masque itself.

41. Dunbar, *A House in Chicago,* pp. 47–48, quoting a communication from Alice Corbin Henderson.

42. Moody to Robinson, August 25, 1899. This passage and the following (in the text) are from the Isaacs-Robinson Collection; Manuscript Division; The New York Public Library; Astor, Lenox and Tilden Foundations.

43. For Robinson's full response, see his letter of August 27, 1899. Fussell, "Robinson to Moody," pp. 174–76.

44. Olivia Howard Dunbar quotes a letter from Miss Dupree in "William Vaughn Moody," p. 123, TPPM. Miss Dupree married William P. Sedley in 1900, and the dedication reads, "To E. D. S."

45. September 30, 1899, PPH.

46. Ibid. The major portion of Miss Peabody's letters to Moody do not survive. They were probably destroyed.

47. The poem was in draft much earlier than October 1899, and was surely one of those included in the rejected volume. Miss Peabody lists receipt of poetry from Moody in her diary, October 1899, and this poem is the most likely candidate, PPH.

48. [October 1899], MPH. No letter of transmission for the above poem exists. This letter is undated, and its generality of reference makes conclusive dating by content impossible. Since Moody mentions his return to Chicago, other possible dates are limited, but references, attitude and tone suggest October 1899 as its most probable date.

49. December 2, 1899, MPP.

50. Such an arrangement is suggested through the Moody-Lovett correspondence of the next few years. See below, ch. 6, n. 2, and ch. 7, n. 31.

51. Introduction, *Some Letters,* p. xviii.

52. February 12, 1900, Herrick Papers, Chicago.

53. This document is in MPC.

54. Lovett, Introduction, *Selected Poems,* p. xliii.

55. In treating the ode in his edition of Milton, Moody wrote that stanza xix and the five following stanzas were "not only magnificent and flawless," but "are also pitched in a key before unheard in England, and colored with the light of a new mind." *Complete Poetical Works of John Milton,* p. 6.

56. He held to this view as late as 1902. See William Vaughn Moody

and Robert Morss Lovett, *A History of English Literature* (New York, 1902), p. 160.

CHAPTER 6: BILLIARD—WORK WITH THE WESTERN WORLD

1. In the work of Moody and his friends, Howard Mumford Jones finds early signs of this century's increasing emphasis on intensity as a literary value. Jones recognizes Moody as a precursor of youthful writers of the 1920s who rebelled against materialism in the name of art and spiritual values. A similar rebellion in American life and art has characterized the 1960s, and Jones's early analysis has seemed increasingly trenchant (see *The Bright Medusa* [Urbana, Ill., 1952], pp. 57–64, et passim). More recently Jones discusses Moody's work as one of the most significant and subtle indices to several American cultural currents of his period (see *The Age of Energy* [New York, 1971], pp. 36, 56, 366–68).

2. This fact has been obscured in Moody criticism because of inaccurate dating of a number of early poems.

3. About two-thirds of the volume was Moody's work: chs. 1–3, 5–7, the Milton and Bunyan section of ch. 7, "The Revival of Romanticism" in ch. 12, and chs. 13 and 14. The extensive final revision of the proofs was Moody's work as well. This statement of the division of labor, substantiated by Moody's letters to Lovett and by differences in style and focus in sections, is fuller and more accurate than that in Henry, *Moody,* pp. 41–42. Henry's source is a Lovett letter written some thirty years after the book's publication. *A History of English Literature* has proved to be a work of unusual endurance. Brought up to date in its mid-career by Fred B. Millett, the history has been in print for seventy years and is now in its eighth revised edition.

4. Passages are quoted in the text below from the text of the poem in Manly, *Poems and Plays,* rather than from its first publication in the *Atlantic Monthly,* 85 (May 1900), 593–98. My treatment of the historical and political contexts of the poem is indebted to the careful work of Francis J. and Adaline Glasheen, "Moody's 'An Ode in Time of Hesitation,'" *College English,* 5 (1943), 121–29.

5. Robinson to Mason, in Ridgely Torrence, ed., *Selected Letters of Edwin Arlington Robinson* (New York, 1940), p. 29.

6. Fussell, "Robinson to Moody," pp. 176–77.

7. Ibid., p. 178. Criticism has developed both sides of Robinson's ambivalent response. In "Moody's Ode: The Collapse of the Heroic," *Texas Studies in English,* 36 (1957), 80–92, Frederick Eckman finds the poem's dominant mode "heroic" and distastefully alien to the concepts and language of the modern reader. He prefers the idiom of John Berryman's "Boston Common." But more recently Robert Bly, a poet himself, argues for the current need of political poetry in America, and he selects Yeats, Neruda, Whitman, and Moody for

consideration as significant and praiseworthy political poets. See "On Political Poetry," *Nation*, 204 (April 24, 1967), 522–24.

8. For the comments of Bliss Perry and Oswald G. Villard, see Dunbar, "William Vaughn Moody," pp. 142–43, TPPM. I have been unable to locate the original sources of their statements.

9. Quoted by G.M.H., "Writers and Books," Boston *Evening Transcript*, January 2, 1901, p. 12. For this information and that in the following sentence, I am indebted to Wallace Ludwig Anderson, "Some Critical Attitudes Toward Poetry in America as Reflected in the Development of the Reputation of William Vaughn Moody as a Poet: 1900–1912," Ph.D. diss. (University of Chicago, 1948), p. 17.

10. See Robinson's comments and his playful circus sonnet, written in response to a letter from Moody which must have mentioned "The Menagerie." Fussell, "Robinson to Moody," pp. 178–79.

11. "The Menagerie," undated manuscript draft in ten numbered pages, signed "William Vaughn Moody," MPC.

12. Moody to Mason, December 2, 1899, MPP.

13. I have developed Halpern's happy suggestion that the woman and child were major characters in the play's first version. See his *William Vaughn Moody*, p. 46.

14. Mason, *Music in My Time*, p. 124.

15. Robinson to Miss Peabody, November 25, 1900, PPH. For Robinson on Moody's "Temperament," see his letter to Miss Peabody, January 1, 1901, PPH.

16. Moody to Mason, November 14, 1900, MPP.

17. Robinson to Miss Peabody, December 10, 1900, PPH.

18. Torrence, *Selected Letters*, p. 38.

19. See Robinson's comments to Moody. Fussell, "Robinson to Moody," p. 181.

20. For N. Hapgood on poetic drama, see his *The Stage in America*, p. 53.

21. Mason, *Some Letters*, p. 130.

22. November 30, 1900, MPP.

23. November 25, 1900, PPH. But by January 17, 1901, Robinson had clarified his response. In a letter to John Hays Gardiner he observed that Moody's masque contained six to eight "entirely damnable" verses. But he now felt that it was "an astonishing work of art and almost flawless in construction." Torrence, *Selected Letters*, pp. 37–38.

24. Mason, *Some Letters*, pp. 131–32.

25. Ibid., p. 133.

26. "Gloucester Moors," *Scribner's*, 28 (December 1900), 727–28; "The Brute," *Atlantic Monthly*, 87 (January 1901), 88–90; and "On a Soldier Fallen in the Philippines," *Atlantic Monthly*, 87 (February 1901), 288.

27. For his careful and thorough work on the critical reception of Moody's poetry, I am indebted to Anderson, "Some Critical Attitudes," both

here and in later discussions. The letters to the *New York Times* are treated by Anderson, pp. 7–9.

28. G.M.H., "Writers and Books," Boston *Evening Transcript,* January 2, 1901, p. 12.
29. Issue of January 29, 1901.
30. The receptions of *The Masque of Judgment* and *Poems* (1901) are considered together in Anderson, "Some Critical Attitudes," pp. 19–103.
31. *Atlantic Monthly,* 87 (March 1901), 420.
32. *Outlook,* 68 (April 13, 1901), 875.
33. January 19, 1901.
34. Mrs. Hovey to Moody, January 9, 1901, MPC.
35. Letter of April 18, 1901, MPC.
36. *Nation,* 72 (March 28, 1901), 259–60.

CHAPTER 7: THE SUBSTANCE OF THINGS HOPED FOR

1. "A Poet of Promise," *Outlook,* 68 (July 20, 1901), 664–65.
2. The Poetry of Mr. Moody," *Dial,* 30 (June 1, 1901), 365, 367.
3. "Mr. William Vaughn Moody's Poems," *Atlantic Monthly,* 88 (July 1901), 132–33.
4. Unsigned review, Chicago *Tribune,* May 11, 1901.
5. "A New Poet," *Critic,* 39 (September 1901), 226.
6. An unidentified review of 1901, quoted in Anderson, "Some Critical Attitudes," p. 3.
7. Mabie to Moody, May 13, 1901, MPC.
8. Other uncited but important reviews I quote from are: [Lewis E. Gates], "Recent Verse," *Nation,* 73 (August 22, 1901), 154; and George B. Rose, "William Vaughn Moody," *Sewanee Review,* 9 (July 1901), 332–33. For a much fuller treatment, see Anderson, "Some Critical Attitudes," pp. 19–103 passim.
9. "Yoked to British Ways," Chicago *Evening Post,* June 8, 1901.
10. Fussell, "Robinson to Moody," pp. 184–85.
11. Torrence, *Selected Letters,* p. 49.
12. Moody and Lovett, *A History of English Literature,* p. 330.
13. Scholarly comment on the entire body of Moody criticism, including that on possible influences operating in Moody's various poems and plays, is fully presented in both Henry, *Moody,* and Halpern, *William Vaughn Moody.* A recent description and appraisal of Moody scholarship and criticism is Maurice F. Brown, "William Vaughn Moody (1869–1910)," *American Literary Realism: 1870–1910,* in press.
14. Much of the critical comment on Moody since 1925 seeks to define the stylistic problems in his work. F. O. Matthiessen has anticipated my approach, identifying Moody's characteristic tendency to "over-abundance" and suggesting that his diction and figures seem "too strenuously sought after." Matthiessen admired the solidity of Moody's

ideas and "the range and energy of his conception of life" but felt Moody never really found his true voice (*The Responsibilities of the Critic* [New York,], pp. 93–97). Ludwig Lewisohn finds Moody "often too traditional in execution" and "insensitive" to the pressing need for stylistic "refreshment" in his period. But Lewisohn is more interested in Moody's ideas. I have developed his suggestion that Moody's work holds "in germ all or nearly all the chief ideas and creative motifs of modern literature" (*Expression in America* [New York, 1932], pp. 302–9). R. P. Blackmur's is the essential analysis of Moody's style from the point of view of the New Criticism. He maintains that Moody is of significance only to those interested in the tradition or to readers who like poetry which evokes familiar emotional experience in realms of the "vague and beautiful." Moody's problem is insufficient "impersonality": personal emotional experience never finds genuine objective embodiment in precise verbal structures. The result is detached rhetoric and mere impassioned summoning of subject ("Moody in Retrospect," *Poetry*, 38 [1931], 331–37).

15. Torrence, *Selected Letters*, p. 38.

16. March 20, 1901, Moody file, President's Papers (Harper), University of Chicago Library.

17. See Moody to Harper, May 8 and 20, 1901, Moody file, President's Papers (Harper), University of Chicago Library.

18. Harriet Moody was known under the name of her first husband, Brainard, until her marriage to Moody in 1909. Manly's error in spelling the name has been repeated in a number of accounts. For details of Harriet Moody's life before her meeting with the poet, I rely principally on Dunbar, *A House in Chicago*. On Moody's life she is unreliable, however, and her treatment of the relationship of Will and Harriet leans to romantic fictionalization when information is unavailable. I follow her description of the first meetings of Moody and Harriet (pp. 47–48), which rests on a letter from A[lice] C[orbin] H[enderson] in TPPM. Percy MacKaye records a "tradition" in which the Little Room is identified as the place of first meeting (*LH*, 437).

19. My account of Harriet's accident follows a letter from Ferdinand Schevill to Percy MacKaye, quoted in *LH*, pp. 6–7, and on Moody to Lovett, May 19, 1901, MPC. Detail here and in the following text pages has been drawn from *LH*, pp. 415 and 416, and from Dunbar, *A House in Chicago*, pp. 54–60.

20. Here and throughout, except in one or two cases otherwise noted, I quote Moody's letters to Harriet from MacKaye, *Letters to Harriet*. The originals are in the Henry E. Huntington Library. Unlike Mason's *Some Letters*, MacKaye's volume is almost complete. I supply notes only when insufficient identification in the text would present difficulties to a reader interested in consulting the context. Harriet's letters to Moody were destroyed, but the poet often gives suggestion of their content in his own.

21. This sequence of events is given in Moody to Herrick, September 5, 1901, Herrick Papers, Chicago.

22. Compare Lovett's delicate treatment of Moody's promotion at Chicago, Introduction, *Selected Poems*, p. xliv.

23. Moody to Herrick, September 5, 1901, Herrick Papers, Chicago.

24. MacKaye quoting a letter from Garland, *LH*, p. 17.

25. A somewhat fictionized account of the trip is in Hamlin Garland, *Companions on the Trail* (New York, 1931), pp. 87–93. Garland exaggerates Moody's helplessness and his own competence, omitting reference to his injury, attested by Moody's letters to Harriet and to Mason. His chapter on Moody must be consulted with caution.

26. *LH*, pp. 79–80.

27. MacKaye quoting a letter from Garland, *LH*, p. 18.

28. MacKaye quoting a letter from Schevill, *LH*, p. 6.

29. Moody had earlier made his view of Homeric Greece clear in a comment on Pope's translation of the *Iliad*, writing: "into that country, so distant, so mysterious, into the midst of that race, so strangely compounded of the childlike and the heroic, of the savage and the lofty minded, Pope can never conduct us, for he has never journeyed thither himself." W. W. Cressy and W. V. Moody, eds., *The Iliad of Homer* (Chicago, 1900), p. 38. For Moody's authorship of the introduction, see Henry, *Moody*, p. 45.

30. The account of Moody's trip is based on his letters to Harriet, to Charlotte Moody, to Lovett, and on the Lewis E. Gates correspondence (PPH) for this period. Passages quoted without identification are *LH*.

31. MacKaye cites Torrence's memory of Moody's description of his fall on Parnassus (*LH*, p. 418). The account, which dates from thirty years after the event, does not agree with the record of Moody's letters, even if his desire not to alarm Harriet is taken into consideration. According to Torrence, "Moody said that he had climbed within a few feet of the very summit of the peak and was reaching upward, clutching the rock with both hands, his eyes fixed on the top just beyond, when he suddenly slipped and fell about fifteen feet into a crevice, where his fall was broken by a sharp projection which struck into his thigh on the very spot operated upon three years later by Dr. Bull." MacKaye goes on to mingle ambiguously a statement Moody made about his operation in 1905, giving the impression that Moody was "wounded" in Greece (*LH*, p. 418).

32. *LH*, p. 134, corroborated in part by references in Moody's letters from Greece. Manly's frequently repeated statement that Moody read all of the Greek drama in Paris (Introduction, *Poems and Plays*, I, p. xxxi) is incorrect. In fact, Moody probably read no more than three or four plays. He and Stickney spent some time discussing the structure of the chorus in Greek drama and of the Pindaric ode.

33. See Moody to Lovett, May 21 [1902], and June 19 [1902], MPC.

34. The trip with Gates is not mentioned in Moody's letters to Harriet,

and it must have contributed to Moody's strain. Gates's condition was precarious, and he resigned his Harvard position within the year to place himself under medical care. A few years later he entered a mental institution, where he remained until his death in 1924. See Gates to Lionel Marks, March 3 [1902]; April 25 [1902]; and September 14 [1903], PPH. And see Coolidge, "Lewis E. Gates," pp. 23–24.

35. *LH*, p. 134.

36. By the summer of 1902 Stickney was nearing the end of his long Paris residence. He had essentially completed his dissertation in Latin, "De Hermolai Barbari vita atque ingenio dissertationem" (Paris, 1903), and was in the midst of his thesis for the Sorbonne doctorate, "Les sentences dans la poésie grecque d'Homère à Euripide" (Paris, 1903). Stickney's increasing involvement in Sanskrit literature resulted in a translation of the Bhagavad-Gita in collaboration with Sylvan Levy. It was published in Paris in 1938, many years after his death.

37. Notebooks One and Two, MPC.

38. In a letter of October 4 [1903], *LH*, p. 163.

39. The four letters Moody wrote Charlotte from Europe had been shy of detail but filled with reassurance that he had regained his health; it was "excellent now"; he was "entirely well." Of his actual condition and his injury in Greece he told her nothing. TPPM.

CHAPTER 8: *The Fire-Bringer*

1. Manly writes (Introduction, *Poems and Plays,* I, p. xiv) that Moody ceased to teach in the university after 1902. He was obviously thinking in terms of the 1902–3 academic year.

2. Paul Shorey, "The Poetry of William Vaughn Moody," *Record* (University of Chicago), 13 (July 1927), 190, 195.

3. *LH*, p. 153. Details on income from *A History of English Literature* are given in Moody to Lovett, September 29, 1903. See ch. 9, n. 5, below.

4. To Miss Peabody, September 30, [1903], PPH.

5. The letters to Charlotte Moody (TPPM) and Mary Mason (MPP) are both of October 14, 1903.

6. Letter to Mary Mason, October 14, 1903, MPP.

7. Notations referred to below in the text were made in Notebook One, MPC, in which Moody continued to make entries at least as late as 1906.

8. Torrence to Miss Peabody, December 30, 1903, PPH; and *LH*, p. 172.

9. The poem was first published in *Scribner's,* 40 (October 1906), 405. Following my standard procedure, I quote from the text in Manly, *Poems and Plays.* Of the several changes Moody made in the manuscript he sent Harriet (MPC), one is of particular interest: the line, "This is not the shepherd old," originally read, "I am not your father old."

10. Stickney's letter to Moody does not survive. See *LH*, p. 179.

11. Ibid., p. 223.

12. The final stanza of "Gloucester Moors" is made up entirely of questions. It begins, "But thou, vast outbound ship of souls,/ What harbor town for thee?"

13. Thomas Riggs, Jr., has oversimplified and I think misread the play, missing Moody's Neoplatonism. He finds only "cheerful reaffirmation of the idea of progress" here (see "Prometheus 1900," *American Literature*, 22 [1951], 422). Halpern's treatment is sounder, though he presents the profound paradoxes of act 3 in terms of a "final optimism" set against Moody's "temperamental pessimism" (see Halpern, *William Vaughn Moody*, p. 112), missing the philosophical synthesis Moody achieves.

14. This plot outline and four pages of a first act are a manuscript in Moody's hand, written on the reverse of a manuscript fragment of *The Masque of Judgment*, pages numbered 36–42, MPC. The manuscript is undated and could well be earlier than the dating suggested by its place in my narrative.

15. *LH*, p. 178.

16. Ibid., p. 185.

17. Ibid., p. 188.

18. Ibid., p. 180.

19. Ibid.

20. Torrence to Miss Peabody, December 30, 1903, and August 24, 1904, PPH.

21. As inspiration for the Western trip, there were the literary and dramatic success of Bret Harte's work, which Moody had reviewed; of the Western novels of the period, Owen Wister's *The Virginian* is a famous example; and of Augustus Thomas's recent Broadway success, *Arizona*. Interest was high in Moody's circle as well. Harriet Monroe had joined a group of Chicagoans who witnessed the Hopi snake dance in 1901. See her *A Poet's Life*, pp. 172 ff., and her article "Arizona," *Atlantic Monthly*, 89 (June 1902), 780–89.

22. Moody to Mason, March 29, 1904, MPP; Moody to Charlotte Moody, April 8, 1904, TPPM. For details of the arrangement, see Moody to Robinson, March 29 and June 1, 1904, Isaacs-Robinson Collection; Manuscript Division; The New York Public Library; Astor, Lenox and Tilden Foundations.

23. *LH*, p. 195. Unless otherwise noted, phrases quoted in the following paragraphs are from letters to Harriet in this period.

24. In reviews by Edwin L. Schuman, Chicago *Record-Herald*, March 30, 1904, p. 8; and by an unidentified reviewer, Boston *Herald*, May 7, 1904. My treatment of the critical reception of *The Fire-Bringer* is indebted to Anderson's "Some Critical Attitudes," pp. 104–89. Anderson tabulated approximately seventy reviews or comments on Moody's poetry, written between 1904 and 1908. Over sixty of these were reviews of *The Fire-Bringer*. Of the seventy items, Anderson

identifies nine as negative in tone, nine as mixed, and the remainder as favorable (see his footnote, p. 105).

25. "The Poetry of Mr. Moody," *Dial*, 30 (June 1, 1901), 365. For fuller comment on the controversy, see Anderson, "Some Critical Attitudes," pp. 111–15.

26. H.A.L. in the San Francisco *Argonaut*, March 18, 1904.

27. Chicago *Record-Herald*, March 30, 1904, p. 8.

28. Los Angeles *Express*, April 16, 1904.

29. "The Fire-Bringer," Philadelphia *Ledger*, May 8, 1904.

30. "Mr. Moody's Poetry," *New York Times*, May 7, 1904, p. 30.

31. H.A.L., "Who Is the Greatest Living American Poet?" San Francisco *Argonaut*, March 18, 1904.

32. "William Vaughn Moody's 'The Fire-Bringer,'" *New York Times*, September 17, 1904, p. 62.

33. *LH*, p. 179.

34. Thomas H. Briggs, Jr., Baltimore *Sun*, May 12, 1904.

35. Opinions have been cited and short phrases quoted from the following as well: J[oseph] B. G[ilder], "The Poetry of a Poet," *Critic*, 45 (December 1904), 571; "Some Genuine Poetry," Baltimore *News*, April 30, 1904; [Lewis E. Gates], "Recent Poetry," *Nation*, 78 (June 23, 1904), 498; "Prometheus Again in Drama," New York *Literary Digest*, January 14, 1905; "The Fire Bringer," Minneapolis *Journal*, May 13, 1904; William Morton Payne, "Two Poetic Dramas," *Dial*, XXXVI (May 16, 1904), 323; "A Stately Poem," Boston *Advertiser*, April 11, 1904; and George B. Rose, "Two Dramas," *Sewanee Review*, XII (July 1904), 346–53.

36. *LH*, p. 197.

CHAPTER 9: REVISIONS

1. *LH*, p. 201.

2. Dunbar, *A House in Chicago*, p. 69.

3. Ibid., p. 62.

4. Ibid., p. 52.

5. The statement that income from *A History of English Literature* allowed Moody to retire from teaching (Manly, Introduction, *Poems and Plays*, I, p. xiv; and Halpern, *William Vaughn Moody*, p. 93) is incorrect. Income from the book was disappointingly insufficient until 1906. See Moody to Lovett, September 29, 1903, and May 23, [1905], MPC. In November 1905 Scribner's informed Moody that sales had "substantially increased" (*LH*, p. 240), and in March 1906 Scribner's sent a check for sales of both Moody and Lovett texts, "justifying" the statement of November (*LH*, p. 257). Moody had not taught for almost three years.

6. *LH*, pp. 206–7.

7. Notebook One, MPC.

8. Notebook Four, MPC.

9. See pp. 8–15 of the manuscript of sixteen numbered pages, "The Return of Eve" [January 1904], MPC. The new song appears in the poem's publication as "The Death of Eve," *Century*, 73 (December 1906), 270–77.

10. *LH*, p. 203. Reference to the "Great Idea" first appears in an unpublished passage of a letter to Harriet of July 16, [1902]. Moody wrote, "I rest in the sheltering silence of your heart, where there is no whisper of reproach or scorn, but only the murmur of the four mystic fountains of love, the stones of which are carved [with] the four words, sister, wife, mother, child." Moody Papers, Henry E. Huntington Library.

11. See *LH*, p. 106.

12. Ibid., p. 207.

13. Ibid., p. 208.

14. See especially Robinson to Miss Peabody, August 27, 1904, and November 15, 1904, PPH.

15. Torrence to Miss Peabody, August 24, 1904, PPH.

16. Riggs, "Life of Stickney," pp. 263–74.

17. *LH*, pp. 206–13 passim.

18. *A Victorian in the Modern World*, p. 192. Hapgood's perception has been echoed in different ways by several recent critics. Bernard Duffey discusses "The Brute" as an embodiment of the "ethical realism" of America in 1900 and finds its commitment to an optimistic attitude toward evolutionary process intellectually superficial (see *The Chicago Renaissance in American Letters* [East Lansing, Mich.], pp. 105–9). Hyatt H. Waggoner sees the problem of "Gloucester Moors" as a "dissociation of sensibility." Because implications of the poem's imagery are not developed, the speaker's questioning is empty rhetoric. Since Waggoner unaccountably thinks "Gloucester Moors" is Moody's best poem, he concludes Moody had no capacity for genuine imaginative response to experience. (See *American Poets* [Boston, 1968], pp. 249–54.) Both critics ignore matters of voice, audience, and Moody's visionary intent in these poems.

19. *LH*, p. 211. For Adams's interest in Conservative-Christian-Anarchy, see his speculations in ch. 27 of *The Education of Henry Adams*.

20. *LH*, p. 211.

21. Robinson to Torrence, November 11, 1904, TPP.

22. Harper to Moody, November 14, 1904; Manly to Moody, November 10, 1904, and November 25, 1904. Department of English file, President's Papers (Harper), University of Chicago Library.

23. Moody to Harper, December 2, 1904. Moody file, President's Papers (Harper), University of Chicago Library. Harper responded in a letter of December 8, 1904.

24. Manly, Introduction, *Poems and Plays*, I, p. xvi.

25. These poems have been dated by references in Moody's letters and by examination of the manuscripts in MPC. Only in the case of "The Counting Man" is the dating particularly problematic, for no manu-

script exists and Moody's letters do not refer to the poem. It was completed by February 1906 when, according to MacKaye, Moody recited it to Arvia MacKaye (*LH*, p. 66). I place it in the fall of 1904 primarily because "Cross Tag" is listed after "The Fountain of Youth" and before "Pourquoi" [*sic*] as a poem subject in Notebook One, MPC.

26. *LH*, p. 112.

27. Ibid., p. 208.

28. This distinction has not been noted by Moody's critics; in fact, too little attention has been paid this poem and Moody's poem, "The Death of Eve."

29. The manuscript (MPC), untitled and unsigned, is undoubtedly the one sent to Harriet in early September 1904 and referred to in a letter of [September 5, 1904] (*LH*, p. 204). Moody writes that he has "already rewritten the opening and close," a revision which would account for major changes in the first and last stanzas of the poem as published in *Century*, 71 (December 1905), 310–12, and for a transposition of two stanzas which had immediately preceded the final stanza in the manuscript (MPC). Moody placed these stanzas in the body of the poem. Two stanzas were added to the poem for publication in 1905 as well.

30. "Old Pourquoi" exists in four versions: 1) manuscript of seven numbered pages signed "William Vaughn Moody" [late September 1904], MPC; 2) the poem as published in the *Reader*, 5 (December 1904), 101–4. For publication Moody changed a number of words and occasionally an entire line. 3) Unsigned manuscript of thirteen stanzas in Moody's hand, with stanzas clipped from version two pinned into the manuscript [January 1905?]. The first four stanzas of version two are deleted in this revision, and the manuscript stanzas represent major changes in the poem; 4) the poem as published in Manly, *Poems and Plays*. This is version three with ten editorial alterations, nine of which are minor.

31. Notebook One, MPC.

32. *Saint Nicholas*, 36 (August 1909), 882. See n. 25, above.

33. The process of editing Stickney's poetry is treated more fully in Riggs, "Life of Stickney," pp. 274–80. Riggs works from Moody's letters to George Cabot Lodge, which have recently been placed in the Lodge Papers, Massachusetts Historical Society. Lodge's intended preface for the volume is not lost, as Riggs states, but exists in page proofs in the Lodge Papers. It tells more of Lodge than of Stickney and was cut from the book just before publication at Moody's insistence.

34. The manuscript of "Musa Meretrix," MPC, much revised, is undated. In addition to thematic echoes of the poem in Moody's letters of January 1905, the manuscript paper is the same as that used for the dated draft of "The Moon-Moth" (see n. 40, below).

35. Harriet first saw the poem as published in the *Reader*, 7 (May 1906), 573. See *LH*, p. 272.

36. *LH*, p. 215.

37. See Moody's listing of the subject in Notebook One, MPC.

38. *LH*, p. 163.

39. I base this statement on Moody's extensive revision of "Old Pourquoi" (see version three, briefly described in n. 30, above).

40. "The Moon-Moth" (an earlier title, "Acrocorinthos," is canceled in the manuscript), a ten-page manuscript in Moody's hand, dated "New York, Feb. 14, 1905," and signed "Wm. Vaughn Moody." The manuscript is twice revised, both times fairly extensively, and presents serious editing problems which Manly solved nicely for the poem's first publication in *Poems and Plays*.

41. See Moody's notes on Greek mythology, Notebook Two, MPC.

42. The second version of the manuscript poem described in n. 40, above, lightly cancels the last two stanzas. Manly wisely ignored the suggestion.

43. In addition to the earliest version in the manuscript "The Return of Eve," described above in the text and in n. 9, there is a six-page manuscript, much revised, in Moody's hand: "I Am the Woman," MPC. Undated and unsigned, the manuscript is written on two different papers. Its first two pages are watermarked "Crane's Japanese Linen 1904," the paper used for drafts of "A Prairie Ride" and "The Three Angels," discussed in the text below. The paper of pp. 3–6 is used only for p. 10 of "The Fountain" manuscript, probably representing a final late revision of the closing section of that poem. "I Am the Woman," MPC, is essentially the poem, with a few editorial changes, published in *Poetry*, 1 (October 1912), 3–6, and in Manly, *Poems and Plays*. I follow my standard procedure and quote in the text below from Manly's text.

44. The poem's first draft was done in January 1904 when Moody was completing his work on *The Fire-Bringer*. "The Fountain" was written some eight months later.

45. The poem's last line troubled contemporary readers (see Robinson to Harriet Moody, in Torrence, *Selected Letters*, p. 73); its vision now seems a particularly modern one.

46. I place the experience referred to in this poem in the visit to Indiana of July 1904. The undated manuscript, MPC, is on the 1904 bond paper described in n. 43, above. The poem's central incident and tone are anticipated in a letter Moody wrote Harriet from the Grand Canyon, April 4, 1904: "My longing to have you here increased three-fold the moment I felt a horse's sinewy back between my legs. We must ride! And we must do it in this country where one's liberty is conterminous with the horizon, and the horizon is farther away than anywhere else in the world." *LH*, p. 416.

47. The only reason I can suggest for Robinson's feeling that this poem was "unfinished" (Torrence, *Selected Letters*, p. 73) is that its structural openness was alien to him. Moody's dramatic handling of the form of the lyric ode represents a gesture toward the poetry of our own time.

48. The undated manuscript, "The Three Angels," much revised, MPC,

is probably that from which Moody made the copy he sent to Harriet, May 17, 1906 (see *LH*, p. 270).

49. A date for any of these poems later than spring or summer 1905 is highly improbable, although there may have been some revision after that period. Moody was working toward a second volume of lyrics and had read a number of his new poems to Robinson, who expected a new volume in the fall of 1905 or spring 1906, at the latest. (Robinson to Miss Peabody, September 5, 1905, PPH.) Harriet Moody, not fully sympathetic to Moody's involvement in the theatre, maintained after Moody's death that he had positively decided to return to poetry in his later years (see Manly's use of this assertion, Introduction, *Poems and Plays*, I, pp. xliv–xlv, and Henry, *Moody*, p. 218). There is no evidence to support such an assertion; indeed, the evidence indicates that Moody's own inclination was quite the reverse.

CHAPTER 10: NURSINGS OF AMERICAN DRAMA

1. P. 351.
2. For MacKaye's sense of ferment in American drama, see *LH*, pp. 33–38.
3. For example, see Edmund Gosse, "Revival of the Poetic Drama," *Atlantic Monthly*, 90 (1902), 156–66; William Dean Howells, "New Poetic Drama," *North American Review*, 170 (1901), 794–800; Henry Tyrrell, "The Dramatic Outlook," *Forum*, 37 (1905), 212; H. W. Boynton, "Poetry and the Stage," *Atlantic Monthly*, 92 (1903), 125.
4. *LH*, p. 219.
5. Ibid., p. 218.
6. The date of this first meeting is obscure. MacKaye's dating in the autumn of 1904 (*LH*, p. 24) is clearly incorrect, for Torrence was in Xenia, Ohio, throughout the fall of 1904 and Moody did not see him again until January 1905 (*LH*, p. 218). In addition, Moody to MacKaye, August 5, [1905], quoted in *LH*, p. 24, is misdated 1904 by MacKaye: On August 5, 1904, Moody was packing to return to New York; in the following year he planned, as he tells MacKaye, to return in November, and so he did. The meeting at the Stedmans of Torrence and MacKaye (Introduction, *LH*, p. 25) must have occurred early in 1905, and Moody and MacKaye have been introduced briefly in February or early March. Moody seems to have spoken to Harriet of MacKaye and *Fenris the Wolf* on his visit to Chicago in April (his first reference to MacKaye in *LH* comes on May 5, [1905], p. 230). In a typed transcript, Moody to MacKaye, January 11, 1906, MPP, Moody arranges the visit he, Robinson, and Torrence made to Cornish in February, observing that he looks forward to the opportunity to get to know MacKaye better. (The earliest letter in this collection is January 6, 1906.)

7. Introduction, *LH*, p. 31. MacKaye treats the formation of the dramatic "Fellowship" on pp. 30–32.

8. Ibid., p. 23.

9. *Marlowe* was presented at Radcliffe College, June 20, 1905, with George Pierce Baker in the title role.

10. Robinson to Torrence, November 11, 1904, TPP; and to Miss Peabody, November 15, 1904, PPH.

11. MacKaye did not meet Robinson in 1904, as he states in *LH*, p. 27, but in November 1905. MacKaye to Torrence, September 21, 1905, TPP, expresses a desire to meet Robinson, and the meeting could not have occurred until MacKaye's trip to New York of November (see MacKaye to Torrence, November 15, 1905).

12. *Fortune and Men's Eyes* (Boston, 1900), and *Marlowe* (Boston & New York, 1901).

13. *El Dorado* (New York & London, 1903); and *Abelard and Heloise* (New York, 1907).

14. *Fenris the Wolf* (New York, 1905); *The Canterbury Pilgrims* (New York, 1916). For the staging of the later play as the Gloucester Pageant, see *LH*, p. 427; for that of the St. Gaudens Masque, see *LH*, p. 67.

15. An unidentified review of 1901, quoted in Anderson, "Some Critical Attitudes," p. 3.

16. *Critic*, 45 (December 1904), 571.

17. Stedman to Moody, January 4, 1904 [error for 1905], MPC.

18. Ibid.

19. *LH*, p. 424.

20. "A New Poet," *Atlantic Monthly*, 95 (June 1905), 748.

21. *LH*, p. 225.

22. Mason, *Some Letters*, p. 153.

23. The scenario is in Notebook Three, MPC.

24. See *LH*, p. 213. Dunbar's treatment of the creative history of the play in *A House in Chicago*, p. 64, is grossly inaccurate.

25. *LH*, p. 213.

26. Ibid., p. 221.

27. Ibid., pp. 228–29. Dr. Bull's bill, enclosed in Bull to Moody, January 12, 1906, MPC, is for removal of a "tumor" and for attendance, April 19 to June 10 [1905].

28. Mason, *Some Letters*, p. 156.

29. *LH*, p. 230.

30. Torrence to Miss Peabody, May 11 [1905] (filed under group 19——), PPH. He quotes her phrase in his letter.

31. Ibid.

32. Letter of [June 5, 1905], MPP.

33. Moody to Charlotte Moody, July 20, 1905, TPPM. See Robinson to Miss Peabody, September 5, 1905, PPH.

34. *LH*, p. 235.

35. Moody to Mary Mason [June 5, 1905], MPP.

36. Moody to Robinson, March 31, 1905, in Introduction, *LH*, pp. 27–28.
37. Details are drawn from Hagedorn, *Robinson*, pp. 210–14.
38. Moody to Mary Mason [June 5, 1905], MPP.
39. Moody to Miss Peabody, June 10, 1905; and *LH*, pp. 234, 235.
40. *LH*, pp. 230–31.
41. Ibid., p. 237.
42. Ibid., p. 236. In a letter of February 5, 1906, Moody wrote R. W. Gilder that *The Fire-Bringer* was scheduled for production in Chicago during the next winter season (Mason, *Some Letters*, pp. 160–61). Moody's commitment to the Chicago New Theatre project was a major one; see *LH*, pp. 240–41 and 250.
43. Moody to Charlotte Moody, July 20, 1905, TPPM.
44. *LH*, p. 237.
45. See the bill with notation of payment in Bull to Moody, January 12, 1906, MPC.
46. In Notebook One, MPC.
47. *LH*, pp. 243, 244. Moody spent some of his time in November working on a review of *The Poems of Trumbull Stickney* (Boston & New York, 1905), of which he had been a coeditor. His review appeared in *North American Review*, 183 (November 1906), 1005–18.
48. Torrence to family, letters of November and December 1905 passim, TTP.
49. Robinson to Miss Peabody, December 1, 1905; and see, among the undated letters, another [early November 1905], PPH.
50. *LH*, p. 245.
51. Torrence to family, November 16, 1905, TPP.
52. *LH*, p. 245.
53. *The Divine Fire* (New York, 1905). I quote below in the text from the novel.
54. *LH*, pp. 245, 246.
55. Ibid.
56. "Three American Poets of To-Day," *Atlantic Monthly*, 98 (September 1906), 325–35. Passages which follow in this paragraph in the text are from this source.
57. See Hagedorn, *Robinson*, p. 212.
58. Torrence identified himself as the subject of this poem in Torrence to family, November 28, 1905, TPP.
59. So Moody reported to Harriet in November (*LH*, p. 241). Scribner's had reprinted Robinson's *The Children of the Night*, and the president had published his famous review of the book in *Outlook* in August.
60. *LH*, p. 242.
61. Torrence to family, November 14 and November 20, 1905, TPP.
62. *LH*, p. 242. For the arrangements, see MacKaye to Torrence, November 15, 1905, TPP; and Torrence to family, November 23, 1905, TPP. For Robinson's reaction, see his letter to Miss Peabody, December 1, 1905, PPH.

63. *LH*, pp. 242–43.
64. Moody's report to Harriet, not included in the text of *LH*, but quoted in Introduction, *LH*, p. 37.
65. Robinson to Miss Peabody, December 1, 1905, PPH.
66. *LH*, p. 420.
67. Ibid., and quoted without correction by MacKaye. Quinn's account of the creative history of the play in his *The American Drama*, II, p. 12, and Lovett's account in his Introduction, *Selected Poems*, pp. liv–lv, are also corrected in my treatment, above in the text. Moody announced the play's completion in a letter to Charlotte Moody, January 24, 1906, TPPM. Considering the fairly frequent meetings of Moody, Torrence, and Robinson in November and December, it is amazing that Moody did not talk of the play in which he was so fully involved. His only discussion of his work seems to have been in letters to Harriet and to Charlotte Moody.
68. Until February, Moody had been calling his play "the Zona play," after the name of his heroine, later changed (e.g., *LH*, pp. 244, 246). In February he gave the play the title, *A Sabine Woman* (see *LH*, p. 253), under which it was premiered in Chicago in April. It became *The Great Divide* in late June or early July (*LH*, p. 290; the date of this letter should read [July 13, 1906]). See MacKaye on the choice of the title, Introduction, *LH*, p. 46.
69. MacKaye quoting Moody, Introduction, *LH*, p. 41.
70. *LH*, p. 250.
71. Mason, *Some Letters*, p. 160.
72. *LH*, p. 255.
73. Ibid., p. 253.
74. Notebook One, MPC.
75. *LH*, pp. 257–58.
76. A cliché of the theatre world, to be sure, but this was Miss Anglin's story, appearing in an interview of the fall, cited in Henry, *Moody*, p. 171. Moody gave a similar if briefer account to Mason, preserved in a manuscript in Mason's hand, "Notes on first performance of The Great Divide," dated "The Judson, May 6, 1906," MPP. The notes are a Boswellian record of Moody's account to Mason of the events of the week of the premiere in Chicago. Minor changes in the manuscript, including addition of the title, above, were later made by Mason, probably some years after the date of the original.

    Of published accounts of the premiere of *A Sabine Woman*, only Henry's (*Moody*, pp. 171–73) is reliable. Errors in the accounts of Garland (*Companions on the Trail*, pp. 92–93) and Lovett (Introduction, *Selected Poems*, pp. liv–lvii) are generally ignored, below. But because MacKaye's is the account of one involved in the production and is the fullest treatment, some corrections of his narrative (Introduction, *LH*, pp. 42–45) are suggested. For treatment of the public events of the week I am primarily indebted to Henry; for information on Moody's actions and attitudes I am indebted to Mason's record. The former is based on work with public documents contemporary with the premiere; the latter is substantiated at a number of points by these public documents and by Moody letters cited below.

77. Introduction, *LH*, p. 42. MacKaye's lectures became the basis of his *The Playhouse and the Play* (New York, 1909).

78. Not Wednesday, "the eve of the opening," as MacKaye states (*LH*, p. 42). In Moody to Torrence, "En Route Pennsylvania Limited, Monday noon [April 9, 1906]," TPP, Moody wrote: "I have a chance to place my playlet (with Margaret Anglin) and am making an All-of-a-Sudden-Willy trip to Chicago for that purpose." In Mason, "Notes on first performance," MPP, Moody identifies the day of arrival as Tuesday.

79. Mason, "Notes on first performance," MPP. A typescript of *A Sabine Woman* [February 1906], with corrections in Moody's hand, is my basis for comment on that play.

80. MacKaye (*LH*, p. 43) writes that it was "a house packed by all the notables of Chicago." I follow Henry (*Moody*, p. 172), who was working from reviews of *A Sabine Woman* in the Chicago newspapers. Garland (*Companions on the Trail*, p. 193) has written that he attended the premiere. Masters, as quoted by MacKaye (*LH*, p. 35), and Monroe (*A Poet's Life*, p. 196) state that they saw the play in Chicago. In his account of the premiere, Lovett does not say he was present, though MacKaye places both Lovett and Garland in the audience (*LH*, p. 421).

81. I follow Henry and Mason, who tell essentially the same story, one recorded in a review of the play, Chicago *Evening Post*, April 13, 1906.

82. Henry does not deal closely with the events of this conference. I follow Mason's account. Mason and MacKaye both place the conference in the box office of the theatre. In his account, MacKaye excises Robertson from the *dramatis personae* and steals the scene (*LH*, pp. 43–45). Garland, Lovett, and MacKaye all err in placing the conference between the first two acts of the play (though MacKaye, contradicting himself, refers to Miss Anglin's "holding the last-act's curtain" [*LH*, p. 45])!

83. Mason, "Notes on first performance," MPP. On a major change Moody had demanded in the contract, one reserving to Robertson the right of Chicago production of *A Sabine Woman*, see *LH*, p. 264.

84. Mason, "Notes on first performance," MPP. See Herrick's fictional treatment of a play's premiere in *Chimes*, pp. 118–22.

85. Chicago *Evening Post*, April 13, 1906.

86. New York *Globe*, April 13, 1906, p. 13. The mounted clipping is filed with the letters of Moody to Miss Peabody, MPH.

87. See *LH*, p. 300.

88. "For the City Editor, (name of paper)" [cancelled heading], [April 13, 1906], manuscript of cover letter and three pages in Moody's hand, signed "W. V. Moody," MPC. The letter as printed here in the text represents the final version of this much-revised manuscript. Moody complained to Mason (see "Notes on first performance,"

MPP) that only one newspaper [Chicago *Evening Post,* April 13, 1906] had printed his letter and that it had garbled his text.

89.   MacKaye uncritically accepts Miss Anglin's statement without reservation (Introduction, *LH,* p. 45). While she was probably interested only in her option on the play, the complex contract Moody signed under protest was not returned to him in exchange for a "simple option." At breakfast, May 6, 1906, he told Mason he was in New York "trying to get the contract . . . changed" (Mason, "Notes on first performance," MPP); and that contract was still in the hands of Miss Anglin at least as late as May 8 (*LH,* p. 264). Moody suggests by inference that Shubert would not have been displeased by the first contract (see *LH,* p. 263), and the business manager with whom Moody dealt at the Garrick may well have been more interested in observing Shubert's wishes than the simpler desire of Miss Anglin.

90.   Mason, "Notes on first performance," MPP.

91.   *LH,* p. 260.

92.   Ibid., pp. 262–63.

93.   Ibid., p. 261. Moody reports almost daily on the negotiations (ibid., pp. 261–67, from which details below in the text are drawn). In the light of these documents, MacKaye's treatment seems excessive: "No sooner did Miller set eyes on the contract which Moody had signed in Chicago, than he tore it up in wrath. 'Get your own lawyer and dictate your own terms,' he said to Moody . . ." (Introduction, *LH,* p. 46).

94.   Moody to Charlotte Moody, May 9, 1906, TPPM; and *LH,* p. 263.

95.   See *LH,* p. 272. This contract is in the Berg Collection, The New York Public Library.

CHAPTER 11: *The Great Divide*

1.   This passage and others quoted without annotation in the following paragraphs in the text are from *LH* in this period.

2.   Moody to Charlotte Moody, July 3, 1906, TPPM. Moody here describes Cornish life as "charmingly simple and free from stiffness, the people both open-hearted and clever." Cf. Harriet Monroe's different experience in Cornish that summer and the next, described in her *A Poet's Life,* pp. 183–92.

3.   Torrence to Moody, [May 29, 1906], and [June 13, 1906], TPP; and Moody to Torrence, May 31, [1906], TPP.

4.   Monroe, *A Poet's Life,* pp. 183–84.

5.   *LH,* p. 283; and Moody to Charlotte Moody, July 3, 1906, TPPM.

6.   *LH,* p. 273; and MacKaye, Introduction, *LH,* p. 22.

7.   Robinson to Miss Peabody, July 4, 1906, PPH. The writing of this poem is generally incorrectly assigned to October 1906, following the New York premiere of *The Great Divide.*

8.   MacKaye treats the obscurity of the reference to the rape of the Sabine women and describes the way the play's new title was chosen, Introduction, *LH,* pp. 43, 46. And see ch. 10, n. 68, above.

9. Moody quoting Miller to Charlotte Moody, July 21, 1906, TPPM. His sister was working in Saranac Lake, New York, on a private nursing assignment.

10. MacKaye, Notes, *LH*, p. 425, citing a passage from his wife's diary.

11. Moody to Harriet, July 26, [1906]. The relevant passage is not in *LH*, but is published in Dunbar, *A House in Chicago*, pp. 65–66. The original letter is in the Henry E. Huntington Library.

12. *LH*, p. 277; also see p. 281.

13. Moody to Charlotte Moody, September 3, 1906, TPPM.

14. In *LH*, p. 296. Unless otherwise noted, passages quoted below in the text are from *LH*, September 1906.

15. Moody characterizing and quoting Shubert, *LH*, p. 299.

16. Moody to Charlotte Moody, September 20, 1906, TPPM.

17. *LH*, p. 304.

18. Ibid., p. 305.

19. Passages in the text below are quoted from the text of *The Great Divide* in Manly, *Poems and Plays*.

20. *A Sabine Woman* [February 1906], typescript with corrections in Moody's hand, TPP.

21. Moody's earliest work on the play coincided with a vision of Western character in terms of the Dionysian motif in *Hedda Gabler*. Moody's Arizona friends appeared "with vine leaves in their hair." *LH*, p. 221. Like Lövborg, Ghent is associated with liquor and the vine. Ruth may be seen as a distant cousin to Hedda, especially as she appears in *A Sabine Woman*.

22. Mason, *Some Letters*, p. 160.

23. Moody to Mason, October 12, 1906, MPP.

24. I am indebted to the work of David D. Henry on the critical reception of *The Great Divide*, in his *Moody*, pp. 173–95 passim. His work on the contemporary criticism of Moody's drama parallels Anderson's on the poetry in "Some Critical Attitudes." Like Anderson, Henry worked primarily with Harriet Moody's large collection of reviews, MPC.

25. Moody to Charlotte Moody, October 7, 1906; and *LH*, p. 306.

26. Mason, *Some Letters*, p. 161.

27. Moody to Charlotte Moody, October 7, 1906, TPPM.

28. Moody quoting Miller, *LH*, p. 306.

29. A review of October 4, 1906.

30. Hapgood to Moody, December 2, [1906], MPC.

31. For a fuller treatment, see Henry, *Moody*, pp. 173–95 passim.

32. New York *Tribune*, June 3, 1907.

33. "To William Vaughn Moody," in Percy MacKaye, *Collected Poems* (New York, 1916); and cf. Robinson's "The White Lights," Robinson's *Collected Poems*, p. 340.

34. *LH*, pp. 307–8.

35. Ibid., p. 310.

36. Daniel Gregory Mason, "Moody, W. V. (Personalia) October, 1906,"

manuscript in Mason's hand, MPP. Notes taken on the occasion of Moody's visit, October 21–24, 1906. Mason drew on these notes for his published accounts, Introduction, *Some Letters,* p. xxiv, and *Music in My Time,* p. 137.

37. MacKaye, Notes, *LH,* p. 424.
38. *LH,* p. 316.
39. Ibid.; and, on the New Theatre's first season, Quinn, *The American Drama,* II, p. 3.
40. F. Greenslet to Moody, September 15, 1906, MPC.
41. Norton to Moody, August 25, 1906, MPC.
42. Moody to H. P. Judson, September 26, 1906, Moody file, President's Papers (Harper), University of Chicago Library.
43. Moody to Howe, January 25, 1907, Houghton Library, Harvard University. (This item is separately catalogued.)

CHAPTER 12: MOODY AND HIS CIRCLE

1. *LH,* pp. 320–21. Unidentified passages above in the text are quoted from *LH,* pp. 318–20.
2. Moody's sense of the book's implications, *LH,* pp. 318–19.
3. Ibid., p. 323.
4. Mason, *Music in My Time,* pp. 139–40.
5. See ch. 10, n. 58, above. I quote from Robinson, *Collected Poems,* p. 351.
6. See MacKaye's "Uriel," *Uriel and Other Poems* (Boston & New York, 1912), pp. 1–13.
7. Ibid.
8. Ibid., and cf. MacKaye, Introduction, *LH,* pp. 26–29.
9. Robinson, Torrence, and the Masons were living at the Judson on Washington Square. Mason's account of their association (*Music in My Time,* pp. 137–40), and Hagedorn's treatment (*Robinson,* pp. 239–46) have both been drawn upon. In a letter to Miss Peabody, October 24, 1906, PPH, Torrence writes that Robinson has completed a one-act modern prose play and has started another play in three acts. The second was probably his rewriting of "Ferguson's Ivory Tower" as *Van Zorn.*
10. "The White Lights," *Collected Poems,* p. 340.
11. Robinson to Miss Peabody, March 6, 1907, PPH.
12. Mason, *Music in My Time,* p. 140.
13. See n. 9, above. Robinson spoke to Moody of *Van Zorn* in January 1907 (*LH,* pp. 319–20, 323). For his earliest work on *The Porcupine,* see Robinson to MacKaye, April and July 1907, quoted in Introduction, *LH,* p. 23.
14. See *LH,* p. 319.
15. Mason, *Music in My Time,* p. 140; and *LH,* p. 320.
16. Mason, *Music in My Time,* p. 138.
17. Moody attended pre-Broadway tryouts of the play in Philadelphia in

mid-October and Chicago in mid-December (Introduction, *LH*, pp. 50–52). On the play's New York run, see Quinn, *The American Drama*, II, p. 31.

18. MacKaye to Torrence, December 14, 1906, TPP; and Robinson to MacKaye, April 1907, quoted in Introduction, *LH*, p. 23.
19. See Quinn, *The American Drama*, II, pp. 18–19.
20. See Moody to Charlotte Moody, March 3, 1907, TPPM; and Robinson to Miss Peabody, July 15, 1907, PPH.
21. *LH*, p. 318.
22. Ibid., p. 323.
23. Ibid., p. 424.
24. Ibid., p. 322.
25. Moody to Harriet, February 28, [1907] (misdated 1905), Introduction, *LH*, p. 48.
26. Moody to Charlotte Moody, March 3, 1907, TPPM.
27. Stedman to MacKaye, quoted in *LH*, pp. 38–39.
28. *LH*, p. 326. Moody's reactions on this trip are cited from letters to Harriet of this period unless otherwise indicated. For the activity and itinerary of the two men I have also drawn on Torrence's letters to his family in this period and from Torrence Diaries: Notebook One, in which an expense account is kept for the period March 1907–May 1907, TPP.
29. Torrence to his family, April 23, 1907, TPP.
30. Notes, *LH*, p. 418, MacKaye citing a communication from Torrence.
31. According to Torrence to his family, May 3, 1907, TPP.
32. *LH*, p. 335.
33. Ibid., p. 334.
34. Moody to Torrence, August 27, [1907], TPP. To MacKaye (September 13, 1907, MPP) Moody wrote, "I am crawling along with the *Eve* play, but finished? Brass-boweled man, have pity! It is just barely so to say begun, and before it is finished I shall be leaner."
35. Mason, *Some Letters*, p. 151.
36. Introduction, *LH*, p. 24.
37. In *LH*, p. 306.
38. E.g., the attitude expressed in Moody to Mrs. Toy (Mason, *Some Letters*, p. 169).
39. In "On the Introduction of the Chorus into Modern Drama," *Harvard Monthly*, 14 (1892), 142–51.
40. In October 1906. See Mason, *Music in My Time*, p. 137. Compare Moody's comments of March 1908 on the problem in Debussy's setting of Maeterlinck's *Pelléas et Mélisande*, *LH*, pp. 357–58.
41. As called for by his scenario, "The Death of Eve," a typescript of sixteen numbered pages, MPC. Moody had followed a similar procedure in writing *The Fire-Bringer*, the lyrics were written last.
42. I follow the text of the play in Manly, *Poems and Plays*. The play should not be confused with the poem of the same title.
43. Scenario, "The Death of Eve," MPC, p. 5.

44. I follow Moody's scenario, "The Death of Eve," MPC, in the description of the projected acts 2 and 3, below in the text.
45. Scenario, "The Death of Eve," MPC, p. 13.
46. *LH*, p. 341.
47. Ibid.
48. Torrence to Moody, August 31, 1907, TPP. The extent of Robinson's commitment to the theatre in this period has not been fully treated. And the late date of publication of *Van Zorn* and *The Porcupine* has led some scholars to place Robinson's work on them in 1914 and 1915 (e.g., Hyatt H. Waggoner, *American Poets from the Puritans to the Present* [Boston, 1968], p. 286).
49. *LH*, pp. 342; 343.
50. Ibid., pp. 343–44. See also Moody's note to Robinson, October 12, 1907, Isaacs-Robinson Collection; Manuscript Division; The New York Public Library; Astor, Lenox and Tilden Foundations.
51. I follow MacKaye's account of the tryouts and opening of the play, Introduction, *LH*, pp. 54–57.
52. *LH*, p. 345.
53. Notes, *LH*, p. 423; and Hagedorn, *Robinson*, pp. 233–34.
54. Mason, *Music in My Time*, p. 145.
55. Grace Elliston to Moody, November 9, [1907], Box 23 [*sic*], Herrick Papers, University of Chicago Library.
56. Garland, *Companions on the Trail*, p. 94.
57. So Mason felt in late October 1906 (*Music in My Time*, p. 136). A similar observation is made in Torrence to Miss Peabody, October 24, 1906, PPH.
58. Introduction, *LH*, p. 26.
59. Notes, *LH*, p. 424.
60. *LH*, pp. 346–47.
61. The anecdote is Torrence's, as quoted in Notes, *LH*, p. 422.
62. *LH*, p. 349.
63. Ibid., p. 351.
64. Moody quoting Mrs. Davidge, ibid., pp. 351–52.
65. *LH*, p. 352.
66. Ibid., p. 353.
67. Ibid., p. 356.
68. Dunbar, *A House in Chicago*, p. 69.
69. Torrence to his family, June 8, 12, and 17, 1908, TPP; and *LH*, p. 362.
70. *Yale Alumni Weekly*, 17 (July 8, 1908), 983. I am indebted to Anderson, "Some Critical Attitudes," for this information.
71. Torrence to his family, July 6, 1908, TPP.
72. Miller had a copy of the play, which he wished to try out in San Francisco in the early summer (*LH*, pp. 360, 361–62). But Moody wanted to rewrite act 3 before the play was staged. Miller postponed his production and instead premiered MacKaye's *Mater* on August 3 in San Francisco. The play opened on Broadway September 25, 1908.

73. Introduction, *LH*, p. 63.
74. The incident is described in Hagedorn, *Robinson*, pp. 230–31. See also *LH*, p. 369; and Introduction, *LH*, pp. 63–64.
75. Torrence to Miss Peabody, July 12, 1908, PPH.
76. Fussell, "Robinson to Moody," p. 187.
77. Ibid.
78. Hagedorn, *Robinson*, p. 250.
79. Torrence to Moody, October 27, 1908, and February 17, 1909, TPP.
80. *LH*, pp. 371–73.
81. *The Faith Healer* (Boston & New York, 1909), published to obtain a British copyright, is a play in four acts which Moody was to revise drastically.
82. Moody had been working on revision of *The Great Divide* since November. For his final revision of the play, see Mason, *Some Letters*, pp. 164–65, 167.

CHAPTER 13: ON THE RAGGED EDGE

1. Moody to Torrence, February 13 [postmarked the 12th], 1909, TPP; and to Charlotte Moody, February 17, 1909, TPPM.
2. E.g., see Moody's letters of the early Chicago years. He wrote Lovett (May 23, [1905], MPC) that he has omitted their academic titles from the title page of *A First View of English Literature;* he asked if Lovett wished to reinsert his title, however, "as a concession to the powers that be."
3. He wrote, "Moody was especially fortunate in securing Prof. [*sic*] Lovett to collaborate with him . . . for Moody probably could never have written it alone." Notes, *LH*, p. 416.
4. Wright's interview, which appeared in the Los Angeles *Daily Times* [February 1908?], is cited in Henry, *Moody*, p. 15.
5. Moody to Charlotte Moody, [January 15? 1909], misdated November 5, 1908, TPPM.
6. Mason, *Some Letters*, p. 169.
7. Ibid.
8. Schevill in a letter of 1935 to MacKaye, quoted in Introduction, *LH*, pp. 61–62.
9. I am indebted here and below in the text to Henry's work on the reception of *The Faith Healer* (*Moody*, pp. 195–214). See Moody's own description of the St. Louis premiere in Moody to Charlotte Moody, April 30, 1909, TPPM. MacKaye published this letter in Introduction, *LH*, pp. 62–63.
10. Introduction, *LH*, pp. 62–63. Moody wrote that the critics had found his hero to be "a 'Christ figure' (whatever that is)."
11. Introduction, *LH*, pp. 62–63. In addition, Moody rewrote act 3 yet once more in New York in April.
12. What follows in the text is a comparison of the version published in 1909 with the final version in Manly, *Poems and Plays*. The play also exists in a three-act typescript draft in MPC.

13. Moody to Charlotte Moody, April 30, 1909, TPPM.
14. *LH*, p. 377.
15. Dunbar, *A House in Chicago*, p. 76.
16. Moody to Miss Peabody, August 12, 1909, MPH.
17. Moody to Mary Mason, August 10, 1909, MPP.
18. I am indebted to Henry's work on the London reception of the play, treated together with the New York reception (*Moody*, pp. 173–95 passim).
19. London *Sunday Times*, September 19, 1909.
20. Other reviews from which phrases are quoted above are from the *Morning Post*, September 16, 1909; London *Daily Mail*, September 16, 1909; London *Era*, September 18, 1909; and *Weekly Dispatch*, September 19, 1909.
21. Dunbar, *A House in Chicago*, p. 81.
22. Notes, *LH*, pp. 427–28. According to MacKaye, Moody was in the hospital for the following periods: October 6–17, October 28–November 10, and November 25–29, 1909.
23. Notes, *LH*, pp. 427–28.
24. *LH*, p. 386.
25. Ibid., p. 387.
26. Dunbar, *A House in Chicago*, p. 82.
27. I cite the text of the play in Manly, *Poems and Plays*.
28. Once again Moody is straining against the conventions of his period —here those of the realistic theatre. To fulfill his vision of drama as liberating ritual, Moody needed a different kind of theatre entirely— one in which audience and the crowd of waiting believers could become one body. Moody's dramatic impulse in *The Faith Healer* has only recently been effectively handled, particularly in productions of *Hair* and The Living Theatre's *Paradise Now*. Moody would immediately have understood the intent of these theatrical experiences. And, like his own work, they protest against restrictive social and moral codes while reaffirming a vision of human sexual, emotional, and spiritual fulfillment.
29. Notes, *LH*, p. 428.
30. Ibid., pp. 428–29.
31. See New York *Evening Post*, January 20, 1910.
32. New York *Press*, January 20, 1910.
33. *New York Times*, January 20, 1910.
34. New York *Evening Sun*, January 20, 1910. Compare reviews of the same date in the New York *Mail* and the *Brooklyn Eagle*.
35. New York *Evening Sun*, January 20, 1910.
36. Ibid.
37. Notes, *LH*, p. 429.
38. Ibid., p. 430.
39. Ibid., p. 429.
40. *LH*, p. 391.
41. Moody to Mason, February 9, 1910. A letter written in Harriet's hand, dictated by Moody, MPP.

42. See his *The Playhouse and the Play*.
43. Quinn, *The American Drama*, II, p. 17.
44. Torrence, *Selected Letters*, pp. 67–68.
45. Harriet to Miss Peabody, August 9, 1911, PPH. The first issue of *Poetry* in 1912 affords literary historians a symbolic link between poetic generations and a brief index to stylistic revolution. It lists Harriet Monroe as editor and Ezra Pound as foreign correspondent. Published posthumously, Moody's "I Am the Woman" appears followed immediately by two Pound poems—"To Whistler, American" and "Middle-Aged" (*Poetry*, 1 [1912], 3–8). Miss Monroe's gesture may well have been intentional. In the second issue she reviews Manly, *Poems and Plays*, from a perspective that has shifted since 1901. "The Fountain," Moody's anticipation of the motifs of T. S. Eliot's "The Wasteland," is singled out for praise. She values the "spontaneity" of Moody's masque and the "simple austerity" of *The Death of Eve*. Miss Monroe still admires Moody's achievement, but she now sees it only as "the beginning of great things" to come in American poetry. ("Moody's Poems," *Poetry*, 1 [1912], 54–57.)
46. Quoted by Lovett, Introduction, *Selected Poems*, p. lxii.
47. Moody to Mason, [October 2, 1895], MPP.
48. John Unterecker, *Voyager: A Life of Hart Crane* (New York, 1969), pp. 40–42, et passim. Harriet gave Crane a copy of the newly published *Some Letters of William Vaughn Moody* and was of crucial importance to him early in his career. Crane surely knew Moody's poetry and was influenced by it and by the sense of Moody's personality and dedication communicated by Harriet, but no definitive estimate of the direct influence of Moody's work on Crane has been made.
49. Moody's influence on O'Neill was probably minor or nonexistent, but it has not been investigated. For Baker on Moody, see his "William Vaughn Moody," *Harvard Graduates Magazine*, 19 (1910), 258–61.
50. *LH*, pp. 393–94.
51. Ibid., p. 394.
52. As quoted in Notes, *LH*, p. 418.
53. Mason to Torrence, October 24, 1910, TPP.
54. Torrence, *Selected Letters*, p. 69.
55. Here and below in the text I follow Schevill's diary, as quoted in *LH*, pp. 397–98.

INDEX